Batman Unmasked

Gray:

Song and Dance Man, 3rd Edition

Harper:

Women in British Cinema

Jones and Jolliffe:

The Guerilla Film Maker's Handbook, 2nd Edition

Macnab:

Searching for Stars

Rayner:

The Films of Peter Weir

Vincendeau:

Stars and Stardom in French Cinema

BATMAN UNMASKED

Analysing a Cultural Icon

Will Brooker

Continuum
London and New York

Continuum
The Tower Building
11 York Road
London SE1 7NX

370 Lexington Avenue
New York
NY 10017-6503

www.continuumbooks.com

First published in 2000

British Library Cataloguing-in-Publication Data
A catalogue record for this book is available from the British Library

ISBN 0-8264-4949-2

Typeset by YHT Ltd, London
Printed and bound in Great Britain by Biddles Ltd, *www.biddles.co.uk*

Contents

Acknowledgements   vii

Introduction: 1978   1

1 1939–1945: Origins and Wartime   33

2 1954: Censorship and Queer Readings   101

3 1961–1969: Pop and Camp   171

4 1986–1997: Fandom and Authorship   249

Conclusion: 1999   308

Bibliography   334

Index   353

Acknowledgements

Thanks to:

Denny O'Neil and Alan Asherman at DC Comics, who generously shared their time, their archives and their memories.

Roberta Pearson for her support, her encouragement and her example.

Deborah Jermyn for buying me Roberta's *The Many Lives of the Batman* second-hand in 1995.

John Hartley for his inspiring background presence and for always finding the money.

David Barker at Continuum for his unflagging faith and enthusiasm.

Fiona Graham for the index.

Justine Davis, who loyally assisted with the New York research.

Liz Brooker, who proofread my first Batman story in 1978.

Pete Brooker, who brought home *The Dark Knight Returns* in 1985.

Joe Brooker, boy wonder.

Will Brooker
Cardiff – New York – London
May 1999

Twinkle, Twinkle Little Bat
How I Wonder what You're at

(Lewis Carroll, *Alice's Adventures in Wonderland*)

Gloria Hunniford: Do you regard yourself as a cultural
                  icon . . . Adam?
Adam West: . . . it . . . doesn't matter.

(Adam West with Will Brooker and Gloria Hunniford,
Open House with Gloria Hunniford, Channel 5, 14 April
2000)

Introduction

1978

What are now called 'Departments of English' will be renamed departments of 'Cultural Studies' where Batman comics, Mormon theme parks, television, movies and rock will replace Chaucer, Shakespeare, Milton, Wordsworth and Wallace Stevens (Harold Bloom, *The Western Canon*, London: Macmillan (1994), p. 519)

1. Hunt the Dark Knight

I have kept a diary consistently since I was very young – since the age of seven, but more of that below – and on 29 July 1992 I pasted in two photographs, one from the *Guardian* and one from the Greenwich and Woolwich *Mercury*. The first is a snatched image of a man and a woman running, hand in hand. The woman clutches a bag and seems to be panting; the man is grim, focused, wearing shades and a jacket. Beneath his jacket, half-concealed, is a Batman t-shirt. The caption explains: 'On the run: a couple sprint across a Sarajevo intersection where snipers often attack civilians.'

The second photograph is a posed portrait. A boy of about five years old sits on a hospital bed, slightly cross-eyed and bewildered, bravely giving a thumbs-up at the camera. To his left is a figure in a Ninja Turtle outfit, bending over the bed: to his right is a teenage boy

1

dressed in an amateurish Batman costume. 'Welcome!' reads the caption. 'Batman and Ninja Turtle drop in for a slice of the action.' Above these two photos I added the legend 'Hunt the Dark Knight', a quotation from Frank Miller's seminal Batman comic series of 1986.[1]

With retrospect I believe that was the point at which the writing of this book began; with that spontaneous impulse to record and preserve two texts which in turn record and preserve the signifier of the Batman in such intriguing circumstances. I wanted to know how the Bat-symbol had infiltrated those places, those moments, and what it meant to the man sprinting across a sniper junction in Sarajevo, to the older boy dressing up for his terminally ill brother in a children's ward of Greenwich Hospital. These images, linked across time and circum-stance by the single icon of a stylised black bat in a yellow circle, retain their fascination and crystallise my wider project.

This book is an investigation, a detection, a 'forensic examination'[2] of the disparate texts which have borne the signifier 'Batman' over sixty years, in an attempt to reconstruct their context and hence recover the meanings carried by this cultural icon at key moments in his history. The scope of my research, from the character's first published appearance in May 1939 to the comic books published around his anniversary in May 1999, is broad enough – even with a focus primarily on American cultural history alone – to draw in a range of texts from World War Two propaganda posters through 1960s Pop Art to the online fangroups of the Internet. My questions, though, remain consistent regardless of period. What does the Batman signify in this cultural moment? What wider context surrounds this particular inflection? What different interpretations govern this meaning, and within which matrix of imposed, 'dominant', delimiting and counter-definition is it situated?

The issues raised by these questions lead me to examine the fundamental relations between cultural power and textual interpreta-tion, but they are always grounded in the concrete: and all these questions, all these issues are loaded in these two photographs linked

---

[1] Frank Miller, Klaus Janson and Lynn Varley, *Batman: The Dark Knight Returns*, New York: DC Comics (1986).
[2] See John Hartley, *The Politics of Pictures*, London: Routledge (1992).

by a logo – the man in the t-shirt promoting Tim Burton's Batman film of 1989, its spin-offs reaching even Sarajevo, and the boy in the cheap costume, either lovingly home-made or rented from a fancy-dress agency somewhere in Woolwich. From corporate merchandise to localised creativity, the adult consumer to the primary-school fan, the warzone crossfire to the leukaemia bed – Batman got there, somehow, and the questions raised by these death-marked images alone are enough, I feel, to justify this book's existence.

2. Confession: I Love Batman

It has become common – even fashionable – for academic writers to declare their own cultural 'positionality' in relation to the texts they are addressing. In some cases – for instance, Andy Medhurst's foregrounding of his age, gayness and lack of any fannish investment in the character at the start of his essay 'Batman, Deviance and Camp'[3] – this is worthwhile and useful; indeed, there are studies – Paul Willis's *Learning to Labour* and Janice Radway's *Reading the Romance*, for example – where the authors' failure to consider the bearing of their own gender and class position to their research subject seems a genuine failing.[4] For a white, male, heterosexual and middle-class researcher to 'come out' in this way, however, still has an air of self-indulgence which more recent confessionals like Fred Pfeil's *White Guys* have not helped to dispel.[5]

Nevertheless, I am convinced that my own exceptional position in relation to my subject must be declared; however I struggle for objectivity, I am so far 'inside' the Batman myth as to be its subject myself, and an examination of readings and interpretations is inevitably affected by my own preferences, even as I try to regard the fan-self

---

[3] Andy Medhurst, 'Batman, Deviance and Camp', in Roberta Pearson and William Uricchio (eds), *The Many Lives of the Batman*, London: Routledge (1991).
[4] See Paul Willis, *Learning to Labour*, Farnborough: Saxon House (1977); Janice Radway, *Reading the Romance*, London: Verso (1987).
[5] Fred Pfeil, Introduction to *White Guys: Studies in Postmodern Domination and Difference*, London: Verso (1995), pp. vii–xx.

from the separate identity of the outsider and objective researcher. In this sense I feel the cultural experience which has woven me into Batman fandom is a benefit to my work, offering me a subject to examine intimately; but this requires a degree of honesty and self-interrogation both here and throughout.

I first wrote on Batman on Monday, 13 February 1978, in five colours of felt-tip pen. This story about the Penguin, written at the age of seven, is a document as significant in its way as those two photographs.

> Bruce Wyane was reading a book about sailors when he saw some light on a biulding. It had a black shape on it. Suddenly he knew. It was the bat signal!
> 'Quick, Robin to the batpoles'! was the next thing he said.
> He raced away in the Batboat and Robin went in the Bat plane. Batman saw a bird's head. He thought it was a swan but it was the Pengiein's boat.
> He made a signal to Robin and robin swooped down in the plane and picked up the penguin.
> Batman went to the commisoners office with Robin, and the penguin got locked up.[6]

Based on the 'imposed' framework I'd received from DC annuals, second-hand comics from the early 1970s and re-runs of the ABC TV series of the previous decade, this story constitutes an experiment within a rigid framework, a working 'in the gaps' as Michel de Certeau would put it.[7] From a distance of over twenty years it is possible to reconstruct a context for this two-page story and trace the juxtaposition of learned conventions – the batsignal, batpoles and vehicles from the television series, the coda at the Commissioner's

---

[6] Will Brooker, unpublished story (13 February 1978).
[7] See Michel de Certeau, *The Practice of Everyday Life*, Berkeley: University of California Press (1984).

1978

Monday, 13th Febuary

Bruce wyane
~~Batman~~ was reading
a book abou sailors when
he saw some light
on a biulding. It had
a black shape on it.
Suddenly he knew.

It was the bat signal!
"Quick, Robin to
the Batpoles" was the
next thing he said.

He raced away
in the Batboat and
Robin went in
the Bat plane.

Bat Man saw a
bird's head. He thought
it was a swan but

6

office from the comic books – with odd, individual whimsies like Batman mistaking the 'Pengiein's' boat for a swan, Bruce reading a book about sailors, and the apparent nod to a contemporary advertising slogan in the reference to 'pick up a penguin'.

The story is suggestive partly in its indication that Batman was a major figure in my creative, fantasy life by age seven – a reminder that an attempt on my part to pretend detachment from the character would be fraudulent, however academically proper – but also in its conflation of references to both the 1970s comic and the 1966 TV series. As will become clear in my third chapter, these two texts are now commonly held at opposing poles by the majority of comic fans. The comic of this period, embodying Denny O'Neil and Neal Adams' relaunch of the character in a more serious and 'adult' mode, is frequently held as good object and defining text, while the television show epitomises the 'campiness' which many comic fans detest and treat as an aberration. I made no such distinction. The TV Batman was, in my seven-year-old life, a gripping and involving adventure as 'serious' as the comics, with the cliffhangers cause for a day's suspense and the theme tune a cue for energetic dancing or play-fighting.

This early experience has stayed with me. Though I recognised the broad comedy of the series when re-viewing it in the 1980s, and later became aware not just of its links to Pop but of the gay associations it had acquired, I cannot share the distaste of many other comic readers for Adam West's portrayal, and this is not merely because I know the series saved the comic from cancellation, or because I disagree with the kind of 'reading' which attempts to prioritise one interpretation and dismiss others as 'corrupt', or because I am dismayed by the homophobia which often accompanies the prejudice against the series. It is also because I used to dance in raptures to the theme music.

So I have my prejudices, a whole raft of them, bound up with the role Batman has played in my cultural life. Like many fans' experience of the character, mine went through phases of contact with various forms, including a lapse from comics during early adolescence followed by a thrilled rediscovery in Frank Miller's *The Dark Knight Returns* of 1986, regular cycles of anticipation and disappointment around the four recent blockbuster films, and a loyalty to the comic-book Batman – or rather, the 'mature readers' titles like *Legends of the Dark Knight*, for there are subtle distinctions in this field with which Bourdieu could have a field day[8] – lasting through to the present, when my increasing academic involvement with the character has led me back to the texts of the Batman's first three decades and the 'original' of 1939.

I have my prejudices, then – a vague sense of the character's 'betrayal' by Hollywood, a preference for comics in the Frank Miller style, an affection for the Warner Brothers animated series – and they are complicated prejudices, incorporating a nostalgia for the 1960s series and a knowing enjoyment of the 1950s comic's kitsch. My pleasures in Batman are manifold, combining various, often mutually incompatible interpretations from over twenty years' exposure to the character at impressionable ages.

Inevitably, like most fans, I also treasure my own platonic ideal of what the Batman would 'really be like': a personal myth bound up with my own notions of fatherhood, the city and moral duty, and wearing Clint Eastwood's face. This myth has only become more potent for me as I immerse myself academically in the character's history and surround myself with his image, his symbol, his totems. I have an emotional investment in Batman which I would guess exceeds that of Tony Bennett and Janet Woollacott for James Bond, or Ken Gelder for Dracula, or even Roberta Pearson and William Uricchio for my own subject; and so this book cannot be quite like theirs, and it is better to admit as much. If there is in my work, to take just one key example, a particular sympathy with 'queer readings' of Batman texts and an insistence on the value of this interpretation, it has its origin in that first exposure, when my ideal of Batman as father-protector – massive in his love and strength as a father can only be to a seven-year-old boy – was formed. As a white, male, heterosexual and middle-class researcher, I love that man: I love Batman.

3. Batman as Cultural Icon

In a sixty-year career, including encounters with Houdini, Judge Dredd, Hitler and the Predator, the Batman has, it seems, come face to face with every major cultural icon but James Bond. An episode in the

---

[8] See Pierre Bourdieu, *Distinction*, vol. 2, London: Routledge (1994).

1940s saw him transported back to Robin Hood's Merrie England,[9] while *Detective Comics* of March 1987 and the prestige-format *Red Rain* brought him together with Sherlock Holmes and Dracula respectively.[10]

There are of course other reasons, aside from these intriguing moments of intertextuality, why a study of the Batman's changing meanings over a historical period owes a debt to existing research on James Bond, Robin Hood and the vampire; particularly the latter two cultural icons, whose meanings long ago escaped the anchorage of whatever 'original' text brought them into being, and whose identity is no longer inseparably tied to an individual author – as, say, Tarzan, Sherlock Holmes, Hamlet and Don Quixote are still – but exists somewhere above and between a multiplicity of varied and often contradictory incarnations, both old and recent, across a range of cultural forms from computer games to novels.

The landmark texts on these cultural figures – Tony Bennett and Janet Woollacott's *Bond and Beyond*, Ken Gelder's *Reading the Vampire*, Stephen Knight's *Robin Hood*, and of course Roberta Pearson and William Uricchio's *The Many Lives of the Batman* – do not constitute guidebooks or exemplars for my own research in anything but a general sense. Each, however, has offered valuable lessons for my project, not so much in terms of detail as in the broad parallels the authors suggest on the level of approach and method, and has played an important role in terms of contextualising Batman within a family of contemporary cultural icons.

Figures such as these, whose associations have changed over their histories – whether during the shifts from one medium to another, as a result of a changing audience or in response to a new social context – offer more interesting possibilities for study with every year of their development as they transform and resurface in new guises, carrying meanings which increasingly toy with and sometimes overturn the conventions of the 'original'. Robin Hood, for instance, was used for

---

[9] 'The Rescue of Robin Hood', *Detective Comics* #116 (October 1946). Thanks to Howard Stangroom for this reference.

[10] *Detective Comics* #572 (March 1987); Doug Moench, Kelley Jones *et al.*, *Batman/Dracula: Red Rain*, New York: DC Comics (1992).

his radical, anti-establishment connotations in a strip from the comic *Crisis* which linked the rise of 'heritage' myth and theme-park history in contemporary England with the suppression of modern uprising like the poll tax riots.[11] Even James Bond's resurrection in *Goldeneye* was notable for its critique of Bond's outdated Cold War values, his sexism countered by a female M and proto-feminist Girls. As such, they serve a similar role to Batman, adapting with the historical moment as certain aspects of their iconic personae are foregrounded and others pushed back.

Robin Hood's relevance to the Batman mythos, for instance, stems partly from both characters' ambiguous relation to society, leading directly to the perceived necessity on the part of the 'dominant' controllers of meaning to limit and direct the character's signification at various key points in its history. The 'enfeebled ballad-operas'[12] which began in the 1590s and established a 'constricted' version of Hood for the next two hundred years, and the use of the character as safe 'heritage' nostalgia from the 1800s to the present day, can be compared with the consistent attempts to divert any gay associations from Batman through the introduction of Batwoman, Batgirl and Aunt Harriet and the killing-off, however temporary, of Alfred and Robin. Ken Gelder's study of the vampire, on the other hand, is an obvious reference point for a study of another 'bat-man', a gothic figure whose identity is subject to transformation and has, like the vampire, entered the popular realm of cartoons, games and films while retaining traceable roots to an authored 'original'.

It will, however, become clear from the following chapters that, partly because of DC Comics' and more recently Warner Brothers' canny hold on the character, Batman does not yet occupy the same cultural role as Dracula and Robin Hood. While evidence of his appropriation by audiences for purposes unintended by the comic book producers dates back to the early 1950s – by the late 1960s he was being liberally borrowed for 'unofficial' use in fashion, art and political satire – Batman and his meanings are still tethered to a multinational

---

[11] Michael Cook and Gary Erskine, 'The Real Robin Hood', *Crisis*, London: Fleetway (1991).

[12] Stephen Knight, *Robin Hood*, Oxford: Blackwell (1994), p. 219.

institution, rather than floating freely in the public domain. I will suggest in my conclusion, however, that with sixty years behind him Batman has now reached the point where he could live on in the cultural imagination, as myth, if that institution decided to cut him free.

Bennett and Woollacott's use of the key terms 'texts of Bond', comprising a range of related sources – 'fanzines, magazine articles, advertisements and the like'[13] – all of which, as intertextual frames, cue an audience's reception and understanding of the character, and 'moments of Bond', which pinpoint shifts in the character's meaning from anti-Communism in the 1950s to a symbol of 'swinging' sexuality in the 1960s and an increasingly parodic figure in the 1970s, has obvious links with my own approach. One passage deserves to be quoted in full, for it applies equally to my object of study – indeed, to any comparable popular hero – as to Bond, and with a minimal effort to change the names could stand as a definition of my own project.

> If Bond has functioned as a 'sign of the times' it has been as a moving sign of the times, as a figure capable of taking up and articulating quite different and even contradictory cultural and ideological values, sometimes turning its back on the meanings and cultural possibilities it had earlier embodied to enunciate new ones. . . . Indeed, it has been the very malleability of Bond in this respect, his ability to be changed and adapted with the times, that has constituted the basis of his continuing – but, at the same time, always modified – popularity . . . it is not the popularity of Bond that has to be accounted for so much as the popularity of different Bonds, popular in different ways and for different reasons at different points in time.[14]

What Bennett and Woollacott are to Pearson and Uricchio, so *The Many Lives of the Batman* is to my work; in many ways groundbreaking within the field, it serves the fundamental purpose of validating further

---

[13] Tony Bennett and Janet Woollacott, *Bond and Beyond*, London: Macmillan (1987), p. 19.
[14] Ibid., pp. 19–20.

research. The academic study of Batman is still met with 'more snickers than serious reflection',[15] as I discovered when the media picked up on my story,[16] but my debt to Pearson and Uricchio remains. After them, to cite Dziga Vertov on D.W. Griffith, 'it then became easier to talk.'[17]

Which does not mean that, after Pearson and Uricchio, there was nothing more to say. *The Many Lives of the Batman* is a courageous, eclectic anthology, admirably covering a range of bases and demonstrating the character's relevance to a variety of cultural approaches, yet inevitably unable to sustain an extended argument or trace a line of enquiry throughout the book. Above all, Pearson and Uricchio's volume invites 'poaching' from the various pools,[18] and my debt to specific essays will be obvious throughout the following chapters.

Lynn Spigel and Henry Jenkins offer provocative research on the reception of the 1960s series and its context of Pop and camp, while Andy Medhurst returns to the 1950s, putting anti-comics campaigner Fredric Wertham in the dock and scathingly interrogating his assessment of Batman's corruptive 'homosexuality'. Wertham has become a familiar Aunt Sally in discussion on comics, yet there is a danger here of received ideas building on each other, constructing a myth from secondary texts. A return to Wertham's *Seduction of the Innocent* reveals a more complex and subtle writer than is usually assumed, whose highlighting of the gay overtones in the 1950s comic effectively, if paradoxically, brought that important meaning to light, rather than repressing it. My chapter on the campaigns of the 1950s examines Wertham's text in more detail than Medhurst's polemic allows.

Many cultural theorists of the 1980s and 1990s have been tempted to embrace the possibilities for multiple readings as an example

---

[15] Pearson and Uricchio, op. cit., p. 1.
[16] An issue I deal with in the Conclusion.
[17] See Annette Michelson (ed.) *Kino-Eye: The Writings of Dziga Vertov*, London: Pluto (1984).
[18] I poach the term itself from Henry Jenkins, who poached it from Michel de Certeau.

of audiences 'beating the system' – the term, characteristically, is John Fiske's[19] – and finding some kind of 'empowerment' in the micro-politics of their daily lives through this resistance. Eileen Meehan's article in *The Many Lives of the Batman* is a rare but useful account of the lengths to which the 'system' – in this case Warner Brothers – will go in order to provide spaces in the text for the maximum number of 'subordinated' groups, reach for a crossover market and multiply its profit. The relationship between producers and audiences is of course fundamental to my study and Meehan's evidence is a particularly timely caution to the celebration of utopian audience 'resistance' through textual readings; as Medhurst is to the 1950s Batman and Spigel and Jenkins to the 1960s, so Meehan is to the Batman of the late 1980s.

Finally, while neither James T. Kirk, Jean-Luc Picard or The Doctor may yet hold the status of cultural icon, the various texts of *Doctor Who* and *Star Trek* offered useful parallels with my research, particularly in terms of the active and dedicated fandom which surrounds them. Indeed, John Tulloch and Henry Jenkins' *Science Fiction Audiences* – coupled with Jenkins' exemplary solo work on TV fandom, *Textual Poachers* – proved more immediately relevant to my own project than the case studies of Stephen Knight and Ken Gelder. Jenkins is particularly valuable in his discussion of queer readers, stressing that despite the pleasure taken in interpretive games which foreground homoerotic moments between Kirk and Spock or Q and Picard, despite the erotic 'slash' fiction and the fan rewrites, *Star Trek*'s gay viewers are still disillusioned that their readings remain aberrant, 'deviant', and have never been sanctioned by adoption into the 'official' text of *The Next Generation*. This resentment, emerging from ethnographic study, again reminds us that the voices of 'resistant' readings are always limited in the face of the repressive cultural power imposed by the 'dominant' meaning. However, pressure from active fan-groups has occasionally built into a collective voice loud enough to force at least token changes within the programme itself, such as the

---

[19] See John Fiske, *Reading the Popular*, London: Routledge (1991) and *Understanding Popular Culture*, London: Routledge (1991).

Next Generation or the *Star Trek: TNG* episodes which discuss homophobia through allegory and metaphor.[20]

Something of the same process seems to have been at work with Batman, as gay readings of the Batman and Robin relationship progressed through a forty-year progress from the taboo – the confessions of young boys in a 'Readjustment Center' – to the tongue-in-cheek – an ironic, in-crowd enjoyment of the TV show's camp – and finally achieved an 'out' public status with Robin/Chris O'Donnell's transformation into a gay pin-up. As the mainstream voice of gay magazines reminds us that 'queer' readings of the Dynamic Duo are an open secret, so DC Comics seems in recent years to have responded by nodding to a romantic love between Batman and his sidekick within 'official' comic book texts. I look more closely at this development towards the end of my second chapter.

As noted, such important studies often inform this book at a background level – reassuring that it can be done, that such work is academically valid, and suggesting ways to approach the role of a cultural icon in his historical context – rather than through direct intervention. The same is true of a body of other texts which have undoubtedly filtered through to this project without always being directly cited. Janice Radway's *Reading the Romance*, like John Fiske's *Reading the Popular* and its sister-volume *Understanding Popular Culture*, is another of those milestones which overshadow any contemporary study of popular texts and their audience, and I am indebted to both writers even as I argue below against what I see as their sometimes over-enthusiastic celebration of 'resistant' readings.[21]

On a more specific level, Toby Miller's *The Avengers* fed into my study of 1960s television's intertextual relations with Pop, fashion and indeed with itself,[22] while Richard Powers' *G-Men* in many ways paralleled my own research in its tracking of the FBI hero and his changing image from the grim avenger of 1930s pulps, comics and

---

[20] See Jenkins, 'Out of the closet and into the universe', in John Tulloch and Henry Jenkins, *Science Fiction Audiences*, London: Routledge (1995), pp. 237–265.

[21] See Janice Radway, *Reading the Romance*, Chapel Hill: University of North Carolina Press (1991).

[22] See Toby Miller, *The Avengers*, London: BFI (1997).

radio to the 'domesticated' family man and team player of late 1950s and early 1960s popular culture.[23] David Lavery, Angela Hague and Maria Cartwright's *Deny All Knowledge* and Lavery's anthology *Full of Secrets* do for *The X-Files* and *Twin Peaks* what Pearson and Uricchio did for Batman; in particular, Henry Jenkins' chapter on 'alt.tv.twinpeaks' and Susan J. Clerc's cyber-ethnography of online *X-Files* audiences provided a framework for my study of Internet Batman fandom.[24]

In terms of method, however, I found myself referring back to less obvious texts. Most fundamentally, the model of 'reading' as interpretation which I apply throughout this work has emerged from the theory of Stanley Fish, after taking account of Roman Ingarden, Wolfgang Iser and E.D Hirsch, and weighing up the reader-response models offered by John Fiske, Janice Radway, Stuart Hall, David Morley, Michel de Certeau and Henry Jenkins.

I discuss my debt to these texts in the final section of this introduction; the first, to Fish, is particularly important as it explains my position on interpretation which will then tacitly inform everything that follows.

4. Structure

My structure is very simple. It is chronological. The four chapters correspond to four key moments in Batman's history; moments of transition or struggle over meaning, which I then examine in the light of surrounding cultural issues.

The first chapter deals with Batman's origins, and at this early stage attempts to lay down a basic template for the character which I argue has remained constant, so far, throughout all his incarnations. In this

---

[23] Richard Gid Powers, *G-Men*, Carbondale: Southern Illinois University Press (1983).

[24] Henry Jenkins, 'Do You Enjoy Making the Rest of Us Feel Stupid?', in David Lavery (ed.) *Full of Secrets*, Detroit: Wayne State University Press (1995); Susan J. Clerc, 'DDEB, GATB, MPPB, and Ratboy' in David Lavery, Angela Hague and Maria Cartwright, *Deny All Knowledge*, London: Faber and Faber (1996).

chapter I seek to demonstrate that, contrary to what we might expect, the first years of the Batman's history – since the introduction of Robin in 1940 – are characterised by consistency rather than malleability; a surprising discovery, and one which I explain through the institutional concept of 'establishing a brand'. During the Second World War, then, Batman did not adapt to the patriotic propaganda monologue which surrounded him as readily as many popular histories make out; rather, it seems that his writers – in both comic books and film serials – adapted the war context to suit the established template of the character.

The second chapter looks at Dr Fredric Wertham's criticism of Batman in *The Seduction of the Innocent*, and re-examines both Wertham and Batman within the early- to mid-1950s. Through a reconstruction of the frameworks which governed homosexuality during this period, I seek to reconsider Wertham, setting aside the stereotypes of homophobic ogre and lunatic quack which dominate most discussion of his work, and ask how his reading of Batman can be understood in context. Having suggested ways in which the 1954 'gay reading' of Batman could be justified and defended, I go on to trace the development of this reading throughout later decades, from the apparently self-conscious camp of the 1960s TV show to the embracing and reclaiming of this interpretation by gay men in the 1980s and 1990s. As noted above, I also suggest that the 'mainstream' texts of Batman are now incorporating elements of this previously censored meaning.

The third chapter focuses on the 1960s and on the issues surrounding the ABC TV series which debuted in 1966. I argue here that far from an 'aberration' which corrupted the meaning of the comic book, the TV series was a closer adaptation of the mid-1960s comics than is often admitted, and that the 'campiness' derided by many comic fans can readily be found in the 'original' text. I look at the complex matrix of appropriation between advertising, Pop art, television and comics and locate Batman's place in this network: and I go on to examine the multitude of different readings drawn from the TV series, again reconstructing the possible framework for these interpretations from the secondary texts of the period. Once more, I suggest that although the 'camp Batman' became as much a bad object for comic fans and writers as the 'gay Batman', this aspect of the character also seems to have crept back into mainstream texts of recent years, and is perhaps being revalued as an integral part of Batman's history.

The fourth chapter is about issues of Batman fandom and authorship, discourses which I argue became public at the same time, in the early 1960s, and developed in tandem. I begin by bridging the gap between the 1960s and 1980s with a survey of fandom's development through lettercolumns, zines and conventions, and its constant links to comic book authorship; but my main focus here is the period 1986-1999, covering the rise and fall of the 'graphic novel' and the debates surrounding the Warner Brothers franchise of Batman films. Having outlined the institutional context for the 'cult of the author' in post-1986 Batman comics, I examine the way this authorship is constructed by contemporary Internet fandom, and go on to suggest ways in which we might discuss the multiple authorship – writers, editors, pencillers, inkers, letterers – which is unique to the comic medium. In the last section I look at Tim Burton and Joel Schumacher's Batman feature films in the context of authorship, and discuss their relation to comics fandom.

My conclusion returns briefly to autobiography, and bookends the story of myself as Batman fan in 1978 as I examine my own treatment by the media as 'Dr Batman' in the spring of 1999. I also go back to issues raised in the second and third chapters as I ask whether DC Comics and Warners may be relaxing the template of 'Batman' at the end of his first sixty years and allowing the character to embody contradictions and difference, rather than attempting to contain his meanings. Finally, having hypothesised about the routes Batman's owners may take him down in the next few years, I propose that he has now transcended the role of institutional product and could survive independently, albeit in a different form, as twenty-first-century myth.

Epilogue: Reading the Bat-signifier

As I have suggested, I myself have a double identity in terms of my approach to the Batman, as both fan and academic. Much of the time, the interests of these two personae coincide: there should be no contradiction in analysing something you love. I trust, then, that this book will be of interest both to fans who may be unfamiliar with cultural studies theory – although they will doubtlessly have practised it themselves – and to academics who may be fascinated by the role of the cultural icon in history, though they abandoned Batman at an early age.

Sometimes, however, the fan and the academic interests diverge slightly, and the following section is a case in point. It serves to outline my approach to intepretation and its relationship to cultural power, illustrated through a Batman story which seems to explore the same themes. It is integral to the theoretical basis of this book. On the other hand, it tends to interrupt the narrative of Batman's evolution and development.

So I present it here as a supplement, an option. Imagine you can click on a hypertext link in this paragraph and skip straight to Batman's genesis in the late 1930s, if you feel so inclined; but remember that you can also skip back later.

The story titled 'The Batman Nobody Knows' appeared in *Batman* #250, 1973.[25] Bruce Wayne has taken a trio of 'ghetto-hardened kids' on a weekend retreat to the country. A bat flits in silhouette across a yellow moon, forming for an instant an echo of Wayne's symbol, and the boys begin to relate their own experiences, or readings, of the figure represented by that signifier. We soon realise that these readings differ not only from each other but from our own reading, the Batman we 'know'. To Mickey, the Batman is a demon, literally half-bat; he possesses x-ray vision and can pass through solid walls, 'but – heh! – when the Batman connects, it's with a fist of iron!' Ronnie, however, sees him as 'a real live dude', a secret agent figure with a hoverpack and trick gadgets: 'the Batman is Muhammed Ali – Jim Brown – Shaft – an' Superfly all rolled into one!' Finally, Ziggy tells of a ten-feet tall shadow, with 'big bat-ears – what could hear a pin drop miles away!'

These three boys, then, clearly represent different audiences in microcosm, coming away from the 'text' of Batman with very different responses. Bruce Wayne, of course, is in a position of authority here – socially because of his age and status, and most pertinently because of his 'authorship' of the Batman – and is therefore viewed within this

---

[25] All quotations from this story refer back to Frank Robbins and Dick Giordano, 'The Batman Nobody Knows', *Batman* #250, New York: DC Comics (1973), reprinted in *The Greatest Batman Stories Ever Told*, New York: DC Comics (1988).

story as a 'dominant' source of official meaning; until the twist at the
end of the narrative. At this point, Wayne sees himself as the holder of
'true' meaning, commenting to himself on Ziggy's story, which the
boy heard from a reformed criminal, 'Hmm, maybe now we'll get a
true picture of "me"! Willie the Horse should know ... I collared
him!'

Ziggy's version, more obviously than the other two, seems to fit
Roman Ingarden's notion of the reading process. 'The literary work is
a formation that is schematic in various aspects, containing "gaps",
spots of indeterminacy, schematised aspects, etc ... some of its
elements demonstrate a certain potentiality ... [a] "holding-in-
readiness" ... '[26]
Willie the Horse's story, it seems, involved the detail that the
Batman was able to hear Willie 'even though [he] was wearin' hush-
sneakers!'; Ziggy fills in the gaps with what seems to him the only
explanation – 'With big bat-ears ... that's how he spotted Willie–.' As
Ingarden goes on to state, 'the spots of indeterminacy contained in the
work itself (the aspects held in readiness) are transformed into
actualities in the concretisations ... '[27] Note that despite Ingarden's
allocation of a certain power over meaning to the reader, he maintains
the concept of a 'true' version which can be corrupted by misreadings.

> If this [inappropriate] concretisation is considered a concretisa-
> tion of the original work, we get a characteristic phenomenon
> of obscuration. A literary work can be expressed for centuries
> in such a masked, falsifying concretisation until finally someone
> is found who understands it correctly, who shows its true form
> to others.[28]

Ingarden would understand the pained expression on Wayne's face
when he moans quietly 'Oh ... no! Willie sure piled it on thick to
make himself look good!'

---

[26] Roman Ingarden, *The Literary Work of Art*, Evanston: Northwestern University
Press (1973), p. 331.
[27] Ibid., p. 336.
[28] Ibid., p. 340.

Wolfgang Iser offers an extension of Ingarden's model with an account of the text's 'schematised views' being 'realised' through individual readings. Iser draws up two poles, the 'artistic' – the authorial intention – and the 'aesthetic' – the reading – claiming that 'from this polarity . . . the literary work cannot be completely identical with the text, but in fact must lie halfway between the two'.[29]

This theory on the face of it marks a shift towards even greater control on the part of the reader, who now has an equal role to play in the creation of meaning and fulfilment of the text's 'potential'. 'The convergence of text and reader brings the literary work into existence . . . '[30] Here, text is only a 'framework' for a variety of meanings – alone it is 'just . . . sentences, statements, information, etc'[31] – and can be activated by the reading into 'several different realisations'.[32] While, as a study of Fish's later work will show, this is hardly pushing audience participation to an extreme, it seems more liberal than the model Bruce Wayne is employing.

In fact, Wayne's anguished response as 'author' clinging to 'true' meaning would probably find more sympathy with E.D. Hirsch than with the other theorists discussed here. It is Hirsch, then, who comes to the rescue when even Batman is losing control. His key phrase – 'the defense of the possibility of knowledge in interpretation' – boils down to an obligation, an ethical duty, placed on the interpreter to seek and value the authorial intention as 'true' meaning. The word 'meaning' has specific connotations in Hirsch's work – one could say a special significance, had he not also commandeered that word to connote something very different. 'Meaning' is Bruce Wayne's idea of the Batman; 'significance' is what Ziggy, Mickey and Ronnie think they know. The latter may vary from individual to individual, historical period to historical period, value system to value system, but the former must remain stable.

Hirsch's project is to prove that it is possible to discover this 'true'

---

[29] Wolfgang Iser, *The Implied Reader*, London: Johns Hopkins University Press (1974), p. 274.
[30] Ibid., p. 275.
[31] Ibid., p. 278.
[32] Ibid., p. 280.

meaning despite our difference in perspective from the conditions of authorship. Meaning must be agreed on; and by 'meaning' Hirsch insists on the author's meaning, the 'original' meaning, although it is then possible in his view to hold a 'double perspective' – 'that of the author and that of the interpreter. The perspectives are entertained both at once, as in normal binocular vision.'[33] So it seems that Ziggy and his friends' first obligation is to find and agree on the 'real' meaning of the Batman. Only then will they be permitted to entertain their interpretations of a giant, a demon or a superpowered special agent, and then only if they hold these readings in 'binocular vision' with the true meaning. To Hirsch, authorial meaning is almost always 'the original and best'.

What happens next in the Batman story seems to constitute Hirsch's worst nightmare of 'cognitive atheism'. Bruce disappears into the darkness and springs back attired in his Batman costume, landing a little awkwardly with the words 'Let me tell you what I think, fellas . . . the Batman looks like THIS!'

But the kids are not impressed; the authorial meaning is derided, mocked, exposed as just another 'reading' and a pretty feeble one at that. 'Aw, c'mon – Mr Wayne!' says Ziggy with a dismissive wave. 'You're too big for that kinda kid-stuff!' Mickey yawns and prepares to sleep, as Ronnie points out that 'every costume-cat' thinks he knows the true Batman. Bruce's entrance, intended as the final word, turns out to live up only to his statement 'Let me tell you what I think . . . '; an offer of interpretation which is rejected.

This is what Hirsch would term the 'affective fallacy' scenario where control over meanings is unleashed and power donated haphazardly to readers. Street kids challenge and mock their adult benefactor, just as Hirsch fears that students, if the concept of an absolute 'truth' in meaning is denied, will hold an equal authority to their lecturers. No readings are valid, and all readings are valid; anarchy, or solipsism, rule the debate.

Yet that worst-case scenario does not, in this portrayal, look as bleak as Hirsch paints it; rather, it is the academic world of a Stanley Fish, where demonstration of 'truth' is impossible but persuasion is

---

[33] Ibid., p. 49.

entirely valid. To Fish, there is no core of 'determinate meanings', but that does not mean the holder of each interpretation cannot believe wholeheartedly that it is the best – as far as they know, and with the proviso that they may change their minds in the future.[34] Faced with a difference in interpretation, the kids tell their own stories, attempt to convince but prepare to modify their opinions – 'How straight can y'get? Believin' a con-man like "The Horse" ...' 'Well, I dunno, Ronnie ... let's ask Mr Wayne what he thinks!'

This little seminar group of Mr Wayne's chimes not with Hirsch's doom-laden predictions but with the vision of Robert Crosman in his essay 'Do Readers Make Meanings?'[35]

> Imagine, if you will, a group of friends discussing Words-worth's poem. Each has an interpretation that is in some respects at variance with the others, and some of their interpretations are diametrically opposed ... is the result of this failure to agree a battle royal, a war of all against all, in which furniture is smashed and bodily injury sustained?
>
> Of course not. Depending on the degree of respect these people have for each other, they may part on more friendly terms than they began ...
>
> [...] This is not to deny that readers generally believe, whatever interpretation they make of a text, that they have discovered the author's intended meaning.[36]

'Hmm,' says Bruce as Batman, musing over the sleeping children. 'Whatever else it proves – the Batman's frightening image scares the guilty ... not the innocent!' That is, the 'creature of the night' message is directed towards a specific 'ideal reader' – the criminal element, described in the Batman origin sequence as 'a superstitious

---

[34] See Stanley Fish, *Is There A Text In This Class?*, Cambridge, MA: Harvard University Press (1980), pp. 359–360.

[35] See Robert Crosman, 'Do Readers Make Meanings?', in Susan Suleiman and Inge Crosman, *The Reader in the Text*, Princeton: Princeton University Press (1980).

[36] Ibid., pp. 160–161.

cowardly lot'.[37] This alternative community of readers – the innocent – fails to receive the message in the same way as the intended group – the guilty.

It also proves, of course, that the Batman image is open not just to two but to a multiplicity of readings; and that no reading, however absurd it seems to Wayne, can be ruled out. It merely requires, in Fish's term, an interpretive strategy to enable or activate it. Ziggy's view of the Batman as a giant with super-hearing is, after all, prompted and supported by the testimony of Willie the Horse. Mickey's demonic vision is mocked by Ziggy – 'what you don't know about the Batman would fill a book!' – but could also be 'proved' with reference to intertextual sources; within Gotham's diegesis exists a creature called the Man-Bat with a distinct visual similarity to Mickey's concept.[38]

This is to illustrate that despite Bruce's reaction to the 'alternative' versions of the Batman presented here, they can all be 'supported' and argued for with equal validity. As Fish points out in his discussion of William Blake's 'The Tyger', we cannot definitively prove the authority of our version through reference to the text itself, or to intertextual material; two of the theories in Fish's account use the same word, 'forests', as key evidence in opposing cases, just as in this story the kids build the same textual elements – crimefighting, flight, bat-ears – into very different pictures.

We might ask whether there is a limit to these readings; whether a line must be drawn beyond which interpretation cannot go. Similarly, Fish asks whether we could have a reading of 'The Tyger' as an allegory of digestion, and Crosman whether Ezra Pound's 'In a Station of the Metro' could be read as meaning 'that we should drink milk regularly'. Both persuade successfully that these readings, however absurd they initially seem, could be argued within a certain discourse. It is a small leap to imagine a scenario whereby Blake's poem could be interpreted as a tract on digestion, a description of forbidden tiger meat 'burning

---

[37] Bob Kane et al., Detective Comics #33, New York: DC Comics (November 1939).
[38] See for instance Jamie Delano and John Bolton, Batman: Man-Bat, New York: DC Comics (1995), and Frank Robbins, 'Man-Bat over Vegas', Detective Comics #429 (1972), reprinted in The Greatest Batman Stories Ever Told, op. cit.

bright' in the gut;[39] and Crosman convinces that to link 'petals on a bough' and 'beautiful faces' with an orchard for milch cows and a healthy diet 'is no more radical a translation of Pound's words than is a standard reading like "in the midst of technological ugliness mankind is still beautiful".'[40]

Could we imagine a reading of Batman as, say, a flying fish, a reincarnation of Joan of Arc, an advertisement for Pepsi? Undoubtedly, given that we were provided with an appropriate interpretive strategy and context, and Fish's examples suggest that these are not so hard to construct. Consider the readings that Batman has already been subject to, both within the diegesis of the text and without. In the graphic novel *Night Cries* he is seen as a child abuser,[41] in the comic book story 'Shaman' he is Chubala, the tribal totem of the Bat.[42] To the character Ra's al Ghul he is always 'the Detective', to the Hitman he is 'Batboy'.[43] To viewers of the BBC series *Only Fools And Horses*, the Bat-costume and 1960s theme tune provided a ridiculous comic finale for Del-boy and Rodney;[44] to the poet Simon Armitage, Batman was a lonely bachelor, brooding over Robin's departure:

> Batman, it makes a marvellous picture:
> You without a shadow, stewing over
> Chicken giblets in the pressure cooker,
> Next to nothing in the walk-in larder,
> Punching the palm of your hand all winter . . .[45]

The readings roll on. Reverend Robert Terwillinger, writing in *Catholic*

---

[39] Fish, op. cit., p. 348.

[40] Crosman, op. cit., p. 153.

[41] Archie Goodwin and Scott Hampton, *Night Cries*, New York: DC Comics (1992).

[42] Dennis O'Neil, Edward Hannigan and John Beatty, 'Shaman', in *Legends of the Dark Knight* #1-5, New York: DC Comics (November 1989–March 1980).

[43] See Dennis O'Neil *et al.*, 'The Demon Lives Again!', *Batman* #244, New York: DC Comics (September 1972); Garth Ennis and John McCrea, *Hitman*, New York: DC Comics (1997).

[44] In the Christmas Special of BBC Television's *Only Fools and Horses* (December 1996).

[45] Simon Armitage, 'Kid', *Kid*, London: Faber and Faber (1992).

World, saw Wayne's recreation of himself out of tragedy as an example of God's grace.[46] Andy Medhurst insists that Batman is Robin's lover.[47] Andrew Ross, in 'Ballots, Bullets or Batmen' sees Batman as implicitly racist, donning 'a costumed disguise in the grand old tradition of the Klan'.[48]

All these interpretations will seem ridiculous to some; many will be inclined to deny or argue against them. They can all, however, be 'proven' with reference to the text in whatever form. They do not necessarily require a 'double perspective', a knowledge that there is an original meaning – whose, in this case? 'Original' creator Bob Kane, the writer or artist of a specific comic book, or the director of a film or television text? – in contrast to which this new reading is merely 'significance'. They are not necessarily a filling in of gaps left open by the author – the writers of 1950s Batman comics quite probably did not intend to leave gaps for a queer reading, and the producers of the 1943 serial surely did not intend to leave their film open for camp interpretation – but this does not affect the objective 'validity' of the reading compared to any other. On this evidence, it seems that the idea of drawing lines is misguided, that the theory of texts imposing restraints cannot stand. There is, I would argue, potentially no limit to the many lives of the Batman.

We should also note that all the readings listed above are not generated from a single individual outside society, but from what Fish calls an interpretive community, or a subject within that community. Medhurst, as noted above, states candidly his position as 'an interested outsider, armed with a particular perspective [of] homosexuality . . . I'm male, white, British, thirty years old . . . '.[49] The same is true of the readings within the Batman story. The kids are all younger than Wayne, of a different class and with a different social status. Moreover, Mickey is white, Ziggy is a Native American and Ronnie is black. Ronnie's interpretation is particularly interesting in this context

---

[46] Robert E. Terwillinger, 'The Theology of Batman', *Catholic World* (November 1966), p. 127.

[47] Medhurst, op.cit., p. 162.

[48] Andrew Ross, 'Ballots, Bullets or Batmen', *Screen* vol. 31, no. 1 (Spring 1980).

[49] Medhurst, op. cit., p. 150.

because, as I have refrained from mentioning before, it constructs the Batman as a black man; as Ronnie puts it, when he dismisses Wayne's costumed entrance, 'the ''Man'' – the real ''Black Batman''!'

Ronnie's reading is supported by intertextual material from his own cultural experience: what we can perhaps borrow Derrida's term to describe as the *hors-texte*.[50] The Batman, to him, is situated in terms of other black heroes from 1970s America, both real and fictional – 'Muhammed Ali – Jim Brown – Shaft – an' Super-Fly all rolled into one!' When Wayne, with something of an amused smile, attempts to gain a 'double perspective' – 'so you see the Batman as a super-mod crime-fighter, Ronnie' – Ronnie takes a position of authority to set him straight. 'Not super, Mr Wayne! He's one down-to-earth hip-dude!'

Note that Wayne asks how Ronnie 'sees' the Batman, implying a 'reading', a 'significance' in Hirsch's term: Ronnie replies that this is how the Batman 'is'. As Fish argues, we do not receive a meaning and then proceed to interpret, or impose a new one. Rather, meaning is made only in reception. In Fish's favourite example of the student asking 'Is there a text in this class?', the lecturer 'immediately apprehended what seemed to be an inescapable meaning, given his prestructured understanding of the situation'.[51] Thus to Ronnie, his version of the Batman is not an interpretation but common sense.

> 'Like wow, Ronnie – you make the Batman sound like a ''brother''!'
> 'What else could a cool cat like him be, Ziggy?'

It seems irrelevant, if we agree with Fish, to treat this as a reading 'against the grain', a subversion of a text which is 'structured in dominance'. The Batman text is directed towards an ideal, implied reader, who will – as most Batman stories show – understand the text as the producer intended it; that is, Wayne intends the message to reach 'a superstitious cowardly lot' where it will be read as a

---

[50] The term, translated as 'outside the text', usually refers to the role of intertextual frames in the production of meaning. See Julian Wolfreys, *Deconstruction: Derrida*, London: Macmillan (1998), p. 79.
[51] Fish, op. cit., p. 306.

frightening image. That does not mean, however, that Wayne's intention is actually inherent in or built into the text. Indeed, the Bat-text of a man in a cowl and cape, with a grey stretch costume, has been received as 'inherently' comical by viewers of the TV series and indeed by many who feel comics are not worthy of adult study.

Wayne's intention, then, can be seen as just another reading; as is Bob Kane's, or that of the writers Frank Miller and Denny O'Neil, or the directors Tim Burton and Joel Schumacher. A reading like Ronnie's need not be distinguished from these by the term 'resistant' or 'subversive', although we might want to retain the terms 'majority' and 'minority' simply to indicate the size of the interpretive group which shares a specific interpretation; a lot of people saw the 1960s Batman as camp, while the group which views Batman as the reincarnation of Joan of Arc is probably much smaller.

It is worth asking, though, if a reading like Ronnie's is in any way politically 'subversive' or 'resistant', in the way John Fiske or indeed Janice Radway might use the words. The detail of Ronnie's interpretation is interesting. Clearly, it undermines Wayne's role as the bourgeois white protector in making it 'obvious' that Batman is black. Moreover, this Batman is 'down-to-earth'; Ronnie's vision shows him breaking up a gang fight, presumably cleaning up the neighbourhood Ronnie lives in. This in fact implies a very different project to Wayne's, whose crime-fighting often seems to involve a merely personal catharsis from beating up petty thugs like the one who killed his parents, rather than an attempt to alter the society which produced those criminals. Indeed, Andrew Ross in the article cited above sees blackness in Batman's world displaced onto the villainous Joker, who parodies 'minstrel blackface', 'speaks in rappish rhymes and moves his body in a shapeless jive'.[52] Ronnie's 'Black Batman', we can assume, would tackle crime with a different agenda to that employed by Wayne.

In Fiske's terms, this would be a 'resistant' reading; but does it imply any real change on a level above the 'micro-political'? The reading has, as Fish would agree, shaped Ronnie's subjectivity just as Ronnie shapes the text – 'meanings, in the form of culturally derived

---

[52] Ross, op. cit., p. 31.

interpretive categories, make readers'.[53] In this sense, Ronnie may go on to become an activist, resisting 'Mr Wayne's' benevolent patronage and his imposition, as Batman, of a personal vendetta onto the city's ghettos under the guise of 'crime-fighting'. For all we know this could be the catalyst that begins his own training to become 'the real "Black Batman"' of Gotham; a story, perhaps, that cries out to be told.

As it stands, though, Ronnie's interpretation changes nothing in terms of the 'ownership' and 'production' of the Batman. Wayne will continue to dispense his own justice based on the elimination of petty criminals for personal vengeance, consoling himself by taking a few kids to the country every now and then. Ronnie's reading, on this level, is hard to see as a political act for social change.

I have come to the conclusion, then, that while meanings can be seen as existing in a democratic system of persuasion and co-existence, this freedom to construct meanings specific to one's interpretive community should not necessarily be seen as having any power in itself to transform society according to the same utopian system. My approach, in short, could be characterised as Fishean but not Fiskean.

As already indicated, the Fish-eye view of a democracy of meanings, in addition to robbing the author of authority, problematises existing writing on 'subversive' or 'resistant' readings. If a text is not inherently 'structured in dominance', to use Stuart Hall's term[54] – that is, if the meaning intended by authors or producers is just one voice in a Babel of equally valid interpretations – can we still celebrate 'resistant', 'counter' or 'anti-hegemonic' readings? Can a reading be valorised as 'against the grain' if texts have no built-in 'grain'? These questions unsettle the assumptions of many recent cultural commentators; not just of John Fiske, but of Janice Radway, David Morley and to some degree Henry Jenkins, each of whom champions the ability of audiences to form their own localised meanings counter to the producers' intention. Through a critique of Jenkins, Michel de Certeau's 'textual poaching' also loses some of its radicalism and romance.

[53] Fish, op. cit., p. 336.
[54] Stuart Hall, 'Encoding, Decoding', reprinted in Simon During (ed.), *The Cultural Studies Reader*, London: Routledge (1993), p. 99.

To clarify my own stance, I feel it is necessary to shift away from celebrating audience readings *per se*, and towards investigating issues of cultural power and the role of these interpretations within the networks of cultural discourse. To pick the kind of example John Fiske churns out in spades, if a working-class family in Brazil were to read *Baywatch* as a satire of white American consumerism, this might afford them a certain pleasure never anticipated by the show's producers; but this 'subversive' reading does not change their lack of genuine cultural power, for all Fiske's talk in *Reading the Popular* of 'micro-politics' and 'weakening the system from within'.[55] The same must be said for Radway's American housewives who draw from the romance 'a strategy for making her present situation more comfortable . . . rather than a comprehensive program for reorganising her life'[56] and for Morley's television viewers who 'negotiate' or oppose the discourse of *Nationwide* but whose cultural power does not extend beyond their own living rooms.[57]

The point to be drawn, then, is that while any number of valid interpretations is possible – and so the celebration of these multiple readings for their own sake is misguided – these various, contradictory meanings need to be argued for and supported if they are to extend beyond the microsphere of the individual reading, and certain groups are more forceful in disseminating their own interpretations than others. Even in the interpretive democracy of Fish's Babel, corporate voices are able to shout far louder, drowning the opinions of individuals; while it may be a democratic pond of meaning in theory, in practice some readers are tiddlers and some are sharks.

This would be the distinction Uricchio and Pearson make between 'authorised' and 'unauthorised' interpretive communities,[58] which in turn broadly delineates the position of producers and audiences: if DC Comics wants to insist that Batman is heterosexual it can reinforce this

---

[55] Fiske, op. cit., p. 11.

[56] Radway, op. cit., p. 215.

[57] See David Morley, *The 'Nationwide' Audience*, London: BFI (1980).

[58] William Uricchio and Roberta Pearson, *Reframing Culture*, Princeton: Princeton University Press (1993), p. 197.

interpretation by ordering the diegetic introduction of a girlfriend for Wayne or killing off Robin, while if a gay teenager is convinced of the opposite, he would – without Internet access at least – have little power to argue his case. In this instance I think the terms 'resistant' and 'dominant' to describe the two sides would be warranted for the sake of convenience, with the caution that the ability to read a text contrary to the producer's intentions has no relation to social power or the ability to 'change the system', and should not itself be read as such.

With exceptions. As Henry Jenkins' accounts of science fiction fan culture indicate, a fan-group can build a cultural power out of the reach of individuals, and campaign for its own meaning against that of the producers through letter-writing, protest and creative networks on a national level.[59] The Internet has given this culture a worldwide scope, and it forms an important part of my study in terms of the massive fan resistance to Joel Schumacher's Batman films in particular. This online campaign, like Jenkins' 'Gaylaxian' group, appears to have succeeded in persuading the governing institution to modify its approach: in this case, to reshoot or at least re-edit scenes from the theatrical trailer of *Batman and Robin*, and also to encourage the release of a 'darker' director's cut of *Batman Forever*. In this context the term 'resistant' has a wider meaning and almost acquires a political association; the Gaylaxians' protests must surely be understood in terms of a more general struggle for gay rights, for instance.

It should be noted, though, that the opposing sides in these debates do not always conform to expectation; in the case of *Batman and Robin*, the fan resistance is fuelled largely by a homophobic prejudice against the camp spectacle and *double-entendre* of Schumacher's interpretation. In this specific conflict over textual meaning, then, 'queer reading', with the cultural power of Warner Brothers behind it, has surprisingly become what we must call the dominant.

While these questions of meaning and interpretation may seem merely academic, then, they are grounded throughout this book in

---

[59] See for instance Tulloch and Jenkins, op. cit., pp. 8–10, on the original *Star Trek* letter-writing campaign.

specific examples of 'real' audiences at particular historical moments. Ziggy, Ronnie and Mickey may serve as here a useful metaphor for a discussion of abstract theories, but as the next chapter shows, young readers like them were pivotal in the changes to the evolving Batman 'mythos' in 1940. If the *circa* Second World War counterparts of Ziggy and his pals had rejected the cheerful crimefighter, complete with sidekick, who replaced the more fearsome 'Bat-Man' in spring 1940, the *Batman* comic might well have failed, the nascent franchise would have faltered, and a promising comic book character might never have become a popular icon: certainly, we would not have had a Robin.

In my second chapter we see that the interpretations of children were central to the 1950s controversy over what Batman was allowed to signify. In this context, a debating of the boundaries of legitimate meaning – in a brutally homophobic society, the reading of a children's character as homosexual cannot be permitted to flourish – involves very real questions about cultural power and the policing of 'subversive' interpretations. Similarly, in the late 1990s, the question of how young people read Batman comics is once again at the heart of institutional concerns, as DC Comics seems to be adapting the style and content of its regular comics once more – as it did in 1940 – in order to retain the crucial juvenile market. As my conclusion suggests, readers like Ronnie could, as such, be seen as the child-rulers in the contemporary arena of meaning-making, indirectly dictating the decisions of a multinational institution through their choice of purchase. This example again problematises a conventional view of cultural power, as the form of Batman comics seems in a sense to be controlled from 'below', and the 'readers' thus have a strong claim to be regarded as 'producers' not just of their own meanings but of the 'official' text.

Finally, I argue that even if the production of Batman texts from 'above' became commercially untenable, the nature of that production would undergo a fundamental shift rather than collapse. Batman would, I propose, become the sole property of his audience, freed from the structures of institution, and would thrive in popular consciousness, his stories remembered, misremembered and retold alongside new ones in the contemporary equivalent of the folktale. Such stories would be more likely to circulate on the Internet than around a camp fire, but here finally we would have a true democracy of meaning where visions of a ten-foot-high demon or a black secret agent could freely be shared and enjoyed without any risk of censorship from 'Mr Wayne'.

1939-1945

ORIGINS AND WARTIME

We tried to console ourselves with Bat Man, but he was really too 'bad'. It appeared that one of his main pleasures was to scare women in their sleep . . . Bat Man gave no comfort. (Heinrich Böll, *Irisches Tagebuch*, Cologne: Kiepenheuer & Witsch (1957))

Ba. What is that flying about? Swallow? Bat probably . . . Like a little man in a cloak he is with tiny hands.[1]

We open with a paradox. Batman's survival as a cultural icon over sixty years can be attributed to his ability to adapt and change with the period. Yet for the first four years of his existence, the opposite appears to be true. The Batman of this period is notable more for his consistency and adherence to an established template than his fluidity; a fact made all the more remarkable when we consider that the surrounding culture was undergoing the profound changes of the Second World War.

This consistency in the face of change seems at first glance entirely

---

[1] James Joyce, *Ulysses*, Harmondsworth: Penguin (1922), p. 309.

contradictory to expectations. Perhaps this is why more than one popular history of the Batman chooses to misremember these first years, glossing them into a more convenient framework in keeping with the overall notion of the Batman as an inherently fluid signifier; in an earlier piece I was even guilty of perpetuating this 'official' version myself.[2] I now believe this reading to be an oversimplification, and hope to offer a more complex interpretation informed not merely by secondary texts but by a study of the original comic books and the Columbia film serial of 1943. This reading will of necessity involve many more questions, tentative theories and multiple possible solutions than it will present definitive answers.

We can establish certain facts. Batman made his public debut in the May 1939 issue of *Detective Comics*, issue #27. Robin first appeared in the issue of *Detective* dated April 1940; the first issue of *Batman*, the spin-off comic book, was dated April–May of the same year. Japan bombed Pearl Harbor on 7 December 1941. The Columbia film serial *Batman* was released in 1943.

Around these key dates, America witnessed a massive shift in its popular culture as the majority of commercial forms – films, advertisements, posters, radio, comics – were given a common focus and enlisted into the war effort.[3] My argument in this first chapter will be that Batman proved remarkably immune to the wartime 'recruitment' process, and largely managed to retain his own unique style while so many other popular texts – and certainly most comic

---

[2] See Will Brooker, 'Batman: One Life, Many Faces', in Deborah Cartmell and Imelda Whelehan (eds), *Adaptations*, London: Routledge (1999); Bob Kane and Tom Andrae, *Batman and Me*, California: Eclipse (1989); Mark Cotta Vaz, *Tales of the Dark Knight: Batman's First Fifty Years 1939–1989*, London: Futura (1989).

[3] See in particular George H. Roeder, *The Censored War: American Visual Experience During World War Two*, New Haven: Yale University Press (1993); Anthony Rhodes, ed. Victor Margolin, *Propaganda, the Art of Persuasion: World War Two*, London: Angus and Robertson (1976); John W. Dower, *War Without Mercy: Race and Power in the Pacific War*, New York: Pantheon (1986); Thomas Doherty, *Projections of War: Hollywood, American Culture and World War Two*, New York: Columbia University Press (1993); Phillip M. Taylor, *Munitions of the Mind*, Manchester: Manchester University Press (1995).

book characters – were drawn in to serve as part of a propaganda monologue.

I will argue that the Batman 'brand' – the forms and conventions governing Batman and his world, and all the primary aspects of the Batman 'mythos' – were established by the time America entered the war, and were largely adhered to during the next three years. During this period we might speak of Batman adopting elements of his surrounding culture, rather than adapting to it. There are propaganda messages within Batman comics of the war years, but these are almost entirely along the lines of war bond appeals rather than militaristic or anti-Japanese content, and furthermore are in the great majority of cases restricted to cover images. That these very rarely bear any relation to the stories in the comic itself suggests a form of tokenism or a meeting of minimum requirements, whether set by editors, publishers, audience or even government: a lip-service to the wartime context which almost feels tacked on to the very different agenda of the established Batman 'mythos'. Similarly, while the Columbia serial is described by Bob Kane as a crude 'propaganda vehicle'[4] and by Bill Boichel in turn as 'a blatant vehicle for World War II propaganda' – that is, as a co-opting of the Batman character to serve as an anti-Japanese patriot – the propaganda aspects of this film also seem bolted-on, mainly confined to voice-over or even, at a greater remove, 'imposed' upon the film through its secondary publicity material.[5]

While the consistency of the Batman style and mood during this period of great flux may on the surface seem contradictory, I will suggest a simple explanation. During the first years of the Batman's existence the character proved a great commercial success, as is indicated by the launch of his solo comic book in early 1940, a syndicated newspaper strip in 1943 and related merchandise such as

---

[4] Kane with Andrae, op. cit., p. 127; see also Bill Boichel, 'Batman: Commodity as Myth', in Roberta E. Pearson and William Uricchio (eds), *The Many Lives of the Batman: Critical Approaches to a Superhero and his Media*, London: Routledge (1991), p. 10.

[5] My subheading below, 'The Mighty Red-Blooded American Hero', is taken from a film poster reproduced in James van Hise, *Batmania II*, Las Vegas: Pioneer Books (1992), n.p.

cut-out Batplanes and stick-on transfers,[6] to say nothing of the extent to which the formula was imitated by other comic publishers.[7] Once the initial 'brand' was established by late 1940, it was in the interests of National Periodical Publications, later to be renamed DC Comics, to retain the elements which made Batman popular, and also, crucially, to differentiate it from the rest of the superhero market. In turn, when Batman was adapted to cinema, Columbia's producers marketed the serial explicitly on the back of the comic book[8] and clearly saw the importance of keeping to the key elements of the Batman 'mythos', while including sufficient 'propaganda' aspects to locate the film within the contemporary patriotic-adventure genre and so to draw on a larger audience than merely dedicated comic fans. The details of this process require us to consider the roles of readers, writers, artists, editors and producers in the creation and subsequent governing of the Batman narrative, and thus explain the various factors behind Batman's resilience, consistency and fidelity to a strangely removed ideal of urban crime-fighting while the rest of his culture went to war.

1. Establishing the Brand: Year One

In June 1998, some fifty-nine years after the publication of *Detective* #27, Denny O'Neil – group editor of DC Comics' Batman titles – gave me a printout of the current *Bat-Bible*. This ten-page loose-leaf document outlines 'everything the present editor thinks new writers and artists need to know to do basic Batman stories'.[9] As such it represents an updated version of the manuscript viewed by Roberta Pearson and William Uricchio in April 1989, which in turn forms the basis for much of their discussion in the concluding chapter of *The Many*

---

[6] See Chip Kidd, *Batman Collected*, London: Titan Books (1996), pp. 26–27.
[7] 'It was only after the arrival of Batman in 1939 that the deluge of superheroes began,' claims Bob Kane, in Kane with Andrae, op. cit., p. 99.
[8] Newspaper advertisements for the film serial used Bob Kane artwork, while the film poster incorporated drawings of Batman and Robin rather than photographs of the actors in costume. See Kidd, op. cit, p. 29, and van Hise, op. cit, n.p.
[9] Denny O'Neil, 'A Brief *Bat-Bible*: Notes on the Dark Night Detective', unpublished manuscript (June 1998), n.p.

Lives of the Batman.[10] Pearson and Uricchio outline 'five key components [which] constitute the core character of the Batman: traits/attributes; events; recurrent supporting characters; setting and iconography'.[11] O'Neil's 1998 *Bat-Bible* follows similar categories, with no-nonsense headings: 'Who He Is', 'Where He Lives', 'The Batcave', 'His Associates', 'His Character', 'Bruce Or Batman?' 'His Gear', 'His City'.[12] Some of these categories have evolved in their detail since Pearson and Uricchio's 1989 meeting with O'Neil; Tim Drake, the third Robin in current 'continuity', was introduced in 1990, while the supporting cast of Gotham City's police force has also developed during the last ten years. These changes, however, do not invalidate their basic summary:

> the character remains a rich man who dresses in an iconographically specific costume (cape, cowl and bat-logo). Because of the murder of his parents, he obsessively fights crime, using his superb physical abilities in combination with his deductive capacities. He maintains his secret identity of Bruce Wayne, who lives in Wayne Manor in Gotham City. He is surrounded by a supporting cast of friends and foes.[13]

Pearson and Uricchio find their 'lowest common denominator of longlasting and recurrent components' echoed in a cereal box panel of 1989, where the same key elements – 'Who He Is', 'Where He Lives', 'His Character' – are once again repeated, albeit in melodramatic style and, curiously, in the past tense:

> His name was The Batman. A dark, mysterious character of the night, stalking the streets, defying criminals with intelligence, athletic powers and state of the art gadgetry, terrifying enemies who dare cross his path. The Batman had a secret identity, that

---

[10] Pearson and Uricchio, op. cit.

[11] Ibid., p. 186.

[12] O'Neil, op. cit.

[13] Pearson and Uricchio, op. cit., p. 186.

of Bruce Wayne[TM], wealthy playboy. At a very young age his parents were killed on the streets of Gotham City[TM] . . .[14]

The same basic template, the key codes which identify Batman and distinguish him from any other character in popular culture, can be found in a multitude of Batman texts in various forms and for various audiences, whenever a brief definition is required. The entry on Batman from the 1986 *History of the DC Universe*, intended for comic book fans, adopts a yet more hyperbolic prose style but incorporates the same essential points:

> In Gotham City, the child orphaned by a killer's gun sharpened both his mind and body to a keen razor's edge. With his young partner Robin, the Boy Wonder, Bruce Wayne became a cancer on the underworld in the form of the Dark Knight Detective. The Batman.[15]

In turn, *The Super Dictionary*, an educational volume using DC superheroes which I bought with my own birthday ten-dollar note back in 1978, introduces the character to its projected audience of under-tens:

> *Batman* is an inventor. In his secret cave, he made his car, his helicopter, and many other things. Some of the bad people he fights are the Penguin, the Joker, and Catwoman, His other name is Bruce Wayne.[16]

This privileging of Batman's 'inventions' over his detective abilities is unusual, but even here we are given the traits of intelligence and physical skill, while the character's dual identity, war against crime, supporting characters, location and accessories are also suggested or

---

[14] Box side panel, Batman[TM] Cereal, quoted in Pearson and Uricchio, ibid., p. 183.
[15] Marv Wolfman, *History of the DC Universe*, New York: DC Comics (1986), p. 13.
[16] Mary Z. Holmes (ed.), *The Super Dictionary*, New York: Holt, Rinehart and Winston (1978), p. 14.

stated outright. Finally, the same characteristics are vividly presented in a media studies textbook for further education students, as part of a case study of Batman:

> He has never had superpowers. He succeeds through ingenuity, skill and integrity as he faces everything the criminal world can throw at him ... he is a man dressed as a bat who seeks revenge on the criminal community who murdered his parents in cold blood in front of him when he was a child.[17]

If I seem to labour the point that Batman can be reduced to key characteristics, it is because so much that follows will threaten any sense of consistency or constancy around the character. I feel the necessity to establish a simple collection of defining traits as a raft to cling to before embarking on sixty years during which the Batman undergoes so many transformations, and is subject to so many competing, often contradictory interpretations, that any defining essence sometimes seems eroded: the character seems to become merely a name and logo adopted by a multitude of different 'Batmen', each representing a different facet of a specific cultural moment and taking on the concerns of a period or the tastes of an audience. Although it will be my argument in the chapters that follow that Batman is to a significant extent a fluid signifier, and that this has ensured his continued popularity for six decades, part of the character's cultural resonance must be attributed to the fact that the societal concerns or audience meanings which the Batman has carried are not merely absorbed by the yielding, malleable figure of a man in a bat-mask, but fitted within a quite rigid and consistent template which specifies not just the character's appearance but his location, associates, motivation and attributes. Whether Columbia wants to produce a patriotic wartime Batman, or Dr Fredric Wertham wants to argue that Batman has a homoerotic relationship with Robin,[18] or Grant Morrison

---

[17] 'Batman: The Case of the Caped Crusader', in Barbara Connell, Jude Brigley and Mike Edwards, *Examining the Media*, London: Hodder & Stoughton (1996), p. 65.
[18] Fredric Wertham, *Seduction of the Innocent*, London: Museum Press (1955).

and Dave McKean want to portray the Batman as a wraithlike figure tormented by inner demons,[19] the interpretation must correspond to a minimal defining structure, or it is simply not recognisable.

The character's position as a cultural icon is, then, due to the extent to which he can adapt within key parameters. He must remain familiar while incorporating an edge of novelty; he must keep the loyalty of an older generation who remember their childhood through him and secure his place in popular memory,[20] while constantly pulling in the younger audience who constitute his primary market. He must always serve the concerns of the present day, while retaining an aura of myth.

This sense of myth and resonance which still surrounds the Batman has its source not in the specifics of his changes over time, but in the opposite, in those elements which never change. The myth lies not in the details of continuity debated by fans, but in the narrative which has entered popular consciousness. I could stop anyone on the street and ask them what they knew about Batman, with a virtual guarantee of hearing back the same list of key traits, the same story.

Indulge me. This is what I would have told you about Batman when I was five years old: *Batman is Bruce Wayne, a millionaire who dresses in a bat-costume and fights crime. He has no special powers but is very fit and strong, and very intelligent. He lives in Gotham City. He fights crime because his parents were killed when he was young. He is often helped by his sidekick, Robin. He fights villains like the Joker.*

This may seem childishly basic. I am fumbling to express a vision of the Batman as I think 'popular consciousness' remembers him: vaguely, naïvely, mythically, as it might remember the story of Jesus or Dracula, Robin Hood or Sherlock Holmes,[21] As Denny O'Neil has argued,

Batman and Robin are part of our folklore. Even though only a

---

[19] Grant Morrison and Dave McKean, *Batman: Arkham Asylum*, New York: DC Comics (1989).

[20] See for instance Lynn Spigel and Henry Jenkins, 'Mass Culture and Popular Memory', in Pearson and Uricchio, op.cit.

[21] With reference to Dracula and Robin Hood and their place in popular culture, see Ken Gelder, *Reading The Vampire*, London: Routledge (1994) and Stephen Knight, *Robin Hood*, Oxford: Blackwell (1994).

tiny fraction of the population reads the comics, everyone knows about them the way everybody knows about Paul Bunyan, Abe Lincoln ... Batman and Robin are the postindustrial equivalent of folk figures. They are much deeper in our collective psyches than I had thought. Because these characters have been around for fifty years, everybody in the country knows about them. They have some of the effect on people that mythology used to and if you get into that you can't avoid the question of religion.[22]

Pearson and Uricchio's 'reductionist articulation', quoted above, is more that of a comic book fan or film viewer, whereas mine, reducing yet more and aiming lower, could I think be articulated by someone who had never picked up a comic or even seen Batman on screen,[23] just as I could come up with two or three things I know about Jesus without having read the New Testament, or tell you Sherlock Holmes' address without knowing who wrote his stories or played him in the movies.

Yet this basic definition nevertheless rings true for the Batman of every decade since the 1940s, whether his surrounding culture was engaged with World War Two, McCarthyism or Pop Art: and it remains true of – or at least is not contradicted by – the versions of the Batman in every media form he has taken thus far, from Bob Kane's comic books to Frank Miller's graphic novels, from the ABC television series with Adam West to Warner Brothers' animated cartoon of the 1990s, from Columbia's *Batman* (1943) to Joel Schumacher's *Batman and Robin* (1997). It fits Denny O'Neil's interpretation. It fits Fredric Wertham's interpretation. It fits Grant Morrison and Dave McKean's interpretation.

Whether this template will remain applicable for as long as the

---

[22] Denny O'Neil, quoted in Pearson and Uricchio, 'Notes from the Batcave', in Pearson and Uricchio, op. cit., p. 23.

[23] The 'tearful grandmothers' and others who phoned O'Neil to protest about the 'death of Robin' storyline – believing that Dick Grayson had been killed – had clearly never read the comic book itself, which identifies the victim as Jason Todd. Pearson and Uricchio, op. cit., p. 22.

character survives is open to debate. Warner Brothers' *Batman Beyond* cartoon series, for instance, imagines a future where the older Bruce Wayne mentors a young 'Batman', and it seems possible that this scenario, or one similar, will be adopted by DC Comics as the 'official' solution to the character's ageing. The implications of such decisions on the part of producers, and their consequences for the Batman's 'key traits', will be discussed in my final chapter. For now, though, I want to return to the other end of the Batman's history, and establish the process through which the basic template was established during the first year of the character's publication.

(i) Batman is Bruce Wayne, a millionaire who dresses in a bat-costume and fights crime

In this bold statement we have encompassed the character's name, iconography, (dual) identity and – in the Proppian sense – his sphere of action;[24] as Pearson and Uricchio assert, Batman is defined primarily by his 'iterative actions' as 'the man who fights crime'.[25] All of these traits were established to the readership by the end of the first episode; yet their evolution, of course, took place prior to the publication of *Detective Comics* #27. The name 'Batman' itself, which would later become the trademark for one of Warner Brothers' largest franchises, first saw print in *Detective Comics* #26, April 1939, as a preview line at the top of a page.[26] Bob Kane claims to have first drawn a 'Bat-man' in the mid-1930s, although the page of sketches he presents in his autobiography, dated '1/17/34', may strike the cynical viewer as being just too neat a piece of evidence, with an air of mannered carelessness that suggests an 'ur-text' conjured up after the fact rather than scrawled by a teenager in the Bronx and lovingly, presciently 'stored in an old trunk'.[27] Intriguingly, a recent article in the *Boston Globe*

---

[24] See Vladimir Propp, *The Morphology of the Folktale*, Austin: University of Texas Press (1968).

[25] Pearson and Uricchio, op. cit., p. 195.

[26] See Kidd, op. cit., p. 25.

[27] See Kane with Andrae, op. cit., pp. 34–36.

reported that a Boston resident, Frank Foster, had also kept some drawings from 1932 in an old trunk; these sketches of a masked superhero are titled 'Batman' and 'Nightwing'.[28]

Be that as it may, Kane openly admits to the number of influences which shaped his creation of the character's appearance, identity and iconography. Like most elements of the Batman 'mythos', the character's name was both original and derivative. Previous years had seen a silent movie called *The Bat* (1926) and its remake *The Bat Whispers* of 1931;[29] *The Spider* magazine from November 1935 also included a Bat Man in its story 'Death Reign of the Vampire King'.[30] The Bat, played by Chester Morris, 'was a detective who tried to track down the mysterious Bat, and was revealed to be the killer himself at the end of the film';[31] he announced his next victim by projecting a 'bat-signal' onto the wall of their home. A similar 'hidden identity' device was used in *The Mark of Zorro* (1920), in which Douglas Fairbanks played both the wealthy fop Diego and his masked alter ego, whose secret cave had its exit behind a grandfather clock in Diego's living room. Each of these pulp texts – in combination with the radio show *The Shadow*, Bela Lugosi as *Dracula*, the syndicated feature *The Phantom* and of course the success of *Superman* in 1938 – contributed to the Bat-Man's evolution.

Kane's friend Bill Finger, the first writer of the Batman stories, suggested changes to the detail of the costume, which Kane claims to have developed from Leonardo da Vinci's sketches of a flying-machine. Following Finger's advice, the character acquired a hood with blank eye-slits instead of a 'small domino mask', a dark grey costume – rather than Kane's original red and black design – a cape rather than rigid wings, and gloves to avoid fingerprints.[32]

The Bat-Man's first appearance in print, and the explanatory

---

[28] See Diego Ribadeneira, 'A Cape Crusader', *The Boston Globe* (20 August 1998), p. B1. Thanks to Elizabeth Garrells for this clipping.

[29] See Kane with Andrae, op. cit., p. 38.

[30] Ibid., p. 45.

[31] Ibid., p. 38.

[32] Ibid., p. 41. Although Kane tends to play down Finger's authorship of the character, it seems clear from his own admissions that without Finger, Batman would have looked more like Robin.

paragraph immediately below, illustrates the extent to which the basic template for the character was in place at this earliest point, and how little the essential concept has changed: the image of a winged silhouette on a city rooftop, against a full moon, could stand at the opening of any Batman comic published today, and the caption would need only minimal tweaking. 'The "Bat-Man", a mysterious and adventurous figure fighting for righteousness and apprehending the wrong doer, in his lone battle against the evil forces of society . . . his identity remains unknown.'[33] Here we are given the name, much of the iconography – winged cape, cowl with pointed ears, dark costume – and a description of his essential behaviour which could stand for the next sixty years. Batman's real identity is 'unknown', 'mysterious'. His stories are in the genre of adventure and action – he is 'fighting for righteousness', not campaigning for social change – and he operates within a primal code of morality, rather than the letter of the law – 'righteousness' implies justice, not necessarily legality. While we have yet to learn his origin or motivation, this is already a personal, 'lone battle' which places Batman outside institutionalised crimefighting. He is not a form of costumed policeman doing his job, but a crusader dedicated to a large-scale and potentially endless mission not against individuals but an abstract concept of 'evil forces'. At the same time, the rooftop with its lit window, and the skyscrapers clearly visible behind, place Batman firmly within a modern urban milieu rather than the historical gothic setting which the caption might otherwise suggest, and the episode title, 'The Case of the Chemical Syndicate', anchors the character to a more pragmatic sphere of business deals, while giving him an angle of detection – if the picture recalls Dracula, the title could almost head up a Sherlock Holmes story – to accompany the action and adventure implied above.

In the first panel we are introduced not to Bat-Man, but to Bruce Wayne, the 'young socialite' and friend of Commissioner Gordon. Within three frames, Wayne's personality is established as he lounges in Gordon's armchair, chin in his hand and a pipe firmly in the corner of his mouth – when Gordon invites him to come investigate a murder,

---

[33] Bob Kane and Bill Finger, 'The Case of the Chemical Syndicate', *Detective Comics* #27, New York: DC Comics (May 1939), p. 1.

Wayne can only muster 'Oh well, nothing else to do, might as well.'
This lazy socialite is explicitly distanced from the Batman himself, who
haunts this scene only as a rumour, his mystery even to the police
emphasised once again.

> Bruce: Well, Commissioner, anything exciting happening these
> days?
> Gordon: – No – o – except this fellow they call the 'Bat-Man'
> puzzles me![34]

The next panels continue the narrative within the sphere of
contemporary – that is, late 1930s – city police procedural. The
frames are heavy with dialogue as Gordon interviews a suspect, and
include a flashback to the murder scene. Bruce Wayne hovers in the
background of these ten panels, saying not a word until he announces,
knocking out his pipe, 'Ho hum! I'll leave you here to finish your work
. . . I'm going home.'[35] His secret identity is saved for a surprise ending
in the last panel, when Wayne returns to his room in civvies and
emerges in costume.

Three panels after Wayne's initial departure, the Bat-Man appears.
This is the first time we have seen him in the light, rather than in
silhouette, and the essential iconography which would remain in place
for the next sixty years is already there – a blue-black cowl topped
with small ears which covers half his face, and matching cape, boots
and trunks worn over a light grey body-suit. The plain black bat-
symbol on his chest would be a constant until 1964's 'New Look'
added a yellow oval to the design.

Batman stands with his arms folded, waiting for two crooks to turn
and see him. He needs to say nothing. His image is clearly already
familiar, and feared, in the criminal underworld: they whirl, eyes
wide, as one of them cries 'The Bat-Man!!!' And then, for the first
time, the Batman 'fights crime'.

---

[34] Ibid.
[35] Ibid., p. 2.

(ii) He has no special powers but is very fit and strong, and very intelligent

Having demonstrated the power of Batman's appearance alone – the caption describing him as a 'menacing figure' – the next three panels go on to establish the character's physical abilities. 'The Bat-Man lashes out with a terrific right . . . he grabs his second adversary in a deadly headlock . . . and with a mighty heave . . . sends the burly criminal flying through space . . .'[36] These three panels are significant in that they show not just the Batman's strengths, but his limitations. He is not Superman, who we have seen on the cover of *Action Comics* tossing an automobile above his head. His 'terrific right' does not sever the criminal's head from his body; his 'mighty heave' sends the other man over his shoulder, but not into the next state. Batman is clearly a man with extraordinary combat skills, but not a superhuman with unexplained powers. In theory, his abilities are such as any reader could achieve with the right dedication and training. Furthermore, they are not limited to physical brawn or martial arts. The Batman dispatches the criminals not as a means in itself – that is, to put two crooks temporarily out of action – but, as we see in the next panel, in order to obtain a clue to the murder in the form of the document they were carrying. By the bottom of the page Batman is speeding away in his car, 'a grim smile' playing on his lips as he reads the document, while Gordon and his men bustle ineffectually around the crime scene.

It is clear, then, that Batman works independently from the 'official' police force – by striking first at the crooks, he acquires the evidence which would have been vital to their research. He is, moreover, apparently considered an outlaw. When the police arrive we see Gordon yelling 'It's the Bat-Man! Get him!' as an officer shoots at the silhouetted form on a rooftop. This panel enforces the distinction between the Batman's 'righteous' mission against 'evil forces' and the more conventional pursuit of lawbreakers embodied by Gordon, although his ambiguous status in relation to the police would subsequently be 'cleaned up' and the character effectively made less threatening, as discussed below.

---

[36] Ibid., p. 3.

On the next page Batman arrives just in time to rescue another businessman from the 'chemical syndicate', who is about to be placed in a gas chamber. In four panels we see Batman display not just physical agility, strength and courage, but quick thinking and resourceful improvisation. The captions run as follows:

> At that moment the 'Bat-Man' leaps through an open transom . . . the 'Bat-Man' seizes a wrench from a table and leaps for the gas-chamber . . . the 'Bat-Man' quickly plugs the gas-jet with a handkerchief, as the gas chamber descends entirely over them . . . he then unties Rogers, and with a powerful swing . . . [37]

Batman smashes the glass with the wrench and frees them both, just as the attempted killer returns. By the bottom of the page, he is addressing the criminal mastermind behind the case, revealing in his longest speech yet that he understands every detail of the plan. As the crook struggles free and draws a gun, Batman swings again – a terrific left, this time – and his enemy falls into a tank of acid. 'A fitting end for his kind', Batman concludes grimly; again, this apparent relish in the death of criminals is characteristic of the early episodes, and would later be modified.

Most of the key traits, however, are established in this first episode. Batman is not merely a strongman but a detective who uses his deductive mind and resourcefulness to fight crime. This framework is crucial to his differentiation from the ranks of superheroes who would follow in the next few years, and the unique 'brand identity' it builds around Bob Kane's character must have proved a strong reason – in the eyes of both DC's editors and Columbia's producers – for keeping the formula almost entirely intact.

(iii) He lives in Gotham City

Well, not originally. The name 'Gotham City' was first used in

---

[37] Ibid., p. 4.

Detective #48, in February 1941;[38] Batman's locale was previously referred to as 'Metropolis',[39] 'downtown Manhattan'[40] and simply 'New York'.[41] Of course, for all intents and purposes it is still New York, and more specifically Manhattan: Denny O'Neil goes even further, virtually giving grid references and the weather forecast in his definition of Gotham as 'Manhattan below Fourteenth Street at 3 a.m., November 28 in a cold year'.[42] Bill Finger had previously admitted as much, explaining that he found the name 'Gotham Jewellers' in a phone directory and chose it over the alternative titles 'Civic City' or 'Coast City'. His reasons for shifting Batman's world to a fictional metropolis were apparently commercial, based on a notion of audience engagement. 'We didn't call it New York because we wanted anybody in any city to identify with it. Of course, Gotham is another name for New York'[43] – or, as O'Neil calls it, 'its mirror-world counterpart'.[44] And of course, New York is the capital city of the world, the 'city which signifies all cities, and, more specifically, all modern cities, since the city itself is one of the signs of modernity'. The description is Richard Reynolds', from *Superheroes: A Modern Mythology*. To Reynolds, New York is

> the place where . . . the author takes the reader in order that something may be made to happen. [. . .] New York is a sign of fictional discourse for the imminence of such possibilities – simultaneously a forest of urban signs and an endlessly wiped slate on which unlimited designs can be inscribed – cop shows, thrillers, comedies . . . and cyclical adventures of costumed heroes as diverse as Bob Kane's *Batman* and Alan Moore's *Watchmen*.[45]

---

[38] Bill Boichel, 'Batman: Commodity as Myth' in Pearson and Uricchio, op. cit., p. 9.

[39] Ibid.

[40] *Detective Comics* #33, New York: DC Comics (November 1939).

[41] *Detective Comics* #31, New York: DC Comics (September 1939).

[42] Denny O'Neil, unpublished lecture (January 1989).

[43] Quoted in Kane with Andrae, op. cit., p. 44.

[44] Denny O'Neil, unpublished lecture (January 1989).

[45] Richard Reynolds, *Superheroes: A Modern Mythology*, London: B.T. Batsford (1992), p. 19.

Gotham is New York – despite Finger's attempts at disguise, any reader encountering Gotham City's 102-storey 'State Building' in 1941[46] would have realised that. And Gotham 'is' Batman.

> As the Riddler put it, 'When is a man a city? When it's Batman or when it's Gotham. I'd take either answer. Batman is this city ... That's why we're here. That's why we stay. We're trying to survive in the city. It's huge and contradictory and dark and funny and threatening.'[47]

Huge, contradictory, dark, threatening, even occasionally funny – echoing Reynolds' remark that New York serves as a backdrop for comedies, as well as cop shows – as the Riddler well knows, the adjectives could apply equally to Batman and his narratives as they do to Gotham itself.

(iv) He fights villains like the Joker

He fought the Joker in *Batman* (1966), and in *Batman* (1989); he fought the Joker in *The Killing Joke*, *Arkham Asylum*, *The Dark Knight Returns* and scores of other stories over the last sixty years. But he didn't fight the Joker in 1939.

The villains of Batman's first year were, like Batman himself, an odd but effective hybrid of two cinematic modes which shared a visual style if not a cultural background: the Hollywood gangster cycle of the 1930s, and the German Expressionist movement. Kane was a fan of *Little Caesar* and *Public Enemy*,[48] and explicitly aimed for a 'Warner Brothers look'[49] in the early stories, even going so far as to include a Cagney lookalike in 'Public Enemy #1', a story from *Batman #4*. This

---

[46] *Detective Comics* #43, New York: DC Comics (July 1941).

[47] Pearson and Uricchio, op. cit., p. 187; the authors are quoting Neil Gaiman's 'When Is A Door? The Secret Origin of the Riddler', *Secret Origins Special* #1, New York: DC Comics (1989).

[48] Kane with Andrae, op. cit., p. 7.

[49] Ibid., p. 111.

influence is subtly evident in the first year of Batman adventures, despite the lack of such obvious homages: from the opening frame of 'The Case of the Chemical Syndicate', with its silhouetted rooftop and backdrop of Manhattan skyline, we are clearly located in the urban milieu. The second story also opens on a rooftop, with the vents, pipes and bricks inked as carefully as the figures; the backgrounds enjoy equal attention, with a sometimes dizzying perspective of office windows providing a stage for Batman's acrobatics. Bruce Wayne's world is, in turn, one of policemen, business deals, petty thugs and crooked magnates, a world where information about his alter ago circulates in the headlines of the 'Tribune' — 'Batman Eludes Capture By Spectacular Leap'[50] — or more discreetly, in the public notices column — 'Batman . . . go to General Post Office and ask for a letter addressed to John Jones.'[51]

By the third story, however, an element of the exotic had entered Batman's diegesis in the form of a crazed scientist and his giant Indian manservant Jabah; Doctor Karl Hellfern, 'later to be more widely known as Doctor Death',[52] was the first of Batman's foes to be given an evocative 'supervillain' codename, and the first to come back from the dead in a sequel — this time with a giant Cossack manservant called Mikhail — even if his reincarnation occurred just four weeks after his apparent demise. The fifth adventure, though, took a new slant entirely as Batman travelled first to Paris, then to Hungary, after a new villain called 'The Monk'. Not only did the Monk adopt a stylised costume like Batman — a red gown and hood — but his henchmen were werewolves, vampires and a giant ape. For the first time, the uncanny seeped into Batman's previously realist adventures, and the rooftops of the city gave way to stilted trees against a looming moon, crooked castle turrets and gothic spires; a *mise-en-scène* far more reminiscent of *The Cabinet of Doctor Caligari* than of *Little Caesar*.

By the time Batman's origin appeared in episode six, then, the 'mythos' had begun to combine contemporary 'realism' with elements

---

[50] *Detective Comics* #28, New York: DC Comics (June 1939).

[51] *Detective Comics* #29, New York: DC Comics (July 1939). Interestingly, 'John Jones' was later used as the alias of Batman's colleague The Martian Manhunter.

[52] Ibid.

of the supernatural, or apparently supernatural. It was this hybrid mode that enabled the introduction of humans in stylised costumes like Catwoman (*Batman* #1, Spring 1940) alongside deformed 'freaks' like the Penguin (*Detective* #58, December 1941), Two-Face (*Detective* #66, August 1942), Clayface (*Detective* #40, June 1940) and the Joker (*Batman* #1).[53]

The genesis of these villains[54] emphasises once more the importance of both Hollywood and Expressionist cinema to Batman's milieu – Catwoman came from Jean Harlow in *Hell's Angels*, Clayface from Lon Chaney in *The Phantom of the Opera* and the Joker from Conrad Veidt in *The Man Who Laughs*.[55] The case of the Joker in particular also brings up significant debates over authorship.

Kane has, of course, a strong claim to have 'created' Batman in his early sketches, with the proviso that many of his ideas were derivative and were in any case refined by Bill Finger before the character was presented to DC's editors. According to Kane, he subsequently 'discovered' the seventeen-year-old artist Jerry Robinson in the Catskill Mountains[56] and hired him as an assistant. He then took on George Roussos, one of many who responded to an ad in the *New York Times*,[57] to draw just backgrounds to the strip.

Despite Kane's haziness and the DC-authorised line that Jerry Robinson arrived 'three issues into the Batman's run',[58] any comparison between Kane's technically clumsy, cartoonish solo work and the Batman of *Detective Comics* #28 indicates that Robinson was already involved with the strip a month into its publication, either

---

[53] I am indebted to Bill Boichel, op. cit., pp. 8–9, for pinpointing these dates, although he cites the year of Clayface's first appearance incorrectly as 1949.

[54] The inspiration for Batman's gallery of villains did not come solely from the cinema, and Chester Gould's *Dick Tracy* strip was another important influence. See *Batman: The Sunday Classics*, New York: Kitchen Sink Press/DC Comics (1991), p. 208.

[55] Kane with Andrae, op. cit., pp. 107–110.

[56] Ibid., p. 101.

[57] Ibid.

[58] Marschall, op. cit., p. 5. We must assume that DC editors approved this version of the authorship history, as it appears in a prestige archive edition of their most important franchise's first adventures.

pencilling for Kane to ink over or taking charge of the art himself.[59] Furthermore, although the officially sanctioned history has DC's veteran scripter Gardner Fox joining the Batman team 'later' – which suggests four or more issues into publication – Kane himself remembers that Fox was responsible for the first use of Batman's utility belt, in the Doctor Death story. The panel he refers to can be found in *Detective* #29, just two months after Batman's first appearance.

By all accounts, then, it seems that Kane and Finger were replaced, albeit temporarily, by the second and third episodes respectively of Batman's career. Despite their joint claims to 'creation' – which Kane in any case attempts to slant towards himself, Finger having passed on by the time Kane wrote his autobiography – it could well be argued that the evolution of Batman's appearance and iconography, and by extension perhaps a good measure of the character's commercial success, has as much to do with Jerry Robinson and Gardner Fox as with Kane and Finger. Fox not only introduced Batman's utility belt but, in *Detective* #31 of September 1939, the Batarang and the Batgyro, which Kane claims to have 'designed' himself[60] from the writer's more pedestrian 'boomerang' and 'Autogyro' – despite the appearance of the former terms in that episode's captions.[61] Similarly, Kane argues against Jerry Robinson's claim to have 'created' the Joker from the inspiration of a playing card, overriding Robinson's version of events with the 'actuality' of his own account. 'I do not doubt that my ex-assistant is sincere in believing that he did, in fact, create the Joker, but time has eroded his memory.'[62]

In this and in many other cases, it is impossible to discern the various hands at work behind the ubiquitous signature 'Bob Kane', which was stamped on every Batman product until the mid-1960s. We can be sure, though, that while the myth of a sole creator aided by the valiant and underrated Bill Finger serves the purposes of Bob Kane and

---

[59] It is very difficult even for the trained eye to discern the exact contribution of penciller and inker respectively to a finished comic book page.
[60] Kane with Andrae, op. cit., p. 103.
[61] *Detective Comics* #31, New York: DC Comics (September 1939).
[62] Kane with Andrae, op. cit., p. 105.

the potted histories of DC Comics, it is indeed a myth, in the common sense of 'falsification'. The 'actuality' of Batman's authorship is far more complex, far less neat, and will probably never be known in full.[63]

(v) He fights crime because his parents were killed when he was young

Readers had to wait half a year before the origin of the Batman was revealed: for six issues, the character simply fought crime with no apparent motivation. In November, though, the event which turned Bruce Wayne into the Batman was finally revealed, and his unique skills explained as a result of dedicated training. Pearson and Uricchio shrewdly note that 'the origin story establishes the four central attributes/traits of the character: obsession; deductive abilities; physical prowess; and wealth'.[64] Four frames tell the story, following from the death of Thomas and Martha Wayne.

'Days later, a curious and strange scene takes place', reads the caption. The young Bruce kneels by his bed, hands clasped and cheeks wet, praying by candlelight. 'And I swear by the spirits of my parents to avenge their deaths by spending the rest of my life warring on all criminals.' This is no conventional prayer, but a 'curious and strange scene'; the boy is not turning to God for comfort in his loss, but vowing on the 'spirits'. This is a personal vendetta, as DC's Dick Giordano has noted, founded in 'emotion that is primal and timeless and dark. The Batman does what he does for himself, for *his* needs. That society gains from his actions is incidental . . .'[65]

'Deductive abilities' are conveyed by showing Bruce, years later, dressed in a white coat and goggles and peering at a test tube; 'physical prowess' is demonstrated in the next panel as Bruce, stripped to blue

---

[63] Joe Desris makes a valiant attempt to detect authorship in his 'Introduction' to *Batman: The Sunday Classics*, op. cit., pp. 6–12. This struggle by a comics historian shows just how difficult it is to identify the creators behind unsigned comic strips.

[64] Pearson and Uricchio, op. cit., p. 195.

[65] Dick Giordano, 'Growing Up With The Greatest', *The Greatest Batman Stories Ever Told*, New York: DC Comics (1988), pp. 7–8: also quoted in Pearson and Uricchio, op. cit., p. 194.

trunks, thrusts a massive barbell over his head in a one-handed grip. The detailed laboratory of the previous panel, wafting with smoke and decorated with carefully-drawn stands, racks and a bunsen burner, is replaced here with a flash of yellow light around Bruce's muscled body, exploding with dynamic energy. Finally, we move to the lavish *mise-en-scène* of the Wayne Manor interior. Bruce is a mere silhouette in an armchair, facing the fire and a large portrait, presumably of his father. 'Dad's estate left me wealthy', he muses. 'I am ready . . . but first I must have a disguise.'

The following image of Bruce – an adult now, chin in his clasped hand with firelight glowing on the wall behind him – is a subtle echo of the frame at the top-right corner of the page, with the boy Bruce in the same posture by candlelight. As the boy had ominously sworn to spend 'the rest of my life warring on all criminals', so the man's vision is equally dark: 'My disguise must be able to strike terror into their hearts. I must be a creature of the night, black, terrible . . . a . . . a . . .'[66]

'The sequence is completed', Pearson and Uricchio conclude, 'when the bat flies in at the open window and Bruce derives his inspiration.'[67]

We should note that this origin story, conveyed with perfect economy in twelve elegant panels – three for the murder, with the rest of the sequence in a neat nine-panel grid – and unchanged for sixty years, was never presented with a fanfare: the cover of *Detective* #33 makes no mention of it, and the sequence is merely a prelude to an unremarkable ten-page adventure called 'The Dirigible of Doom'. Whenever the sequence is reproduced, in fact – in *The Penguin Book of Comics*,[68] or *Tales of the Dark Knight*,[69] for instance – the artwork is taken from *Batman* #1 (1940), where a half-page image of the Batman from *Detective* #34 was superimposed over the mildly incongruous drawing of the 'dirigible' which initially headed the story.

---

[66] *Detective Comics* #33, New York: DC Comics (November 1939).

[67] Pearson and Uricchio, op. cit., p. 195.

[68] George Perry and Alan Aldridge, *The Penguin Book of Comics*, Harmondsworth: Penguin (1967), pp. 170–171.

[69] Cotta Vaz, op. cit., p. xiii.

As Pearson and Uricchio note, 'writers have repeatedly returned to the scene of the crime and restaged the origin much as it "happened" in 1940 [*sic*]'.[70] The previously anonymous killer was revealed to be Joe Chill, who was then revealed to be in the employ of Joe Moxon; more recent continuity of the 1990s returns to the notion that the murder was a senseless mugging, the editors having realised that Batman's war against crime can find no satisfying conclusion in the punishment of a single individual. Meanwhile almost every self-contained Batman 'graphic novel' since Frank Miller's *Batman: The Dark Knight Returns* of 1986 has sought to tell the same story again, with a fresh angle or treatment. Miller reduced the origin to a series of fragmented, silent flashback panels, the visions of gun barrels and bullets breaking up finally into a mosaic of pearls:[71] Brian Augustyn took the setting back to a nineteenth-century highway robbery.[72] Dave Gibbons emphasised the parallels with Superman's origin, stressing the childhood trauma and loss of family which unites the two men,[73] and Denny O'Neil, having extended the telling of Bruce's teenage years to involve FBI training and Zen Buddhism, wryly restaged the primal moment with the Waynes as ice statues and Joe Chill as a murderous snowman.[74]

But the first revisiting of the origin was far earlier and came only five months later, in *Detective* #38. A young boy, his eyes wide, watches helplessly as his parents fall, crying 'Mother! Father!' Yet this time there was someone to comfort him and take him under a dark wing. 'I'm the Batman! I want to help you!'[75] This time the boy was Dick Grayson, soon to become Robin, the Boy Wonder.

---

[70] Pearson and Uricchio, op. cit., p. 194. Strictly speaking, if the 1939 version states that Thomas and Martha Wayne were killed 'some fifteen years ago', Bruce must have been orphaned in 1924.

[71] Frank Miller, *Batman: The Dark Knight Returns*, New York: DC Comics (1986).

[72] Brian Augustyn and Mike Mignola, *Batman: Gotham by Gaslight*, New York: DC Comics (1989).

[73] Dave Gibbons and Steve Rude, *Superman/Batman: World's Finest*, New York: DC Comics (1992).

[74] Denny O'Neil, 'The Man Who Falls', in *Secret Origins*, New York: DC Comics (1990); 'Shaman', *Legends of the Dark Knight* #1, New York: DC Comics (1989).

[75] *Detective Comics* #38, New York: DC Comics (April 1940).

(vi) He is often helped by his sidekick, Robin

'The sensational character find of 1940'[76] had a profound effect on Batman, his stories and his mythos. According to Bill Finger and Bob Kane, Finger had been toying with the idea of including a Watson to Batman's Holmes for reasons of narrative variety: 'Batman didn't have anyone to talk to, and it got a little tiresome always having him thinking.' Kane, meanwhile, announced that he was planning to 'put a boy in the story to identify with Batman'.[77] We can only conclude that a two-step process of identification must have been intended, because Kane goes on to explain that he 'imagined that young boys reading about Batman's exploits would project their own images into the story and daydream about fighting alongside the Caped Crusader as junior Batmen. I thought that every young boy would want to be like Robin.'[78] As it turned out, a number of boys did want to be like Robin and daydreamed about living with Batman; they told Dr Fredric Wertham their daydreams, and he reported them in *The Seduction of the Innocent*. But that's a story for another chapter.

'The introduction of Robin', Kane continues, 'changed the entire tone of the Batman stories.'

> Robin lightened up the mood of the strip and he and Batman would engage in punning and badinage as they defeated their adversaries. The brightness of Robin's costume also served to brighten up the visuals and served as a counterpoint to Batman's somber costume. More significantly, the addition of Robin gave Batman a permanent relationship, someone to care for, and made him into a fatherly big brother rather than a lone avenger.[79]

The evolution of the Batman mythos has always been subtle, evolving over a few months at least, and changes can rarely be pinpointed to a

---

[76] Ibid.

[77] Kane with Andrae, op. cit., p. 46.

[78] Ibid.

[79] Ibid.

single issue. Even in his second appearance, Batman had smiled grimly, announcing to two startled policemen 'So sorry, gentlemen, but I'm afraid I have to go now . . .' before leaping from a roof,[80] and he was given to wisecracks during fight scenes – 'So, you still want to play, eh!', 'I hate to do this, buddy!',[81] 'Let's pretend I'm the ball and you're the bowling pins!'[82] – for several issues prior to Robin's appearance. The Boy Wonder's debut, however, coincided with and consolidated changes to Batman's 'moral code' during 1940.

Most notable of these was the character's depicted attitude towards firearms and the taking of human life. In *Detective* #29, Batman had announced to two goons 'Your choice, gentlemen! Tell me! Or *I'll* kill you!'[83] in *Detective* #32, we saw him loading a pistol with which to finish off an army of sleeping vampires at point-blank range. The next issue showed Batman drawing his handgun again, though only to shoot at a gas vial – 'I hope I don't get blown up'[84] – while issue #35 included a half-page image of the hero wielding a smoking revolver. The first issue of *Batman*, dated Spring 1940 and therefore published at around the same time as Robin's first appearance in *Detective*, upped the ante by having Batman pick off criminals with the Batplane's machine gun. 'Much as I hate to take human life, I'm afraid *this time* it's necessary!'[85] Even when the death of wrongdoers was an accident, Batman had grimly approved this brand of rough justice. In his first issue, he comments 'A fitting end for his kind' as the mastermind plunges into an acid tank; a few months later he watches a scientist perish in flames, and pronounces 'Death . . . to Doctor Death!'[86]

By the end of 1941, as Mark Cotta Vaz notes, the Batman's moral code was firmly in place, and there were no exceptions to the rule: 'The Batman never carries or kills with a gun!' stated a caption in *Batman* #4.[87] At the same time, the character's iconography and

---

[80] *Detective Comics* #28, New York: DC Comics (June 1939).

[81] *Detective Comics* #35, New York: DC Comics (January 1940).

[82] *Detective Comics* #36, New York: DC Comics (February 1940).

[83] *Detective Comics* #29, New York: DC Comics (July 1939).

[84] *Detective Comics* #33, New York: DC Comics (November 1939).

[85] *Batman* #1, New York: DC Comics (Spring 1940).

[86] *Detective Comics* #29, New York: DC Comics (August 1939).

[87] Quoted in Cotta Vaz, op. cit., p. 13.

appearance was subtly being modified to suit his new role as father-protector rather than lone avenger. 'I wanted to give him a more handsome countenance', Kane explains, 'and make him less vampirish and ominous-looking.'

> I began drawing the cowl higher up so that his face showed more, and had him smile and look less grim. Over time, I also shortened his ears, which were originally quite long and made him look somewhat Satanic.[88]

'Help! The devil himself,' cries a citizen as Batman appears before him in *Detective* #31;[89] and indeed, the hero of these first episodes, roaming the older worlds of Paris and Hungary in addition to New York on his grim pursuit of vampires, monks and other Gothic horrors, sometimes seems a more terrifying figure than the villains. Little wonder that Commissioner Gordon repeatedly declares to Wayne 'I tell you Bruce, if I ever catch the Batman!'[90] Yet by the end of Robin's first appearance, with Dick Grayson describing the episode as 'fun' – 'Say, I can hardly wait till we go on our next case. I bet it'll be a corker!'[91] – this morally ambivalent element of the character was slowly but decisively being phased out. The reasons for these changes are several, and operate on at least three levels – the interplay between authorial and editorial control, the institutional consideration of audience response and sales, and the external discourses of a contemporary debate over comics' corruptive effects, articulated through journalism.

As indicated above, the idea of bringing in a boy sidekick came from Finger and Kane in tandem, and so represents a joint authorship despite Kane's characteristically blithe remarks about 'when I created Robin'.[92] At this point, however – which, from the available evidence,

---

[88] Kane with Andrae, op. cit., p. 47.

[89] *Detective Comics* #31, New York: DC Comics (September 1939).

[90] *Detective Comics* #35, New York: DC Comics (January 1940).

[91] *Detective Comics* #38, New York: DC Comics (April 1940).

[92] Kane with Andrae, op. cit., p. 45.

we can locate in early 1940[93] – authorial interpretations of how Batman 'should' be were coming into conflict with editorial or institutional readings for the first time in the character's history. Kane reports that his editor, Jack Liebowitz, was against the idea of Robin's introduction, for the reasons of 'branding' I suggested above: 'He said that Batman was doing well enough by himself and felt we shouldn't tamper with it.'[94] Author and editor compromised on this occasion and agreed to run Robin for a single issue only.

> But when the story appeared, it really hit: the comic book which introduced Robin (Detective Comics #38, April, 1940) sold almost double what Batman had sold as a single feature. I went to the office on Monday after we had gotten the figures and said 'Well, I guess we had better take Robin out – right, Jack? You don't want a kid fighting with gangsters.' 'Well,' he said sheepishly, 'Leave it in. It's okay – we'll let it go.'[95]

This debate over meaning, then – which comes down to a quite fundamental and long-running distinction between the two opposing visions of Batman as dark loner and Batman as benevolent father-figure, with all the connotations both figures carry – was settled by audience response. In this case, the readers' approval manifested itself simply as sales figures, as there were no letters pages and no real forum for feedback of any kind: Alan Asherman, DC's current librarian, suggests that the claims of 'careful research into just what sort of features your readers demand'[96] published in *Detective* were pure gimmickry. The company did have postcards printed to send to those fans who wrote

---

[93] Although the creative process from writing to art to the comic's publication was by all accounts a rapid one, we can imagine that two to three months must have passed between Kane presenting the Robin concept to his boss and the character's first appearance in the April 1940 issue of *Detective*.

[94] Kane with Andrae, op. cit., p. 46.

[95] Ibid.

[96] Advertisement for *Star-Spangled Comics* #1, in *Detective Comics* #41, New York: DC Comics (July 1940).

in, but there were no DC letters pages until the ones Asherman himself edited in the 1960s, and so little way for us to discern what form of reaction Batman invited from his young fans.[97]

However, we know that letters did arrive at the DC offices on 480 Lexington Avenue, New York,[98] because a significant number were from concerned mothers whose opinion, Kane remembers, had a significant effect on editorial policy. This further regulation of Batman's behaviour occurred in spring 1940 – at around the same time as Robin's debut, and with the same effect. It concerned Batman's use of a machine gun in the first issue of his solo title. According to Kane, 'the editors thought that making Batman a murderer would taint his character, and that mothers would object to letting their kids see and read about such shootings'.[99]

Again, shifts in Batman's character were debated between authors – the creative impulse behind the character – and their superiors – the institutional body controlling him. In this case, there was no room for compromise, and guidelines were imposed onto Batman's behaviour from 'above'. 'I goofed,' confesses Bill Finger. 'I had Batman use a gun to shoot a villain, and I was called on the carpet by Whit Ellsworth. He said, "Never let us have Batman carry a gun again." He was right.'[100]

Frederick Whitney Ellsworth was editorial director for all DC titles from 1940 to 1953;[101] his interest in Batman, we can surmise, was inevitably of a different nature from that of Bob Kane and Bill Finger, who come across as being a trifle naïve. 'We didn't think anything was wrong with Batman carrying a gun', Kane admits, 'because the Shadow used one. Readers found this use of a gun deplorable.'[102]

Although Kane is vague about how this reader concern was expressed, we can see why Ellsworth would take any such criticism of one of his properties seriously if we consider the context of general concern and suspicion which surrounded comics even in the early

[97] Alan Asherman, personal conversation (29 June 1998).
[98] This was the address given for DC Comics in the mid-1940s.
[99] Kane with Andrae, op. cit., p. 45.
[100] Quoted in Kane with Andrae, op. cit., p. 45.
[101] See Batman: The Sunday Classics 1943–46, op. cit., p. 14.
[102] Kane with Andrae, op. cit., p. 45.

1940s. Tom Andrae has described it as a 'moral panic based on fears that the superhero was a violent, authoritarian figure like Hitler, and that comics were corrupting the minds of youth'.[103] Although we might argue that the concern over comics did not escalate into a fully fledged 'moral panic' until it was linked during the post-war years to juvenile delinquency, and taken up by psychiatrist Fredric Wertham in particular,[104] there was nevertheless a significant discourse around the dangers of comic books which emerged from similar concerns around the dime novel, the Sunday 'funnies' and the cinema,[105] and was undoubtedly linked to the emergent research into the 'effects' of advertising and propaganda on audience response and public opinion.[106]

Amy Kiste Nyberg, in her social history of comics censorship, *Seal of Approval*, reports that

> The first national attack on comic books came from Sterling North, literary critic for the *Chicago Daily News*. In an editorial on May 8, 1940, headlined 'A National Disgrace', North noted that almost every child in America was reading comic books. Nearly ten million copies were sold every month, taking a million dollars from the pockets of children. He examined 108 comics available on the newsstands, concluding that at least 70 percent of them contained material that no acceptable newspaper would think of accepting. He argued that the old dime novel could be considered classic literature compared to the comic book ... [107]

North's editorial, with its description of comics as a 'hypodermic injection of sex and murder' and accusations that any parent who failed

---

[103] Tom Andrae, personal correspondence (27 September 1997).

[104] See Amy Kiste Nyberg, *Seal of Approval: The History of the Comics Code*, Jackson: University Press of Mississippi (1998), p. 18.

[105] Nyberg, ibid., pp. 2–3.

[106] The two most celebrated examples of this 1940s research remain Robert Merton's *Mass Persuasion*, New York: Harper and Brothers (1946), and Paul. F. Lazarsfeld's *The People's Choice*, New York: Columbia University Press (1944).

[107] Nyberg, op. cit., p. 4.

to provide an antidote to the 'poison' of comic magazines was 'guilty of criminal negligence', was reprinted in over forty newspapers and magazines and distributed in schools and churches across the country. Apparently, the *Daily News* received twenty-five million requests for copies of the article and even a year later was still being asked for reprints at the astonishing rate of one thousand a day.[108]

The editorial was published in May 1940. *Batman* #1, with the eponymous hero squinting down his machine-gun sights – 'Much as I hate to take human life, I'm afraid *this time* it's necessary!' – was dated April–May 1940. It does not seem too far-fetched to imagine that some parents perhaps looked at a comic book for the first time after reading North's accusations, and picked up the first issues of Batman's solo title; nor that some of those parents, stung by North's insinuations about 'criminal negligence', may have assuaged their conscience by sending off a letter to the editor of the offending comic. If one thousand people were writing to the *Daily News* each day with requests for the article, it seems possible that F.W. Ellsworth may have received a substantial mailbag of complaints during May 1940. It is hardly surprising, then, if he called Bill Finger 'on the carpet' that month and began to impose his own rules for the Batman's character and behaviour.[109]

> The new editorial policy was to get away from Batman's vigilantism and to bring him over to the side of the law. We made him an honorary member of the police force who was outside the law but still working with it. And, to avoid violence, we made Batman into more of an acrobat who used his physical prowess rather than weapons to defeat villains.[110]

These subtle but important shifts, which cumulatively had a profound effect on Batman's behaviour, storylines and the overall mood of the

---

[108] Ibid.

[109] It is perhaps ironic though that, according to Kane, Ellsworth was responsible for the return of the psychotic, mass-murdering Joker after his apparent 'death' in *Batman* #1. See Kane with Andrae, op. cit., p. 107.

[110] Ibid., p. 45.

strip, were therefore the result of audience response – emphasised by a surrounding journalistic discourse of moral concern – to which the institution of DC Comics in turn responded by making demands of the two authors. 'I never had complete control over the *Batman* strip', Kane admits, 'and the editors placed increasing limits over what Bill and I could do.'[111] In fact, the machine gun incident in *Batman* #1 led indirectly to the drawing-up of the first internal comics code – specific to DC, rather than to the industry as a whole – which every writer and artist had to follow. 'It forbade any whippings, hangings, knifings, or sexual references. Even the word "flick" was forbidden because the lettering (all in block capitals) might run together.'[112]

DC's new editorial policy, however, went further than merely banning undesirable behaviour and images; it sought to promote Batman as an 'honorary member of the police force', an upstanding social figure and by extension as a laudable role model for the juvenile readership. This agenda, too, is linked to the contemporary journalistic debate on comics. Twinned with the discourse about the dangers of comic books was a 'lively dialogue'[113] in the professional journals of teachers and librarians, about the challenge comics presented to educators. One response would have been to ban them; another was to substitute 'good' reading matter, such as novels about 'Heroes and Supermen', for superhero comics. In place of Batman, then, children were recommended 'Robin Hood ... and Paul Bunyan'.[114] A third strategy, however, was to use comics themselves for educational purposes. *True Comics*, launched in March 1941, and its competitor *Classic Comics*, which followed in the Fall, featured 'real life' heroes such as Winston Churchill, and appointed eminent figures from psychology and academia as advisory board members. *Picture Stories from the Bible*, and *Topix Comics*, which focused on leading saints of the Catholic Church, were launched in 1942.[115]

By this point a wider discourse about the possible 'positive' uses of

---

[111] Ibid., p. 44.
[112] Ibid., p. 46.
[113] Nyberg, op. cit., p. 5.
[114] Ibid., p. 6.
[115] Ibid., pp. 6–8.

the comic form is apparent in the *New York Times* of the period. These articles only start to cluster in the *Times* during the mid-1940s – there is only one story on comic books during 1941, and one in 1942 – but we can assume that the discussion may reasonably have taken a couple of years to filter through from the more specialist library and educational journals to the agenda of a national newspaper. By contrast, we might note that for the period July 1941 to June 1943 there are fifteen articles listed in the *Reader's Guide* which relate to comic books, ranging from 'Let children read comics: Science gives its approval' in the *Science News Letter* through 'They like it rough: In defense of comics' in the *Library Journal*, to 'Why not? Give them what they want!' in *Publisher's Weekly*.[116]

The *New York Times* articles, while on the whole expressing concern, nevertheless admit to the possibility of 'positive' effects from comic books. The article 'Children and the Comics', from July 1943, suggests that there are both 'good' and 'bad' comics,[117] while a follow-up piece by the same author is titled 'Positive and Negative'; subsequent articles make the relatively mild complaint that 'Some Comics Books [sic] Are Called Shocking', or even report that 'Educators Uphold Children's Comics'.[118] In addition to the notion that comic book adaptations might lead children to read the 'classics',[119] there develops an idea that even superhero comics can instil positive values in children and have a worthwhile social effect. 'By admiring the courage, bravery and honesty of the hero, we develop these traits', one boy suggested in a *New York Times* 'youth forum'.[120]

This was clearly the response which DC's editors hoped to produce by imposing an ethical template onto the previously ambiguous figure of the Batman, and restricting what Kane and Finger could or could not

[116] 'Let Children Read Comics: Science Gives its Approval', *Science News Letter* (23 August 1941); 'They Like it Rough: In Defense of Comics', *Library Journal* (1 March 1942); 'Why Not? Give Them What They Want!', *Publisher's Weekly* (18 April 1942).
[117] Catherine Mackenzie, 'Children and the Comics', *New York Times* (11 July 1943); 'Parent and Child: Positive and Negative', *New York Times* (31 October 1943).
[118] 'Educators Uphold Children's Comics', *New York Times* (2 February 1944).
[119] 'Some Comics Books [sic] are called Shocking', *New York Times* (14 February 1946).
[120] 'Influence of Reading on Youth Discussed', *New York Times* (16 December 1945).

do with the character. Rather than simply forbidding the elements to which concerned parents might object, they sought to relocate Batman within a new discourse of 'positive-effect' comic books.

Batman #3, from August–September 1940, contained a manifesto titled 'The Batman Says' which stressed the character's new aims and social ideals, explicitly constructing him as a form of costumed teacher or even pastor. The no-nonsense tone was still there, but from now on Batman's adventures were clearly no longer to be read as exciting yarns but as moral lessons: his war against crime had become not just a personal vendetta but a patriotic duty.

> I think Robin and I make it pretty clear that WE HATE CRIME
> AND CRIMINALS! [. . .] Why? Because we're proud of being
> AMERICANS – and we know there's no place in this great
> country of ours for lawbreakers! That phrase 'CRIME DOES
> NOT PAY' has been used over and over again to the point
> where I hesitate to repeat it. But remember this: IT'S JUST AS
> TRUE NOW AS IT EVER WAS – AND THAT'S PLENTY
> TRUE! Robin and I hope that our adventures may help to 'put
> over' that fact. We'd like to feel that our efforts may help
> every youngster to grow up into an honest, useful citizen. [. . .]
> If you do this, if you are definitely on the side of Law and
> Order, then Robin and I salute you and are glad to number you
> among our friends![121]

Batman was by no means the only character who was moulded into a slightly more acceptable form following the rise of public concern over comics in 1940. Superman, too, was put through subtle changes to tame his lawlessness and faintly radical edge, and transform him into a more unambiguously patriotic hero.[122] As Superman's co-creator Jerry Siegel remembers it, he was explicitly asked to remodel his character after Batman in terms of shifting Superman's focus from social reform

---

[121] 'The Batman Says', *Batman* #3 New York: DC Comics (August–September 1940), quoted in Cotta Vaz, op. cit., p. 15.
[122] Tom Andrae, 'From Menace to Messiah: The Prehistory of the Superman in Science Fiction Literature', *Discourse* #10 (Summer 1980).

– fighting slum landlords, for instance – to a less ambivalent form of crimefighting;[123] an ironic move when we consider that the Superman of recent graphic novels often plays the naïvely moralistic 'boy scout' to Batman's darker form of justice.[124]

DC's new comic code, in turn, affected every single writer and artist in its employ, and so imposed its rules about whipping, hanging, knifing and 'flicking' on each of the company's characters. By the mid-1940s the 'positive effect' discourse around comic book characters had gained enough credence that even the priest who warned of the 'perils' posed by comics – reported in the *New York Times* of 24 August 1946 – also recognised the ambiguity they contained when superheroes 'do such commendable things as helping the Red Cross drive, or during the war, aiding the war effort'.[125]

It was in this latter respect that many publishers of comic book superheroes found their best hope of gaining at least a measure of public approval, as they were able to show their characters promoting war bonds or physically fighting the Axis, and therefore protest that the comic books in question not only presented an upstanding social ideal for children but actively supported the American war drive. As such they were almost in a position to argue that, *contra* North's editorial, parents had a moral duty to buy these patriotic titles for their children's edification. Batman, in the event, did his bit for both the Red Cross drive – in *Batman* #28, April–May 1946 – and war bonds – for instance, on the cover of *Batman* #17, June–July 1943.

However, by December 1941 Batman's template had already been established. A successful formula was in place, with an evocative fictional diegesis, a fully fledged supporting cast of allies and enemies, a sidekick whose first appearance had doubled sales figures and consolidated the brand's success, and a convincing agenda of social and patriotic duty to ward off any more complaints from parents and

---

[123] In a letter to Tom Andrae, reported in Andrae, personal correspondence (1 October 1997).

[124] See Dave Gibbons and Steve Rude, *Superman/Batman: Worlds' Finest*, New York: DC Comics (1992), and Frank Miller's *Batman: The Dark Knight Returns*, op. cit.

[125] 'Priest Warns of Perils in Comic Books', *New York Times* (24 August 1946).

critics. There was no reason to fundamentally change the Batman formula. Not even if the country went to war.

2. Life during Wartime

In order to understand why an author like Mark Cotta Vaz would be tempted to depict the Batman of the war years as a propaganda figure who 'took to the patriotic calling with a surprising fervor' to 'protect the home front',[126] and in order to fully appreciate the remarkable extent to which Batman – in my reading, at least – in fact remained immune to this propaganda discourse, we have to consider the intertextual factors surrounding the character during this period.

As George H. Roeder, Jr has extensively documented in *The Censored War*, one of the prime tasks of the US Office of War Information during 1941-1944 was to make every American citizen feel involved in the military effort. 'World War II was the first movie every American could be in . . . World War II offered each citizen the dual role of spectator and participant.'[127] Virtually every form of popular culture was co-opted into a wartime propaganda monologue, with the shared agenda of presenting a united front to the consumer public. Cinema was used for educational shorts such as Frank Capra's seven-part *Why We Fight* series,[128] subtly partisan news and information series such as *March of Time*,[129] the government-made *Army-Navy Screen Magazine* for servicemen,[130] patriotic cartoons like Disney's *Der Fuehrer's Face* with Donald Duck,[131] and of course Hollywood feature films loaded with appropriately upbeat ideology – *The Fighting Sullivans, Objective Burma, Bombadier, 30 Seconds over Tokyo, Tender*

---

[126] Cotta Vaz, op. cit., p. 33.

[127] George H. Roeder, *The Censored War: American Visual Experience during World War Two*, New Haven: Yale University Press (1993), p. 43.

[128] See Roeder, ibid., p. 50.

[129] See Anthony Rhodes, *Propaganda: The Art of Persuasion: World War Two*, London: Angus and Robertson (1976), p. 152.

[130] See Rhodes, ibid., p. 158, and Roeder, op. cit., p. 52.

[131] Rhodes, ibid., p. 159.

Comrade, *Pride of the Marines* and *Hail the Conquering Hero*, to name but a few.[132]

The radio was employed for similarly pedagogic series such as the nationwide broadcast 'This Is War', which reached twenty million Americans every Saturday night for thirteen weeks with its blend of information, inspiration and plain anti-Axis scare-mongering. 'By 1943', reports Anthony Rhodes in *Propaganda: The Art of Persuasion*, 'of the twenty NBC serials which went out weekly, only five were unconnected with the war.'[133] And 1943 proved a landmark year for radio war bond drives, in the form of singer Kate Smith's marathon effort which was both celebrated and analysed in Robert Merton's *Mass Persuasion*.[134] Meanwhile, songwriters and swing orchestras kept up the patriotic spirit with 'Ballad For Americans', 'Goodbye Mama – I'm Off to Yokahama' and 'Praise the Lord and Pass the Ammunition', all of which were available on record or in sheet music form;[135] and war bond drives were supported by celebrity galas and street parades as 'urban spaces became huge stage sets intended to remind citizens that responding to war needs should be their preoccupation'.[136] Even the packaging of consumer goods became an issue of patriotism; Lucky Strikes 'went to war' by giving up its traditional green dye, while Campbell's and Coca-Cola 'ran advertisements that emphasized the similarity between the "uniform" worn by brand-name products and those worn by soldiers'.[137]

To talk of a propaganda monologue, then, is no exaggeration. It would have been hard for any American citizen to walk ten minutes from her home without coming into contact with several messages, whether borne by radio, cinema hoardings or soup cans, exhorting her either directly or subtly to keep up the fight on the home front. Most pertinent to our discussion here, though, is the use of visual printed

---

[132] See Thomas Docherty, *Projections of War: Hollywood, American Culture and World War II*, New York: Columbia University Press (1993).
[133] Ibid., p. 150.
[134] Merton *et al. Mass Persuasion: The Social Psychology of a War Bond Drive*, New York: Harper & Brothers (1946).
[135] See Rhodes, op. cit., p. 148.
[136] Roeder, op. cit., p. 69.
[137] Ibid., p. 60.

material for propaganda purposes: specifically, the extensive use of comic book-style images. This material can be categorised into several distinct camps. It is worth documenting briefly in order to stress the extent to which comic books and cartoons were decisively recruited into the war effort: and again, ultimately in order to indicate by contrast the unusual status of the Batman comics during this period.

Firstly, while a great deal of American poster art of the war years included photographic montage or realist painting in a sentimental or heroic mode – Norman Rockwell providing perhaps the best examples of this latter trend[138] – the use of comic book images and conventions was also prevalent. The posters by 'Holmes' encouraging recruitment into the Glider Troops, of which Rhodes provides an example,[139] employ breezily stylised artwork of guys and gals with speech balloons emphasising the '50% extra pay' available; the pen-and-ink drawing is, as Rhodes recognises, clearly in the mould of contemporary comics.

As the cartoon for Eveready batteries reprinted by George H. Roeder indicates,[140] art in the comic book mode was also being used to sell consumer goods while nodding towards the war effort at the same time – by pointing out the need for batteries in times of conflict, Eveready gains itself a reputation for social responsibility as well as brand quality. A glance through *Detective* of the early to mid-1940s shows a range of 'topical' wartime advertisements in cartoon form – for instance, a doughboy 'polishing up his Jap lingo so he knows how to ask for Wheaties when we hit Tokyo', a sailor courting girls with Babe Ruth candies, with the slogan 'send a box to your boy in service', and a GI nicknamed 'R.C.' starring in one-page adventures for Royal Crown cola. Even discounting the short comic strips reminding readers to buy war bonds which appeared in virtually every issue, it is clear that the use of comic book form and conventions for advertising purposes was an established trend, and that these advertisements frequently took on a patriotic slant in the years 1941–45.

Political newspaper cartoons, of course, employed a very similar visual form to more pointed satirical ends – Bill Maudlin's 'Willy and

---

[138] Ibid., p. 71.
[139] Rhodes, op. cit., p. 150.
[140] Roeder, op. cit., p. 74.

Joe' strip has a weary soldier telling his Red Cross colleague 'Just gimme a coupla aspirin. I already got a Purple Heart'[141] – and for more explicitly militaristic purposes, as in the cartoon which gives John W. Dower's *War Without Mercy* its title: the phrase is attached to the ammunition which a sailor labelled 'US Navy' intends to shoot into a grim Rising Sun located somewhere over Hawaii.[142] Countless further examples could be found, as Dower illustrates, in every issue of the *Chicago Tribune*, *Washington Post*, *Philadelphia Enquirer* and *New York Times*, to say nothing of *Life*, *Collier's* and the US Marines' own magazine, *Leatherneck*.[143]

The immediacy and accessibility of the comic book form also lent themselves well to the propaganda leaflets which the US Government distributed across Europe to undermine Nazi morale. As Rhodes testifies, 'the vast American airfleets that dominated the skies literally swamped the enemy with paper ... a special squadron of Flying Fortresses was set aside to do nothing but carry out leaflet raids.'[144] The Imperial War Museum in London still holds many of these original leaflets, which display a remarkable talent for German doggerel in addition to an almost universal adoption of the familiar comic book format. In one, a caricatured Hitler climbs up to Stalin's window only to be knocked on the head with a hammer, while a bayonet waits for him below: in another cartoon, Goebbels canoodles with a film starlet, oblivious to his soldiers' hardship. The meaning is obvious even if we ignore the bawdy rhyming captions in German.

This simple visual appeal of comics and cartoons, barely requiring a basic literacy for comprehension, made them ideal entertainment for the American army as well as effective propaganda reading for the Nazis and the occupied French. William W. Savage's *Comic Books and America 1945-1954* estimates that 'hundreds of thousands of comic books were shipped to American service personnel around the world'.

---

[141] See Rhodes, op. cit., p. 151.
[142] John W. Dower, *War Without Mercy: Race and Power in the Pacific War*, Pantheon: New York (1986), p. 181.
[143] See ibid., pp. 181–189.
[144] Rhodes, op. cit., p. 146.

they satisfied the requirement which dictates that popular culture appeal to the lowest common denominator, in this case the individual with limited language skills and the capacity to respond to only a narrow range of cultural symbols. The mobilization of a total of some 16 million Americans by war's end suggested a number of possibilities to comic-book publishers, and they made every effort to capitalize on them.[145]

'Cartoon books popular as gifts for servicemen', testifies the *Publisher's Weekly* from September 1944, while a story in the *Saturday Evening Post* urges readers to send 'cartoons to overcome soldier's mail-shortage problem'.[146] Although they were provided with ample cartoon entertainment in the many humour magazines – such as *First Class Male* and *Riggin' Bill*[147] – which were sent out to the US military in great number, American servicemen nevertheless had the wherewithal, despite Savage's disparaging comments about their cultural limitations, to 'appropriate' from the material they were given and create their own in the same spirit. The most successful of these, George Baker's 'Sad Sack' – originally running in the Army's own *Yank* magazine[148] – became a national institution, earning several mentions in the *Reader's Guide* from 1941 to 1945 as various journals from the *New Yorker* to the *Saturday Evening Post* discovered the 'real Sad Sack' or celebrated the 'G.I.'s favorite comic'. Yet even when they had no hope of publication, servicemen continued to satirise their own situation through cartoons in the George Baker style, as demonstrated by a *Life* article from 1942 which declares 'This Is How U.S. Boys Look and Laugh at Camp Life', complete with illustrations by privates in service.[149]

---

[145] William W. Savage, Jr, *Comic Books and America 1945–1954*, Oklahoma: University of Oklahoma Press (1990), p. 11.

[146] *Publisher's Weekly* #146 (30 September 1944), *Saturday Evening Post* #214 (20 June 1942).

[147] See Dennis Gifford, *The International Book of Comics*, London: Hamlyn (1988), p. 152.

[148] Ibid.

[149] 'This Is How U.S. Boys Look and Laugh at Camp Life', *Life* #12 (23 March 1942).

The GIs lapped up superhero comics at the same rate, and according to anecdotal evidence appropriated from these texts as well, naming planes and tanks after DC's characters and painting vehicles with comic art.[150] William Savage is once again dubious about the qualities of both the medium and the intellect of its readers.

> Sending comic books to military personnel testified to the utility of the medium in raising morale through patriotic fervor ... laden as they were with unlikely role models, comic books could still inform about unity on the home front and indicate the extent to which American soldiers were glorified in a predominantly domestic medium. Even an illiterate could discern from comic books the virtue of the American cause and the sterling qualities of the American fighting man.[151]

Savage is partly justified in pouring scorn on the simplistic values of the wartime superhero comic. The covers of *Captain America, Daredevil Battles Hitler, USA Comics, Wonder Comics, Speed Comics, Major Victory* and *Young Allies*, all launched between 1941 and 1944, constitute a manic display of brutal violence and desperately wishful thinking: brightly costumed American heroes trample hordes of Japanese, free handsome officers from Nazi ghouls, upturn entire subs of baffled Germans and cheerfully leave Adolf Hitler himself either tied to a pole or beaten and cowering.[152]

Comics and cartoons, then, were used for propaganda purposes in domestic advertisements, on recruitment posters, in satirical news-paper features, in leaflet drops for allies and enemies, in humour strips shipped out to servicemen and in the superhero titles read at home and on the front. There was, to put it mildly, a strong precedent for Batman to be 'recruited' into the war effort. It is perhaps unsurprising that a journalist like Mark Cotta Vaz desperately wants it to have happened, to the extent that he creates a history which meets his and the reader's expectations. 'During World War II everyone in America

---

[150] Alan Asherman, personal conversation (29 June 1998).

[151] Savage, op. cit., p. 11.

[152] See Gifford, op. cit., pp. 134–135; for *Speed Comics*, see Rhodes, op. cit., p. 167.

was called to action ... America's superheroes were also pressed into service.' And so Batman was called into service, to gain 'patriotic, as well as crime-fighting renown'.[153]

His version makes sense. It is, however, largely contradicted by a study of the original comics from 1941 to 1945. Before considering why this might be so, I want to illustrate the extent to which Batman comics differed from the surrounding discourse of superhero titles during those years, and more generally the ways in which the character remained isolated from the propaganda monologue which had affected so many aspects of wartime popular culture.

Cotta Vaz runs a convincing argument. He reprints several original covers from *Detective*, *Batman* and the Superman/Batman title *World's Finest* which show Batman and Robin selling war bonds from a stall,[154] passing a new rifle to a grateful doughboy,[155] riding in an Army jeep,[156] flying on the back of an American Eagle,[157] crouching behind an artillery piece,[158] straddling a gunboat's cannon[159] and even flinging tennis balls at caricatures of Axis leaders.[160] 'Keep the American Eagle Flying', the heroes urge,[161] or with slight variation, 'War Savings Bonds and Stamps Keep Em Rolling!'[162] and 'Keep Those Bullets Flying! Keep On Buying War Bonds and Stamps!'[163] The captions are a precise echo in tone, almost in wording, of propaganda posters which appeared in every American city during 1942, exhorting the public to 'Keep 'Em Firing!',[164] and indeed of *Keep 'Em Flying*, one of 1942's most popular films.[165] It seems patently clear from this evidence that

---

[153] Cotta Vaz, op. cit., p. 33.
[154] *World's Finest* #8, New York: DC Comics (Winter 1942).
[155] *Batman* #30, New York: DC Comics (August–September 1945).
[156] *Batman* #12, New York: DC Comics (August–September 1942).
[157] *Batman* #17, New York: DC Comics (June–July 1943).
[158] *Batman* #15, New York: DC Comics (February–March 1943).
[159] *World's Finest* #7, New York: DC Comics (Fall 1942).
[160] *World's Finest* #9, New York: DC Comics (Spring 1943).
[161] *Batman* #17, op. cit.
[162] *Batman* #12, op. cit.
[163] *Batman* #15, op. cit.
[164] Poster reprinted by Rhodes, op. cit., p. 173.
[165] See Docherty, op. cit., p. 301.

Batman did lend his voice to the chorus of war bond promotion, and took an active part in the ongoing propaganda campaign.

I was seeking to support this reading with further evidence when I began my research into original Batman comics in the archive of London's Victoria and Albert Museum, and continued it in the library of DC Comics in New York. After little more than an hour, my initial line of enquiry was already in question: my own notes from the Victoria and Albert break off to ask 'why aren't there *more?*'

The fact is that Cotta Vaz has not just taken a sample of patriotic Batman covers to prove his point: he has reprinted just about every patriotic Batman cover which saw print between 1941 and 1945. Even if we include the four additional examples mentioned by Amy Handy in *Bat Man in Detective Comics* – *Detective* #65, where Robin introduces the Boy Commandos, *Detective* #78 and #101, and *Batman* #2, with the title 'Blitzkrieg Bandits'[166] – we are still left with a ballpark figure of eleven 'topical' cover images. Bearing in mind that during these four years Batman appeared monthly in *Detective*, bi-monthly in *Batman* and quarterly in *World's Finest*, eleven patriotic covers from all three titles is not a significant proportion from a grand total of eighty-eight. If more exist, they are not in DC Comics' archive; and I doubt that there are many more.

Further, there is a marked distinction between a patriotic cover and a patriotic content. We have already seen that Kane, Finger and their 'assistants' gradually lost a degree of control of Batman during 1940, as editors like Whitney Ellsworth imposed their own concepts and frameworks on the character according to notions of audience response and a surrounding journalistic discourse which was suspicious, to say the least, of comic books' potentially 'negative' effects. It seems highly likely that Ellsworth or his colleagues would have seen the need to show Batman fighting on the home front and promoting war bonds, in order to stress the character's uses as a positive role model and evade further criticism from parents and educators. Tom Andrae supports this theory with his comment that 'I've interviewed Jerry Robinson and he indicated to me that he picked the cover subjects he drew, not his editors. However, I think it is highly possible that an

---

[166] See Amy Handy, *Bat Man in Detective Comics*, New York: Abbeville Press (1993).

editor may have suggested something like a war bond cover.'[167] In fact, it seems that Ellsworth may even have drawn some of these covers himself: he is documented as having sketched the 'dummy' layout for several *Batman*, *Detective* and *World's Finest* covers during 1940 and 1947.[168]

My argument that the war bond covers were 'imposed' upon the character from an editorial level, almost as lip service to the war effort, stems mainly from the fact that these covers – in every case I have seen – bear absolutely no relation to the stories in the comics themselves. Take the cover of *Batman* #30, for instance, as reprinted by Cotta Vaz and mentioned above. Batman and Robin appear in the jungle to hand a new rifle to a weary private. Batman declares 'Here's a new gun from the folks back home, soldier!', while Robin chirps up 'Yep! The folks that're backing the 7th WAR LOAN!'[169] Inside, however, is a story about the Penguin, with no reference to loans or wars; neither is there any mention of the ongoing conflict in the back-up strip about Batman's butler, Alfred. The only way a reader could locate this issue historically, if we tore the cover off, is from the Kellogg's Shredded Wheat advert with 'US Navy Craft Hot-Iron Transfers', and a short strip advertising paper collection as a 'weapon of war'.[170]

This isolation from war issues is typical of the Batman titles of 1941–1945. While it would be impossible to cite every available story, we can get a sense of the stability and self-contained identity of Batman narratives during this period of immense global change merely by comparing comics from specific key dates. In the months preceding Pearl Harbor, while other comic books were gleefully anticipating America's entry into the conflict,[171] Batman was fighting gangsters and gunmen in a funhouse (*Detective* #52, June 1941), and helping an understudy actress impress her parents (*Detective* #53, July 1941). In

---

[167] Tom Andrae, personal correspondence (1 October 1997).
[168] See *Batman: The Sunday Classics 1943–46*, op. cit., p. 15.
[169] *Batman* #30, New York: DC Comics (August–September 1945).
[170] Ibid.
[171] Most patriotic comic book heroes debuted during 1941, rather than 1942; *National Comics* #18, on the stands during November 1941, even 'depicted the Japanese attack on Pearl Harbor that would not happen until a month later'. Savage, op. cit., p. 9.

the issue of *Detective* dated the month of the Pearl Harbor bombing, Batman was stopping the Penguin from stealing a diamond (*Detective* #58, December 1941). Even allowing for the discrepancy between cover dates and the actual month of publication, we might have expected the Batman stories of early 1942 to make some reference to an America on the brink of war; but in the February issue, we find Batman once again preventing a diamond theft. The only difference is that this time the culprit is the Joker (*Detective* #60, February 1942). Two years into the conflict, very little had changed; in May 1944, Batman fights the Penguin again (*Detective* #87), and the Joker crops up once more a few months later, in September 1944 (*Detective* #91).

These stories are characteristic in their parochialism, in their focus on petty crime and their stock cast of thugs and outlandishly costumed villains. These are tales of Gotham City, not of the world at war: they smack more of the late 1920s or early 1930s, the milieu of *Little Caesar* and *Scarface*, than of *Pride of the Marines* and *Hail the Conquering Hero*.

This is not to say that there were no topical references whatsoever within the Batman comics of 1941–1945. Much of Mark Cotta Vaz's thesis that Batman took on a patriotic role is based around the story 'Swastika Over The White House', from *Batman* #14 (December–January 1943), in which Batman and Robin foil a Nazi gang by trapping them under their own giant swastika. Cotta Vaz also reprints pages from 'The Two Futures' from *Batman* #15 (February–March 1943) and 'The Bond Wagon' (*Detective* #78, August 1943), billed as 'a timely patriotic story with real punch'. Both, as the headings suggest, address topical issues within the device of time travel and historical fantasy.

Amy Handy provides one further example of a patriotic Batman from the comic itself, rather than the covers; in *Detective* #101, Alfred chases a hapless criminal who finally gives in and attempts to come clean: 'Okay, Alfred, y'tracked me down! I'll confess – I did it!' Batman and Robin look on, beaming, as Alfred protests 'Did WHAT, old boy?!? I only wanted to urge you to back the 7th WAR LOAN!'[172]

Four stories which could be regarded as war-related, then, over

---

[172] *Detective Comics* #101, New York: DC Comics (July 1945), reprinted in Handy, op. cit.

four years. Again, it is not a large figure in proportion to the total number of Batman adventures over that period, most of which ignored the war entirely. Moreover, of these patriotic moments from the overall Batman text of 1941–1945, only one can be considered actively militaristic. 'Swastika Over The White House' is something of an anomaly in that it shows Batman and Robin actively engaging in combat with Nazis, albeit Nazis on American soil; the others, like all but one of the covers cited by Cotta Vaz, are far more concerned with urging readers to support War Bond campaigns rather than demonstrating the ease with which American champions defeat the enemy. We can contextualise this by referring back to the covers of the superhero comics mentioned above. *Speed Comics* #31 shows Captain Freedom clutching a squirming Hitler under one arm as he leaps a barricade.[173] *Major Victory* #1 has the eponymous hero launching himself barehanded onto two Nazi officers, while the *Captain America Special* shows Cap and his sidekick Bucky wading through a battlefield of enemy soldiers, dealing out uppercuts and shooting down attacking aircraft.[174] Even *Detective Comics'* own 'Boy Commandos' strip had its team of young soldiers smashing German spies in the face and breaking through enemy lines to help their Russian allies;[175] while Superman played his part by capturing Hitler and Stalin in a two-page strip entitled 'What If Superman Ended The War?'[176]

That imaginary tales of glorified violence against the enemy – often featuring Hitler himself – were not the exception but the rule for superhero comics during the war years is indicated by Denis Gifford's list of stories within just one issue of a *Daredevil* title from July 1941:

Following the title story came 'The Claw Double Crosses Hitler', 'Daredevil and Lance Hale Fighting Hitler and His Jungle Hordes', 'Daredevil With Dickie Dean, Boy Inventor, Smash Goebbels' Spy Net', 'Daredevil and Cloud Curtis

---

[173] See Rhodes, op. cit., p. 167.
[174] Gifford, op. cit., pp. 134–135.
[175] *Detective Comics* #88, New York: DC Comics (June 1944); *Detective Comics* #89, New York: DC Comics (July 1944).
[176] 'What If Superman Ended the War?', *Look* magazine (1943).

Wreck Goering's Sky Fighters', 'Daredevil and the Pirate Prince versus Von Roeder, Nazi Sea Raider', and a pictorial postscript biography entitled 'The Man of Hate: Adolf Hitler, Dictator of Germany'.[177]

By contrast, from the available evidence it seems that Batman came into direct contact with Hitler just once, on the cover of *World's Finest* #9 (Spring 1943). Rather than a scene of carnage and vengeance as appeared so regularly across the board of superhero comic books, this was an almost playful scenario where Batman and his friends pelt Hitler and his colleagues with tennis balls. Once again, the main purpose of this sideshow is to promote war bonds: 'Knock out the Axis with War Bonds and Stamps', reads the slogan.

Batman's role as a fighting American, then, was limited to say the least. What patriotic elements there were in the Batman comics take the overriding form of war bond promotion rather than militaristic aggression. Yet this makes perfect sense within the context of Batman's existing 'positive image', which as I argued above was firmly established by late 1940. Batman had been rewritten from Kane and Finger's more ambivalently gothic figure as a social crusader, a role model for decency and fair play. Encouraging readers to support the war effort on the domestic front was a logical extension of this image; appearing on the battlefield to trample Hitler and his minions would have been out of keeping with both Batman's established character – which had been built around a hatred for crime rather than overt nationalism – and the framework of his stories, with their urban location, regular cast and overtones of 1930s gangsterism. As such, stories like 'The Merchants of Misery' from *Detective* #88, where Batman deals with a crooked racketeer who terrorises poor families,[178] and 'Batman Goes To Washington' from *Detective* #91, in which Batman and Robin lead a crusade to rehabilitate criminals as worthwhile citizens,[179] are far more representative of the 'fair play' and 'social justice' forms of patriotism which DC had already sought to

---

[177] Gifford, op.cit, p. 134.
[178] *Detective Comics* #88, New York: DC Comics (June 1944).
[179] *Detective Comics* #91, New York: DC Comics (September 1944).

associate with the character than is the 'Swastika Over The White House' episode on which Cotta Vaz bases his argument.

What Batman effectively did during 1941 to 1945 was adapt to the wartime discourse, but entirely on his own terms. Rather than go to the front, he made occasional appeals from Gotham: rather than battle Nazi hordes, he campaigned for democracy back in the United States. Tom Andrae confirms that 'I do think there was a conscious decision on the part of writers and editors to downplay patriotic themes in Batman. I think this was because they felt that Batman's ethos was primarily located in Gotham City and that going to foreign countries would dilute the dark, urban quality of the strip.'[180]

There is a remarkable contrast here to the process we saw at work during 1940, when Batman was considered malleable and bent to the pressures of audience concern. While the brand is being established, a cultural figure like Batman is apparently seen by his producers as fluid, open to change; but when he seems to have taken on a successful and profitable form, his owners may choose to place him on a pedestal above the surrounding ideological tide, rather than allowing him to be immersed and shaped by it, and so risk the erosion of the brand's identifying characteristics. There emerges an intriguing distinction, then, between the first years of a popular character's development, when his defining traits are treated as fluid and disposable, and the status he subsequently achieves when he garners enough of a regular following for those traits to harden into a proven, bankable formula. In Batman's case we can pinpoint the moment when this balance tipped fairly accurately, sometime between 1940 and 1941; we might also ask in passing, though, when this change might have occurred for similar heroes such as James Bond, Sherlock Holmes and the cast of the first Enterprise.

As to the reasons for this phenomenon in Batman's case, we can make informed guesses with reference to frameworks of institution, authorship and audience respectively. Firstly, it would have been entirely within the interests of DC Comics' editors – like Whitney Ellsworth – to keep the established Batman brand as consistent as possible during 1941–1945. We must remember that Captain

---

[180] Tom Andrae, personal correspondence (1 October 1997).

Freedom, Major Victory and their like were launched at least two years subsequent to Batman: while the former were created specifically for a wartime market eager for patriotic heroes, and thus could be based around a simple character trait of victory at all costs, Batman had already been firmed into a coherent figure with recognisable character traits, a fictional locale and supporting cast. This formula, which was refined and effectively finalised with the introduction of Robin and the accompanying shifts towards greater social responsibility, had proved extremely successful. As noted above, by 1943 the character had become a franchise in itself, springboarding into a Columbia film serial and a syndicated daily and Sunday strip, in addition to various merchandise. If the deals for these Batman spin-offs were in progress during 1942, DC's editors would have been well aware of the standing formula's evident marketability just months after America's decision to join World War II.

While sales figures and audience surveys are now almost impossible to find[181] and even harder to verify, the titles in which Batman appeared – *Detective*, *Batman* and *World's Finest* – ran to 3 million issues every month in 1943, and were estimated to be read by eight times that number.[182] The estimated monthly circulation of all comic magazines in 1940 has been placed at 3.7 million, although the figure rockets to 28.7 million in 1944.[183] If we guess that the total monthly circulation of comics in 1943 was somewhere between the two, say at 20 million, Batman titles would constitute a significant amount of that total. A press release booklet from 1943 indicates the potency of the Batman concept in the early 1940s and gives a sense of its popular appeal. Note that history has already been rewritten here to retrospectively include Robin within the original 'brand' and thus gloss over Batman's first year of vampires and vigilantism.

---

[181] 'Most of the information I've seen has come from fans digging up old promotional and advertising material and from a few academic studies,' writes Tom Andrae, in personal correspondence (2 October 1997).

[182] McClure Newspaper Syndicate Promotional Book, distributed 1943, reprinted in *Batman: The Sunday Classics 1943–46*, op. cit., p. 29.

[183] Patrick Parsons, 'Batman and His Audience: The Dialectic of Culture', in Pearson and Uricchio, op. cit., p. 68.

Born May 1939 ... within a few short months the innate appeal of these characters forced circulation up and up; popularity polls ranked Batman and Robin extremely high in fan-following. *Detective Comics*, now featuring these two great characters on its cover, became one of the world's two largest monthly comics. Less than a year later – in April, 1940, the clamorings of comics readers led the publishers to devote a complete new magazine to Batman and Robin ... the sales of Batman Magazine spurted upward ... soon made it one of the world's largest bi-monthly comics. [...] King of Serials – in late 1942, three major film studios bid for the serial rights to Batman and Robin – after observing the meteoric rise of these comic heroes. [...] Now, available to newspapers for the first time, Batman and Robin is assured of broad, immediate and enthusiastic acceptance. This strip is unique in that it has been tested and proved by actual mass acceptance in those two other mass media, magazines and movies. [184]

Quite simply, Batman wasn't broke, so why fix him? Remember the words of Kane's editor, Jack Liebowitz, on the introduction of Robin: 'He said that Batman was doing well enough by himself and felt we shouldn't tamper with it.' Now that Robin had doubled sales and the 'socially responsible' Batman was doing great business, Liebowitz and his superiors must have been even more firmly inclined to let well alone, and perhaps – within the framework of social acceptability they had imposed onto Kane and Finger's more ambivalent character – to trust the judgement of the creators who had, after all, come up with both Batman and Robin in the first place.

Denny O'Neil, while of course only making guesses himself, supports my own conjecture. The relative lack of topical references in the Batman comics of the period, he proposes, was 'probably down to

---

[184] McClure Promotional Book, op. cit., pp. 30–37.

Finger', who 'probably wanted to keep that noir feel . . . Finger wasn't drafted, as far as I know.'[185]

O'Neil is right. Finger was classified 4F – that is, excluded on health grounds – presumably because of a history of scarlet fever. In fact, if we cross-reference the biographies in *Batman: The Sunday Classics 1943-46*, it becomes clear that as DC's artistic 'bullpen' gradually lost its creative staff to the draft during the Forties, most of those left behind had been classified exempt from war service on health grounds. Writer Alvin Schwartz, a friend of Bill Finger's, had chronic asthma;[186] artist Stan Kaye, who worked on *Batman*, *Superman* and *World's Finest*, retained scar tissue on his lungs from childhood TB,[187] while Dick Sprang, who pencilled, inked and lettered Batman in the 1940s, had 20/400 vision.[188]

It does not seem too far-fetched to imagine that Finger may have felt little interest in penning scripts about the frontline action in which he was never going to participate and of which he had no experience. Better, surely, to write from what he knew – a childhood in the Bronx and a lifelong immersion, during periods of sustained illness, in cinema and pulp fiction.[189] His friends and collaborators on the various Batman projects would have been in much the same position, and his editor Whitney Ellsworth was apparently giving the Batman team *carte blanche*, give or take a few covers, to carry on doing what they had so profitably achieved before Pearl Harbor. In turn, Finger's immediate superior Jack Schiff – story editor of all DC titles from 1943 to 1945 – was something of a liberal who would later write one-page superhero strips for the National Social Welfare assembly, promoting brotherhood, education and fair play.[190] Rather than attempt to steer Finger's strips towards the bloodthirsty, militaristic tone so evident in other

---

[185] Denny O'Neil, personal interview (30 June 1998). Alan Asherman also concluded in personal conversation (29 June 1998) that the phenomenon could be attributed to 'preferences of the writer'.
[186] *Batman: The Sunday Classics 1943–46*, op. cit., p. 21.
[187] Ibid., p. 17.
[188] Ibid., p. 22.
[189] Ibid., p. 15.
[190] Ibid., p. 20.

titles of the war years, it seems far more likely that Schiff would have encouraged stories like 'Batman Goes To Washington' and 'The Merchants of Misery'; or even have suggested the ideas for them himself.

Finally, what of the audience – those 24 million readers who supposedly read every issue of *Batman*, *Detective* and *World's Finest* every month in 1943? What of the significant proportion of adults – 41 per cent of males and 28 per cent of females – who were reading comics that year,[191] and the 'hundreds of thousands' of servicemen and women who received comics while on active duty?[192]

Trying to guess the appeal of a comic character to audiences of almost sixty years ago is clearly impossible, given that there were no letters pages or published fan mail in the comic books of that period. We know that Batman did sell, and was apparently very popular, during the war years, in spite of its deviation from the conventions of the 'patriotic' superhero comic as established by the surrounding titles. Perhaps this differentiation was one of the reasons for the character's success: in a market of nearly identical militaristic heroes, the Batman stories stood out as having a pre-war identity of their own. The consistency of this identity must surely have played a part in the Batman's success; the 1939–1941 stories had, after all, attracted an established fanbase 'ranging high into the millions'[193] who presumably had no particular wish to see the milieu, tone and familiar personality of their favourite character go through drastic changes, war or no war.

It might not be too much to suggest, then, that the stability of the Batman's 'mythos' during a period of cultural upheaval and anxiety may have had a deep-seated appeal to both juvenile and adult readers. While the fairly regular bond appeals would have enabled an active participation on the part of young fans, who could identify with their hero through saving for war stamps or collecting waste paper, the dominant mode of the wartime Batman stories is, as noted above, an ahistorical one: or, better, carries an aura of previous decades, whether the late 1920s of actual gangster activity or the early 1930s, when the

---

[191] According to a survey of reading habits in 1944; see Parsons, op. cit., p. 69.
[192] Savage, op. cit., p. 11.
[193] *Batman: The Sunday Classics 1943–46*, op. cit., p. 29.

fictional gangster began his rise in cinema. To the nineteen-year-old private serving in Japan, the monthly adventures of an avuncular hero fighting costumed villains and thugs in a thinly disguised New York, with no reference to the ongoing conflict, may have proved strangely comforting; more so than seeing Major Victory stroll through a facile version of the battlefield whose reality was all too immediate. In this light, *Batman* may almost have seemed like a letter from home.

Life went on back in Gotham City. The Joker and Penguin would be locked up to escape again, and Batman would declare again that he hated all crime, and Robin would grin 'that goes double for me!' For the half-hour it took to read the comic, we were back in a paradoxically safer world, a world of predictable rules even to its crimewaves, a reassuringly nostalgic world: a world where, crucially, there was no war. It is not difficult, from this perspective, to imagine Batman's appeal to both children and adults between 1941 and 1945.

3. 'The Mighty Red-Blooded American Hero'

The Columbia film serial *Batman*, which ran in fifteen episodes during 1943, is not easy to find in the late 1990s. A string of megastores and specialist outlets across Manhattan can testify to my search for a video copy, and archive services in both the US and UK were equally unable to supply any leads. By the time I found myself lacing a 1940s print of Episode One onto a Steenbeck viewer in the basement of London's BFI offices, I was nearing the very end of my research, and my expectations of this final elusive text had been significantly coloured by the framework of intertextual material I had been obliged to rely on in place of the original.

As noted above, Bill Boichel's brief history of Batman texts dismisses the serial as 'a blatant vehicle for World War II propaganda'. Bob Kane is equally scathing in his description of a visit to the studios:

> my enthusiasm soon turned to disappointment. My frustration began with the casting, or should I say miscasting, of Batman and Robin. The actor playing Batman was an overweight chap called Lewis Wilson, who should have been forced to go on a diet before taking the role. Robin, played by Douglas Croft,

was equally miscast . . . the car that was supposed to be the Batmobile was an ordinary gray convertible . . . the film was a quickie, completed in a few weeks. [. . .] The story was one of those typical propaganda vehicles for bolstering up the war effort.[194]

I approached the serial, then, expecting to find a reading of the comic book which could be considered 'aberrant' in terms of the original mythos; an imposition, by Columbia's writers and director, of patriotic ideology onto Kane and Finger's relatively neutral framework, using Batman as a mere 'vehicle' for contemporary propaganda. Certainly this is how Kane sees the serial, and as such Columbia's *Batman* represents the first significant case of dissent over the character's meaning, with the 'author', Kane, asserting that director Lambert Hillyer and the three writers responsible for the screenplay – perhaps the casting director and whoever chose the 'gray convertible' also fall within his condemnation – have 'misread' the original texts of Batman.

As with the wartime comic stories, however, I discovered that the framework of expectations through which I approached the film serial actually found little textual support, and I was once again obliged to reassess my approach after engaging with the primary text as opposed to secondary material. While Kane's interpretation of the serial as a 'misreading' remains significant and interesting, I ultimately found myself agreeing with an alternative view of the film chapters, from James Van Hise's popular history *Batmania II*: 'Overall this is a very faithful adaptation of Batman for the time, although it ignores all of his traditional foes, many of whom had already been introduced in the comic books by 1943.'[195]

The primary difference between *Batman* the comic book and *Batman* the serial is, as Van Hise notes, the choice of villain. While Batman had in fact fought a 'Dr Deker' who stole a brainwashing machine, in *Detective* #55 (September 1941), the choice of a Japanese scientist called Dr Daka as the serial's arch-villain added unprecedented overtones of militaristic racism to Batman's agenda. As I argued above,

---

[194] Kane with Andrae, op. cit., p. 127.
[195] Van Hise, op. cit., n.p.

such associations were largely absent from the Batman comics of the period, whose recurrent use of the grotesquely clownlike Joker and Penguin kept Batman's focus on parochial crimefighting rather than patriotic militarism.

I suggested various reasons why Batman remained unique during the early 1940s in terms of his relative immunity to wartime propaganda discourses; the individual concerns of the creators involved, for instance, and the institutional willingness of DC Comics to let this flagship title continue its unprecedented success along much the same lines as were established in 1940, while loading the burden of a more contemporary wartime message onto other titles, stories and characters such as the 'Boy Commandos'.

The Columbia film studio was, however, not in exactly the same position as DC Comics. *Batman* the film serial needed to appeal to an audience beyond that of the comic books and to reach a wider viewing public than the established Batman fan-base. By locating the serial within the national discourse of anti-Japanese propaganda, Columbia was able to position *Batman* as a contemporary patriotic adventure in keeping with so many other films of the early 1940s. At the same time, the producers clearly sought to capture the audience of comic readers and to promote their version of the hero on the back of Batman's existing familiarity, rather than as a new character.

Thus Batman was billed on the 1943 film poster as 'the mighty red-blooded American hero',[196] a far cry from the 'tall, cloaked figure' in a 'weird, close-fitting costume ... the man that is "the eyes of night" ', as the comics were describing him in 1941.[197] On the other hand, the poster caption goes on to stress that the serial is 'based on the Batman Comic Magazine Feature appearing in Detective Comics and Batman Magazines', from which the red-blooded hero 'comes to thrilling life'. Rather than use a shot of Lewis Wilson or Douglas Croft, the poster is based around a painting of Batman and Robin which bears little resemblance to either of the actors, although it adopts a 'realistic' style compared to the more cartoonish mode of Kane, Robinson and their colleagues; similarly, a painting by DC's Jack Burnley was used to

---

[196] See Kane with Andrae, op. cit., p. 127.
[197] *Detective Comics* #52, New York: DC Comics (June 1941).

illustrate the film in the 'King of Serials' paragraph of the McClure Promotional Book cited above.[198] Finally, the 'Batman' title, splashed dramatically in the centre of the film poster, makes no attempt to echo the distinctive logo which had been established in the comic books.

The poster, then, neatly embodies many of the contradictions of the film serial; careful to retain the familiar traits of the comic book character and not alienate his faithful and substantial existing readership, it also attempts to subtly reposition Batman for a wider national audience with the label of 'American hero' and its implications of a patriotic crusade. The film chapters follow much the same pattern. What remains surprising to the late-1990s viewer prepared for a 'propaganda vehicle' is the extent to which the the propaganda element is kept separate from the Batman 'mythos', and consists primarily of voiceover, or of scenes which exclude Batman himself. The twin concerns of the producers – to adapt a comic book and incorporate a 'contemporary' plot – manifest themselves in the serial as remarkably autonomous elements. We are given 'propaganda', and 'Batman', but never an integrated vision of the 'propaganda Batman'. I shall examine this curious distinction below, but I want firstly to discuss the ways in which the serial displays 'fidelity' to the comic book, contrary to Kane's complaints, and subsequently the relation of the anti-Japanese narrative to, respectively, the Batman comics of the time and the surrounding cultural discourse.

Episode One of the serial, subtitled 'The Electrical Brain', opens with a Batman logo behind the credit sequence. The first shot establishes Wayne mansion from a distance, dark and framed by trees. The voiceover is deep, brooding, portentous; it echoes the hyperbole and rhetoric of the comic book captions, just as it was itself later to be parodied in William Dozier's voiceover for the 1966 TV series. 'High atop one of the hills which ring the teeming metropolis of Gotham City, a large house rears its bulk against the dark sky.' Foreboding chords swell. We dissolve to a shadowy interior and discover Lewis Wilson as Batman, centrally framed at a large desk. He gazes directly ahead, pensive and motionless; gloved hands support his chin. As the camera slowly dollies in, the voiceover continues: 'Deep in the

---

[198] See Kidd, op. cit., p. 31.

cavernous basement of this house, in a chamber hewn from the living rock of the mountain, is the strange, dimly lit, mysteriously secret Bats Cave – hidden headquarters of America's number one crimefighter – Batman.'

This opening is true to the established Batman mythos in both detail and tone. Wilson's costume reproduces all the key iconographical elements of Kane's early drawings – the long-eared cowl, the grey bodysuit emblazoned with a black bat, the cape and gauntlets. We are given the precise locale of Gotham City – never supplied by the comic books until February 1941 – and drawn into a dark, melodramatic atmosphere very much in keeping with the character's earlier 'gothic' adventures.

'Yes, Batman', the voiceover repeats for effect. 'Clad in the somber costume which has struck terror into the heart of many a swaggering denizen of the underworld. Batman – who even now is pondering the plans of a new assault against the forces of crime . . .' The script here virtually quotes directly from Kane and Finger's origin story – 'my disguise must be able to strike terror into their hearts' – and as such demonstrates a significant degree of 'fidelity' to the source. Moreover, the next moments provide a remarkable dramatisation of the changes Batman was put through in spring 1940, as Robin bounds into the scene from left of frame. The music takes on a light, playful air and the Boy Wonder leans close to his mentor, waking Batman from his ponderous reverie. The transformation is startling. Wilson beams widely and leans back in his chair, suddenly relaxed. Rising, he slips an arm around Douglas Croft's shoulder and they both run out of shot to the left. A neater summation of the shift from the 'grim' lone vigilante of 1939 to the avuncular, cheerful crimefighter of the 1940s could hardly be imagined.

At the end of the first scene, in which the heroes cuff two criminals and call the police to pick them up, we are privy to Batman and Robin pushing back their masks and revealing their secret identities. The next scene has Bruce and Dick in civvies – although their first names are not given until the second episode – talking to Bruce's girlfriend Linda. Now we discover Bruce's façade of foppish idleness, made clear in Robin's *sotto voce* question 'Why don't you let her know who you really are, instead of letting her think you're just a . . . good for nothing playboy?' The screenwriter's luxury of having an entire five-minute scene to fill with dialogue, as opposed to the comic scripter's need to advance plot in every panel and reduce conversation to the bare minimum of exposition, allows a subtlety of characterisation which was impossible in the 'original' text. Wilson's delivery as Wayne is educated and somewhat effete, while his interaction with Croft suggests a suave intimacy reminiscent of nothing so much as the male lovers in Hitchcock's *Rope*. The covert exchanges of the two men while Linda leaves the room – 'You're liable to carry that masquerade too far', Dick hisses, as Bruce gazes implacably ahead – give subsequent dialogue with Linda an undercurrent of irony, while the bantering performances lend an air of romantic comedy. 'You've had your usual busy day, I suppose,' Linda remarks to Bruce. 'Yup,' he replies blithely, 'Up at the crack of noon, a brisk walk to the corner, and then the club for a rugged afternoon of gin rummy.'

While there are departures from the letter of the comic book – Commissioner Gordon is bizarrely renamed Captain Arnold – there are also many instances of direct citation, such as the 'terror into the heart' voiceover, and elaborations on the comic book's framework, as in the case of Bruce Wayne's characterisation. Overall, I would be more than inclined to agree with Van Hise as regards the 'fidelity' of the adaptation; indeed, it can be argued that the comic book in turn adapted to some degree from the serial. The cliffhanger between Episodes Two and Three, for instance, where Batman appears to fall from a burning wire between two rooftops and saves himself with his own rope, was apparently borrowed by the writer of the syndicated comic strip in an episode from November 1943.[199] More fundamentally, it seems that William Austin's portrayal of Alfred, Batman's batman, affected the character's shift in the comic books from a short, bumbling figure to the tall and more sophisticated butler familiar from the mid-1940s onwards,[200] and even that the 'Bats Cave' of the serial was the first use of the term; Cotta Vaz reproduces frames from a 1941 comic which refer only to an 'underground tunnel', and states that the

---

[199] See *Batman: The Sunday Classics*, op. cit., pp. 6–7.
[200] Alan Asherman, personal conversation (29 June 1998).

'discovery of the Bat Cave was still years away'.[201]

The replacement of Batman's usual villains with Dr Daka, though, is a move of major significance, especially when we consider the total absence of Japanese villains in the Batman stories of the war period. [202]

As John W. Dower vividly demonstrates in *War Without Mercy*, American popular culture of the 1940s treated the 'Jap' with a pathological disgust which even the Nazis were spared. Dower shows that American poster art portrayed Hitler and Mussolini as individuals, however caricatured: the 'Jap' was simply a generic creature. A *Washington Post* cartoon reproduced by Dower makes the point well, illustrating 'sharply contrasting American images of the enemry – an ape representing all "Japs" imitates "Hitler" '.[203] This distinction is echoed in the popular song 'There'll Be No Adolph Hitler Nor Yellow Japs To Fear', whose cover is reproduced by Rhodes.[204]

The Nazis were at least human: the 'Jap' was vermin, his familiar stereotyped features – bright yellow skin, round glasses over slit eyes, protruding teeth – often degraded further into images of lice or monkeys, whether the brutish ape from the *New York Times* of April 1943, the foolish chimpanzee of a *Colliers* cover from May of the same year, or the grotesque insect labelled 'Louseous Japanicas' pictured in *Leatherneck* from March 1945.[205] Even when he took human form, the 'Jap' was a horrific, twisted figure, smirking 'Go Ahead, Please – Take Day Off!' in a Texaco poster from 1943, complete with mock-'Oriental' script and pidgin English.[206]

Terms demeaning and abusing the Japanese were used without apology at every level of American discourse, from popular songs – 'We're Gonna Have to Slap The Dirty Little Jap'[207] – through journal articles and newsreels to military analysis: Dower reports on a

---

[201] Cotta Vaz, op. cit., p. 97: he sources the artwork to *Batman* #4 of Winter 1941, which seems incorrect given that *Batman* #7 was dated October–November 1941, and #9 February–March 1942.
[202] See Brooker, 'Batman: One Life, Many Faces', op. cit.
[203] Dower, op. cit., p. 182.
[204] Rhodes, op. cit., p. 164.
[205] See Dower, op. cit., pp. 181–189.
[206] Rhodes, op. cit., p. 164.
[207] Ibid., p. 148.

lieutenant colonel's psychological approach to the Japanese which began 'let us look into one of these yellow heads and see what it contains'. The phrase 'little yellow men ... became an everyday expression in discussions of the Japanese enemy ... in one American newsreel, the Japanese were simply reduced to "the LYBs," shorthand for "little yellowbellies".'[208]

This discourse of unashamed hatred for the racial 'other' was enthusiastically taken up by many superhero comics of the period. The comic book covers discussed above – from *Captain America*, *Major Victory* and so forth – echo the popular shorthand of the time in their depiction of grotesque 'Jap' soldiers with bright yellow skin and buck teeth. More pertinently, *Detective Comics* embraced the same stereotypes and racist slurs, in virtually every strip but Batman. In the early 1940s, this treatment extended equally to the Chinese, who were popularly regarded in the Fu Manchu mould as part of a generalised Oriental 'Yellow Peril',[209] before any need arose to distinguish between 'friendly' Chinese and 'enemy' Japs.[210] *Detective*'s Cliff Crosby, for instance, walks through Chinatown as 'slanted eyes follow his every move', and punches out an Asian thug with the words 'Take your monkeys and go deliver your laundry!' The Chinese in turn are reduced to stilted dialect, both here and in the accompanying strip 'The Crimson Avenger': 'We look much, but no see melican!', 'We all same catch im spy out side – good flighter, but we catch!'[211]

In the years following America's entry into the war, the explicitly Japanese stereotype becomes more widespread in *Detective*. An episode of the Boy Commandos features Japanese soldiers invading an island, their leader identified through squint eyes, round glasses and large teeth: 'We build secret submarine base! Submarines sink many American ships!' Brooklyn, one of the heroes, observes an American professor discussing flowers with the enemy captain, and snarls 'Japs!

---

[208] Dower, op. cit., p. 162.

[209] Ibid., pp. 158–159.

[210] See 'How To Tell Japs From the Chinese', *Life* (December 1941); 'How to Tell Your Friends from the Japs', *Time* (December 1941); 'No Certain Way to Tell Japanese from Chinese', *Science News Letter* (December 1941).

[211] 'Cliff Crosby', and 'The Crimson Avenger', stories in *Detective Comics*, New York: DC Comics (March 1940–February 1941).

Why, da doity rat! Playin' up to da Nips to save his own skin.' Yet the situation is clearly resolved. 'I was t'inkin' maybe ya liked da Japs!' Brooklyn protests once the enemy is defeated, to which the Professor replies firmly 'I do like cherry-blossoms . . . but I DON'T like Japanese militarists!'[212]

A few issues previously, a text story had emphasised the same message in the tale of Marine Private Erwin Sanders, nicknamed 'Lucky' and 'built for good American laughter'. Lucky cheerfully relates that 'it wouldn't be long before the Marines rolled the little yellow bellies into the sea', and affirms that he wouldn't swap the tough life at Parris Island for anything – 'not unless it happened to be an extra crack at the Japs'. A cartoon strip earlier in the issue gives the reader the opportunity to get a crack at the Japanese from the home front, by purchasing more war bonds. In the first frame we see a slant-eyed businessman standing before a Rising Sun flag, rubbing his hands over the statue of an American citizen. 'Excellent statue of true friend of Japan!' he exclaims, as a Japanese boy grins 'American patriot buy few war bonds – then SELL them!' In the next panel a GI offers a grim reminder: 'Don't let em erect a statue of YOU in Tokio! BUY war bonds – and HOLD ONTO THEM!'[213]

By contrast to both the immediate surrounding of Detective, and the wider cultural discourse of newsreels, songs, posters and magazine articles, the Batman stories of this period – from my reading, which cannot hope to be exhaustive but nevertheless attempts a thorough analysis of the incomplete DC Comics archive – contain one use of the word 'Jap', in Detective #88 of June 1944. Even here it is an evil racketeer, rather than Batman, who exclaims 'It shouldn't happen to a Jap!' as the Caped Crusader's punches rain down on him.

It can be contested that Batman and Robin do fight pigtailed 'mongols' in Detective #52 (June 1941), the 'giant Indian' Jabah in Detective #29 (July 1939) and turbanned 'Hindus' in Detective #35 (January 1940). 'Mongols' in particular are a regular choice of villain, recurring several times in the first year of publication alone. There is little point in arguing that these thugs are not depicted according to

<hr/>

[212] *Detective Comics* #91, New York: DC Comics (September 1944).
[213] *Detective Comics* #87, New York: DC Comics (May 1944).

racial stereotype; they spout cod-'Chinese' characters in their speech balloons, are described in captions as 'tricky' and speak in a Fu Manchu dialect, if at all: 'Ah! Yes! Hee Hee!'[214] It can at least be pointed out, though, that the thugs' skin colour is never a caricatured bright yellow, as was the convention in many other forms of popular entertainment and information,[215] and that the terms used to describe them never become more demeaning than 'Chinaman'. In fact, the portrayal of 'Orientals' in Batman during the opening months of the 1940s – a time when, as noted above, Chinese and Japanese were frequently conflated in an anti-Asian discourse – is relatively subtle on closer inspection, and clearly avoids pathologising the villains purely on the grounds of race.

Gotham's Chinatown – 'a city within a city – where the mystery of the East comes to the streets of the West' – is populated by good citizens as well as greedy thugs, much like the rest of the city. The 'unofficial mayor', Wong, is described as a 'wise, honorable man'; when he places a personal advertisement in 'Chinese style' type, Batman responds immediately 'to help a friend'.[216] In turn, the villainous Sin Fang – a slit-eyed schemer with a long moustache – is revealed in a significant twist to be not what he seems: 'Suddenly the Oriental begins peeling off the skin of his hands – revealing white flesh underneath ...' The real Sin Fang, we learn, has been killed and impersonated by a white Chinese-speaker called Sheldon Lenox. Even the Oriental henchmen, Batman informs us, were 'fake Hindus'.[217]

In the second tale set in Chinatown, issues of ethnic identity are once again shown to be more complex than they first appeared: the Fu Manchu style villain, it transpires, assumed that the police 'would probably hunt for white gangsters and never suspect a Chinese of kidnapping'. It takes Batman's knowledge of Oriental combat to reveal that 'one of his men spoiled the plan by killing the chauffeur with a hatchet! Only the Chinese hatchet man would use that type of weapon!' In the penultimate panel of this story we cut to a Chinese

---

[214] *Detective Comics* #39, New York: DC Comics (May 1940).
[215] See Dower, op. cit., p. 161.
[216] *Detective Comics* #39, New York: DC Comics (May 1940).
[217] *Detective Comics* #35, New York: DC Comics (January 1940).

household where a young girl asks her mother 'why should I pray for the well-being of one called the BATMAN?' 'Because, little one,' the woman replies, 'he has saved the souls of many of our people.'[218]

As in the case of Batman's isolation from overtly militaristic discourse, we can only guess at the reasons behind this relatively liberal, even-handed portrayal of 'Orientals' during the year preeceding Pearl Harbor, and the apparent absence of any anti-Japanese content in the stories of 1941–1945. Again, it can probably be attributed to a combination of the creative freedom afforded to Batman's writers by the editors at DC and the personal beliefs of Finger and his colleagues, who after all had grown up as working-class New Yorkers and may well have seen Chinatown as no more 'exotic' or 'other' than the Bronx.

The question is, then, how the film serial attempted to reconcile an anti-Japanese discourse with the conventions of a typical Batman narrative, given that it remained 'faithful' to the established codes of the comic book character in most respects. The simple answer is that it didn't. As such, the Columbia film serial initiated a mode of operation which was taken up where necessary by Batman's writers and producers for the next fifty-five years. As I outlined at the start of this chapter, certain traits surrounding and defining the Batman must be kept intact to retain a sense of 'continuity'. If Bruce Wayne became a hobo who dressed in a rat costume and commited crime, he would become a very different character – 'Ratman', perhaps. At a less extreme level, if the Batman is removed from his crusade against urban crime many of his key characteristics are placed in question: his costume, origin and motivation all stem from a mugging in Gotham City and the vow against the symbolic figure who murdered his parents. The Batman of 1943, despite his popularity, did not have the status of a recognisable cultural icon. His producers, therefore, could not allow themselves the luxury of experimenting with his proven formula without running the risk of losing an audience which, after all, had only been established over the previous four years.

With sixty years of tradition behind them, the current editors of Batman can afford to play with readers' expectations of the character

---

[218] *Detective Comics* #39, New York: DC Comics (May 1940).

and experiment with those basic traits, treating them as variables rather than fixed tenets. Batman can be portrayed as a down-and-out who only hallucinates his life as a crimefighter,[219] or as a vampire with the associated 'special powers' of Dracula.[220] However, such departures are almost always confined to the 'Imaginary Story' or 'Elseworld' narrative, which remain outside 'continuity'. If a set of obligations are imposed on the character within a 'continuity' story which threaten to contradict one or more of the basic traits, Batman's producers can choose not to change the character but to adapt the scenario to suit him.

This is how Denny O'Neil reacts when a science fiction 'crossover' story, involving all of DC Comics' characters, seeps into the Batman titles of the late 1990s; as editor, O'Neil proposes, he would 'play it so the visiting alien is after a gadget in an alleyway',[221] and so retain the urban tone of the Batman story while incorporating the literally alien element. And this, apparently, is what screenwriters Victor McLeod, Leslie Swabacker and Harry Fraser did in 1943.

Dr Daka, as played by J. Carrol Naish, is clearly located within the contemporary stereotype of the 'Jap', as far as the conventions of realist cinema can approximate the caricatures of poster art: on their first meeting, Batman is able to exclaim 'Aha, a Jap!' from one glance at his enemy. Daka is short and sallow, hair slicked back and lips dark; his delivery is stilted and robotic, combining unthinking servitude to his master and a contempt for American values. This is his first speech, with a faithful reproduction of Naish's accent:

I am Dr Daka – humble servant of his majesty Hirohito – heavenly ruler and prince of da *Riiising* Sun. By divine destiny my country shall destroy da democratic forces of evil in da *Uniiited* States to make way for da new *or*-dah. An order dat will bring about da liberation of da enslaved people of A*mer*-ica.

---

[219] See Bryan Talbot, 'Mask', *Legends of the Dark Knight* #39–49, New York: DC Comics (November–December 1992).
[220] See Doug Moench, Kelley Jones and Malcolm Jones III, *Batman/Dracula: Red Rain*, New York: DC Comics (1992).
[221] Denny O'Neil, personal interview (30 June 1998).

Yet Batman was the hero who fought petty criminals, not the forces of Japan. For him to engage directly with the wartime enemy would require a significant deviation from the conventions established during the comics' first four years, and would potentially alienate an audience who had come to watch an adaptation of Batman, not just another war adventure. We should remember that this audience, unlike that of Tim Burton or Joel Schumacher in the 1990s, had to be hooked for fifteen separate episodes, rather than one ninety-minute whole; if the serial began to disappoint viewers in its lack of resemblance to the familiar and popular 'original', theatres could have been empty by the fifth instalment.

So rather than Batman going to war, the war is brought to Batman, in the most indirect manner conceivable. Incredible as it may seem, Batman does not meet Daka until the very last episode of fifteen, although the villain is introduced to the viewer in Episode One; several hours previously in terms of total screen time, or weeks before in the context of a Saturday morning serial. Until that final point, the two storylines and by extension the two associated discourses of 'Batman adventure' and 'Japanese plot' run virtually parallel to each other, converging almost by accident. Rather than being transformed into a patriotic, all-American crusader, Batman is drawn gradually into the intrigue through his normal duties of fighting crime; it is pure coincidence that Dr Daka happens to be behind this particular crime, and then only at several removes.

The villain is first mentioned by members of the Collins gang, while Batman cuffs them in the first scene – 'Dr Daka'll make you regret this!' warns one hood, to which Batman replies in bewilderment 'Who's that?' A few scenes later Linda's Uncle Martin, just released from prison, is kidnapped by thugs and taken to Daka, who explains that he is recruiting 'dishonored' Americans for his league of spies. Prompted by loyalty to his girlfriend, Bruce decides to investigate Martin's disappearance, and in the process of pursuing the kidnappers as Batman, retrieves a radium gun which belonged to Daka. It takes a voiceover to explain that 'Daka, the sinister Jap spy, believes Linda knows the whereabouts of the powerful radium gun'; the villain's interest then turns to Martin's niece, and Batman naturally seeks to rescue her when she is captured by Daka's men.

It is only in Episode Three that Daka first hears of Batman, when his thugs report back from a fistfight with the heroes, and even now he hardly seems to rate his opponent as a patriotic hero. 'Batman is a rank amateur!' he lectures them. 'Get rid of him!' Finding that Bruce has placed a newspaper advertisement in an attempt to trace the owner of the radium gun, his reaction is equally dismissive. 'Obviously Batman is trying to set a trap for us!' Batman, on the other hand, doesn't know or much care about the mastermind behind this outfit; he merely wants Linda's uncle back, for her sake. Far from undertaking a patriotic mission, he is following a personal agenda for his girlfriend, and beyond that simply 'fighting crime', as he always has; the goons he engages with are white Americans, rather than Japanese. This gulf between the two spheres of hero and villain is emphasised to the point of comedy in a scene from Episode Four, where the two speak on the telephone without knowing the other's identity; Batman adopts a 'Hindu' accent, posing as 'Swami Dhar', yet it is he who remarks 'strange voice' as he puts the phone down.

The patriotic element of the serial, then, has to find expression in forms other than Batman himself. To an extent this burden is carried by the secondary American characters who come into contact with Daka. Uncle Martin, for instance, responds vehemently to the suggestion that he would join the villain's league: 'Listen, Daka – or whatever your name is – I owe my allegiance to no country or order but my own. I'm an American first and always! And no amount of torture conceived by your twisted Oriental brain will make me change my mind!' Similarly, Daka's henchman Foster delivers a fiercely patriotic speech when the Doctor threatens to feed him to a pit of alligators.

> I don't need any . . . handwriting on the wall to tell me who's going to win *this* war – because it's written as plain and black as . . . death in every newspaper. That's what I came back to tell you; cause I'm not afraid of you. You've shot your *bolt*, Daka – you and *all* your Axis cronies.

Other than these declarations, made as if by proxy for Batman by stand-ins for the hero, the propaganda message is carried entirely by voiceover. This device is interesting in its literal imposition of a meaning over the image of Batman; the voiceover is by its nature added after the fact of filming, and so comes across as an afterthought, tacked-on almost in contradiction to what we are being shown. The introductory montage, for instance, is 'neutral' in propaganda terms, showing Batman and Robin crashing through a window to fight crooks, chasing criminals in a car and punching two men who are attempting to steal a safe. The voiceover subtly adds connotations of patriotism to this crime-fighting sequence, culminating in explicit references to the ongoing global conflict which actually bear no relation to the accompanying images of petty crime. The sequence begins immediately after the shot of the 'Bats Cave' discussed above, with the two heroes leaving to the left of frame, and the words 'Robin, the Boy Wonder':

> They represent American youth – who love their country, and are glad to fight for it. Wherever crime raises its ugly head – to strike with the venom of a maddened rattlesnake – Batman and Robin strike also! And in this very hour, when the Axis criminals are spreading their evil over the world, even within our own land, Batman and Robin stand ready to fight them to the death.

While there is an interesting attempt even here to construct the Axis as 'criminals', and so bring the Japanese within the boundaries of Batman's established 'war on crime', the propaganda message nevertheless fails to integrate with either the images shown or the portrayal of Batman and Robin that follows in this and subsequent episodes. As such it serves much the same function as those war bond covers discussed above, which bore no relation to the issue's actual storyline. Both pay the required lip service to wartime propaganda on their surface – whether on a comic book cover, or within the first two minutes of a serial – before letting Batman get on with what he did best. To change that would have been to change the nature of the character at the height of his early popularity, to change the brand just when it was selling to three million readers every month in comic books and reaching a nationwide audience daily through newspaper syndication. Batman was the man who fought crime, and that, almost without exception, was the way it stayed until 1945.

Epilogue: Post-bellum

There is another paradox in the fact that it took the end of the war to prompt a major shift in the tone and style of Batman stories. Unlike the case of other superheroes, though, the change was not directly related to the cessation of hostilities – which makes sense, as Batman had rarely engaged with the issues of a precise historical moment. While many of the characters created specifically to fight the Axis themselves folded with that enemy's defeat, and others adapted to meet the demands of a changed world – the Boy Commandos were reduced to pre-VJ Day flashbacks and domestic capers, as *Detective*'s new hero Johnny Everyman stepped in to ask searching questions about racism, democracy and world hunger – the post-war shift in Batman stories was again less to do with topicality than with the process of branding.

Batman had now run succesfully for six years across three different media forms, building a readership from juvenile fans through army personnel to, presumably, a sizeable proportion of that 41 per cent of males and 28 per cent of females who admitted to enjoying comic books in 1944. It seems feasible that the brand was now considered well-enough established to tolerate some playful testing of the familiar codes and conventions: and so, in *Batman* #24 (August–September 1944), the opening caption asks 'if some magic wand could waft the Batman and Robin back across the bridge of years to a distant past, what thrilling adventures would confront the streamlined crime-smashers of the 20th century? Well, here's the answer! A pulse-pounding story of ancient Rome . . .' Eight issues later – easily long enough to judge whether the departure from contemporary Gotham had affected sales – the device is reprised. In *Batman* #32 (December 1945–January 1946), 'Batman and Robin flash back through the mists of time to a swashbuckling romantic adventure with the Three Musketeers!' Flash-forward another six issues to *Batman* #38, and once more the time is deemed right for a historical tale: 'Back 25 centuries to the glory that was ancient Greece flash Batman and Robin to play a thrilling part in the historic Olympic Games . . .'

In the mid-1940s, then, Batman had undergone a second shift. Created as a lone vigilante, he had been refined into a cheerful costumed lawman; now his stories escaped their familiar boundaries and became playful experiments, fantasies in which Batman and Robin were sometimes the only constant.

These fantasies were avidly consumed by the teenage boys and young men who made up a major part of Batman's audience. Unfortunately for Batman, they were also read by the psychiatrist who treated some of those boys and young men in the 'Quaker Emergency Service Readjustment Center' for 'overt homosexuals'.[222] The consultant's name was Dr Fredric Wertham.

---

[222] See Fredric Wertham, *Seduction of the Innocent*, London: Museum Press (1955).

2

1954

CENSORSHIP AND QUEER READINGS

Who ever let you out of the nut house must have been
bats. (Letter to Dr Fredric Wertham, 1950s)

Nineteen fifty-four was the publication date of Fredric
Wertham's *Seduction of the Innocent*. The book was mainly
an attack on horror comics, but has also become notorious for
its argument – across four pages which are often narrowed down in
discussion to a single, much-quoted paragraph – that Batman and
Robin's adventures had homoerotic overtones. This was the text, then,
which brought to light the 'gay readings' of the character which had
previously been hidden and, paradoxically in terms of its repressive
project, caused those readings to circulate in popular culture for the
next forty-five years.

Despite the focus on this single date in my heading, the historical
scope of this chapter is actually far wider than that of the previous
section. Because the importance of Wertham's writing on Batman can
only be read backwards through its effect on discourses around the
character in subsequent decades, I am employing a framing device at
either end of the chapter. The first examines the almost universally
negative – even personally vehement – reaction to Wertham on the
part of comics fandom, including the response of comic-book historians
to *Seduction of the Innocent*. These readings frequently mobilise a subtle,
or sometimes blatant, homophobic prejudice in their efforts to decry

Wertham's interpretation of a homoerotic relationship between Batman and Robin.

As I have discussed elsewhere, however,[1] the arguments against Wertham are made more interesting and problematic by the fact that they come from two very distinct camps: the homophobic criticism of presumably heterosexual commentators, and the equally vicious mockery from critics who locate themselves within the approach of 'queer' reading and therefore attack Wertham for his own supposed homophobia.

This contradiction led me to re-examine both *Seduction of the Innocent* and the actual Batman texts of the 1950s, which few of those who attack Wertham from either side appear to have done at all thoroughly. My project from here on is twofold.

Firstly, through a reconstruction of the cultural framework governing homosexuality in the 1950s, and with reference to the personal testimonies available from gay men who lived through that decade, I propose that rather than embodying a homophobic project of witch-hunting Wertham expresses a concern for the sexuality of his young interviewees which although naïve was entirely understandable in context.

Secondly, through a reading of the Batman comics on which Wertham and his sources would have based their opinions, again with reference to contemporary cultural structures, I argue that the interpretation of the Batman and Robin scenario which was made visible by Wertham is by no means as absurd as his critics want to suggest.

Finally, in the second book-end of my framing device, I demonstrate through a variety of references to a 'gay Batman' from the late 1950s onwards that Wertham's highlighting of a few boys' homoerotic interpretation actually made this reading widespread and caused it to circulate, rather than dampening and repressing it. While the notion of gayness in association with Batman and Robin was frequently a cause for parody and homophobic jibes, I show that the

---

[1] Will Brooker, 'Containing Batman: Rereading Fredric Wertham and the Comics of the 1950s', in Nathan Abrams and Julie Hughes (eds), *Containing America*, Birmingham: Birmingham University Press (forthcoming).

reading made visible by Wertham has also been taken up again by gay audiences in a less condemnatory social context, and in turn has been incorporated by the producers of mainstream Batman films and comic books into scenarios of love and trust between men.

1. Framing Device: Dark Legend[2]

Wertham was not the first to see a homoerotic relationship between Batman and Robin. His own study of the comics over four pages of his best-known work, *Seduction of the Innocent*, was prompted by the earlier research, 'several years ago', of a 'California psychiatrist', and also, significantly, by the testimonies of 'overt homosexuals' being treated at the 'Quaker Emergency Service Readjustment Center'[3] who had drawn their own fantasies from the pages of Batman comics. These more complex discourses are, however, usually conflated into the single figure of Fredric Wertham, and his four pages concentrated down to a single passage which is quoted without fail whenever the question of a 'gay Batman' arises.

> At home they lead an idyllic life. They are Bruce Wayne and 'Dick' Grayson. Bruce Wayne is described as a 'socialite' and the official relationship is that Dick is Bruce's ward. They live in sumptuous quarters, with beautiful flowers in large vases, and have a butler, Alfred. Bruce is sometimes shown in a dressing gown. As they sit by the fireplace the young boy sometimes worries about his partner . . . it is like a wish dream of two homosexuals living together.[4]

It is this passage which a contributor to the Internet *Mantle of the Bat*

---

[2] *Dark Legend* was one of Wertham's earliest works, published in 1941: the title chimes intriguingly both with Batman and with the bogeyman reputation of Wertham himself. See Amy Kiste Nyberg, *Seal of Approval*, Jackson: University Press of Mississippi (1998), p. 88.
[3] Fredric Wertham, *Seduction of the Innocent*, London: Museum Press (1955), pp. 189, 191.
[4] Wertham, op. cit., p. 190.

Bat-Board clearly had in mind when he answered my query in May 1997. I had posted a message to the bulletin board which stated simply that I had heard Batman could be perceived as gay, and asked for response. This was my longest reply.

BATMAN GAY? I DON'T THINK SO ... LOOK AT THE EVIDENCE

Fear not, my friend, I have had this argument many times before and I can categorically assure you that it is total BOLLOCKS ... this whole 'subversive sexuality' nonsense found its genesis in the 50s under the auspices of that ball-less, soulless, joyless, guilt-ridden, pro-Censorship and all-round 'Protector of our Morality' (Arrogantly Self-Proclaimed) Dr Frederic Wertham, who wrote a book on this so-called 'affliction' to superhero comics entitled 'Seduction of the Innocent' (1957). [*sic*] In short – Our Man is staunchly heterosexual. Hope this helped: in short, he's not Gay.[5]

This post, with its interesting appeal to heterosexual 'male bonding' as it offers help to a new friend, does not in fact offer the 'evidence' promised by the heading. Some textual reference was supplied in a second answer:

NO HE'S NOT GAY!

If he is Gay, then he has an awful lot of girlfriends! But he's not Gay, unlike other superheroes, he doesn't stick to one partner, everytime you see him, he has a new trophy on his arm!!! He's a cool geezer.[6]

This reading, despite the lack of detail in the 'proof' offered, does hold some currency in terms of the comic book text. Bruce Wayne has indeed had a number of girlfriends, from his fiancée Julie Madison

---

[5] BatDan, post to *Mantle of the Bat Bat-Board*, http://www.cire.com/batman (May 1997).

[6] Dawg, post to *Bat-Board*, ibid.

onwards. We might note in passing, though, that these have never lasted long, while Robin has been by his side in one form or another for fifty-nine years.

A third answer was even more direct, even aggressive:

WRONG GUY!
Batman isn't Gay. He is a heterosexual man. Get it?[7]

While these responses may seem crude, they are not a great deal less sophisticated than those offered by critics whose work has found publication through conventional means rather than on the Internet. This stolid denial of the 'Gay Batman' reading, and its sourcing to the scapegoat figure of Wertham, is a constant in virtually every history of comics I have come across,[8] and that line, 'a wish dream of two homosexuals living together', becomes a recurring motif to be heavily repressed whenever it raises its head.

'Wertham', says Paul Sassienie in *The Comic Book*, 'deliberately, or otherwise, missed the point, that in truth Bruce Wayne and Dick Grayson's relationship was no more than that of father and son.'[9] Reinhold Reitberger, in *Comics: Anatomy of a Mass Medium*, calls Wertham's interpretation 'a libellous propaganda campaign' and stresses that 'Batman has now sent teenage-wonder Robin to college where he seems to show a normal and lively interest in the opposite sex.'[10] E. Nelson Bridwell, introducing *Batman from the 30s to the 70s*, bristles at 'a certain psychiatrist [who] decided that a man and boy living together spelled homosexuality', calling it 'one of the most irresponsible slurs ever cast upon our heroes',[11] while Mark Cotta Vaz, in *Tales of the Dark Knight*, cites the opinion that 'if they had been actual

---

[7] Number 2, post to *Bat-Board*, ibid.

[8] The two most academically rigorous accounts of the 1950s anti-comics campaign, ironically, pass no comment on Batman. See James Gilbert, *A Cycle of Outrage*, New York: Oxford University Press (1986) and Nyberg, op. cit.

[9] Paul Sassienie, *The Comic Book*, London: Ebury Press (1994), p. 58.

[10] Reinhold Reitberger and Wolfgang Fuchs, *Comics: Anatomy of a Mass Medium*, London: Studio Vista, (1972), p. 123.

[11] E. Nelson Bridwell, *Batman from the 30s to the 70s*, New York: Crown Publishers (1971), p. 12.

men, they could have won a libel suit', derides Wertham's 'unfounded rumors' and concludes 'it was sad that Wertham got so much mileage out of his unwarranted attacks on Batman. This was the same Batman who had fought Nazi spies and aided the War Bond effort . . . '[12] Cotta Vaz calls upon the power of authorial meaning, stressing that 'Bob Kane has dismissed the notion of Batman and Robin as homosexuals, aghast that anyone would read into his characters some subliminal ode to homoeroticism. After all, Bruce Wayne regularly squired the most beautiful women in Gotham City and presumably had a healthy sex life.'[13] Similarly, Ron Goulart's *Great History of Comic Books* claims that Wertham's accusations about Batman and Robin's relationship 'caused DC . . . anxiety and anguish'.[14]

Roger Sabin, in *Adult Comics*, is equally critical but on the whole less sensationalist, if we take his claim that *Seduction of the Innocent* was the '*Mein Kampf* of comics' with a pinch of salt. He too overturns Wertham's identification of 'homo-erotic undercurrents (especially in the case of Batman's relationship with Robin)' with his challenges that *Seduction of the Innocent* employed a 'suspect' methodology and ultimately contained 'no evidence . . . that comics were a corrupting influence'.[15] Similarly, William Savage derides Wertham as a 'monocausationist' and his work as 'pompous, polemical, biased and poorly documented'.

> The doctor's research confirmed the view (which he attributed to others) that stories about Batman and Robin were 'psychologically homosexual' . . . and only 'someone ignorant of the fundamentals of psychiatry and of the psychopathology

---

[12] Mark Cotta Vaz, *Tales of the Dark Knight: Batman's First Fifty Years 1939–1989*, London: Futura (1989), p. 47.

[13] Ibid.

[14] Ron Goulart, *Great History of Comic Books*, Chicago: Contemporary Books (1986), p. 270.

[15] Roger Sabin, *Adult Comics: An Introduction*, London: Routledge (1993), pp. 157–158.

of sex' would say it wasn't so – a splendid ploy for preempting the layperson's criticism of the critic.[16]

Martin Barker is equally dismissive in his study of 1950s comic censorship, *A Haunt of Fears*, which surprisingly has only four lines of comment on Wertham's interpretation of Batman. *Seduction of the Innocent*, says Barker offhandedly, 'repeats the old story about the homosexual relations between Batman and Robin . . . apparently some of Wertham's patients got quite a thrill from imagining this relationship!'[17]

As indicated above, Wertham has also been ridiculed and lambasted from the opposite direction, for his supposedly rampant homophobia. The best-known example of this tendency remains Andy Medhurst's 'Batman, Deviance and Camp', whose very title would incite many Batman fans to outraged denial. Medhurst brands Wertham a 'crazed' homophobe with a project of 'shrill witch-hunting', quotes the infamous paragraph about Bruce and Dick at home, and responds

> To avoid being thought queer by Wertham, Bruce and Dick should have done the following: never show concern if the other is hurt, live in a shack, have only ugly flowers in small vases, never share a couch, keep your collar buttoned-up, keep your jacket on and never, ever, wear a dressing-gown.[18]

In a remarkable echo of Medhurst's retort, Freya Johnson, in an article on the 'queer supratext' of *Batman Forever* from the on-line journal *Bad Subjects*, picks out the same passage and comes up with the same reply.

> Obviously they must be fags: otherwise they'd have a butler named 'Butch', live in cramped quarters littered with beer-

---

[16] William W. Savage, *Comic Books and America: 1945–1954*, Norman: University of Oklahoma Press (1990), pp. 96–97.

[17] Martin Barker, *A Haunt of Fears*, London: Pluto Press (1984), p. 68.

[18] Andy Medhurst, 'Batman, Deviance and Camp', in Roberta E. Pearson and William Uricchio (eds), *The Many Lives of the Batman*, London: Routledge (1991), p. 151.

cans, wouldn't show concern for one another's injuries or be caught dead in a dressing-gown and cultivate only (what?) cactuses in small ugly metal pots? [19]

I have one more example of a text which engages with and comments on Wertham's 'dressing-gown' paragraph, and it takes a curiously, provocatively ambiguous position in its criticism; indeed, it sometimes seems not to disagree with Wertham at all. Burt Ward – Robin, in the 1960s TV show – even provides his own elaborate reworking of the 'wish dream' scenario in the chapter of his autobiography titled simply 'Are Batman and Robin Gay?'

> A mature man, unmarried and rarely seen in the company of women, takes a naïve teenage boy under his wing. The boy isn't adopted, so there is no father/son relationship – and there has never been any such intention. [...] They share many secrets and spend long hours together alone in remote areas – undisturbed in a massive, impenetrable cave.[20]

Ward goes on to virtually reproduce the passage from Wertham on Wayne and Grayson's interior decoration, although his own description is clearly informed by the TV show's *mise-en-scène* as well as that of the comic books:

> They live together in opulence befitting a baron. Exquisitely manicured grounds, a grand staircase leading to unknown rooms upstairs, spacious downstairs living areas decorated with macho furnishings – suits of armor in the foyer, heavy bookcases in the library, an imposing bust of Shakespeare, and

[19] Freya Johnson, ' ''Holy Homosexuality Batman'': Camp and Corporate Capitalism in ''Batman Forever'' ', *Bad Subjects* #23, http://english-server.hss.cmu.edu/bs/23/johnson.html (December 1995).
[20] Burt Ward with Stanley Ralph Ross, *Boy Wonder: My Life In Tights*, Los Angeles: Logical Figments Books (1995), pp. 81–82.

enormous round vases in various sizes and shapes . . . HOLY
HOMOPHOBIA![21]

It is difficult to guess the extent to which Ward is attempting irony
here. Much of his autobiography consists of detailed sexual adventures
with groupies which have more than an air of wish-fulfilment about
them, and his prose style is enthusiastic but clumsy. When he links
'macho furnishings' to 'homophobia', we can hardly tell who or what
he is parodying, if anything. If this description is meant as a satire of
Wertham, like Medhurst's and Johnson's witty inversions, Ward's
intention is belied by the passage cited above, which draws parallels
between Batman and Robin's relationship and a 'gay' scenario more
explicitly than Wertham ever did.

   If in turn Ward himself seems ignorantly homophobic in his
apparent association of 'manicured grounds', 'an imposing bust of
Shakespeare' and 'enormous round vases' with 'homosexual' tastes, his
efforts to answer the title question again reveal ambiguities as he boasts
of his close, quasi-sexual relationship with co-star Adam West:

> No question that we've . . . made love in front of each other
> and next to each other on many occasions . . . after dark, by the
> time we removed our costumes and makeup – we found a
> common bond in seeking a release of the tensions of our
> plugged geysers. It's true: we share a special relationship and
> chemistry that is hard to define and harder to explain . . . we
> have a lot of love for each other and the memories we've
> shared. Certainly that can't be misconstrued to mean more
> than it actually is and was. Can it?[22]

Ward almost seems to be asking for reassurance, though again it is
unclear which way he wants this admission to be read or what kind of
answer he seeks.

   Paradoxically, Burt Ward – through his nervous boasts, his
protestations of heterosexuality coupled with an inability to resist

---

[21] Ibid., p. 82.
[22] Ibid., pp. 83–84.

suggestions of homoeroticism, and the confusions inherent in his prose style – comes closest of all these commentators to expressing the ambiguity in Batman and Robin's relationship. Ultimately, Ward acknowledges that the traits identified by Wertham in Batman comics – like those he identifies himself in his relationship with West – walk a thin line between the homosocial and the homosexual. While there is no 'correct' way to see this relationship, it can feasibly be read as 'gay'.

Rather than deny or mock this interpretation – which we must remember was not dreamed up by some crackpot doctor in isolation but was put to Wertham by young gay men of the period – it seems more profitable to ask why such a reading would have come about. To do that, we have to attempt to reconstruct some of the historical context of the mid-1950s through which images of 'homosexuality' were derived, and compare these images in turn to the scenario portrayed in *Batman* comics, with reference to primary texts. Wertham's description of Bruce and Dick may seem heavy-handed and based on stereotype: but images of gay men in 1954 were heavy-handed and stereotyped, and these were the images received and internalised not just by heterosexuals but by gay men themselves.

2. Wertham's Agenda

I am not an apologist for Wertham. It is a worthless exercise, however, to set him up as an Aunt Sally and deride him as an idiot or an ogre by the standards of our own very different culture. Andy Medhurst demonstrates the ease of this approach in his article on Wertham, which rejoices in gags such as 'Nightmare On Psychiatry Street: Freddy's Obsession'.[23] Referring to Wertham as 'Doctor Doom' is all well and good, but it could be argued that Medhurst is led into generalisations and accusations for effect, such as the notion that Wertham 'points his shrill, witch-hunting finger at the Dynamic Duo and cries "queer" '.[24] There is, we might suggest, little gain in caricaturing Wertham as an hysterical, evangelical Witchfinder General

---

[23] Medhurst, op. cit., p. 150.

[24] Ibid.

when your own project is meant as a criticism of sterotypes. While he labels *Seduction of the Innocent* 'flamboyant melodrama masquerading as social psychology',[25] Medhurst's response, like the retorts of those critics he refutes – Mark Cotta Vaz, for instance – is also reliant on moral indignation and grand gestures of dismissal which make for a winning style but falter a little under analysis.

Medhurst claims, for instance, that Wertham 'writes with anguished concern about the potential harm that Batman might do to vulnerable children, innocents who might be turned into deviants'. This is simply an exaggeration, and an irresponsible one, for it misrepresents the original text for the sake of making a point more easily. This may well be Medhurst's honest reading of Wertham, but I believe he is wrong, and that the truth is far less convenient.

What Wertham actually says is this:

> Many adolescents go through periods of vague fears that they might be homosexual. Such fears may become a source of great mental anguish and these boys usually have no-one in whom they feel they can confide ... during and after comic-book reading they indulged in fantasies which became seriously repressed. Life experiences, either those drawing attention to the great taboo on homosexuality or just the opposite – experiences providing any kind of temptation – raise feelings of doubt, guilt, shame and sexual malorientation.[26]

We might now quibble with the term 'malorientation', but overall, rather than expressing shock and outrage, Wertham's tone seems one of quite reasonable concern. He does not, in my opinion, come across as 'shrill' or 'anguished'. Rather than advocating a witch-hunt against deviants, he understands that in a climate where homosexuality is a great taboo, gay fantasies might be a source of worry for young men. Moreover, his overall suggestion, at the beginning of his discussion on

---

[25] Ibid.
[26] Wertham, op. cit., p. 189.

Batman, is merely that 'a subtle atmosphere of homoeroticism' pervades the comic; not a scenario of 'deviance', but, in his own words, a 'love-relationship'.[27]

Fredric Wertham was in many ways remarkably unprejudiced for his time. That he detested racism is clear from any thorough reading of *Seduction of the Innocent* alone. To take just one example:

> One of the most significant and deeply resented manifestations of race prejudice in the mores of the United States is the fact that in books, movies and magazines photographs of white women with bared breasts are taboo, while the same pictures of colored girls are permitted. Comic books for children make this same distinction. [. . .] This is a demonstration of race prejudice for children, driven home by the appeal to sexual instincts. It is probably one of the most sinister methods of suggesting that races are fundamentally different with regard to moral values, and that one is inferior to the other. This is where a psychiatric question becomes a social one.[28]

Again, there is no shrillness or anguish here. There is a measured concern about an issue which worries Wertham, just as there was in the earlier passage. Few of us would mock his concerns here, or feel it appropriate to refer to him as 'Freddy' or 'Doctor Doom' for his dislike of racism. If we learn that Wertham's suspicion of Superman comics was based on his discomfort with all aspects of Fascism and his fear that children might learn to admire both physical force and the domination of 'inferior' peoples,[29] his writing on this subject may also make more sense.

It would no doubt surprise many of those who caricature him as a bigot to learn that, during the 1920s, Wertham was one of the few psychiatrists who would treat black patients; that he spent the war years campaigning without result and against great hostility to establish a low-cost clinic in Harlem; that his LaFargue Clinic was finally opened

---

[27] Ibid., p. 190.
[28] Ibid., p. 105.
[29] Ibid., p. 34.

on 113th Street in March 1944 with the help of funding from Ralph Ellison and the support of New York's black ministers.[30]

This sits uncomfortably with the received view of Wertham: but the research which became *Seduction of the Innocent* – social psychiatry with particular reference to juvenile delinquency and its relation to surrounding culture – in fact took its motivation from his work in Harlem. Wertham's campaign against racism, which led to his court testimony for the NAACP against classroom segregation in 1951, ran parallel to his campaign against comics, which in turn led to his attendance at the New York Committee to Study the Publication of Comics in 1949,[31] and to many other subsequent hearings. 'Wertham's expression of disgust for racist overtones in comics before the New York Commission stemmed as much from his work at LaFargue as from his general exploration of social psychology', writes James Gilbert in *Cycle of Outrage*.[32]

In addition to those at the LaFargue Clinic, Wertham's research took in the children who attended his group-therapy sessions at the informal 'Hookey Club', the 'overt homosexuals' of the Quaker Readjustment Center and the young patients at Queens Hospital. With his assistant Hilde Mosse, Wertham 'examined hundreds of cases of juvenile mental illness'.

> Wertham concluded that the evidence pointed to cultural factors. This was demonstrated by strange patterns of children's play into which had crept characters and incidents that could only derive from comic books. Furthermore, children often confirmed this observation by identifying comics as inspiring their beliefs and behaviour.[33]

I am not interested in defending Wertham's methods of analysis, which

---

[30] Gilbert, *Cycle of Outrage*, op. cit., pp. 94–95.
[31] Ibid., pp. 101–102.
[32] Ibid., p. 101.
[33] Ibid., p. 96.

as many others have pointed out[34] were highly personal and impressionistic rather than controlled studies. While his textual analysis and interviews are suggestive, and in fact constitute one of the few attempts to subject the comic form and its readers to serious analysis, both are also undeniably selective and invariably unsourced.

Rather, I want simply to indicate that Fredric Wertham can not be explained away as a narrow-minded fool whose work was informed by prejudice against those who did not conform. Wertham did not conform when he agitated for a Harlem clinic at a time when several childcare agencies refused to accept black children.[35] He did not conform when he testified in favour of more liberal censorship laws in the 1920s,[36] nor when he defended the nudist magazine *Sunshine and Health* in a Post Office obscenity trial of the 1940s.[37] He argued at length against the barrage of advertisements which encouraged vulnerable young people to conform by playing on their fears about weight, skin, health and confidence, with particular sensitivity to stereotypes of women and their effects on teenage girls: it is there over fifteen pages in *Seduction of the Innocent*, for those critics who trouble to read that far.[38] 'Where in any other childhood literature except children's comics,' he asks, 'do you find a woman called (and treated as) a ''fat slut''?'[39]

The great irony is that Wertham, with his 'decidedly liberal politics and associations',[40] was on the whole more progressive than the audiences of the 1950s would have been comfortable with. He achieved his success with *Seduction of the Innocent* by playing down his views on racism and highlighting instead the aspects of his personal agenda which were more to the public's taste.

By emphasizing one element of popular culture, he provided an

---

[34] See for instance Martin Barker, op.cit.; Savage, Nyberg and Gilbert also offer convincing critiques.

[35] Gilbert, op. cit., p. 95.

[36] In the federal trial over the supposed obscenity of *Daphnis and Chloe*; ibid., p. 94.

[37] Ibid., p. 98.

[38] Wertham, op. cit., pp. 196–211.

[39] Ibid., p. 234.

[40] Gilbert, op. cit., p. 108.

explanation for the rise of juvenile delinquency that appealed immediately and concretely to a very large audience of worried adults. . . . Many would have sharply rejected Wertham's belief in racial equality and his affirmation of the rights of adults to read pornographic literature.[41]

Most of us would, if fully apprised of Wertham's views, fall pretty much into accord with his attitudes towards racism and towards the depiction of nudity in adult magazines. We would probably agree with him that it is wrong to exploit teenage insecurities in order to sell bogus 'health' products in the back pages of comic books. That his comments on homosexuality seem misguided or, to some, homophobic, can be very simply explained by the fact that liberal Anglo-American attitudes towards homosexuality have altered quite significantly since 1954. I have little doubt, bearing in mind his political leanings during the 1950s, that were he alive today Wertham would have fundamentally reconsidered the views on homosexuality he expresses in *Seduction of the Innocent*.

In fact, though, Wertham is not saying anything very different about the young men who he feels would be troubled by gay fantasies than he is about the young women plagued by anxieties about their body image. Both, he suggests, could find their worries heightened by the content of some comic books. Here is a typical passage on young girls' susceptibility to unrealistic ideals of women.

> Even girls without neurotic trends are apt to be sensitive about their breasts before and during adolescence. Some girls mature earlier than their classmates and go through agonies because they fear they are conspicuous . . . usually it is difficult for a woman, and much more so for an adolescent girl, to tell even a doctor about such secret preoccupations. [. . .] The ultra-bosomy girls depicted as ideal in comic-book stories and the countless breast and figure advertisements make young girls genuinely worried long before the time of puberty.[42]

---

[41] Ibid.
[42] Wertham, op. cit., pp. 199, 201.

And here is that passage on gay fantasies again.

> Many adolescents go through periods of vague fears that they might be homosexual. Such fears may become a source of great mental anguish and these boys usually have no one in whom they feel they can confide ... during and after comic-book reading they indulged in fantasies which became severely repressed. [...] The Batman type of story may stimulate children to homosexual fantasies, of the nature of which they may be unconscious. In adolescents who realize it they may be given added stimulation and reinforcement.[43]

'May be', 'may become', 'may stimulate'; in fact the passage on latent homosexuality is far more tentative than the other. In both cases, however, the stimulus is not assumed to lead to an automatic response. In a crucial paragraph which has been overlooked by those critics seeking a neat depiction of Wertham as outdated and simple-minded, he states that 'comic books, like other books, can be read at different levels, with different people getting out of them different things. That does not depend only on differences in age; it is affected also by more subtle factors of constitution, experience, inclination and unconscious susceptibilities.'[44] The hint of Freudianism might strike a dubious note, but on the whole this does not seem so far from Stanley Fish's concept, discussed in my Introduction, of 'interpretive communities' which govern multiple possible readings.[45]

What we have here, then, are two passages, both of which express a concern that young and emotionally vulnerable readers may draw from comic book images a reading which in some way builds on their teenage anxieties, and that they may have nobody to turn to about those worries. The first does not seem absurd or reprehensible. Why then should the second? Only if we attempt to judge it from our own

---

[43] Ibid., pp. 189, 191.
[44] Ibid., p. 188.
[45] Stanley Fish, *Is There A Text In This Class?* Cambridge, MA: Harvard University Press (1980).

cultural position, rather than try to relocate it in the context in which it was written.

3. The Great Taboo

Seduction of the Innocent was a canny piece of work, written for a specific cultural moment and audience in a populist, accessible style. Wertham had honed this almost chatty manner in a series of articles on the subject, beginning with 'The Comics . . . Very Funny!' in the *Saturday Review* and *Reader's Digest* of May 1948, and concluding with what was essentially a summary of *Seduction of the Innocent* in *The Ladies' Home Journal* of November 1953.[46] The book was, in a sense, Wertham's Trojan Horse: a vehicle for expressing his intense mistrust of comic books which played down the less fashionable elements of his argument and pushed to the front those aspects which tallied with contemporary fears. As such, *Seduction of the Innocent* deliberately tapped into a wider social project of categorisation and containment which sought to identify, isolate and examine potential threats to the social body of America with the aim of either curing them or cutting them out completely.

Alfred C. Kinsey's vast enquiry into sexual behaviour is part of this culture of classification, even if its attitude towards homosexuality was more liberal than many of the psychological studies of the gay 'problem' which followed it.[47] The McCarthyite hunt for Communists shares the same project of obsessive identification and categorisation. In turn, the investigations into the 'juvenile delinquent' within which Wertham deliberately located his campaign against comics echo this need to pigeonhole and isolate problematic members of society. While homosexuality, communism and delinquency may seem to present very different social 'problems', the discourses surrounding them in the early 1950s were remarkably similar, and were frequently conflated.

---

[46] See Gilbert, op. cit., pp. 98–103.

[47] See Alfred C. Kinsey *et al.*, *Sexual Behavior in the Human Male*, Philadelphia: W.B. Saunders Company (1948).

James Gilbert argues that popular fears in the 1950s were centred around a

> predominant metaphor . . . of contagion, contamination, and infection. In some sense, these were the interchangeable parts of a larger political and social dialogue during the 1950s. An invasion from the outside, from beyond the family, the community, the group, or the nation threatened treasured institutions.[48]

As illustration, Gilbert quotes Senator Hendrickson, addressing the June Conference on delinquency in the year *Seduction of the Innocent* was published:

> Not even the Communist conspiracy could devise a more effective way to demoralize, disrupt, confuse and destroy our future citizens than apathy on the part of adult Americans to the scourge known as Juvenile Delinquency.[49]

We need only to compare the articles on comic books from 1952 to 1955 with those on 'Sex Perversion' – as the *Reader's Guide* for those years terms homosexuality – to see that parallel discourses were in operation. Between 1953 and 1954, *Newsweek* spoke of a 'Delicate Problem', *Time* of a 'Hidden Problem' and 'Unspeakable Crime'.[50] During the same period, *Changing Times* warned against 'Dirt and Trash', the *English Journal* discussed a 'challenge' to society and *Time* was alarmed at 'Horror on the Newstands'.[51] The former refer to homosexuality, the latter to comics, but the same images of threat and illicit deviance resound through both. Homosexuality is a 'problem', comics are a 'challenge'. Homosexuality is a 'crime',

---

[48] Gilbert, op. cit., p. 75.
[49] Ibid., p. 75.
[50] 'Delicate Problem', *Newsweek* no. 43 (1954); 'Hidden Problem', *Time* no. 62 (December 1953); 'Unspeakable Crime', *Time* no. 61 (November 1953).
[51] 'Dirt and Trash that Kids are Reading', *Changing Times* no. 8 (November 1954); 'Comic Books, a Challenge', *English Journal* no. 41 (December 1952); 'Horror on the Newstands', *Time* no. 64 (September 1954).

comics are a 'horror'. Wertham's own article in the *Ladies Home Journal* about 'What Parents Don't Know' only compounds the parallels; the phrase could quite easily refer to a son or daughter being gay, rather than to the danger of comic books.[52]

The echoes between these discourses on comics and deviancy respectively can be traced back well into the 1940s. In February 1946, for example, the State Education department surveyed the 'effects' of comic books on children, concluding that many parents would be 'shocked and horrified' if they knew the books' content.[53] A 'youth forum' on WQXR radio in 1945 asked boys and girls what they thought of comic books, to which one boy responded that 'bad books' were 'immoral', and that 'many of them give a distorted picture of things'.[54] A priest who claimed to have surveyed ten thousand young people on the subject warned of the 'perils' comics posed to children.[55]

In March 1948 a symposium at the New York Academy of Medicine, entitled 'The Psychopathology of Comic Books', condemned comics for 'stirring primitive impulses that retarded the development of socially desirable behavior and attitudes';[56] towards the end of the decade the National Congress of Parents and Teachers were supporting 'decency crusades' against comics, while the editor of the National Education Association Journal described the comic industry as threatening 'indecency . . . the perversion of the child mind'.[57]

'Immoral', 'indecency', 'distorted', 'primitive', 'retarded', 'shocked and horrified', 'influence on youth', 'perversion': all these key words and phrases could equally be found in discussion of homosexuality during the 1940s and early 1950s, the period of Wertham's primary campaign. Most studies of the period, including those of the American Medical Association, regarded homosexuality as a disorder suitable for psychiatric treatment, although others advocated

---

[52] Wertham, 'What Parents Don't Know About Comic Books', *Ladies Home Journal* no. 70 (November 1953).
[53] *New York Times* (14 February 1946).
[54] *New York Times* (16 December 1945).
[55] *New York Times* (24 August 1946).
[56] Nyberg, op. cit., p. 32.
[57] Ibid., p. 37.

shock therapy and hormone replacement to redress a genetic 'vulnerability'.[58] Brown and Kempton's *Sex Questions and Answers* of 1950 provides the characteristic overview that 'in dealing with this problem . . . a complete "cure" is still very rare',[59] while even more liberal studies proposed that homosexuality may be 'better than isolation . . . or it may be an added destructive touch in a deteriorating personality'.[60]

By drawing concerns about the 'deviant' and the 'delinquent' social type so explicitly together, then, Wertham was deliberately exploiting a link which was already implicit within the overarching discourse of social 'problems' and their 'treatment'.[61] That apparently separate moral concerns could very easily be called to serve under a wider banner is indicated by the quotation from Hendrickson above and had in any case already been demonstrated four years previous to the publication of *Seduction of the Innocent*, when Senator Joe McCarthy pledged to purge the Government of not just Communists, but 'queers',[62] and proceeded, to much public acclaim, to weed out both suspected Reds and supposed homosexuals in the State Department for interrogation.

The harassment and persecution of suspected homosexuals under McCarthy's crusade – and the extent, as a partial consequence, of institutionalised homophobia throughout the 1950s – is often overlooked, and yet it closely parallels the more notorious anti-Communist witch-hunts and legislation. Ninety-one employees were dismissed on the grounds of alleged 'sex perversion' in 1950 alone, not one of them daring to appeal. Within the military, the penalty for 'homosexual acts and tendencies' was a dishonourable, 'blue' discharge which stigmatised the bearer for life and barred him from all benefits

---

[58] Quoted in Judd Marmor (ed.), *Sexual Inversion*, New York: Basic Books (1965), p. 6.

[59] Quoted in Donald W. Cory, *The Homosexual in America*, New York: Paperback Library Inc (1951), p. 186.

[60] Dr Clara Thompson, quoted in Cory, ibid., p. 191.

[61] See also Michel Foucault, *Discipline and Punish*, London: Allen Lane (1977).

[62] Robert Griffiths, *The Politics of Fear: Joseph R. McCarthy and the Senate*, Lexington: University Press of Kentucky (1970), p. 89.

promised in the GI Bill of Rights.[63] In the workplace, almost all employment agencies refused to take on 'effeminate' men, and stamped 'a number or a letter on their applications that means "gay", and virtually unplaceable'.[64]

Sexual contact between men, classed as sodomy or simply 'crimes against nature', was illegal in the forty-eight states and ranked alongside carnal knowledge of animals or even birds.[65] Homosexuality itself was technically a sex crime in many areas, punishable by indeterminate and involuntary hospitalisation in a mental institution; as Thomas Szasz notes in Marmor's *Sexual Inversion*, the fact that gay men were rarely incarcerated solely because of their sexual conduct 'does not alter the intent of the legislation or its potential threat'.[66] The US Government's policy of the time, meanwhile, was clearly outlined in a document entitled 'Homosexuals and other Sex Perverts'. The first pages bluntly explain that 'homosexuals are perverts'.

In the opinion of this subcommittee homosexuals and other sex perverts are not proper persons to be employed in Government for two reasons; first, they are unsuitable, and second, they constitute security risks. [...] It is generally believed that those who engage in overt acts of perversion lack the emotional stability of normal persons. In addition there is an abundance of evidence to sustain the conclusion that indulgence in acts of sex perversion weakens the moral fiber of an individual to a degree that he is not suitable for a position of responsibility ... our investigation has shown that the presence of a sex pervert in a Government agency tends to have a corrosive effect on his fellow employees. These perverts will frequently attempt to entice normal individuals to engage in perverted practices.

---

[63] Cory, op. cit., p. 44.

[64] Howard Brown, *Familiar Faces, Hidden Lives: The Story of Homosexual Men in America Today*, New York: Harvest (1977), p. 163.

[65] This wording was used in the statutes of Minnesota, North Dakota, Pennsylvania and Washington in 1951; see Cory, op. cit., Appendix B, pp. 281–291.

[66] Thomas Szasz, 'Legal and Moral Aspects of Homosexuality', in Marmor, op.cit.

The passage concludes that 'one homosexual can pollute a Government office'.[67]

Reconsider the earlier passage from Wertham in the light of this evidence from the same period. Medhurst remarks, having accused Wertham of crying 'queer', that 'such language is not present on the page, of course'.[68] The fact is that we can make no such assumption about texts from the 1950s. Just as government and military literature of the 1940s used 'Jap' without apology, so we have seen that Senator McCarthy had no qualms about using the word 'queers' in a Congressional address to Harry S. Truman in February 1950; indeed, Robert Griffith reports in *The Politics of Fear* that this language 'seemed to have touched a popular nerve'.[69] According to one account of the time, newspapers in certain states '[did] not hesitate to denounce "queers" and "fags" on the editorial page'.[70]

By choosing not to consider its historical context, Medhurst also neglects to recognise Wertham's suggestion that homosexuality in boys could stem from a 'disdain for girls'[71] – a theory which Medhurst derides as 'breathtaking' in its audacity[72] – as a product of its time, and a mild echo of the official government line that the 'active male homosexual often has a dislike for women'.[73] The difference is that Wertham refrains from using the terms 'sex pervert' and 'crimes against nature', favouring far less judgemental language such as 'erotic relationship', 'love-relationship', 'homoerotic sexual curiosity' and 'wish dream'.[74] Once again, I am not seeking to justify Wertham's theories of homosexual development, which remain unquestionably outdated and hopelessly limited in their explanatory power. I merely want to point out that, compared to the viciously homophobic literature which surrounded it, *Seduction of the Innocent* attempts naïvely to understand more than it encourages disgust and contempt.

---

[67] Cory, op. cit., Appendix A, pp. 270–273.
[68] Medhurst, op. cit., p. 150.
[69] Griffith, op. cit., p. 89, p. 103.
[70] Brown, op. cit., p. 30.
[71] Wertham, op. cit., p. 188.
[72] Medhurst, op. cit., p. 151.
[73] Cory, op. cit., Appendix A, p. 272.
[74] Wertham, op. cit., pp. 188–190.

Secondly, consider the effects of this discourse of hatred on the young boys for whom Wertham expresses concern: boys who were going through 'periods of vague fears that they might be homosexual'. Given the above evidence, it hardly seems ludicrous that, in Wertham's phrase, 'such fears may become a source of great mental anguish ... these boys usually have no one in whom they can confide'.[75] In fact, we do not have to imagine the emotional trauma suffered by young men questioning their sexuality in the 1950s, for it is vividly described in a number of personal testimonies from the period.

The histories these men relate about discovering their sexuality in the 1940s and 1950s are characterised by double-lives, secret relationships, platonic infatuations, unspoken love and frequent self-doubt. To take just one example from *Growing Up Before Stonewall: Life Stories of Some Gay Men*, Ed, who was nineteen when *Seduction of the Innocent* was first published, talks of his 'very mixed feelings about physical pleasure coupled with psychological anxieties ... I was annoyed and confused ... it was difficult thinking that I might be a true homosexual. I probably tried to rationalise it away, or was just very confused about it.'[76] Another man, who was aged eleven and at boarding school in the 1950s when his 'crush' on an older boy was discovered, recalls that 'I felt dirty, evil, lost, and for months I spent my time wandering the woods alone.'[77]

Yet another, growing up in the same decade, 'had had homosexual experiences in his adolescence, but ... they had left him feeling so guilty that he had stopped ... "Many mornings I would go to church and pray for help. Eventually I gave that up, and then I gave up believing in God altogether. If there were a God, why wouldn't he help me? My problem was so real and so great."'[78] Christopher, who was nineteen in 1952, did find someone to confide in, but to little avail. His minister assured him that he 'couldn't possibly be queer'. At

---

[75] Ibid., p. 189.

[76] Peter M. Nardi, David Sanders and Judd Marmor (eds), *Growing Up Before Stonewall: Life Stories of Some Gay Men*, London: Routledge (1994), p. 116.

[77] D.J. West, *Homosexuality Re-examined*, London: Duckworth (1977), pp. 18–19.

[78] Brown, op. cit., p. 111.

the age of twenty-one, however, 'Christopher was still worried about his gay fantasies and yearnings.'[79]

These are not the scaremongering reports of a moralistic psychiatrist, as Medhurst tries to depict Wertham ('Wertham quotes this to shock us'[80]), but the evidence given by a gay doctor, Howard Brown, to indicate the difficulties and trauma suffered by those who realised their homosexuality during the 1950s. Remember also that Wertham's theories about the potentially worrying effects of gay fantasies were not his own invention but were inspired by talking to gay men, no matter that they were in therapy with New York's Quaker community at the time;[81] and bear in mind that his attitude towards them was not condemnatory. Wertham does not describe his informant as a sex pervert, but as an 'intelligent, educated young homosexual'; and it was this man, not Wertham, who suggested that gay fantasies would not 'do any harm sexually. But they probably would ruin . . . morals.'[82] The sad truth is Wertham had no need to impose his own concerns on the gay men he met; they had internalised society's judgements to the extent that they themselves viewed homosexuality as at best a guilty secret, at worst a terrible sin.

In another of the testimonies gathered by Brown we hear that Victor, who had a gay relationship in the 1940s when he was sixteen years old, 'did not consider himself homosexual . . . raised to regard homosexuals as monsters, he could not help loathing himself. For five years he considered suicide.'[83] Brown confirms that 'years-long contemplation of suicide is typical of many homosexuals who discovered their sexual identity in the forties and fifties. I know that during my college years, whenever I heard that someone had committed suicide, my first thought was: I wonder if he was homosexual.'[84] Again, in this light Wertham's concern for the 'great

---

[79] Ibid., p. 122.

[80] Medhurst, op. cit., p. 152.

[81] For a brief account of this Quaker rehabilitation centre see Cory, op. cit., p. 56.

[82] Wertham, op. cit., p. 192.

[83] Brown, op. cit., p. 40.

[84] Ibid., p. 41.

mental anguish' of the boys he interviewed does not seem quite so ridiculous or as narrow-minded.

'Where then,' asks Brown, 'can the young homosexual turn for a model of what he might become?'[85] Perhaps to books, or to comics. Wertham's reports from youths whose sexuality was 'awakened' or reinforced through comic-reading finds parallels in other personal narratives of the period. Howard Brown's own 'discovery' of his gayness came in 1946 through his reading, with a roommate, of Gore Vidal's *The City and the Pillar*.

> The characters in it were the first homosexuals I could identify with. Indeed, this novel was the first written evidence I had come across that there were other homosexuals like me. Very tentatively Frank and I discussed the book in relation to ourselves. We both confessed that there were times when we suspected we might be homosexual . . . he suggested that if we studied very hard and never mentioned the subject, it might just go away.[86]

Roger, another correspondent of Brown's, recalls that 'I was five or six. I was lying on the living room floor, on my stomach, looking at a *Tarzan and the Apes* comic book and imagining how it would feel to be overpowered and held in Tarzan's arms.'[87] Compare with the passage from Wertham:

> One young homosexual during psychotherapy brought us a copy of *Detective Comics*, with a Batman story. He pointed out a picture of 'The Home of Bruce and Dick', a house beautifully landscaped, warmly lighted and showing the devoted pair side by side, looking out of a picture window. When he was eight this boy had realized from fantasies about comic book pictures that he was aroused by men. At the age of ten or eleven, 'I found my liking, my sexual desires, in comic books. I think I

---

[85] Ibid., p. 42.
[86] Ibid., p. 36.
[87] Ibid., p. 100.

put myself in the position of Robin. I did want to have relations with Batman ... you can almost connect yourself with the people.'[88]

We are back to the kind of passage for which Wertham is roundly condemned from either side. The critics who so desperately want to rid Batman of any homoerotic associations would squirm at this paragraph much as they do at the 'dressing-gowns' passage, claim once again that Wertham 'deliberately, or otherwise, missed the point, that in truth Bruce Wayne and Dick Grayson's relationship was no more than that of father and son', [89] and bellow 'NO HE'S NOT GAY!' To them we must once more stress the point that these were not Wertham's interpretations, dreamed up in isolation; they were the readings of comic book fans. Medhurst recognises this distinction and expresses his 'admiration' for the boy while retaining his contempt for the mediator, Fredric Wertham.

> What this anonymous gay man did was to practice [a] form of bricolage ... denied even the remotest possibility of supportive images of homosexuality within the dominant heterosexual culture, gay people have had to fashion what we could out of the imageries of dominance, to snatch illicit meanings from the fabric of marginalized desires ... Wertham's patient evokes in me an admiration, that in a period of American history even more homophobic than most, there he was, raiding the citadels of masculinity, weaving fantasies of oppositional desire.[90]

What Medhurst means to celebrate here is the concept of 'reading against the grain'. However, he has already made it clear that only certain readers are entitled to practise this approach. For Wertham's patient to pick up signs of gayness from a Batman comic is 'rather moving';[91] for Wertham to perform the same reading himself earns

---

[88] Wertham, op. cit., p. 192.
[89] Sassienie, op. cit., p. 58.
[90] Medhurst, op. cit., p. 153.
[91] Ibid., p. 152.

him the monicker 'Doctor Doom' and relentless mockery: 'So, Wertham's assumptions of homosexuality are fabricated out of his interpretation of certain visual signs. To avoid being thought queer by Wertham, Bruce and Dick should have done the following ... '[92]

'There is a difference', Medhurst avows, 'between sporting the secret symbols of a subculture if you form part of that subculture and the elephantine spot-the-homo routine that Wertham performs.'[93] Never mind that Wertham never refers to 'homos', that he describes two men as a 'devoted pair', that he passes no judgement on the boy's romantic fantasy: it seems that only gay critics are allowed to discuss gay readings. Here I have to disagree, and would suggest that adequate research can enable any critic to recover the possible frameworks through which a text was read during a historical moment. Andy Medhurst, after all, was no more a gay man in the 1950s than I was.[94]

Yet if Medhurst seems a little sulkily to keep the ball to himself, he does accept the possibilities of play. The critics who attempt to 'prove' that Batman is heterosexual are doing the character a disservice by denying his availability to multiple readings; their denials seek to make Batman a far more boring cultural icon than he really is.

There can be no 'proof' that Batman is gay or straight, of course. What I intend to do now is merely indicate the importance of subtle dress, linguistic and colour codes to gay identity in the 1950s, and with these in mind suggest the hooks in the Batman texts of the period upon which a gay reading could have been hung. My aim is not to argue that this is the 'correct' or only reading of these comics, but to give these readings some context and substance. We know, from Wertham, that such readings were in existence. We do not know – because of the brevity of his transcribed interviews and the vagueness of his textual references – exactly how these readings might have come about, and which elements of the comic books inspired them. To take this investigation further we shall have to do what so few of Wertham's detractors have attempted, and read some old Batman comics.

---

[92] Ibid., p. 151.
[93] Ibid.
[94] He was thirty years old at the end of the 1980s: ibid., p. 150.

4. Being Seen with a Hairdresser

The homophobic culture of the 1950s offered gay and straight people alike a number of keys for spotting homosexuality through visual cues. The US Government document which advised that the 'passive male homosexual' exhibited 'a dislike for women' also described him as effeminate 'in his manner and appearance'.[95] Psychiatrists compounded this received notion by explaining to young men that 'Homosexuals didn't become doctors; they became hairdressers, interior designers, that sort of thing'.[96] The minister to whom Christopher, in the testimony cited above, turned for help followed the same guidelines: 'I was tall and strong and a good athlete . . . and I came from a good family, so I couldn't possibly be queer.'[97]

Many gay men who grew up in the 1940s and 1950s internalised these crude stereotypes to the extent that they were unable to identify themselves as homosexual, or alternatively retained their cover by explicitly avoiding such codes. The president of the Gay Activists Alliance in the 1960s, Bruce Voeller, spent years in a heterosexual marriage before admitting his true sexual preferences even to himself. 'The main reason it had taken him so long to realize his sexual identity, Voeller explained, was that he could not identify with the sterotypical image of the homosexual man ("homosexuals had to be effeminate").'[98] Similarly Larry, who dated girls through his teens while having sexual relations with other boys, 'did not consider himself homosexual . . . "queers were supposed to dress up in dresses and wear makeup and that kind of thing, and we weren't like that"'.[99] Nevertheless, Larry continued to spend the night with pickups from gay bars in Manhattan.

> One night, taking the subway back to the Bronx, Larry suddenly realized that 'if that kid was a homosexual, so was I.

---

[95] Cory, op. cit., appendices.
[96] Brown, op.cit., p35.
[97] Ibid., p. 122.
[98] Ibid., p. 26.
[99] Ibid., p. 44.

But that was terrible. I mean, that meant I was a fairy, a queer, and some of my pals back in the Bronx once beat up a fag, a guy with bleached hair and a fruity walk. That was me?' He simply could not figure out how he fit into the picture. Or what the picture was. As a boy, he had learned to spot and sneer at one set of characteristics – the effeminate set.[100]

As Howard Brown remembers, 'being seen with a hairdresser'[101] or discussing 'such otherwise taboo topics as cooking'[102] were enough to make a man appear suspect. Brown confesses 'I was afraid of revealing my homosexuality by showing the slightest interest in color schemes and the like.'[103]

It does not seem facetious to observe that 1957 saw a story called 'The Rainbow Batman' in which Bruce Wayne proudly displays an entire wardrobe of costumes in pumpkin-orange, lime and canary-yellow, as well as the usual dull grey and blue. 'I must, Robin – I must wear a different-colored Batman costume each night!' he proclaims, fastening his cloak. Although Robin describes this as the red outfit, the cape and trunks Batman has chosen are clearly magenta, and the bodysuit a pale pink.[104] To the boy wondering about 'Batman and Robin living together and possibly having sex relations',[105] this colour cue could well have confirmed his pleasurable fantasy that the two were lovers.[106]

If this only indicates a homophobic stereotype which was internalised by gay men, the gay culture of the 1950s – bars, clubs and in particular the cautious to-and-fro of late-night street conversations – was also built around codes and subtle cues. Donald

---

[100] Ibid., pp. 44–45.
[101] Ibid., p. 51.
[102] Ibid., p. 10.
[103] Ibid., p. 148.
[104] Sheldon Moldoff, 'The Rainbow Batman!' *Detective Comics* #241, New York: DC Comics (March 1957).
[105] Wertham, op. cit., p. 192.
[106] I have been informed by other fans that the 'real' reason for these coloured costumes was to distract the public's attention from the fact that both Dick Grayson and Robin had a broken arm.

Cory vividly describes the 'circumlocutious pathway' followed by men cruising a gay street in the 1950s:

> Some stand idly at a store front, pretending to windowshop, often with hands in pockets. Others walk slowly, turning, looking, staring, walking by, then turning again.
> 'Say, fellow, do you have the time?'
> 'It must be about eleven ...' [...]
> The weather may be the next resort in the search to keep alive the ebbing conversation.
> 'A little chilly tonight, isn't it?'
> 'Not too bad. I've been rather hot myself.'
> A ripple of forced laughter, not in appreciation of humor, but part of the effort to establish a common bond through the double entendre and the laughter of recognition that follows. The two have broken through the façade of pretense and have made their first attempts toward penetrating each other's secret.
> 'Live near here?'
> 'I'm from out of town ... stopping at a place near here ... just down the street and around the corner.'
> 'I wouldn't know. I don't get around to those spots very much.'
> 'You should. It's quite a gay place.'
> *The word* has been uttered, and the rapport has now been established.[107]

Moreover, the strategy of reading novels and movies for a gay 'subtext', whether intended by the producers or not, was apparently well-established by the mid-1950s. Donald Cory, writing in 1951, provides a 26-page list of novels and dramas dealing with homosexuality, some of which are 'about' homosexuality in a more disguised form than others. Kipling's *Stalky & Co*, for instance, like Lawrence's *Women In Love* and Henry James' *The Pupil*, is included

---

[107] Cory, op. cit., pp. 117–119.

because it has been subject to 'homosexual interpretation'[108] for its treatment of close male friendships, and the inclusion of *Moby-Dick* confirms that Cory's reading of these novels as 'gay' is based on a piecing together of textual clues rather than on their explicit depiction of homosexual relationships.

Richard Dyer has famously described this process, after Lévi-Strauss, as 'bricolage'. Significantly, Dyer's account suggests that 'queer readings' of a text were a direct result of the isolation and despair – the 'great mental anguish', perhaps – which many gay men experienced from internalising the stereotypes of a particularly homophobic culture.

> This isolation (and the feelings of self-hate that much of the imagery we learnt in the cinema instilled in us) perhaps also made the need for escape more keen for us than for some other social groups – so, once again, we went to the pictures. Once there, however, we could use the films – especially those *not* directly offering us images of ourselves – as we chose. We could practice on movie images what Claude Lévi-Strauss has termed *bricolage*, that is, playing around with the elements available to us in such a way as to bend their meanings to our own purposes. We could pilfer from straight society's images on the screen such that would help us build up a subculture, or . . . a 'gay sensibility'.[109]

Which is, as Medhurst points out, exactly what Wertham's patients seem to have done with Batman. Indeed, a precedent for a gay reading of what, in the 'official' version, is a 'buddy' relationship – 'no more than that of father and son'[110] – had already been established with reference to a similar mode of homosocial behaviour in Hollywood cinema. Vito Russo reads 'a sweet and very real loving dimension' into a Laurel and Hardy film of 1932, and proceeds to firmly identify 'gay overtones' in the buddy relationships of *Pinocchio* (1940), *Gilda* (1946),

---

[108] Cory, op. cit., Appendix D, pp. 304–305.
[109] Richard Dyer, *Gays & Film*, New York: New York Zoetrope (1984), pp. 1–2.
[110] Sassienie, op. cit., p. 58.

Red River (1948), *Cinderella* (1950), *The Big Sky* (1952) and *Gentlemen Prefer Blondes* (1953).[111] We might question whether these readings were widely recognised at the time – the moment in *Cinderella* is extremely brief, for instance – yet we can be fairly sure that Russo was not the only gay man to draw homoerotic interpretations from the Hollywood cinema of the 1940s and early 1950s.

Russo's discussion of 'code words' for homosexuality indicates that the strategy of reading popular texts as 'gay' was based, like the same process in everyday life, on a set of linguistic and visual cues. *Bringing Up Baby* (1938) contains a rare instance of '*the word*' itself escaping the Motion Picture Production Code – when Cary Grant, discovered in a fluffy nightgown, exclaims 'I've just gone *gay* all of a sudden', the gag depends on audiences understanding the term as 'homosexual' rather than 'happy'.[112] Other cues were more subtle, but just as easily understood. The word 'pansy' was forbidden by the code in 1933, so the flower itself was used as a prop for jokes about 'sissy' gay men.[113] Similarly, use of the word 'lavender', or the colour itself, immediately identified a character as gay.[114]

Batman and Robin's adventures do not, to my knowledge, feature pansies or lavender – although I have mentioned Batman's pink outfit, and there is a moment in a 1951 *Detective* where a passerby remarks of the hero 'Dear – Dear! A masked man – and such a queer costume!'[115] However, it is interesting to note that Batman's 'real' name, Bruce, had strong associations with gayness which date back to the 1940s and have apparently survived several decades. Russo cites *Seven Sinners* of 1940, in which a man is beaten up because his address book lists a telephone number for 'Bruce in Bombay', and *No Small Affair* (1985) where a shy boy is taunted by his classmates: 'I've got this friend. His name is Bruce. He wants to take you to the dance on Saturday night. You can flip to see who wears the dress.'[116] In turn, E. Nelson

---

[111] Vito Russo, *The Celluloid Closet*, New York: Harper & Row (1981), pp. 63–79.
[112] Ibid., p. 47.
[113] Ibid., p. 40.
[114] Ibid., p. 38.
[115] *Detective Comics* #54, New York: DC Comics (August 1951).
[116] Russo, op. cit., pp. 45, 257.

Bridwell, the commentator who huffed at that 'certain psychiatrist' above, lamented in 1971 that 'today, when a comedian calls someone Bruce, you can almost bet he means the guy is a swishy character'.[117] It was for this reason that Bruce Banner, aka The Hulk, was renamed David in the 1977 TV series; Bruce just wasn't a hulky enough name.[118] While it is possible that 'Bruce' had gathered further camp associations from its links with Batman in the 1950s and through the 1960s TV show, the name clearly already carried overtones of homosexuality by the 1950s; and this itself may have been enough to clue in those boys who lingered over 'The House of Bruce and Dick' in their monthly comic book.

Within the context of a 1950s America where covert homosexuality was identified by gays and straights alike – in everyday life and popular culture – through a variety of codes, Wertham's recognition of a 'love-relationship' and 'subtle atmosphere of homoeroticism' through certain visual signifiers does not, to my mind, seem at all absurd. If it is contested that his was a homophobic agenda, his interpretation remains exactly the same as that of the young gay men he quotes. At the very least it must be pointed out that Wertham took the trouble to examine the Batman comics of the 1950s himself and attempted to perform, however clumsily, the same kind of textual reading he believed his patients had opened up. Few of his critics have ever matched this diligence in research.

Admittedly, Batman comics of the early 1950s are rather harder to come by now than they were forty years ago, but they can be found, and they make suggestive reading. In one story after another, Batman and Robin exhibit a love and trust for each other which often extends beyond the generic conventions of the adventure or science fiction narrative, providing ample material to support the relationship described by Wertham and the boys whose testimonies informed his reading. It could be argued, of course, that part of Robin's narrative function – as well as serving as a Watson to Batman's Holmes, and

---

[117] Bridwell, op. cit., p. 12.

[118] Sassienie, op. cit., p. 190. 'During the airing of the TV show, where Bruce (Batman) Wayne was considered by some to be gay, the name Bruce began to be used in a derogatory way to describe gay, or camp, men.'

providing a point of identification for young readers – is to be kidnapped and rescued. The same pattern could regularly be seen in the adventures of Superman and Jimmy Olsen, or Green Arrow and Speedy – or, in the 1940s titles, of Captain America and Bucky, The Human Torch and Toro, Slam Bradley and Shorty Morgan. The difference is, though, that the *Batman* comics extend this hero/sidekick relationship into the domestic sphere. To the best of my knowledge, even Green Arrow and Speedy, who were virtually clone copies of Batman and Robin in these years, were depicted almost exclusively in 'work' situations – preparing their weapons, fighting criminals and discussing their next move – but not in the bedroom, living room or kitchen, and not enjoying each other's company for its own sake. This relationship was clearly a professional one, unencumbered by emotional considerations, and far less complex – far less interesting – than that of Batman and Robin. This 'working relationship' was, from my reading, repeated across the board of the hero/sidekick stories.

Bruce and Dick, however, went out together during the day to combat villains, then came home for a cosy supper and glass of milk before retiring to bed and rising for the newspapers over breakfast. In diegetic terms, they hung out together far beyond the call of duty; there was what we might call an excess of homosociality, at least, to the adventures of Batman and Robin.

Take, as just one instance, 'The Man Who Stole The Joker's Jokes', a story from 1951.[119] The narrative opens with Bruce and Dick at home in Wayne Manor, reclining on the sofa. Bruce is indeed wearing a gown as he reads the newspaper and Dick watches the television. The scene speaks of a relaxed, intimate bonding between two men, similar to that described by Wertham: 'I have seen an elaborate, charming breakfast scene . . . between Batman and his boy, complete with checked tablecloth, milk, cereal, fruit juice, dressing-gown and newspaper.'[120] Admittedly, Wertham cites this image in contrast to those he would like to see in comics, of 'a normal family

---

[119] Various, 'The Man Who Stole The Joker's Jokes', *Batman*, #67, New York: DC Comics (1951).
[120] Wertham, op. cit., p. 236.

sitting down at a meal';[121] but we can at least be sure that scenes of the kind he describes did exist in the comics themselves, rather than merely in his imagination.

'What do you say we go out and see the fair in person, Dick?' Bruce asks. 'A wonderful idea – let's go', exclaims Dick, and they're off. Five pages on and the demands of the crime genre have kicked in, as the Joker catches Robin in the fairground Tunnel of Love and Batman is seen in close-up, rubbing his chin in concern. 'Robin is gone! This is serious . . . he never disobeys an order! Something must have happened to him!' In the next scene Commissoner Gordon receives a ransom note. He and Batman appear in mid-shot in the police office. 'What are you going to do?' asks Gordon. Batman looks away, fist clenched in a melodramatic pose. 'The only thing I can do – surrender! I'd do anything for that kid!'

This explicit declaration of commitment, even devotion, is compounded by the next two panels which again invoke the conventions of melodrama. Robin is shown in the foreground of his prison, with crooks jeering him as he weeps. The next frame depicts Batman in long shot, pacing the cave with his shadow thrown before him, as the caption describes 'a distraught and lonely figure'.[122]

It hardly takes a reading 'against the grain' to see this as a depiction of tenderness and compassion between two men. Indeed, the storytelling comes intriguingly close to the conventions of the romance comic. Batman and Robin are often framed together in tight close-up, with the emphasis on distraught facial expression and emotion instead of action. Even the perfectly shaped tears on Robin's cheeks call to mind the weeping girls Roy Lichtenstein picked out from the pages of heterosexual romance titles.

This story does not, of course, demonstrate that Batman and Robin have a gay relationship any more than it demonstrates that they live as a surrogate father and son, or are simply platonic colleagues. It does, I think, demonstrate the elements in the stories of the early 1950s upon which a gay teenager could readily have drawn his own reading, and

---

[121] Ibid.

[122] Various, 'The Man Who Stole The Joker's Jokes', *Batman*, #67, New York: DC Comics (1951).

that Wertham's examples, albeit sketchily described, are indeed based on textual evidence rather than his own invention.

5. A Thousand Masks

'Society has handed me a mask to wear,' wrote Don Cory, in *Homosexuality*, 'a ukase that it shall never be lifted except in the presence of those who hide with me behind its protective shadows. Everywhere I go, at all times and before all sections of society, I pretend.'[123]

The motif of double lives, and the constant fear of exposure this entailed, is paramount in the testimonies of gay men who passed as straight during the 1950s, and when we look from these testimonies to the Batman comics of the period it becomes striking how often the theme of hidden identity recurs. On the surface, Batman's secret is his alter ego as Bruce Wayne; but it is not hard to imagine that this repeated motif could have acquired a personal resonance for a young man having to hide his sexuality in the early 1950s. Again, a few examples should furnish the context.

Howard Brown reports, for instance, that in 1956 he turned down a promotion for fear of discovery by his prospective boss: 'the thought of Mr. and Mrs. Jacobsen coming by while I was giving a gay party or merely sitting at home with a lover was chilling. If they, or some other straight couple, did not realize I was gay the first time they popped in, they surely would the second.'[124] The consequences of such a discovery were horrific, with every potential to wreck a man's career, undermine his social reputation and poison his relationship with his friends and family. Brown relates the story of Henry, forced to resign from the Air Force when he was accused of being gay; the fact that his address book contained no women's names was all the 'proof' needed.[125] Henry was subsequently refused membership of the

---

[123] Cory, op. cit., p. 11.
[124] Brown, op.cit., p. 144.
[125] Brown, op. cit., p. 152; compare the 'Bruce in Bombay' scene from *Seven Sinners*, cited above.

American College of Surgeons when his sexuality was rediscovered, on the grounds of 'poor moral character'.[126] We also hear of Lloyd, ordered to resign after a private investigator, hired by his employers, interrogated neighbours until they revealed that he lived with a man;[127] and of Daniel, a gay teenager who was brutally ostracised within his small Midwest town and eventually banished by his parents.[128] Jim, a married man who had repeated affairs with men, admits 'I have a thousand masks ... and my wife is getting inside more of them than anyone else ever did.'[129] Of himself, Brown concludes 'I had lived for a long time with the fear of being "discovered". Every homosexual has lived with this fear.'[130]

We might also remember that the standard superhero device of dual identity – Batman comics, like most examples of the superhero genre, featured not just a hero and sidekick split between Bruce/Batman and Robin/Dick, but a whole cast of alter egos from Selina/Catwoman through Oswald/Penguin to Harvey/Two-Face – would have found an immediate echo in the use of false names by gay men in the 1950s. The Mattachine 'homophile' association of that decade was built around fanciful pseudonyms and passwords.[131] Donald Cory felt the need to publish *The Homosexual In America*, and indeed republish it twenty years later, under a false name for fear of blackmail.[132] On a quotidian level, the memoirs of gay men such as Howard Brown testify that giving false names was standard practice in the bars of the 1950s.[133]

With this in mind, consider *Batman* #182 of April 1951, in which the Puppet Master threatens to reveal Wayne's face beneath the mask – 'Now the climax of the show! The unmasking of Batman!' – and *Detective* #188 of October 1952, in which Batman warns Robin that if

---

[126] Ibid., p. 154.
[127] Ibid., p. 152.
[128] Ibid., p. 90.
[129] Ibid., p. 114.
[130] Ibid., p. 4.
[131] See West, op. cit., pp. 143–144.
[132] Cory, op. cit., p. 10.
[133] 'Every bit as frightened as I was, my partner would frequently refuse to give me his real name': Brown, op. cit., p. 52.

Wayne Manor is destroyed, 'our identities will be revealed'. It seems entirely possible that for a young man like Daniel, such stories might have struck a chord; and the parallels would surely be made explicit by *Detective* #194, April 1953, which opens with a revelation – a document stating plainly that 'Bruce Wayne is the Batman!' – and develops into a tense drama based solely around Batman's desperate attempt to keep his hidden life concealed. At the climax, a criminal in possession of the vital document taunts Batman with the ultimate threat: 'I'll tell the world who you really are!', as Batman gulps 'H-he knows my secret!' The suspense of the moment is stressed in a caption: 'Is this the end of Batman's secret identity? Is his secret about to be revealed to the world?' Reassurance comes only when we learn that the document was written in invisible ink, and the villain holds nothing but a blank sheet of paper.

While the motif of hidden identity and discovery obviously takes on a stylised, adventure-serial form here, it nevertheless seems hardly surprising that the boys interviewed by Wertham, their own lives dominated by the very real fear of discovery and its consequences, should have found some appeal and even solace in Batman's fantasy world of intense paranoia coupled with regular sighs of relief; after all, the hero's identity always remains intact, and his sidekick is always returned to him for an embrace in the final frame. As Wertham describes it,

> They constantly rescue each other from violent attacks by an unending number of enemies. The feeling is conveyed that we men must stick together because there are so many villainous creatures who have to be exterminated. They lurk not only under every bed but also behind every star in the sky. Either Batman or his young boy friend or both are captured, threatened with every imaginable weapon, almost blown to bits, almost crushed to death, almost annihilated. Sometimes Batman ends up in bed injured and young Robin is shown sitting next to him.[134]

---

[134] Wertham, op. cit., p. 190.

A study of the adventures of Batman and Robin throughout the 1950s provides more than ample examples of this rescue motif. In 'The Death-Cheaters of Gotham City' from 1952, Batman fakes his own suicide through poison. The scene recalls *Romeo and Juliet*, adapted for a male couple and given a happy ending:

[Panel 1: Bruce falls to the floor]
Dick: Doctor! Come quickly! Doctor! [thinks] Oh, Bruce! Bruce!
[Panel 2: Dick crouches over Bruce's body]
Doc: It's too late, son – Bruce Wayne is dead!
[Panel 3: Dick begins to despair]
Dick [thinks]: He's dead! He's dead! What if I fail? Why did I let him do it? Oh, Bruce – Bruce!
[Panel 4: Bruce twitches, breathes]
Dick [tears on cheek]: It worked! It worked! Thank heaven – it worked![135]

Detective #186, published in the same month of 1952, echoes the Joker story detailed above as Robin is again captured by crooks. Later, in 'the sumptuous suburban home of Bruce Wayne', we see Bruce in profile, musing 'Wonder why *Robin* isn't back yet?' Called to Gordon's office, Batman is shown the kidnappers' note: 'Batman: if you want to see Robin alive again, come to Regan's Baths at once!'[136] 'Do you want my men to move in on Regan's?' Gordon offers. 'No,' replies Batman firmly, 'I don't want to risk anything happening to the boy!' The crooks offer an ultimatum: 'Just sign this agreement that neither Batman nor Robin will set foot in the city for a week, and your kid assistant goes free! If you don't . . . ' Batman, in close up, thinks grimly 'I can't risk *Robin's* life! I have no choice!' before declaring aloud 'I'll sign!'[137]

Detective #194 repeats the same motif – Robin is kidnapped, and

---

[135] *Batman* #72, New York: DC Comics (August–September 1952).
[136] We might note an additional overtone in the choice of location: bath houses were already a meeting place for gay men in the 1950s.
[137] *Detective Comics* #186, New York: DC Comics (August 1952).

we cut to Batman growling 'They got *Robin*! I'll make them pay for . . . ' The theme is revisited in both *Detective* #199 – 'Don't come near me, *Batman*! If you make a move toward me, I'll put a bullet through *Robin*!' – and #200, the following month – 'I'm leaving Gotham City, and I'm taking your young pal with me! Try to stop me, and HE'LL PAY FOR IT!'

Detective #190, from December 1952, works through an intriguing variation on the scenario. Here, Batman is rendered helpless with amnesia and Robin weepily attempts to coax him back to his previous self. Robin is shown in close-up, tears rolling down his cheeks. 'You're a *detective* – the greatest detective on earth! And your career musn't be ended by this amnesia – I won't let it be ended!'

This reversal fantasy, which transforms Robin into the protector and Batman into the child, wrings every ounce of melodrama from its premise. First, Batman insists on taking a vial of chemical antidote as Robin tries to restrain him physically, pleading 'Batman, it's too risky – your guess could be wrong!' The sidekick-as-hostage device is then reprised and subtly altered, as Robin offers to sacrifice himself to the crooks who threaten that unless he accompanies them as a prisoner, 'Batman will lose his life as well as his memory.'

> Robin: I – I guess I'll have to do it! I'll go along!
> Batman [anguished]: No, *Robin* – NO – !¹³⁸

Of course, crime is punished and love prevails: the last panel is a circular vignette of Batman with his arm around Robin in mid-shot, every inch the happy couple.

Finally, there are the stories from the same period which involve not merely Robin's capture or a helpless Batman, but both at once. *Detective* #202 of December 1953 shows Batman and Robin with their wrists tied behind them, forced to step off a rock into the sea at gunpoint. *Detective* #189 from November 1952 features the heroes bound to each other and about to drown on top of a submarine, and *Detective* #182 has Batman and Robin gassed, then roped together by their wrists and ankles.

---

¹³⁸ *Detective Comics* #190, New York: DC Comics (December 1952).

It could be contested with perfect validity that my reading of DC Comics' archive constitutes no more than merely another interpretation; that indeed, I was seeking through my study of these comics, whether consciously or unconsciously, to find textual 'evidence' for my own thesis. There can, in my view – as my Introduction must have made clear – be no absolute form of 'evidence' or 'proof' to support a single interpretation of texts over any other. It does seem, however, that there was more than enough material in the Batman comics of the early 1950s to provide a gay reader, viewing the texts through his cultural understanding of 'gayness' during that period, with fantasies of homosexual romance and stylised echoes of his own situation.

If I had studied the *Batman* and *Detective* comics of 1950–1955 and found no sign of the images and scenarios described by Wertham, I would have found myself arguing contrary to my original expectations – as I did in Chapter 1 with the notion of Batman as propaganda figure – that Wertham misremembered, recreated or simply invented the testimonies of his patients in order to serve his crusade against comic books. Such shrewd calculation would by no means be out of keeping with what we know of Wertham's character: *Seduction of the Innocent*, as I noted above, was written in a deliberately populist style and for a specific purpose, playing down some of the author's personal concerns about racism in order more successfully to tap into a contemporary moral panic about delinquency.

However, this appears not to be the case. The brief testimonies reproduced by Wertham – 'I was put in the position of the rescued rather than the rescuer. I felt I'd like to be loved by someone like Batman,' 'Batman could have saved this boy's life. Robin looks something like a girl,'[139] – clearly ring true in the context of the Batman and Robin stories I have transcribed here. Moreover, they tally with another testimony from a very different source, which confirms me in my belief that these patients' reports are genuine.

'Batman and Robin Made Me Gay' is an autobiographical piece by a gay man, the late Steve Beery, published in *Gay Comix* of September 1986. Beery was 'a kid in the early '60s', but crucially, the comics he read were 'reprints from the 1940s and '50s' – precisely those which

---

[139] Wertham, op. cit., p. 192.

Wertham and his patients were studying. His article bears this out, both in his engagement with the detail of Wayne Manor's furnishings and in his emotional investment with the duo's relationship. 'Some kids wanted to be Batman', says Beery.

> I wanted to be Robin. Batman was the Daddy: accomplished, perfect, remote. Robin was just like me, only more so . . . he got to live in an elegant mansion with sumptuous furnishings and a butler. In the secret Batcave deep beneath the house, he worked out, wrestled and studied crime detection. He drove his own Batcycle and flew his own Whirlybat. Best of all, he had the undivided loyalty of Batman.

Beery speaks of the 'bond that linked the two partners', evident in the 'situations where Robin's life was in jeopardy', and makes plain the 'romantic' nature of his identification. Most significantly, he explains that this long-term romantic drama could be read beneath and beyond the cyclical, episodic crime-and-punishment stories.

> For all the emphasis on detection, on puzzling over clues and chasing the crazy villains, the Batman and Robin stories were about devotion – to their crimefighting ideal and, more importantly, to each other. Unwittingly, and to my undying gratitude, Batman and Robin made me gay.[140]

Beery, of course, was reading the reprints; had he grown up in the 1950s with the originals, his response might have led him into 'readjustment', rather than to San Francisco. Those ten years made a lot of difference. Yet although a reader like Beery might never forgive Wertham's course of action, even by situating it within the very different context of the early 1950s, his every word suggests that he would find no fault with Wertham's detection.

---

[140] Steve Beery, 'One Reader's Story: Holy Hormones! Batman and Robin Made Me Gay!', *Gay Comix* no.8, San Francisco: Bob Ross, publisher (Summer 1986), n.p. I am grateful to Randall Scott of the Michigan State University Library Special Collection for this document.

6. Containing Batman

Others have discussed Wertham's role in the Senate Subcomittee hearings of spring 1954, which investigated the relation of comic books to juvenile delinquency, in such detail that there is little point in my rehashing the proceedings here.[141] Following these 'Kefauver hearings', named after the Senator who presided over them,[142] the comics industry opted to provide self-regulation before legislation could be enforced, and formed the Comics Magazine Association of America on 7 September 1954.

> The result of Wertham's campaign and the industry counter-offensive was victory claimed by both sides. The public-relations counsel to the publishers association, David Finn, declared that the comic book industry had yielded only on insignificant matters. They avoided impending censorship which might have destroyed the comic genre. In retrospect Wertham agreed. Yet this estimate was far too modest, for within a few years of the publication of *Seduction of the Innocent*, twenty-four out of twenty-nine crime comic publishers went out of business.[143]

Wertham was offered the chance to head the association as America's comic 'czar',[144] but declined; the post was taken by Judge Charles F. Murphy on 16 September and the new Comics Code, based partly on cinema's Hays Code, was in place by the end of that year.[145] As Nyberg notes, 'the bulk of the comics code dealt with the two topics which had brought the ire of the public down around the heads of the publishers: crime and horror.'[146]

We have just seen what happened to the crime comic publishers;

---

[141] See Nyberg, op. cit.; Gilbert, op. cit.; Barker, op. cit.

[142] Nyberg, op. cit., p. 53.

[143] Gilbert, op. cit., p. 108.

[144] Ibid., p. 107.

[145] See Nyberg, op. cit., pp. 110–112. The industry had first adopted a code in 1948, following Wertham's earlier assaults on comic books.

[146] Ibid., p. 112.

the main victim within the horror genre was E.C., publisher of *The Crypt of Fears*, *The Vault of Horror*, *Shock SuspenStories* and similar titles. William M. Gaines represented the E.C. group and made front-page news through his debates with Senator Kefauver over the limits of 'good taste' in a comic book;[147] he also came into direct conflict with Wertham about differing interpretations of an E.C. story.[148] Despite organising a protest-letter campaign among his readers, discontinuing his horror titles and establishing a 'New Direction' imprint, Gaines and E.C. struggled in the year following the Code's implementation, and pulled out of the Comics Magazine Association in December 1955.[149] Comic Media, publishers of *Horrific* and *Weird Terror*, and Fiction House, home of *Jungle Comics*, went the same way with less fanfare; both folded in 1954.[150]

DC, however, had – wisely in retrospect – never specialised in crime or horror titles. Although Wertham had specifically criticised characters like Wonder Woman, the Blue Beetle and the Green Lantern as well as Superman and Batman, the adventures of the costumed crimefighters under DC's banner were not obvious targets for Code censorship while more graphically horrific or violent material was being published by other companies. The only aspects of the 1954 Code which seem to relate to Batman are those pertaining to 'Marriage and Sex':

2. Illicit sex relations are neither to be hinted at nor portrayed.
[. . .]
4. The treatment of love-romance stories shall emphasize the value of the home and the sanctity of marriage.
5. Passion or romantic interest shall never be treated in such a way as to stimulate the lower and baser emotions.
7. Sex perversion or any inference [*sic*] to same is strictly forbidden.[151]

---

[147] See Nyberg, op. cit., pp. 59–63.
[148] Ibid., p. 64.
[149] Nyberg, op.cit., p. 124.
[150] Ibid.
[151] See Nyberg, op. cit., p. 168.

Ironically, those Batman comics discussed above, with Bruce and Dick enjoying each other's company over the newspapers or during breakfast, do seem to emphasise the value of the home; but as we have seen, the depiction of love between two men who live together would sadly have fallen into the category of 'sex perversion', and the fantasies this scenario seemed to permit might well have qualified in the eyes of Judge Murphy and his five 'trained reviewers'[152] as 'lower and baser emotions'.

It is hard to judge the precise effect that the Code had on Batman comics after 1954. As usual, there is a received version of events which tends to be reproduced across most popular histories of the character. As we have seen before, these potted biographies tend to perpetuate a narrative of Batman's development which 'everyone knows', and which nobody therefore thinks to check against primary evidence. Further ambiguity results from the fact that these histories seem to conflict with each other in their detail, even when they agree in general that Wertham and the Code effectively 'cleaned up' Batman and reduced him to an anodyne and far less interesting figure.

Bill Boichel's 'Commodity as Myth' in Pearson and Uricchio is typical in its description of 'the sunny Caped Crusader of the 1950s who emerged as a response to pressures on the comic book industry',[153] the phrase finding an echo in his later passage:

> The post-war tendency to a sunnier Batman evident before the Wertham crisis intensified after the Code's introduction. The first Batman titles carrying the Comics Code Authority stamp, *Batman* #90 and *Detective Comics* #217 (March 1955) signalled the inception of a makeover of the Batman mythos. *Detective Comics* #253 (July 1956) introduced the character of Batwoman, a mirror image of Batman, complete with a Batcave and Batcycle of her own. Perhaps intended to ward off further charges of homosexuality, Batwoman functioned as a female presence and potential love interest. Determined to establish

---

[152] Ibid., p. 114.
[153] Bill Boichel, 'Batman: Commodity as Myth' in Pearson and Uricchio, op. cit., p. 11.

both Batman and Robin's heterosexuality, the writers introduced Batwoman's niece as the Boy Wonder's possible girlfriend in *Batman* #139 (May 1961).[154]

There are a couple of interesting points raised here. Firstly, note that Boichel traces the 'tendency to a sunnier Batman' back to the comics of the mid- to late 1940s – precisely the comics which Wertham later identified as not just sunny, but positively gay.[155] Wertham's concern over Batman was not with overt violence or the promotion of crime, but with the mix of light-hearted domestic scenes and emotional melodrama which DC's editors must have thought would keep them out of any further censorship debates: this 'sunnier' Batman, after all, evolved in direct response to the criticism of the early 1940s. We should observe, then, that the Batman who became subject to Wertham's disapproval was in fact the result of an earlier anti-comics campaign, with a different agenda; in 1940 there was too much violence, in 1954 too much love.

Boichel is therefore not quite accurate in his remark that the tendency toward a softer Batman 'intensified' after 1955. Wertham had never accused Batman of being too hard, but of being soft with the wrong person. The post-Code stories surely involved a shift of focus rather than an increased mellowing; the introduction of a 'family' which could more easily be read as heterosexual to replace or diffuse the 'subtle atmosphere of homoeroticism'[156] which had pervaded the Wayne/Grayson household.

Secondly, Boichel's comment that 'the writers' introduced Bat-Girl may be off-hand but does raise intriguing issues. We saw that in the early 1940s it was the editors, responding to pressure from journalism and letters of protest, who instructed Bill Finger and Bob Kane to make changes to Batman's character.

The *New York Times* – which as we saw served as the platform for substantial pro- and anti-comic debate in the 1940s – contains only two

---

[154] Ibid., p. 13.
[155] If we consider Wertham's campaign against comic books to have begun proper with his influential magazine articles of 1948.
[156] Wertham, op. cit., p. 190.

columns on comic books during all of 1954, which nevertheless represents a leap from the one paragraph on the subject in 1953; the 1954 article is a review of *Seduction of the Innocent* by an associate professor of sociology from Columbia University. There is no mention of Batman or of homosexuality, but this is a positive review which begins 'All parents should be grateful to Dr Fredric Wertham for having written *Seduction of the Innocent*', praises the author's 'careful observations and his sober reflections' and concludes 'surely any careful reader of this book can only agree with Dr Wertham . . . it does not seem to me that "further studies are needed" before action is taken against comic book publishers.'[157]

Clearly, this review alone would have played a small part in bolstering Wertham's campaign and alerting DC's editors to the need for damage limitation before a public backlash against their titles threatened sales. This article seems merely a symptom, however, of what Paul Sassienie describes as a 'wave of bad publicity after the Senate report'.[158] The *Reader's Guide* from 1951 to 1953, as noted above, lists eight articles which warn of the 'Challenge of Comic Books',[159] ask 'How Good are the Comic Books'[160] or simply assert that 'Comics Aren't Good Enough'.[161] That the publications in question are largely educational and parenting magazines suggests that concern over comic books would have been building steadily in the early 1950s amongst the social groups most likely to lobby against DC and its fellow publishing companies: Nyberg reports that 'some of the strongest support for legislation against comic books came from the National Congress of Parents and from the National Education Association'.[162]

In the years 1953 to 1955 there are no fewer than fifty-two articles on comics listed in the *Reader's Guide*. Three are by Wertham himself, in the *Reader's Digest*, *Congressional Digest* and *Ladies' Home Journal*. There

---

[157] C. Wright Mills, 'Nothing to Laugh At', *New York Times* (25 April 1954).
[158] Sassienie, op. cit., p. 59.
[159] 'Challenge of Comic Books', *School and Society* no. 75 (5 April 1952).
[160] 'How Good are the Comic Books?' *Parents' Magazine* no. 26 (November 1951).
[161] 'Comics Aren't Good Enough', *Wilson Library Bulletin* no. 26 (January 1952).
[162] Nyberg, op. cit., p. 37.

are five reviews of *Seduction of the Innocent* and twenty-one articles on the Subcommittee hearings, the formation of the Code and appointment of the 'czar', Charles F. Murphy. This discourse on the dangers of comics circulated across the national press, from *Time* and *Life* through *Catholic World* and *Christian Century* to the *Library Bulletin*, *Science News Letter* and *Today's Health*.[163]

In all, it seems entirely likely that DC as an institution would have felt it prudent to adapt the codes and content of one of its flagship characters for a second time in the face of this widespread discourse of concern and condemnation. Even if Batman passed through the Code censors unharmed, there would still be the character's now-tarnished public image to think of, and the introduction of heterosexual love interest might well have seemed a necessary addition to rescue Batman and Robin as respectable cultural icons. We can reasonably assume that, as was the case with the previous significant change imposed from 'outside', these alterations to the Batman mythos were handed down as instructions from editors to writers and artists.

Other accounts of the 'comic crackdown period'[164] are less thoughtful and suggestive. Cotta Vaz, heavily prejudiced against Wertham's 'incredible charges' and 'unwarranted attacks',[165] cites Denny O'Neil's description of the late-1950s Batman as a 'benign scoutmaster' and complains that

> There he was, the former 'weird figure of the night', too often waltzing around Gotham in the light of day. [...] During the decade Batman tales moved away from the original formula of darkness and menace that had set the tone in the Golden Age. [...] Wertham's tactics ... roughed up the Dynamic Duo [166] ...

If we accept the conventional view that the 'Golden Age' of comics ran

[163] *Reader's Guide* (April 1953–February 1955).
[164] Cotta Vaz, op. cit., p. 49.
[165] Cotta Vaz, op. cit., pp. 44, 47.
[166] Ibid., pp. 50–51.

from 1938 to 1945,[167] this argument seems founded on sloppy thinking. Cotta Vaz admits himself just two pages later that as early as 1940 'Robin helped make fighting crime FUN!'[168] and we have already seen that Batman's 'original formula of darkness and menace' had been more or less abandoned by the end of the character's second year in print. If Cotta Vaz means to suggest that the move towards a 'softer' Batman took place in the 1950s, he is contradicted not only by my own research in this and the previous chapter but by Bill Boichel's passage above. The image of Wertham 'roughing up' Batman and Robin also seems to be squarely contradicted by Boichel's theory that the characters were in fact progressively softened up in the years before 1954, and that the Code 'intensified' the process.

Finally, Medhurst agrees that 'crazed as Wertham's ideas were, their effectiveness is not in doubt.'

> And in all of this, what happened to Batman? He turned into Fred MacMurray from *My Three Sons*. He lost any remaining edge of the shadowy vigilante from his earliest years, and became an upholder of the most stifling small town American values. Batwoman and Batgirl [*sic*] appeared (June Allyson and Bat-Gidget) to take away any lingering doubts about the Dynamic Duo's sex lives.[169]

It is curious that Medhurst seems to valorise the 'edge' of the 'shadowy vigilante' Batman over the bland figure who took his place in the late 1950s; he subsequently scorns the 'portentous Dark Knight charade' of the 1980s[170] and mocks the 'humorlessness, fondness for violence and obsessive monomania'[171] of Tim Burton's 1989 *Batman*. Despite his very different project, Medhurst's take on the post-Code Batman ultimately follows similar lines to that of Cotta Vaz and Boichel: 'shadowy vigilante' good, 'benign scoutmaster' bad. The received

---

[167] See Sassienie, op. cit., p. 21.
[168] Cotta Vaz, op. cit., p. 53.
[169] Medhurst, op. cit., pp. 153–154.
[170] Ibid., p. 156.
[171] Ibid., p. 162.

opinion seems to agree, 1940 was a very good year for Batman; Boichel sees the decline setting in very soon after that,[172] while Cotta Vaz, like Medhurst, blames Batman's ruination on Wertham's criticism of 1954. Medhurst finds the character's salvation in the 1966 TV series,[173] while Cotta Vaz seems to prefer the return to a 'darker' tone as epitomised by the Denny O'Neil and Neal Adams comics of the 1970s.[174] All agree, however, that the period 1954–1966 represents, in Medhurst's phrase, 'the retreat into coziness forced on comics by the Wertham onslaught,'[175] characterised by a boringly inoffensive Batman.

To Medhurst, this period involved an attempt to close down gay readings of the texts, most notably through the introduction of Kathy Kane/Batwoman and her niece, Betty Kane/Bat-Girl. He cites an episode from 1963 as an example of the new 'squeaky-clean sexuality', adding a satirical slant to his recreation of the story in order better to serve his argument and mistakenly using 'Bat-Girl' interchangeably with 'Batgirl', thus confusing Betty Kane with the later, very different character whose alias was Barbara Gordon.

> the episode concludes with another tableau of terrifying heterosexual contentment. 'Oh Robin,' simpers Batgirl, 'I'm afraid you'll just have to hold me! I'm still so shaky after fighting Clayface . . . and you're so strong!' Robin: 'Gosh Batgirl, it was swell of you to calm me down when I was worried about Batman tackling Clayface alone.' [. . .] Batwoman here seizes her chance and tackles Batman. 'You look worried about Clayface, Batman . . . so why don't you follow Robin's example and let me soothe you?' Batman can only reply 'Gulp'.[176]

Medhurst comments that 'one feels a distinct Wertham influence here: if Robin shows concern about Batman, wheel on a supportive female,

---

[172] Boichel, op. cit., p. 13.

[173] Medhurst, op. cit., p. 156.

[174] Cotta Vaz, op. cit., p. 51.

[175] Medhurst, op. cit., p. 154.

[176] Ibid., p. 154.

the very opposite of a "morbid ideal", to minister in a suitably self-effacing way.'[177] This is a valid point, and Medhurst's reading of the Bat-Girl/Robin scene as a deliberate editorial attempt to avoid further charges of homoeroticism does ring true; we have, as noted above, seen fairly conclusively that Batman's editors self-consciously changed aspects of his behaviour in order to dodge criticism in the early 1940s. Medhurst then goes on to argue, however, that while

> there no doubt were still subversive readers of *Batman*, erasing Batgirl on her every preposterous appearance and reworking the Duo's capers to leave some room for homoerotic speculation ... such a reading would have had to work so much harder than before. The *Batman* of this era was such a closed text, so immune to polysemic interpretation, that its interest today is only as a symptom ... [178]

I do not believe there is any such thing as 'a closed text ... immune to polysemic interpretation'. Depending on their cultural context and the nature of the interpretive communities who encounter them at that moment, some texts may seem to be more open to more readings than others, but this is a relative, not an absolute quality. This Batman story of 1963 is just as potentially 'open' to multiple readings, including gay readings, as were the texts of the early 1950s discussed above. There seems little doubt that the editors of Batman comics intended to limit the possible meanings of these stories – that is, they hoped that no journalists, psychiatrists, parents or Code authorities would read them as 'homoerotic' – but it seems quite possible that, say, one of the boys interviewed by Wertham could easily have picked up a post-Code Batman title such as this one and found in it the same relationship he had enjoyed in the pre-Code comics. In fact, there is no reason why the editors and writers at DC should have cared if such an interpretation was still circulating among a small section of their teenage readership,

---

[177] Ibid.
[178] Ibid.

as long as it remained on that level and was overlooked by the social institutions – regulators, journalists, lobby groups, Church organisations – who had the power to damage their company.

I would even go so far as to venture that cues for a gay reading might deliberately have been kept in the text – or self-consciously added, if we assume that prior to 1954 the writers were oblivious of Batman's potentially gay overtones – under the cover of heterosexual 'respectability' donated by Kathy and Betty Kane. This can only remain a hypothesis, and it is impossible to know whether the responsibility would lie with editors or individual creators, but it does seem feasible that DC staff might have resented the negative publicity, the unwelcome accusations, the threats of censorship and the patronising Code forced onto their flagship characters, and deliberately cocked a snook at the campaigners and regulators by retaining, or even increasing, subversive overtones beneath the imposed veneer of a Batman 'family'.[179]

It is surprising that Medhurst, who champions reading 'against the grain', sees only one possible interpretation of the Batman story he cites. Why does Batman gulp when Batwoman offers to soothe him, if he has been transformed into an unproblematic heterosexual? In fact, Medhurst has created this 'tableau of terrifying heterosexual contentment' from a montage of scenes within a two-part, sixteen-page story, and so distorts the original to make his point. The 'Oh, Robin – I'm afraid you'll just have to hold me!' dialogue actually occurs eight pages before the end, and the subsequent frame could in fact be read as a mockery, rather than a celebration, of heterosexual courtship: Batwoman turns to Batman and echoes, in a 'sing-song' voice conveyed by musical notes within the speech balloon, 'Oh, Batman – I'm afraid you'll just have to hold me! I'm still shaky after fighting Clayface – and you're so stron-nn-g!'[180] Surely this is a parody

---

[179] According to an Internet report, Bob Kane claimed in the 1980s that, surprised and amused by Wertham's interpretation, he 'eventually decided to play into it, injecting double-entendres into the stories'. Given Kane's selective memory and tendency to relate history to his own advantage, we might want to take this with a pinch of salt. Post from Ontir, *Jonah Weiland's Comic Book Resources*, op. cit. (5 May 1999).

[180] *Batman* #159, New York: DC Comics (November 1963).

of Bat-Girl's feminine wiles which exposes and laughs at heterosexual romantic conventions: Batman's slightly pouty look out 'to camera' as Batwoman flutters her eyelashes at him merely increases the sense of comedy. As I will argue in the following chapter, the 'camp' phase of Batman did not, as Medhurst seems to believe, begin with the TV show of 1966 but in the comics from which the series was adapted; this story from 1963 falls well within that period, and carries the same potential connotations as the TV episodes where Batman has to resist the charms of a female admirer.[181]

Of course, we could note here that there are other textual determinants at work – just as the sidekick is called upon by narrative conventions to be regularly captured and rescued, so the hero of an episodic adventure drama, be he Batman, James Bond or James T. Kirk, cannot become involved in a long-term heterosexual relationship without it fundamentally affecting the genre. We might also observe that the fear of women's debilitating effects on men constituted a discourse of the 1950s which had nothing to do with homosexuality. As was the case above, though, I would suggest that the trope of the 'woman trap' in the Batwoman and Bat-Girl stories is played up through the gulps and dismayed glances to a point of excess, and that the pre-existing Batman and Robin couple – placed under threat by Betty and Kathy's advances – provides extra support for a reading of these scenarios as 'gay'.

The truth is that Medhurst has not really researched widely before making his assertions. The Batwoman story he so freely adapts is his only proof of the post-Code shift towards 'stifling small town American values', and this is a crib from *The Greatest Joker Stories Ever Told*, a 1988 compilation, rather than evidence of a return to primary texts. Of course, it is very difficult to lay hands on original 1950s or 1960s comics; but even the companion volume *The Greatest Batman Stories Ever Told* includes a story from the same year as Medhurst's Batwoman tale which immediately contradicts his pessimistic reading of the post-Code Batman.

---

[181] See Medhurst, op. cit., p. 157.

'Robin Dies At Dawn', from *Batman* #156,[182] places the Dynamic Duo on an alien planet, complete with deadly plants whose tendrils snake out to grab Batman around the waist. 'If only *Robin* were here to help me!' Batman shouts. '*Robin! Where are you, Robin? Robin!*'

'Suddenly, a familiar, sturdy figure races forward ... ' Batman glances toward his sidekick, yelling '*Robin!*' once more for good measure. There is another rescue of the kind we saw virtually every month in the mid-1950s comics; Robin smashes the plant, and the crimefighters flee across the alien landscape only to be attacked once again, this time by a giant statue. Robin taunts their new enemy, trying to lure him into a chasm. It is difficult to read his words – 'Come on, Big Boy! I'm still waiting for you!' as indicative of a 'closed text' which refuses to admit any readings outside those of respectable hetero-sexuality;[183] indeed, it is hard to accept that the anonymous writer[183] was unaware of the potential for double meanings. Indeed, the melodrama of 'Robin Dies At Dawn!' is if anything more overt and exaggerated than that of the mid-1950s stories, as if the shift from an urban/domestic to a fantastical environment of lurid colours and alien creatures had allowed both writer and artist a freer rein.

Robin is felled by a massive boulder flung by the giant statue, cueing Batman to cry his partner's name once more before kneeling over the small body. 'He – he's dead! *Robin's dead!*' The crimefighter cradles his sidekick as a caption elaborates: 'The dawn sun rises, looking down at a man stunned by the shock of a terrible catastrophe!' '*Robin* sacrificed himself for me!' Batman laments. 'He died so I could live! Oh, *Robin ... Robin ...* '

Later, 'crushed by tragedy', Batman begins to lose his reason and shakes his fists at the sky, defying imagined observers: '*Why are you watching me?*' Even the appearance of a bright purple monster fails to bring him to his senses. 'Let it come!' he exclaims, tumbling through the air. 'I don't want to live! It's my fault *Robin* died! I don't want to live!'

---

[182] *Batman* #156 (1963), reprinted in *The Greatest Batman Stories Ever Told*, New York: DC Comics (1988), pp. 131–148.

[183] While this story is signed 'Bob Kane', this was merely convention by the 1960s and provides no guarantee whatsoever that Kane had creative input.

In the next panel we discover Batman writhing on the floor of a laboratory, repeating the same anguished phrases. The alien planet was a dream-sequence produced by a space-flight simulator, and Robin assures him that 'I've been coming in every day . . . to look in on you!' The pair walk out arm in arm, but Batman's hallucinations continue in the next chapter. Soon Bruce is tossing and turning in bed, the covers tangled around his pyjama-clad limbs. '*The tentacles – tightening around me! Help! Robin! Help!*' Dick races into the bedroom, followed by Alfred and Ace the Bat-Hound. 'Gosh! He's dreaming about the tentacle-plant!' Robin exclaims.

Next day it's business as usual – 'get dressed, Dick!' – until Batman suffers another trance. Back at the cave, he strips to his civvies and declares 'while I have these mental blackouts, I endanger your life! I can't ever let that happen again! There's only one thing I can do . . . ' Now we see Bruce's profile in dramatic close-up, with a tearful Robin in the background. 'I must put away my *Batman* costume and retire from crime-fighting!' 'Oh, *Batman!*' Robin weeps. 'Sob!'

Rather than exhibiting a 'subtle atmosphere of homoeroticism', we might want to regard this as hysterical camp, prefiguring the TV series of the mid- to late 1960s in its garish palette, its overblown theatricality and its depiction of a Batman and Robin who take everything with the utmost gravity whatever the absurdity of their surroundings. Instead of discreet signs of a 'love-relationship', we are presented here with what appear to be blatant *double-entendres*, a constant insistence on the devotion between the two men and a sense of 'queerness' which, it sometimes seems, can only have passed the Code regulators and escaped public criticism because it was outrageously fantastical, rather than cosily domestic. Given that, as I shall argue in the following chapter, the comic book audience of the mid-1960s was adept at reading superhero adventures on at least two levels, I would suggest again that the irony which cannot help but strike the late-1990s reader of 'Robin Dies At Dawn!' was not just picked up by part of the contemporary readership but may have been fully intended by the writers involved.

This is far from an isolated example. The first Batwoman and Bat-Girl stories of the late 1950s take a different tone, the 'sci-fi fad' having not yet overwhelmed the Batman titles, yet it would take a very limited reading to conclude that these adventures only offer a 'respectable' heterosexual interpretation. What Medhurst seems to overlook in his reading is that homosexuality is in no way entirely ruled out by the sudden arrival of a girlfriend. In the 1950s, as now, many gay men would have found themselves adopting or forcing themselves into a 'straight' lifestyle, complete with wife and children: Howard Brown alone cites numerous testimonies from married gay men.

If a reader of the pre-Code comics had established that he would like Batman to be gay, the Batwoman stories would do little to deter him or, as Medhurst suggests, make him 'work so much harder'[184] at his interpretation; I would even suggest that the unconvincing heterosexual romances in which Batman and Robin suddenly found themselves embroiled might have confirmed this reader in his opinion. The Dynamic Duo had simply been obliged to become more straight-acting, but the genuine romance would still have been intact and obvious, for those who wished to see it.

The first appearance of Batwoman, for instance, has Robin stumbling in on Kathy Kane and Bruce Wayne together: 'Batman, I – oh! Maybe I'm intruding!' Rather than telling the Boy Wonder to knock next time and pulling Kathy into a clinch, Batman reassures him: 'Don't be foolish!'[185] The very idea of Bruce pairing off with Kathy! Robin clearly has no need to worry.

When Bat-Girl first appears in 1961 and attaches herself limpet-like to Robin, his reaction is much the same as Batman's in the Clayface story cited above; not enthusiasm or doe-eyed adoration, but 'Ulp!'[186] This will evidently, he assumes, bring trouble. In a subsequent 1961 episode he escapes her embrace and fumbles to explain his lack of interest.

> Bat-Girl: Oh, *Robin* – I think you're adorable!
> Robin: B-Bat-Girl, please ... I'm ... er ... devoted to another woman!
> Bat-Girl: Oh, *Robin*! – sob – y-you can't mean that![187]

---

[184] Medhurst, op. cit., p. 154.
[185] 'The Batwoman', *Batman* #109 (1956).
[186] 'Bat-Girl!', *Batman* #139, New York: DC Comics (May 1961).
[187] 'Bat-Mite Meets Bat-Girl', *Batman* #141, New York: DC Comics (July 1961).

Of course, he doesn't really mean that; the 'official' explanation is that he has devoted himself to Gotham's Statue of Justice, but it is easy enough to imagine another reason behind his stammered excuse.

'Prisoners of Three Worlds', from the following year, emphasises the continuing 'double-life' motif from its title onwards, and even extends the theme of dual identity to the previously 'respectable' Kane girls. While Bruce is at work with Commissioner Gordon, Robin strolls about college. Two of his female classmates comment that 'Dick Grayson is cute-looking – but he's such a drag! He isn't even going to the school dance this afternoon!' Next we see Kathy, 'blessed with riches and beauty', sunning herself on the beach. 'I'll never understand why a woman as attractive as Kathy isn't married yet!' remarks a passing male. The four-panel sequence is completed with Betty on a train. All the main characters are single in these frames, and crucially, none of them fit in. The point is made explicitly about Dick and Kathy that they fail, or refuse, to fall in with heterosexual convention; but Bruce and Betty are also somehow 'queer' – Gordon muses that Bruce 'seems to have no goal in life', while Betty can only long to 'see Aunt Kathy again! Exciting things always happen when I visit her!'

The caption announces, however, that 'each of them has a *double* life' and the subsequent two panels pair our foursome – but in same-sex couples, where they finally seem happy and fulfilled in contrast to the 'straight' masquerade of the opening frames. 'Unknown to the world', Robin and Batman dress together, while an exact echo of the scene finds Bat-Girl and Batwoman getting into costume.

During the science-fiction adventure Batman tells Kathy, close to death, that he loves her. He is faced with this confession at the end of the story, when Kathy reveals that 'I *did* hear you admit that you loved me!' As in the Clayface/Joker episode above, Batman's response is to stare out at the reader, this time with 'shock lines' indicating his panic. He thinks 'Whew – I've always managed to escape death-traps – all kinds of danger! But how do I get out of *this*?' The implications of this are surely undeniable. Heterosexual romance is presented as a 'trap', a 'danger' – even admitting that you love a woman is a terrible mistake.

The next panel involves a shift which in cinema would break spatial continuity by 'crossing the line', and convey a momentary disruption: now Batman stands on the left, rather than the right of frame, with Kathy facing him. He playfully chucks her under the chin, and smiles

'Well – er – *Batwoman* – I thought we were going to die – and I wanted to make your last moments happy ones!' Batwoman, unamused, thinks 'Hmmm . . . I wonder . . . '

So this time it is the girl, rather than the boy, who wonders; and she can surely only be asking herself if there's another reason why Batman seems so uninterested in her romantic advances. If she compared notes with her niece Betty, of course, she might get a clearer picture – but then we can't even be sure if Kathy, beautiful and desired by men but never married, is only teasing Bruce for show, or whether Betty has a crush on the aunt who makes her life so 'exciting', rather than on the fumbling, flustered Dick Grayson. We as readers can only wonder what the writers intended, and how many readers wryly identified the 'subversive' romantic narratives I have picked out here from the 'official' adventure. On the whole, however, it seems clear that although the post-Code years are widely considered to have controlled and contained Batman, there are ample examples of Batman escaping the censorship structures which were imposed on him after 1954.

7. Framing Device: Batman and Robin Forever

As is so often the case, multiple cultural determinants shaped the frequent reception of Batman as 'camp' or 'gay' in the decades following Wertham's critique and the subsequent institutional attempts – whether tokenistic, tongue in cheek or entirely sincere – to 'clean up' the character's image.

It was not just due to Wertham and the popular circulation his 'gay Batman' reading had achieved in the previous decade that the 1940s series *Batman*, rescreened in 1965 and early 1966 as an all-night 'Evening with Batman and Robin', prompted audiences to 'provide a ribald commentary on the relationship between Batman and his teenage henchman Robin',[188] jeer and whistle 'if Batman and his boy assistant

---

[188] 'Film Critic', '1943 Serial All At Fell Swoop', *The Times* (3 February 1966).

Robin as much as exchanged smiles',[189] and cry out "'Robin's wearing stockings!" . . . in mincing voices'.[190] The performances, grave voice-overs and stirring music of any 1940s serial would have seemed amusingly dated to a young, high-spirited audience of 1966, who apparently played 'leapfrog in the aisles or poker in the lobby'[191] during the screening and treated the show with a gleeful irreverance. In a context of racial unrest and increasing public distrust over LBJ's handling of Vietnam, an audience of American students and young people would probably have jeered every reference to 'Japs' and national patriots as well: the catcalls at Batman and Robin's intimate smiles would have been just part of a more general pleasurable mockery and scepticism. One reviewer of the time comments with some regret on 'how much we have lost in innocence even since 1939'.[192]

However, it appears likely that the reception of Batman and Robin as 'gay' in this context did have very much to do with the widespread dissemination of Wertham's 'dressing gown' reading, which of all his many arguments about comic books seems to have been the one single theory to grip the public imagination and lodge itself in cultural memory. Jeffrey Blyth, reporting from the US in the *Daily Mail* of December 1965, explains that 'Because he never had a girl friend and Robin, his teenage ward, was his only companion, it was suggested during the big American comic-book clean-up of the 50s that Batman and Robin had homosexual overtones.'[193] Kenneth Tynan, reviewing the all-night screening in the *Observer*, also discusses 'the thesis – advanced by several psychiatrists – that Batman and Robin are queer.'[194] While Wertham's name seems to have slipped from

---

[189] Alexander Walker, 'Stop For A Meal or A Chat!', *Evening Standard* (3 February 1966).

[190] Virginia Ironside, 'Hiss! Boo! Cheers! We Want Batman', *Daily Mail* (16 February 1966).

[191] Walker, op. cit.

[192] 'Film Critic', op. cit.

[193] Jeffrey Blyth, 'Batman Flies Again For 4½ Hours Nonstop', *Daily Mail* (28 December 1965).

[194] Kenneth Tynan, review, *Observer* (6 February 1966).

journalistic discourse ten years after the first publication of *Seduction of the Innocent*, his four pages on Batman clearly live on.

Similarly, we can by no means assume that Wertham's reading of Batman was the sole motivating force behind either ABC's decision to play the 1966 TV series as 'camp', or the fact that a significant percentage of the adult audience enjoyed it as such. Medhurst rightly notes that Batman and Robin were in some ways already ripe material for a camp reworking, simply because of the juxtaposition between 'serious' crimefighting and 'ludicrous' costume, and the fact that the comics were usually centred around a close male couple.[195] We would also have to consider many other factors – the contemporary view of all comics as inherently camp in their Pop straddling of 'high' and 'low' culture; the other TV shows of the period which had already established the profitable formula of a multi-levelled appeal to both an 'ironic' adult and 'naïve' juvenile viewer; the prior existence of a 'camp reading' of Batman and Robin in cinema, as demonstrated by the rescreening of the 1940s serial; and the arguably camp nature of the Batman comic stories from which the TV series was adapted.

We cannot tell, then, whether the TV critic who, discussing Adam West's on-screen relationship with 'Wonder Boy Robin', added wryly 'I like to think they are just good friends', had any direct knowledge of Wertham's 1954 text.[196] Certainly, when a 1966 columnist remarks 'it was even suggested by one sophisticated reviewer that . . . there was a decided suggestion of homosexuality in the relationship of Batman and Robin,'[197] the traces of Wertham himself seem to have been lost, the origins of the 'gay reading' fading as they pass along a chain of vague references in secondary texts. I would argue, however, that Wertham remains the source; we have seen that his name sometimes resurfaces in references to the 1966 show – in Burt Ward's autobiography, for instance – even if much of 1960s culture seemed to simply have absorbed the *Seduction of the Innocent* reading without remembering its author, date or context.

The overarching irony is that while Wertham intended to censor

---

[195] Medhurst, op. cit., p. 156.
[196] Nancy Banks-Smith, review, *Sun* (6 July 1966).
[197] Milton Shulman, review, *Evening Standard* (27 July 1966).

and contain the readings he discovered in the Quaker Readjustment Center of New York City during the late 1940s and early 1950s, he achieved precisely the reverse. Wertham, in highlighting this interpretation, caused it to circulate not just in his own decade but in the popular discourse of the next forty-five years. At the end of the 1990s the joke that Batman and Robin are, or could be gay is something that 'everybody knows', from school playgrounds through academic departments and magazine offices to film studios. Without Wertham, this reading might well have remained confined to a few young men in a New York treatment centre, and gone no further.

It may seem from the evidence so far that the dissemination of the 'gay Batman' reading resulted mainly in homophobic jeering and snide nudges. It might then be argued – and this, indeed, is Medhurst's complaint – that what Wertham made visible was a reading of Batman and Robin from the 'outside', at worst a homophobic equating of gayness with limp-wristed effeminacy and corruptive deviance, at best a simplistic reduction of homosexuality to 'camp', an appropriate subject for faintly sneering jokes like those in *Mad Magazine*'s parody 'Buttman' of 1995, which concludes with the heroes' silhouettes in a heart-shaped Bat-Signal as they discuss their 'little secret tucked away in the deep dark recesses of the ButtCave'.[198] The same tone was adopted by the *Sun* newspaper in its preview of the 1989 Tim Burton film, reporting that

> film bosses decided to end Batman's monk-like life to crush rumours that he was gay ... for years, he and his young sidekick Robin have been the target of malicious jibes. But KRRANG! After Robin is sensationally killed off minutes into the film, 'Big Boy' Batman moves into action.[199]

Even the *Guardian*'s 'Pass Notes' on Batman in June 1995, describing the character's occupation as 'homo-erotic icon', echo Wertham without actually citing him and offer jokey 'proof' of Batman's homoeroticism from a position which, while not hostile, is clearly

---

[198] 'Buttman Ferschlugginer', *Mad Magazine* (July 1995), p. 8.
[199] Piers Morgan, 'Here's Batman and Throbbin', *Sun* (1 February 1989).

located 'outside' gay culture and makes free with lazy stereotypes. 'The suit, the theatricals, the fastidious cleanliness of the lifestyle, the valet. And Robin. No one ever questions the amount of time man and boy spend together in the mansion.'[200]

That the *Seduction of the Innocent* reading has been taken up by heterosexuals with an amusement bordering on homophobia cannot be denied. Nevertheless, there is equal evidence that Wertham's highlighting of his patients' interpretation has informed the reading of Batman by gay men, and been used towards positive and pleasurable ends from an 'insider' position. Consider George Melly's blithe remarks in his *Revolt Into Style* of 1970: 'We all knew Robin and Batman were pouves ... over the children's heads we winked and nudged, but in the end what were we laughing at? The fact they didn't know Batman had it off with Robin.'[201] The 'we' here – not newspaper reviewers or jeering students, but Melly's circle of gay or gay-friendly associates – clearly suggests an 'insider' queer reading in circulation around the TV Batman of the late 1960s.

Comic book historian E. Nelson Bridwell unwittingly confirms Melly's remarks by blaming the sullying of Batman and the name 'Bruce' on the 'gay set' of that decade, who he claims 'eagerly seized on' Wertham's interpretation for their own purposes;[202] and Steve Beery's testimony, with its double-edged memories of the TV Batman being called a 'fairy' at school coupled with the 'blunt sexual urge' invoked by Burt Ward's Robin and his 'strong legs in tights',[203] provides support to Bridwell's argument from a radically opposed position. Wertham's highlighting of the 'gay Batman' reading, then, was indirectly responsible for homophobic jibes at the 1943 serial, the 1966 series and the Batman of subsequent decades, but also, it seems, encouraged a fair degree of pleasure on the part of gay viewers from the 1960s onwards.

Like the jokes about Batman from 'outside', the 'insider' reading

---

[200] Anon., 'Pass Notes', *Guardian* (21 June 1995).

[201] George Melly, *Revolt Into Style: The Pop Arts In Britain*, Harmondsworth: Penguin (1970), p. 193.

[202] Bridwell, op. cit., p. 12.

[203] Beery, op. cit., n.p.

amongst gay men has continued to circulate into the 1990s. Those that mention Wertham by name remain few and far between. An article titled 'Comics 'r' Us' in *Gay Times* – which actually quotes Wertham's 'dressing gown' passage, citing it as home of the 'legendary' rumours about Batman and Robin – is a rare exception and significant for the way in which it uses this paragraph as a springboard for further gay reading rather than for denial. 'The most famous and popular comic book characters have definite parallels with a gay lifestyle,' suggests the author:

> [They] all lead dual lives. If they do reveal their alternative personae to anyone . . . it is usually to their closest friends and their family. They fight a continual battle against prejudice . . . some support the underdog. The parallels with gay experience go further. Superman and a majority of the X-Men were born with their mutant powers . . . but many don't realise they possess such powers until they reach their early teens. Some try to resist the change and deny the urge. Others (take the Boy Wonder for example) embrace the new culture and lifestyle with relish, creating gaudy, vivid apparel and an arrogant attitude.[204]

More common are the references which take for granted Batman's inherent 'gayness' but never question where the 'legendary' rumours began. A 1997 feature in the British gay magazine *Attitude*, for instance, asked readers to confess their childhood crushes on TV characters. Andy, aged 30, chose Burt Ward and Adam West. 'I thought Batman was really hunky . . . and fatherly . . . but I also liked Robin for being cute and boyish. Sometimes I'd fantasise about being one of them, fancying the other one; other times I'd swap round; sometimes I even imagined being a third party in the relationship.'[205] It is striking how vividly this echoes the testimony in *Seduction of the Innocent* of the boy who confesses 'I think I put myself in the position of Robin. I did want to have relations with Batman . . . I felt I'd like to be loved by someone

---

[204] Megan Radclyffe, 'Comics'r'Us', *Gay Times* (November 1996), pp. 18–19.
[205] Murray Healy, 'Tuned In, Turned On', *Attitude* (January 1997), p. 65.

like Batman'.[206] Only the context has changed, from a sad, touching psychological case study to a jokily embarrassed column in a national gay magazine.

It would be naïve to suggest that gay men would never have thought of seeing Batman and Robin as gay were it not for Wertham's promotion of his patients' reading into popular discourse. To some extent, though, we can surely see Andy's fantasies as an extension of the *Seduction* testimonies; not referencing them directly, of course, but perhaps informed by an unconscious background knowledge of the 'gay Batman' reading which Wertham made visible.

We could say the same about a range of diverse cultural artefacts – the personal advertisement in the 'Men Seeking Men' section of the *Guardian*'s 'Soulmates' pages, announcing that 'Batman, 28, seeks soulmate with own cape';[207] or the Internet site of Scott Alcid, who presents the diary of his 'first rustlings of being gay' alongside a pin-up gallery of actor Chris O'Donnell in his Robin suit, admitting that 'the character itself has always been a favorite of mine.'[208] The fact that Chris O'Donnell, a presumably heterosexual married man, has twice earned the place of cover boy for *Attitude*[209] – but only with the release of a new Batman film, and always in costume – must be attributed to the status and connotations of Robin for a contemporary gay audience, rather than solely to O'Donnell's clean-cut good looks and sexualised rubber suit. This again, I believe, can ultimately be sourced to Wertham; while director Joel Schumacher's tendency towards camp and playfully knowing homoeroticism in *Batman Forever* and *Batman and Robin* may have re-emphasised Robin's gay associations, O'Donnell's first appearance in *Attitude*, dated June 1995, precedes the British release of Schumacher's first Batman film. Even the use of Catwoman on a flyer for the 'Kitty Lips' club night in London – 'for gals and their gay guys as guests' – seems to belong to the same reading, appropriated

---

[206] Wertham, op. cit., p. 192.

[207] *Guardian* Soulmates, 'Men Seeking Men' section (29 November 1997).

[208] *Scott's Place on the Web*, http://www.clark.net/pub/salcid/chris/chris.html (18 June 1997).

[209] 'Boy Wonder', cover, *Attitude* magazine (July 1995); 'The Boy's Back', *Attitude* magazine (June 1997).

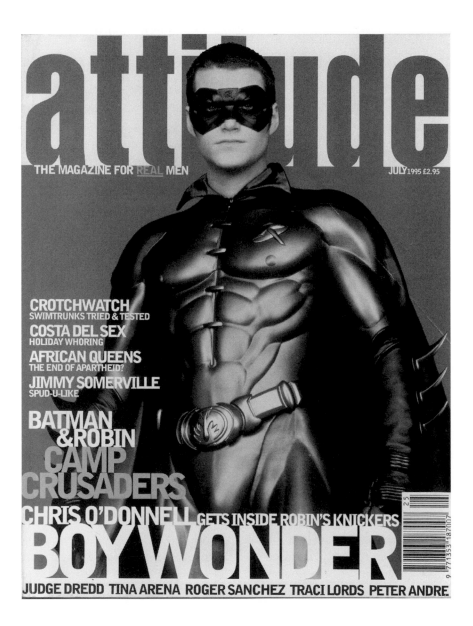

attitude

THE MAGAZINE FOR REAL MEN

JULY 1995 £2.95

CROTCHWATCH
SWIMTRUNKS TRIED & TESTED

COSTA DEL SEX
HOLIDAY WHORING

AFRICAN QUEENS
THE END OF APARTHEID?

JIMMY SOMERVILLE
SPUD-U-LIKE

BATMAN &ROBIN
CAMP CRUSADERS

CHRIS O'DONNELL GETS INSIDE ROBIN'S KNICKERS
BOY WONDER

JUDGE DREDD TINA ARENA ROGER SANCHEZ TRACI LORDS PETER ANDRE

at a distance from *Seduction of the Innocent* and extended this time to a lesbian audience.

Finally, it is possible to argue that the dissemination of the gay readings Wertham identified has also led, after a long period of apparent denial and attempted containment on the part of the producers of both Batman comics and films – the killing off of Alfred the butler in the 1960s and his replacement with Aunt Harriet[210] and a new Batgirl;[211] Robin's departure to college,[212] murder at the hands of the Joker[213] and exclusion from two Tim Burton feature films – to a limited acceptance of these readings and recently to their incorporation in 'mainstream' Batman texts.

Again, Schumacher's two feature films of 1995 and 1997 – which, as I shall discuss in Chapter 4, were widely considered by reviewers and fans to exhibit both camp and homoerotic aspects – played a major part in incorporating the 'gay Batman' reading into 'official' – that is, Warner Brothers-sanctioned – portrayals of the character. Schumacher's films, the first since 1966 to feature both Batman and Robin, exploited the public memory of Burt Ward and Adam West's banter, and more generally the audience awareness of the 'gay Batman' reading, to playful and comic effect. Andy Medhurst's review of *Batman and Robin* recognised Schumacher's teasing, and responded in kind:

> George Clooney and Chris O'Donnell are probably the most ravishing male couple ever to share a house in the history of Hollywood ... better still, two of the central, recurring male characters finally say 'I love you' before kissing. The fact that this exchange involves Bruce Wayne and a sickbed-confined Alfred is, as any devotee of Bat-queer subtexts will attest,

---

[210] In June 1964, *Detective Comics* #328, editor Julius Schwartz killed off Alfred and later replaced her with Aunt Harriet.

[211] In January 1967, *Detective Comics* #359, at the request of TV producer William Dozier.

[212] *Batman* #217, New York: DC Comics (December 1969).

[213] In the 'Death in the Family' story, originally in *Batman* #426. This Robin was Jason Todd, not Dick Grayson, but the death can still be read as a move to break up the 'couple'.

simply displacement. Bruce and Dick are far too busy gazing soulfully into each other's eyes or quarrelling like tetchy long-term lovers to have time to put their deeper feelings into words.[214]

The comic books, on the other hand, seem to take an approach which recalls the 'love-relationship' and 'subtle atmosphere of homoeroticism' of the 1950s comics more than it does the irony and camp of the 1960s Batwoman stories, the TV series which followed or indeed Schumacher's two feature films.

It would be misleading to suggest a trend here. I have only three examples, and these are of moments within comic books rather than entire stories. The first, a photorealistic 'pin-up' painting of Bruce Wayne stripped of his Batman suit and naked to the waist,[215] could be read as a conventional image of narcissistic straight machismo such as we find in Schwarzenegger or Stallone movies, although I was struck by its lovingly detailed portrayal of the nude male form, at once muscular and vulnerable, and its similarities to the fashion spreads in *Attitude*. The second revisits the death of Robin/Jason Todd, giving us access to Batman's stream of consciousness as he kneels, once more cradling his sidekick in his arms. Again, the scene could be read within the conventional structures of the action genre, where 'buddies' are permitted intimacy only in death; and yet the captions read like a romance.

Part of me recalls him putting on his costume that first time . . . the look on his face . . . his smile . . . as if it were yesterday. That first time, I must keep it alive . . . the memory of it. Alive in my heart so that the memory of this . . . here now . . . doesn't destroy me. We're together at least. One last time together . . . as it should be.[216]

---

[214] Andy Medhurst, review, *Sight and Sound* vol. 7 no. 8 (August 1997).
[215] Alec Ross, portrait in *Batman: Black and White*, New York: DC Comics (1996).
[216] James Robinson and Lee Weeks, 'A Great Day For Everyone', *Legends of the Dark Knight* #100, New York: DC Comics (November 1997).

The third doesn't even feature Batman. Robin, the Boy Wonder, has met Superman for the first time. As they perch on a rooftop, the Man of Steel gazes into the distance for a moment. 'Did I say something stupid?' Robin thinks, asking 'What?' 'Oh, it's nothing,' Superman tells him, still staring off at the city. 'I was thinking it must be nice to have a partner. Someone who understands why we do what we do.' Robin looks up at him and smiles. 'Yeah. It *is* nice.'[217]

Just a moment, and very simple. Yet this suggestion of tenderness and intimacy between Batman and Robin has taken over forty years to creep back into Batman texts without bringing with it nudges of camp or layers of irony. Had Wertham discovered this story in 1953, he would no doubt have cited it within his study as another example of comic books' dangerous potential. That it was published in 1998 by DC Comics, who remain fiercely protective of Batman's image, indicates perhaps that we are beginning to come full circle: that the institution controlling Batman is beginning to accept the gay reading as one of the many various, mutually contradictory but equally valid meanings which the character has gathered over the last sixty years, and recognising that this reading means something to a significant proportion of their market.

As I shall discuss more fully in Chapter 4, the fact that overtones which many readers would surely recognise as mildly homoerotic have been allowed into mainstream Batman titles – albeit those for a 'mature' audience – has a great deal to do with the discourse of authorship which became a significant factor within both Batman comics and films during the late 1980s. Just as Mark Waid, in the *Kingdom Come* comic series, is permitted to show Batman twenty years into the future, and Kelley Jones, in *Red Rain* and *Bloodstorm*, is given leave to draw Batman with absurdly long ears and a jagged cloak, so there seems to be room within DC's current definition of the Batman for James Robinson to hint at a romantic love between Bruce Wayne and Jason Todd.[218] There are limits: Denny O'Neil told me that he

---

[217] Kelly Puckett, Dave Taylor *et al.*, 'Fear of God', *Legends of the DC Universe #6*, New York: DC Comics (July 1998).

[218] While writing this passage I discovered rumours on a fan site that Robinson is himself gay, which would provide support to my reading of 'A Great Day For

could never publish a story which explicitly showed Batman to be gay, for fear of the media backlash.[219] A story like Robinson's, however, or the brief exchange in Kelly Puckett's Robin/Superman episode, presents little such risk but at the same time, in my reading at least, can imply that there is more between Batman and Robin than a buddy–buddy work relationship.

Attempting to deny and censor the 'gay Batman' only made this interpretation more visible; accepting it, and drawing it into the mainstream portrayal of the hero as one facet of his complex cultural persona, can only make the Batman more rounded as a fictional character and richer as a popular icon. Some of his online fans are already espousing this position, rather than the homophobic line of the Internet posts cited above. 'Jim', for instance, responded to my initial enquiry as follows:

> As a heterosexual male, I've always been fascinated by the bunch that worry if Batman is gay. They make it sound like if he was, it would make him less of a hero. Nothing could be further from the truth.[220]

To which 'Harley Quinn' added:

> I am bisexual . . . I have many excellent gay friends, and think Batsy is a role model for EVERYONE!! Young and old, gay and straight, whateva. Anyone who is worried . . . well it's just a sign of their ignorance. What you said about Batman's sexuality is totall right, in every respect. I admire you, and I stand by ya! Welcum to the Bat-Board![221]

Everyone'. The rumour was started by 'Xanadude' with his 'Tacky James Robinson Question', *Jonah Weiland's Comic Book Resources*, http://www.comicbookresources.com (6 December 1998).

[219] Denny O'Neil, personal interview (1 July 1998). O'Neil remains particularly wary of media attention following the overwhelmingly negative reaction to DC's 'Death of Robin' phone poll, which took place under his editorship.

[220] 'Jim', post to *Mantle of the Bat Bat-Board*, http://www.cire.com/batman (May 1997).

[221] 'Harley Quinn', op. cit.

Some forty-five years since *Seduction of the Innocent*, it seems that Batman's producers may also be in the process of accepting that an edge of homoeroticism is integral to Batman's relationship with his sidekick, just as an element of camp is invoked, for many readers, by his costume alone. The reading identified by Wertham has been circulating for almost five decades now, and Batman himself has only been around for six; what began with a few boys in the Quaker Readjustment Center has now become an undeniable and valid part of the character's cultural heritage and will, it seems, never be banished no matter how vehemently some fans and critics attempt to censor it.

3

1961–1969

POP AND CAMP

It went on for a period that could have contained without substantial cuts the whole of an evening's viewing from Batman to Closedown. (Kingsley Amis, *Jake's Thing*, Middlesex: Penguin (1978))

1. Aberration

The ABC television series *Batman*, which ran from 1966[1] until 1968, ranks just below Fredric Wertham in the traditionalist's hierarchy of Batman 'bad objects'. The paunchy, portentous Batman played by Adam West, while rarely cast in the Wertham mould as an enemy of the Bat-mythos, is generally seen by comic fans as a clown whose 'inaccurate' version of the character has unfortunately become the predominant image in the mind of the general, non-comics-reading public. Andy Medhurst notes wryly that for the 'unreconstructed devotee of the Batman . . . the West years had been hell',[2] and quotes from the introductions of various 1980s graphic novels, each of which

---

[1] A feature film spin-off, *Batman*, was released in August 1966.
[2] Andy Medhurst, 'Batman, Deviance and Camp', in Pearson and Uricchio (eds), *The Many Lives of the Batman*, London: Routledge (1991), p. 159.

attempt to define their version of the Batman in explicit contrast to the TV show.

> most of them contain claims such as 'This, I feel, is Batman as he was meant to be.' Where a negative construction is specifically targeted, no prizes for guessing which one it is: 'you . . . are probably also fond of the TV show he appeared in. But then maybe you prefer Elvis Presley's Vegas years or the later Jerry Lewis movies over their early stuff . . . for me, the definitive Batman was then and always will be the one portrayed in these pages.'[3]

Alan Moore, author of several 1980s Batman comics himself, takes the same line in his introduction to Frank Miller's graphic novel *The Dark Knight Returns*, celebrating Miller's achievement in giving new credibility to a character who 'sums up more than any other the essential silliness of the comic book hero'.

> Whatever changes may have been wrought in the comics themselves, the image of Batman most permanently fixed in the mind of the general populace is that of Adam West delivering outrageously straight-faced dialogue while walking up a wall thanks to the benefit of stupendous special effects and a camera turned on its side.[4]

Miller himself in turn distances his later work *Batman: Year One* from the ghosts of the TV show: 'If your only memory of Batman is that of Adam West and Burt Ward exchanging camped-out quips while clobbering slumming guest stars Vincent Price and Cesar Romero, I

---

[3] Ibid., pp. 161–162. Medhurst is quoting Kim Newman and Jonathan Ross respectively from the introductions to *Batman: The Demon Awakes*, London: Titan (1989) and *Batman: Vow From Beyond the Grave*, London: Titan (1989).
[4] Alan Moore, 'Introduction', in Frank Miller, *Batman: The Dark Knight Returns*, London: Titan (1986), n.p.

hope this book will come as a surprise. For me, Batman was never funny.'[5]

In fact, my own copy of *Batman: Year One* bears the signature of Adam West on the page just before this introduction – I bought the volume while waiting for West to make a guest appearance at London's Forbidden Planet bookshop in the late 1980s. The actor arrived in a sleek black vehicle and looked pretty cool to my teenage eyes; which perhaps distinguishes me from many of my fellow comic fans, who seem united with Miller, Moore and 'celebrity' fans like Jonathan Ross in their disdain for the TV series and its cast. Posts from the Internet board of *Mantle of the Bat* frequently criticised the then-forthcoming *Batman and Robin* with reference to the TV series which it seemed, from previews and leaked stills, most to resemble.

> People like [screenwriter] Akiva Goldsman are reverting back to 60's Batman. Will someone tell Warner Brothers that even little kids prefer Darknight Batman compared to CapedCrusader Batman as offered in the 60's.[6]

> I think the problem is that the non-batfans can only identify with the 60's series especially the gadgets, thus they look forward to some kind of 'nostalgia' along with a 90's penchant for special effects . . . the others being more in number than us batfans seem to be getting more of Warners' attention . . . thus anyone who doesn't even care for the Batman as a character would like to see this movie.[7]

> I still don't think Joel Schumacher is the right man as I really hate the campyness of the 60's Batman that seems to be slowly trickling into the 90's series.[8]

---

[5] Frank Miller, 'Introduction', *Batman: Year One*, London: Titan (1988), n.p.
[6] Mike, post to *Mantle of the Bat Bat-Board*, http://www.cire.com/batman (25 February 1997).
[7] Nikhil Soneja, post to *Mantle of the Bat Bat-Board*, ibid. (26 February 1997).
[8] BatDan, post to *Mantle of the Bat Bat-Board*, ibid. (27 February 1997).

I will discuss the reception of Schumacher's two feature films more fully in the next chapter: but note that, firstly, these contributors to the *Bat-Board* see themselves as a distinct group of 'batfans', as opposed to and in many ways alienated from the 'non-batfans' who identify Batman with the 1960s television series rather than the more recent comic books. A powerless elite, these writers seem almost to construct themselves as marginalised unfortunates, helpless in the face of institutional decisions and the preferences of a wider, non-fan audience for the 1960s version of 'their' character. Secondly, we can see even from these brief quotations that the terms in which Schumacher's movies and the 1960s series are criticised echo the comments of Miller, Moore and Ross above: burned-out celebrities in tacky, overblown costumes, 'outrageous' dialogue, absurd situations treated with ludicrous gravity, 'slumming' actors, corny jokes. Miller is the only one who says the word; almost spits it. 'Camped-out'. But it takes Malcolm, the third contributor to the *Bat-Board*, to put all this shared feeling into plain language. 'I really hate the campyness of the 60's Batman . . .'

Just as Wertham is detested by fans for his role in bringing the 'gay Batman' reading into public circulation, so Adam West's TV show is disliked for its part in playing up to that interpretation. Accordingly, the vision of the 'dark' Batman – 'that grim crime fighter driven by an obsession born of tragedy', supposedly a return to Kane's 'original'[9] – of the 1970s and 1980s comics, and to an extent the Tim Burton movies, sought to exorcise the 'camp' Batman of the 1960s show as much as it attempted to banish the 'gay' rumours highlighted by Wertham. Paul Sassienie's version of the story suggests with regard to the 1960s show that 'an unintended side-effect of portraying Batman in this "camp" fashion was the re-emergence of the opinion, originally expressed by Dr Wertham, that Batman and Robin were homosexuals'.[10] Accordingly, Denny O'Neil and Neal Adams' 1970s reworking of the Batman comics is seen by Sassienie as a project to

---

[9] See Mark Cotta Vaz, *Tales of the Dark Knight*, London: Futura (1989), p. 95.
[10] Paul Sassienie, *The Comic Book*, London: Ebury Press (1994), p. 91.

revamp and revitalise . . . to return Batman to his darker, more sinister roots, to shake off the image of the TV show which had trivialised Batman on television and caused a corresponding change in the comics. Adams says, 'We made him a bit more angry than he'd been for a while, a bit more vicious.'[11]

Cotta Vaz provides an echo of this image of Adams and O'Neil as the comic's timely saviours in the conclusion to his chapter on the 1960s Batman: the writer and artist 'came together at this critical juncture to take Batman into his postpop period – and back to his Dark Knight beginnings'.[12] Bob Kane, whose autobiography is relatively open-minded in its attitude towards the TV show and reprints a photo of the author arm-in-arm with a costumed West and Frank 'Riddler' Gorshin, reports in turn that

> I've received many letters from comic book fans who didn't appreciate Batman being parodied in the TV series and thought that he should be taken seriously. The letters of indignation were mainly from young readers; adults seemed to enjoy the campy satire of the show. My own opinion is that it was a marvellous spoof, and great for what it was, but it certainly wasn't the definitive Batman. Since the seventies, those who have worked on the series have returned to my original conception of Batman as a lone, mysterious vigilante.[13]

Again, the 1960s series is camp and not 'the definitive Batman'; that honour goes to the later, 'dark' version of O'Neil, Adams and, in the 1980s, Frank Miller and Alan Moore, whose graphic novels *The Dark Knight Returns* and *The Killing Joke* influenced Tim Burton's 1989 film in both tone and some of its detail. Even a contemporary advertisement for *Batman In The Sixties*, a reprint of selected comics from the period, describes them as 'seventeen tales that transformed Batman from Pop

---

[11] Ibid., p. 95.
[12] Cotta Vaz, op. cit., p. 95.
[13] Bob Kane with Tom Andrae, *Batman and Me*, California: Eclipse Books (1989), p. 135.

Icon to Dark Knight';[14] while 'Pop Icon' allows the TV-era Batman a certain dignity, the transition is still presented as a journey towards the character we recognise from the late 1980s and 1990s, the 'Dark Knight' of Frank Miller's graphic novel.

This distinction between 'camp' and 'dark' Batmen was strikingly enforced by DC's lawyers in 1988, when Adam West was forbidden to wear his home-made, powder-blue Batman outfit for public appearances for fear that his performance would be confused with the forthcoming *Batman* movie from Warner Brothers.[15] The latter was, like the graphic novels cited above, already being defined in explicit contrast to the 1960s show, as James Van Hise confirms in his semi-professional volume *Batmania II* under the heading 'Dark Vs Camp'. It should be noted that, unfortunately, the production values of *Batmania II* do not stretch to pagination.

> Many months before, when Warners had announced *Batman*, a journalist asked one of the producers whether Adam West would be involved, and he responded that the only way Adam West would be involved was when he was invited to a screening of the movie. So the producers were attempting to distance themselves from the sixties TV series right from the start . . .[16]

West himself had apparently expressed bitterness about the new movie and his exclusion from any aspect of its production during an interview on the American show *A Current Affair* in May 1989; Van Hise reports that 'one had the distinct impression that . . . he received an irate phone call from someone at Warner Brothers telling him to knock it off',[17] for his later interviews suggested a far more mellow, resigned attitude. 'I am not the Prince of Darkness', West admitted on *Larry*

---

[14] Advertisement in *Batman Beyond* #1, New York: DC Comics (March 1999).
[15] James Van Hise, *Batmania II*, Las Vegas: Pioneer Books (1992), n.p.
[16] Ibid., n.p.
[17] Ibid., n.p.

King Live in June 1989. 'Wayne Manor is not Bleak House ... I don't think people would expect me, having done the other light-hearted, Captain Blood, Crimson Pirate kind of Batman to do this.'[18]

The divisions, then, are clear, whether we draw them from Malcolm's straight-talking Internet post, Miller's contemptuous dismissal, Sassienie's heavily loaded version of the history or West's shrugging admission. Despite, or perhaps because of the fact that most articles about graphic novels or Tim Burton's movies are still headed with a variant of Robin's 'Holy' exclamation, a 'Biff!' or 'Pow!', fans attempt to construct the 1960s TV Batman as virtually a different character, entirely divorced from the ideal which they see as rooted in the comics. The 1960s TV Batman is the Vegas Elvis, the Crimson Pirate; the comic book Batman – in the texts of the 1970s and 1980s at least – is the 'grim crime fighter', the 'lone, mysterious vigilante', who in turn supposedly harks back to the 'original'.[19] The comics show us the 'definitive' Batman; the TV series is at worst an aberration, at best a trivialisation, a 'spoof',[20] a 'tongue in cheek interpretation',[21] a 'parody',[22] a 'satire'.[23] According to Mark Cotta Vaz, 'the biggest influence the TV show had on the comic book was making Batman a campy, lighthearted figure'.[24] James Van Hise also complains, in his chapter on '60s Silliness', that

the TV Batman and the comic book Batman were never even similar. In order to cash in on the TV series and satisfy new readers brought to the comic book by the TV show, the comic book Batman became a bit campy for about a year ... [but] even at its worst, the comic book version was still more

[18] Ibid., n.p.
[19] Notwithstanding that, according to my research, the 'dark' Batman of Kane and Finger's stories lasted precisely one year, from 1939–1940.
[20] Kane with Andrae, op. cit., p. 135.
[21] Cotta Vaz, op. cit., p. 91.
[22] Ibid., p. 95.
[23] Ibid., p. 91.
[24] Ibid., p. 95.

powerful looking and heroic than the TV Batman, who at times acted like a dunderhead . . . [25]

Never is it ventured that the TV show might have been a fairly straight interpretation of the Batman comic books of the early to mid-1960s, or that elements of camp may have been inherent or evident in the 'original' rather than imposed by TV producers. My investigation below should demonstrate that although the comic did change after the TV show's debut, presumably in order to capture a wider audience, the comic was already exhibiting some aspects of both pop and camp – shockingly vivid colour schemes, tongue-in-cheek dialogue and a dual address to both children and adults – at least a year before the series' debut.

My initial aim in this chapter, then, is to suggest that the relationship between the comic book and TV show is more complex than is often claimed, and that it involved a great deal of interdependence. I will explore the network of influences between comics, television, advertising and art which shaped ABC's Batman as both 'pop' and 'camp', referring to reviews and journalistic materials of the time.

The middle section is based around an examination of eight interpretations which circulated around the show, discussing them in relation to the 'interpretive communities' which produced them and the textual 'evidence' on which they were based; I also analyse the *Batman* text itself in relation to its intertextual surroundings and the framework of generic television conventions within which it operated.

Finally, I return to the 1980s and 1990s to discuss the ways in which West's version of the character has been recalled by significant groups of readers not with suspicion or disdain, as in many of the texts cited above, but in a spirit of fond nostalgia. As was the case with the 'gay' reading above, I will suggest that in the 1990s, mainstream Batman texts such as Joel Schumacher's films have begun to reincorporate elements of the 1960s TV Batman, and that this facet of the character may increasingly be gaining a degree of acceptance

---

[25] Van Hise, op. cit., n.p.

amongst comic book writers, artists and fans as one of many possible
and equally valid interpretations.

2. Genesis

Whatever the complaints of some comic fans, Batman would very
probably never have survived beyond 1965 without the help of the
ABC television series. Bob Kane received the bad news about the title's
flagging sales from DC in that year, and from his own account the
predictions were grave enough to plunge him into an identity crisis.

> My publisher informed me that unless sales picked up the next
> year, it would mean the demise of the Caped Crusader. This
> was one of my darkest periods . . . I had built my whole life on
> drawing Batman and it was the only vocation I knew . . . I was
> studying metaphysics then and had delved into meditation, in
> order to figure out what I could do if *Batman* ended. This was
> an especially disturbing problem because I had always felt that
> Batman and I were one: he was my own wish fulfillment alter
> ego. If he ceased to exist, then, in some sense, I felt that a part
> of me would no longer exist.[26]

According to comic writer Mark Waid, the first issue of *Batman*
published after the TV show's debut sold 'a phenomenal 98% of its
1,000,000 print run'.[27] Within a year the second wave of Batmania,[28]
surpassing the merchandising triumphs of 1940–1943, had swept
America, and the *Batman* comics had more than regained their

---

[26] Kane with Andrae, op. cit., p. 134.
[27] Waid claims the issue in question was *Batman* #180, with a cover date of March
1966. My own notes show that *Batman* #181 bears a June 1966 cover date, so there
may be some inaccuracy here. See Mark Waid interview, http://westwood.fortu-
necity.com/mcqueen/309/waid_part1_master.html (14 January 1999).
[28] The term, of course, echoes 'Beatlemania', and as I note below, the *Batman* TV
show shares its Pop aesthetic with the Beatles movies *A Hard Day's Night* (1964) and
Help! (1965).

buoyancy, apparently doubling their sales during 1966–1967.[29] In the simplest marketing terms, then, the TV show saved the character and his comic book incarnation, which is perhaps what unconsciously galls so many traditionalist fans whether they realise it or not.

The TV *Batman* relied on a public awareness of the comic book, of course, although it subsequently stamped its own image of the character indelibly into popular consciousness, associating 'Batman' forever – for many people – with Adam West's moral homilies and cans of shark repellent. Its own success, however, was due less to the established appeal of the comic book than to the series' promotion and reception as 'camp' and 'pop', two words which at that time were often used interchangeably. As Henry Jenkins and Lynn Spigel note, the Pop Art aesthetic, far from being campily tongue-in-cheek, was originally in deadly earnest;[30] but nevertheless, journalistic discourse of 1966 tended to conflate the two terms[31] when discussing the art of contemporary painters like Andy Warhol and Roy Lichtenstein, whose work characteristically employed a deliberately flat style and bright, garish colour, and whose subject matter often appropriated 'throw-away', ephemeral images from advertising and comic books. This perceived overlap between the two aesthetics would have been enforced by Susan Sontag's influential 'Notes on Camp' of 1964, with its checklist of traits and motifs. Note 56 advises that 'one may compare Camp with much of Pop art, which – when it is not just Camp – embodies an attitude which is related, but still very different.'[32] I will return to Sontag, and to camp's slippery evasion of rigid definition, in section five below.

From one angle, then, this looks like a simple process whereby the TV series, jumping onto the bandwagon of Pop Art, revived a dying comic book title. But the relationship between these three forms – pop, comics and television – was in fact significantly more complex,

---

[29] See Kane with Andrae, ibid., p. 135; Van Hise, op.cit., n.p. and Cotta Vaz, op. cit., pp. 89–91.

[30] Lynn Spigel and Henry Jenkins, 'Mass Culture and Popular Memory', in Pearson and Uricchio, op. cit., pp. 124–125.

[31] See Anon., 'Too Good to be Camp', *New York Times* (23 January 1966).

[32] Susan Sontag, 'Notes on Camp', *Against Interpretation*, New York: Dell (1969); the essay was first published in 1964.

involving a multiplicity of criss-crossing appropriations and re-appropriations, borrowings and borrowings-back.

(i) From comics to Pop, and back again

Pop Art's greatest debt may have been to advertising, but its second most important influence was the comic book. As Spigel and Jenkins neatly summarise, 'Pop revelled in cartoonish characters, cheap industrial tools, gimmicky special effects, a flattened-out and exaggerated use of colour, repetitious imagery, and factory-like production';[33] terms which could, of course, equally be applied to the comic book industry. The first artist of the period to take inspiration from the funny papers was probably Jess Collins, who began his pop-style 'Tricky Cad' collage series – transforming Dick Tracy panels into a surrealist visual anagram – in 1953.[34] Andy Warhol, whose best-known work drew on advertising and celebrity portraiture rather than comics, had also grown up with the Dick Tracy comics which his mother read to him, in a thick Czech accent, when he was ill.[35] He exhibited paintings celebrating Tracy, Superman and Batman in 1960, but abandoned this approach when he saw Lichtenstein's more accomplished work in the same vein.[36] Lichtenstein's enlargements of comic panels were largely taken from the romance and war genre, 'As I Opened Fire' (1964) and 'I Know How You Must Feel, Brad' (1963) providing typical examples.[37] In 1963, Richard Pettibone had used an image of the DC comics hero 'The Flash' in a boxed assemblage, and the previous year Batman had again been the subject of a painting, this

---

[33] Ibid., p. 122.
[34] Jess Collins, 'Tricky Cad (Case VII)' (1959); see Lucy Lippard *et al.*, *Pop Art*, London: Thames and Hudson (1966), p. 145.
[35] Klaus Honnef, *Warhol: Commerce Into Art*, Cologne: Taschen Verlag (1993), p. 14.
[36] 'Oh, why couldn't I have thought of that?' Warhol exclaimed on seeing Lichtenstein's use of Ben Day dots. See Janis Hendrickson, *Lichtenstein*, Cologne: Taschen Verlag (1994), p. 23.
[37] Roy Lichtenstein, 'As I Opened Fire' (1964) and 'I Know How You Must Feel, Brad' (1963); see Hendrickson, ibid., pp. 28–29, 12.

time Mel Ramos' celebration of a chunky 'Photo Ring' (1962).[38] Finally, Warhol returned to the subject in a new medium with his movie *Batman Dracula* of 1964.[39]

Pop Art had, then, gained some of its shock value and daring appeal by elevating the previously maligned form of comics to the 'respectable' status of art: but it went on to indirectly repay the favour as comic books latched onto the coat-tails of this new fad and marketed themselves as tongue-in-cheek entertainment for a knowing college crowd, as well as for the traditional juvenile readership. The colours which had inspired Warhol and Lichtenstein were heightened to even more garish hues of turquoise, cerise and emerald; the cover of *Batman* #171, for instance – which, as we shall see below, acquired great significance in March 1965 – has the Riddler in his lime green costume spinning madly against a shocking pink background. Compare with Warhol's 'fauve' Campbell's cans (1965) in arbitrary, clashing shades rather than the authentic red and white,[40] or with Klaus Honnef's account of Warhol's 'pistachio green or bright orange' colour schemes from the early 1960s.[41]

The comic book sound-effects which Pop had echoed in its privileging of word-as-image – in Robert Indiana's 'USA/EAT', 'USA/HUG' slogans and Edward Ruscha's canvas dominated by the 'SPAM' logo,[42] as well as in Lichtenstein's massive 'Whaam' (1963), 'Torpedo . . . Los!' (1963) and 'Takka Takka' (1962)[43] – were also played up, enlarged and exaggerated. In keeping with what was seen by audiences, if not artists, as Pop's sense of camp irony, the comic writers threw in more alliteration, more wordplay and more of the clunky dialogue familiar from Lichtenstein's panels – 'Why, Brad, darling, this painting

---

[38] Richard Pettibone, 'Flash' (1962–1963); Mel Ramos, 'Photo Ring' (1962); see Lippard, op. cit., pp. 146–147.

[39] Starring Baby Jane Holzer, according to the *Internet Movie Database, http://us.imdb.com;* interestingly, this experiment with two cultural icons predated the *Batman/Dracula* prestige comic book by almost thirty years.

[40] See Lippard, ibid., p. 93.

[41] Honnef, op. cit., p. 22.

[42] Robert Indiana, 'USA 666' (1964), Edward Ruscha, 'Actual Size' (1962); see Lippard, op. cit., pp. 123, 150.

[43] See Hendrickson, pp. 22, 23, 20.

is a *masterpiece* . . .'[44] – presumably in the hope that the motto 'so bad it's good', which had worked so well for Pop Art based on comics, would prove equally successful for comic art based on Pop. As Batman was the Caped Crusader, so his colleague the Elongated Man was referred to as the 'Malleable Manhunter'[45] or the 'Stretching Sleuth';[46] not just by editors, but by readers who shared the joke and submitted their own contribution to the comics' new letter-columns.

While many fans would now claim that the campy penchant for puns in Batman comics was an unhappy result of the TV series, a letter published in *Batman* #174, commenting on the Riddler issue cited above, indicates that the tendency started a long while before, and that it was popular with at least one contemporary reader:

> I am a great lover of the pun. Over the years, Robin has been noted for his wild puns but I doubt that the Boy Wonder was ever punnier than he was in this issue. The Riddler should have been returned to the punitentiary instead of the penitentiary! I guess my favorite pun was 'vile inn' . . . but I also 'pealed' with laughter over the orange-bell riddle . . . I thought Robin displayed good horse sense when he decided to 'stirrup' some trouble.[47]

That the reappropriation and exaggeration of the conventions Pop had borrowed from comics hit its mark is further suggested by a letter in *Detective Comics* #331 of September 1964. The writer is Joan Kassman, a female college student – far outside the comics' traditional demographic – who confesses she bought the title 'as a joke' but found it 'enjoyable for a much larger audience than just the children who take it seriously'.[48] Already, then, there existed an ironic, dual

---

[44] Roy Lichtenstein, 'Masterpiece' (1962); see Hendrickson, op. cit., p. 14.

[45] Dee Sloan, letter in *Detective Comics* #336, New York: DC Comics (February 1965).

[46] Kenneth S. Gallagher, letter in *Detective Comics* #336, ibid.

[47] John Pierce, letter in *Detective Comics* #174, New York: DC Comics (September 1965).

[48] Joan Kassman, letter in *Detective Comics* #331, New York: DC Comics (September 1964).

address in circulation around Batman, some fifteen months before the launch of the TV series; and it is confirmed by similar letters, such as the complaint from twenty-five members of Humboldt State College, California, that Batman had used the incorrect symbol 'A' for the chemical Argon. 'How do you expect the inquiring youth of today, such as ourselves, to obtain a greater amount of scientific knowledge from your publications, when only a closed door awaits our enquiry?'[49]

This sense of irony, camp and polysemy was identified by another reader, a man in his late fifties who had never read a comic book before. As it happens, he would have read exactly this letter, just as his eye would have been caught by the pink and green image of the Riddler described above. The man's name was William Dozier, and in March 1965 he picked up a copy of *Batman* at an airport comic stand.[50] Dozier was a veteran TV producer, responsible for *Bewitched* and *Dennis The Menace*; ABC had recently optioned Batman for a possible new series, and asked Dozier if he wanted to take the helm.

(ii) From comics to TV, and back again

Gerard Jones, in *Tales of the Comic-Book Heroes*, imagines Dozier's train of thought:

> A superhero TV show? It could happen, with the right hook. It couldn't hurt to kill a few minutes on a plane reading this Batman with this wild-looking character, the Riddler on the cover. There was a look here . . . It was Pop Art, it was Lichtenstein. And the writing inside was . . . well, not like the old way of writing for kids, it was . . . kooky. Riddles, puns on every page. This stuff could be hilarious if it was read the right

[49] Members of Humboldt State College, letter, *Batman* #171, New York: DC Comics (May 1965).
[50] See Van Hise, op. cit., n.p.; Cotta Vaz, op. cit., p. 90; Joel Eisner, *The Official Batman Batbook*, London: Titan (1987), p. 8; and Gerard Jones and Will Jacobs, *The Comic Book Heroes*, California: Prima (1997), p. 96.

way. It could be . . . high camp. And high camp was happening. Susan Sontag said so.[51]

Of course, Jones' interior monologue is imaginary, written with a sly hindsight especially in its reference to Sontag: but whatever form his musings took, it's a fact that on 12 January 1966, less than a year after Dozier settled in with a comic book on that plane flight, Batman made its debut screening on American television.

It goes without saying that the TV series drew on the comic books for its main characters and many secondary figures, as well as for its settings, iconography and visual style. But it also fed back into the comics to an extent which raises significant issues about the power balance between the 'TV' and the 'comic book' Batman.

It is difficult to reconstruct the exact nature of the relationship between comic book editor Julius Schwartz and the show's producer William Dozier, and by extension between the institutions they represented; DC, in Schwartz's case, and in Dozier's the joint interests of ABC Television, co-producers 20th Century Fox and his own Greenaway Productions.[52] My analysis here and throughout, as I stress below, is based on filling in the gaps and drawing connections between scattered textual clues. From the circumstantial evidence I do possess, though, I conclude that the substantial changes to the comic book Batman during 1966–1967 – in terms of design, dialogue, narrative and character – did serve to make this Batman more similar to the TV character and his aesthetic. In cases like the reintroduction of Batgirl and the return of Alfred, we can confirm from interviews that William Dozier was expressly behind the change. In other instances, such as the comic books' gradual incorporation of 'holy' gags and 'go-go' references, we can only say that the connection between comic and TV show seems very likely. With regard to the exaggerated 'biffs' and full-page fight scenes which appeared in Batman comics during the TV show's run, we can suggest that Dozier's series may well have been one of the influences, with the proviso that *Detective*'s similarity to the

---

[51] Jones and Jacobs, ibid., p. 96.
[52] The show was co-produced by Greenaway and 20th for ABC, according to James Van Hise, op. cit., n.p.

TV aesthetic in this respect may have been a convenient side-effect of DC's move towards Pop styling across all its titles.

We cannot make the easy assumption that ABC or Dozier had DC over a barrel during this period. According to DC's librarian Alan Asherman, who was with the company in the 1960s, DC kept a close rein on the TV series continuity, and forbade transgression of the character's 'rules'. While this seems paradoxical given the show's reputation as a 'corruption' of the comic book, Asherman suggests that the rules enforced pertained more to the fundamental Batman template than to issues of style, dialogue and tone. The TV Batman had to remain upright and moral, he was not permitted to use a gun, and he was not allowed to kill or cause the death of another.

It is intriguing to see which aspects of the character were regarded by DC as sacrosanct and which were open to change during this historical moment – Batman could be portrayed as a pedantic buffoon, as long as he never turned to crime – though again we should bear in mind that the comic books of the early 1960s had already embraced elements of comedy, dual address and self-consciousness, and had exhibited Pop and camp tendencies before the TV series was even in development. It should also be noted that DC did have cause to enforce their own vision of the Batman upon the ABC series, at a very early stage, and that Dozier bowed to it: Batman was originally to have deliberately allowed Jill St John to fall to her death in the first episode, but the comic book editors ruled that he must be powerless to save her.[53] The power relationship between these institutions was, then, not entirely one-sided; DC had not signed away the rights to their character and his representation, and were not legally bound to accept whatever changes Dozier proposed.

Remember, though, that the Batman comic books were – despite their clutching at Pop 'respectability' during the early 1960s – still in severe danger of folding, while the Batman TV show was a commercial success from its first screening. As I have already noted, and will stress again, the process was by no means a straightforward one of single cause and effect; yet it seems that DC's editors did not see any cause to argue with Dozier's quite significant suggestions for the comic. We can

---

[53] Allan Asherman, personal conversation (29 June 1998).

also safely assume that the increased continuity between TV series and comic book would have had significant benefits for DC in terms of attracting and maintaining an increased readership, and that this must have affected DC's decision to go along with the ABC series in terms of tone, style, characterisation and dialogue. In effect, then, I am proposing that the Batman comic books of 1966–1967 were subtly and gradually rebranded and marketed not just as Pop artefacts but as adaptations of the TV series, echoing and advertising Dozier's show just as the show boosted sales of the comic: once more, a complex cycle of mutually advantageous appropriation.

Barbara Gordon, the second Batgirl – alias Barbara Gordon, studying a 'PhD at Gotham State University'[54] – was written into the comic narrative with *Detective* #359 of January 1967. This addition was made by Julius Schwartz, then-editor of the Batman titles, at the explicit request of Dozier, who wanted to bring her into the TV series as a female interest[55] and as a new sop to those persistent rumours that the TV Batman and Robin, like their comic book counterparts, were gay;[56] she debuted, played by Yvonne Craig, in the first episode of the TV show's third season, aired on 14 September of that year.[57]

Alfred the butler, who had been killed off in the comics, was also brought back at Dozier's request – a twist which involved him losing his memory and returning as the mysterious 'Outsider' during 1966. Henry Goldman, a contributor to the letter-column of *Detective* #349, accurately guesses the Outsider's true identity months before it is due to be revealed, and the editor's reply – while refusing to give the guessing-game away – makes Dozier's backroom influence over significant details of the comic book's cast and plot fairly clear. 'Despite Alfred's "demise" in *Detective* #328, he will appear in the Batman-TV series, slated to start in January over the ABC television network. Check your newspaper TV listing for details.'[58] Julius

---

[54] 'The Million Dollar Debut of Batgirl!', *Detective Comics* #359, New York: DC Comics (January 1967).

[55] See Cotta Vaz, op. cit., p. 91.

[56] See Sassienie, op. cit., p. 91.

[57] Eisner, op. cit., p. 136.

[58] Henry Goldman, letter, *Detective Comics* #349, New York: DC Comics (March 1966).

Schwartz's recollection of the exchange between himself and the ABC producers strongly suggests that Dozier and his colleagues, in this instance – or by this stage – held the balance of power. 'It became a very difficult situation when they ... wanted Alfred there and they wanted me to bring him back ... I said, "But he's dead!" They said, "You can think of a way".'[59]

Ironically, Alfred had been written out of the comics, according to Cotta Vaz, as another victim of the post-Wertham clean-up campaign, 'a sacrificial offering to all the whispers about three single men living in a millionaire's manse'.[60] Eventually Dick Grayson's Aunt Harriet, who had first appeared in the TV show, moved across into the comic books to look after the two bachelors and presumably to provide DC with yet more insurance against accusations of latent homosexuality.

Batman comics of 1966 ran full-page ads for Dozier's series inside the front cover, selling the characters and the company on the back of the TV show's success. 'Top TV Comic Stars Come From DC – The House of Hits', boasts one ad from *Batman* #181, June 1966. 'Pow! On ABC TV ... Batman and Robin in Color!' That 'Pow!' motif, which had been lifted straight from the comics to the TV series to give the latter a comic-book 'look', was now being used, paradoxically, to link the comic book back to the successful show. As Julius Schwartz later confessed: 'As long as it was popular on television, we said, "Let's do it in comics, too!"'[61] A glance at the comics of that year shows what he means: a parade of fight scenes punctuated with BIFF-BAM-POW effects, a portentous narrational style in the manner of Dozier's TV voiceover, attempts to squeeze in what one reader called 'a pun a panel'[62] – 'I'll give him something to "chair" him up', announces Batman, swinging said article of furniture at a villain[63] – and editorial boasts that the stories are 'as unrealistic as camp'.[64] Even the addition of 'go-go' checks to the cover of every DC title during 1966 –

[59] Cotta Vaz, op. cit., p. 94.

[60] Ibid.

[61] Ibid., p. 95.

[62] Mike Friedrich, letter, *Batman* #181, New York: DC Comics (June 1966).

[63] Ibid.

[64] Ibid.

and titles like 'Batman's Crime-Hunt a Go-Go!'[65] – can be seen as a homage to Adam West's solemn commentary on the fall of Jill St John in the TV show's first episode: 'What a way to go-go'.[66]

Robin had, to the best of my knowledge and in the opinion of James Van Hise,[67] never used the phrase 'Holy Fourth Amendment', 'Holy Interplanetary Yardstick', 'Holy Hole-In-A-Donut'[68] or any variations thereon in the pre-1966 comics. This 'affectation', as Hise calls it, was not overused in the comic books, but it crops up enough to suggest the books' debt to the TV show for their tone, style, conventions and, we can surmise, much of their recently doubled readership. In *Detective* #353, Robin cries 'Holy Sparklers' about a cache of jewels, and 'Holy Jets' with reference to the Batmobile's speed. This latter instance raised the hackles of a contributor to #356's lettercol, the issue where Alfred finally returned from his exile. The letter, from Rick Wood in Los Angeles, is worth quoting in full as an early example of fan resistance against interpretations imposed from above.

> The reason I didn't like it is one line on page 6, where Robin says 'Holy Jets!' Not only is this not particularly inspired dialog, it is not the sort of thing 'our' Robin says. This is an expression that 23 year-old teen-ager who plays Robin on TV uses. Batman in the comics is *not* so bad that he is good. He is just plain good in the first place. He's been around for almost 30 years. 'Camp' has only been around for one or two years, and already every article on the subject predicts that the fad will vanish in a couple of months. Batman will still be around long after 'camp' is gone, unless he starts trying to be so bad he's good – and winds up so bad he's gone.[69]

---

[65] *Detective Comics* #353, New York: DC Comics (June 1966).

[66] See Eisner, op. cit., p. 17.

[67] Van Hise, op. cit., n.p.

[68] See Eisner, op. cit., pp. 167–171.

[69] Rick Wood, letter, *Detective Comics* #356, New York: DC Comics (October 1966).

The editor's reply is brief and feeble: 'Because Robin doesn't age comics-wise doesn't mean he can't change with the times. So for the present he's going to camp along with the trend.' For the present: that is, while a substantial proportion of *Detective*'s readers were picking it up because of West and Ward, and would – a DC editor might well assume – only keep buying it if they found it to be an adaptation of their favourite show, complete with one-liners and catchphrases. Comic spin-offs from TV series had been running since 1950, with *I Love Lucy*, *Sergeant Bilko* and *Jackie Gleason* faithfully reproducing the gags of the original shows; it seems reasonable to hypothesise that the *Batman* viewer coming to *Detective* for the first time would have expected the comic to fall into this readily accessible genre, rather than being prepared to catch up with long-running narratives and learn the arcana of the Bat-mythos in order to enjoy the title.

Rick Wood was, however, not the only fan to dislike the comics' shift to cater for a wider audience. Gary Collins writes, the following year:

> What is wrong with the TV series? I can sum it up in one word – *Camp!* You see, Batman was always the most believable of your heroes . . . however, the TV show is actually a parody of Batman. The producers admit they are only making fun of Batman. After watching a few of these shows, I was disappointed with it. But I still look forward to your mags. Then I had a horrible thought. What if you copied its camp style? And soon my fears were realized. The . . . main things I noticed were:
> 1. The use of such expressions as Holy Jitters and Holy Wanted Posters! Such expressions are not only ridiculous, but very unrealistic.
> 2. The overexaggerated POWS and OOFS cluttering up the fighting scenes, and the awkward position of clobbered thugs.[70]

Of course, Batman comics had always included fight scenes with visual sound effects, and the set-piece combats of every TV episode made

---

[70] Gary Collins, letter, *Batman* #189, New York: DC Comics (February 1967).

explicit reference to this comic book convention: but the comics of
1966 actually abandon the frame-by-frame storytelling format for the
whole-page 'splash' panel. While I've already indicated that it would
be a mistake to assume a unidirectional causality behind every aesthetic
shift within Batman titles of this period – giant panels rather than
smaller grids recall Lichtenstein and Warhol's oversized enlargements,
after all, and thus provide another example of comic book design
feeding back from Pop – this change also enabled Batman comics better
to approximate the fight scenes of the TV show, which made extensive
use of long shots to show a whole roomful of pugilistic action. Rather
than the grid format unique to comic book narrative, then, we are
given oversized tableaux laden with captions like 'OOF! POW!!
POW! SOCK! KRAK! THUD! ULLG!'[71] Even the typography of
these pages, with their array of 'SOCK', 'RRUNCH' and 'BOP'
almost taking precedence over the pictures of Batman and Robin,
seems to deliberately emulate the visual effects of the TV show.[72]
When a simple advertisement for the Hawkman strip in *Detective* #353
has to be headed with a massive 'WHEET!' and 'CAW!', it is fairly
clear that the sound-effects trend has extended beyond the mere visual
conventions of the fight scene.

   Batman and Robin even seem to make a wryly knowing joke about
the comics' direct lifting from TV in one adventure from late 1966: as
they climb a wall sideways in the manner of West and Ward, Robin
wisecracks 'Shouldn't we have music for this act?' Batman, ever the
sensible mentor, replies 'Shh!'[73] Few moments in *Batman* ever reach
the level of intertextuality shown in the backup strip, 'The Elongated
Man', where the hero's wife gasps 'It wo-wo-worked – just like for
that gal in that *Bewitched* TV program!'[74] *Batman* #183, however,
contains a remarkable episode in terms of its self-conscious
incorporation of the TV show into Batman's 'real' world, explaining
the show as a factual report of Batman's life. On the cover, Batman is
lounging in an easy chair with a bottle of pop, watching 'The

----

[71] See *Batman* #186, New York: DC Comics (November 1966).
[72] See *Batman* #181, op. cit.
[73] *Batman* #188, New York: DC Comics (January 1967).
[74] *Detective Comics* #348, New York: DC Comics (February 1966).

Adventures of Batman'. Inside, Robin explains that the show is a 'TV documentary about you and some of your greatest adventures!' Although the Batman who would rather watch the tube than answer an urgent call from Gordon turns out to be an imposter, it is stressed that the real Batman is the fellow who appears in the TV show, which in Batman's diegesis has become a 'documentary'. Bat-fans would probably already have seen, that very month, a TV commercial for ABC's fall season which also featured Batman and Robin watching their own show, with Robin commenting 'look, our own daring adventures are on twice a week, just like last season!';[75] the comic book story precisely echoes this moment of self-reflexivity.

If any doubts remained in the reader's mind, they are laid to rest by Batman's account of his escape from the lookalike's trap: 'I did the Batusi on that netting'. The reference to another defining moment of the TV series' first episode, Adam West's improvised disco dance at the nightclub, cleverly indicates that the two Batmen from TV and comics are in fact, as far as the producers were concerned, one and the same.[76]

(iii) From Pop to TV, and back again

The cycle of appropriation and cross-reference came full circle when the TV series in turn marketed itself as both camp entertainment – amply demonstrated by the poster for the full-length movie spin-off of August 1966, with its slogan 'Men Die! Women Sigh! Beneath that Batcape – He's All Man!'[77] – and as an extension of the Pop aesthetic. This latter promotional strategy played up the marked visual similarities between the series' *mise-en-scène* – with its orange and chartreuse backdrops and coloured gels over the lights,[78] and the animated sound effects – and the best-known Pop devices such as Warhol's day-glo palette and Lichtenstein's explosive captions.

---

[75] See Van Hise, op. cit. n.p.
[76] See *Batman* #183, New York: DC Comics (August 1966).
[77] Reprinted in Van Hise, op. cit., n.p.
[78] See Van Hise, ibid., n.p.

The sound effects were a genuine innovation and represented quite a financial investment for the producers; costs for the original opticals were 'astronomical', according to post-production coordinator Robert Mintz, and even when it was decided that the effects should instead be cut in rather than superimposed, the show remained expensive.[79] We must also remember that for a TV show to be in 'full color' at all spoke of a deliberate stylistic choice in 1966, and *Batman* made the most of its available palette. Indeed, it would be very difficult to imagine 1966's *Batman* in black and white, and I think it very doubtful that the series would have had anything like the same effect. James Van Hise rambles badly on this theme, but makes the point clearly enough:

> *Batman* was very colorful and very visual for its day. ABC had only had color television shows for about three years at that point, so it was still very experimental. *Batman* exploited color to its fullest advantage . . . the approach to color on the *Batman* series, which was decidedly different from many other color shows of the time, also helped give it a comic book appearance. They used the tilted angles and the bubbles with the POW! and WHAM! signs because that was something that made you think of a comic book. On *The Lone Ranger* or some of the superhero shows which preceded *Batman* you didn't consciously think of it as a comic book. When you watched it, you watched it like a regular TV drama. Dozier and his team wanted that mixture because the Pop Art craze was so big. So it all fit and the timing was perfect.[80]

The move to cash in on Pop was exemplified by ABC's decision to invite the artists of the moment themselves to celebrate the show's launch at a 'cocktail and frug party' in a New York discotheque.[81] The premiere episode was subsequently screened to Warhol, Lichtenstein and their followers in a hotel adorned with Bob Kane artwork, which

---

[79] Eisner, op. cit., p. 10.
[80] Ibid., n.p.
[81] Spigel and Jenkins, op. cit., p. 123.

in turn was labelled 'authentic pop art'.[82] Spigel and Jenkins confirm that 'ABC used the Pop aesthetic as a promotional and publicity vehicle, giving the show cultural status by hyberbolically referring to its Warholian aspects.'[83]

So Pop Art had copied from Batman comics, and Batman comics had copied from Pop Art; Dozier's series adapted the comic book, which then adapted itself further to surf the popularity of the series: and as one reviewer put it in May 1966, the sum of this borrowing was that 'the pop art fad . . . made Batman almost flopproof'.[84]

The TV Batman, then, was born from a whole kaleidoscope of discourses around art, pop, comics and camp. This genesis is fairly straightforward, though, compared to what happened when audiences got their hands on the series. Batman had been intended as a polysemic text, with an appeal on two levels; in the event it was read on levels which William Dozier could never have imagined.

3. Readings

(i) Adults and children

First, there was the twin address actually intended by Dozier, which he explains as follows:

> I had just the simple idea of overdoing it, of making it so square and so serious that adults would find it amusing. I knew kids would go for the derring-do, the adventure, but the trick would be to find adults who would either watch it with their kids, or, to hell with the kids, and watch it anyway.[85]

Even allowing for the alienation of those viewers on the cusp between

---

[82] Ibid.; see also Adam West with Jeff Rovin, *Back to the Batcave: My Story*, London: Titan (1994), p. 87.

[83] Spigel and Jenkins, ibid.

[84] Ibid., p. 124.

[85] Eisner, op. cit., p. 6.

the child and teenage audience – Dozier states elsewhere that twelve- and thirteen-year-olds neither took the show seriously, nor found it funny[86] – this was a pretty impressive demographic, and there was obviously a sound economic logic behind such an approach. As I've already stated, my research method tends towards reconstructing institutions and audiences from textual analysis, rather than trusting in statistics and figures, but there is no doubt that the institutional matrix[87] of 1960s broadcasting had an important role in the aesthetic and style of the Batman series.

Briefly, the American Broadcasting Company, which produced the show, was in direct competition with its longer-standing rivals NBC and CBS. In the face of falling ratings, and informed by the increasing perception of a segmented television audience, ABC had begun to actively court the younger market.[88] The emerging 'teen-age' audience, which was being recognised as a powerful consumer group with both disposable income and the capacity to make or break style trends,[89] was drawn in the early 1960s by girl-centred comedies like ABC's *Patty Duke Show* (1963), and subsequently by the new gimmick-based sit-coms such as *Bewitched, I Dream of Jeannie, The Addams Family, My Favorite Martian* and *My Mother The Car*. In many respects, Batman fits neatly into this established form of what Lynn Spigel calls the 'fantastic sit-com',[90] with the gimmick that the main character was not a witch, a genie or a Martian, but a superhero; it should be noted that the show was Emmy-nominated in 1966 both for Outstanding Comedy Series[91] and for Best Supporting Actor in a Comedy Series, the latter honour going to Frank Gorshin.[92] I shall examine *Batman*'s place alongside other contemporary TV series in more detail below.

---

[86] Van Hise, op. cit., n.p.

[87] See Janice Radway, *Reading the Romance*, Chapel Hill: University of North Carolina Press (1991), particularly pp. 19–45.

[88] Julie D'Acci, 'Nobody's Woman? *Honey West* and the New Sexuality', in Spigel and Curtin (eds), *The Revolution Wasn't Televised*, London: Routledge (1997), p. 80.

[89] See James Gilbert, *A Cycle of Outrage*, Oxford: Oxford University Press (1986), particularly pp. 196–211.

[90] Lynn Spigel, 'White Flight', in Spigel and Curtin, op. cit., p. 58.

[91] Eisner, op. cit., p. 73.

[92] Van Hise, op. cit., n.p.

But despite ABC's promising track record in garnering the teen audience and gaining a 'swinging' reputation,[93] by 1965 the other networks had caught up, and the launch of *Batman* in January 1966 was a calculated gamble. A news report of the time refers to the show as 'the smash that ABC damn well needs'.[94] Dozier knew that if the series only attracted the traditional comics readership, aged from eight to fourteen, it would prove too expensive to run.[95] True, there was already strong evidence that shows could pull twice the viewing figures through a dual address. ABC had successfully followed in Warner Brothers' footsteps with its animated sit-coms *The Flintstones* (1960–65) and *The Jetsons* (1962–63), which were enjoyed by kids for their slapstick humour and by adults on a more satirical level,[96] while shows like *Dennis The Menace* (1959–63) and *Gunsmoke* (1961–75) were recognised by both series writers and audiences as offering different pleasures across the generation gap.[97] More specifically, a generic precedent for tongue-in-cheek detective series had been established by the James Bond films, *I Spy*, *Get Smart* and NBC's smash *Man From UNCLE*, which had managed to attract the much-sought 'egghead set' of 'young, college educated adults' the previous year.[98] A 1966 poster for the *Batman* feature would later make knowing reference to this tradition, with its slogan 'In an age of super-spies . . . super-lovers . . . and super-men . . . make way for Batman who makes the others look like kid stuff!'[99]

Yet despite the success of this genre ABC's most recent venture along the same lines, the female private-eye show *Honey West*, had flopped despite wearing its 'camp, satirical and pop characteristics'[100] on its sleeve. Batman's proposed dual address, then, was far more than just a whimsical, stylistic choice; it was a careful economic decision.

---

[93] D'Acci, op. cit., p. 87.

[94] Anon., 'Too Good to be Camp', *New York Times* (23 January 1966).

[95] Van Hise, op. cit., n.p.

[96] Spigel and Jenkins, op. cit., p. 125.

[97] Ibid., p. 123; Horace Newcomb, 'From Old Frontier to New Frontier', in Spigel and Curtin, op. cit., p. 288.

[98] D'Acci, op. cit., p. 80.

[99] Van Hise, op. cit., n.p.

[100] D'Acci, op. cit., p. 80.

It is never possible to guarantee that the 'authorial meaning', or 'intended reading' of any text will be echoed by the audience interpretation, but in this case there was a remarkably good fit between Dozier's stated intention and the manner in which the show was received by both critics and audiences. Any number of reviews could be quoted to make the point; *Time* reported that while children took him seriously, adults were 'supposed to see Batman as camp',[101] while the *Saturday Evening Post* claimed that 'Batman watching families with eight year-olds in them are torn with dissention because of the ' "Daddy, stop laughing" problem'.[102] Finally, Newsweek explained that 'Adults like [Batman] as a campy put-on. Children thought of him as a hero.'[103] The match between producers' stated intentions and critics' initial response could hardly be tighter if William Dozier had written the reviews himself.

(ii) Comedy

I still feel a slight jolt of misrecognition when I read that *Batman* was Emmy-nominated for Best Comedy in 1966: part of me wonders if the panel somehow made a mistake, chose the wrong genre or the wrong show. I feel strangely put out, suddenly discovering that the joke was on me back in the 1970s; that something had been going way over my head since well before my time. I was one of the 'Daddy, stop laughing' viewers, enjoying *Batman* as, I think, a six-year-old when the show was repeated in Britain. I didn't think it was funny when Batman announced that he'd resisted King Tut's hypnosis by reciting his times tables backwards;[104] I thought it was pretty impressive. I didn't think it was funny when the Neal Hefti theme kicked in and the Dynamic Duo went into POW! THWOK! action; I jumped up myself and started play-fighting my little brother. But then, I didn't think it was funny

---

[101] See Spigel and Jenkins, op. cit., p. 124.
[102] Ibid.
[103] Ibid.
[104] In, I think, episode #42, 'Tut's Case is Shut', first screened 29 September 1966.

when my friend Nathan and I ran down our road with our pants over our corduroy trousers and cardboard ears sewn onto the hoods of our coats.

Because of this I think I know how Bob Kane and William Dozier felt when they discovered their 'straight' creation was being read as a gay romance – obscurely possessive, a little wounded, a little foolish. Because of this, for me to read *Batman* as a comedy is similar in some ways to my reading of the comics as 'gay': my interpretation must be based on a reconstruction of intertextual frameworks and an attempt to place myself in a specific historical and cultural viewing position, drawing only partly on first-hand experience. As an adult watching the series for this research, I found *Batman* divinely funny: but I can still very much remember what it was like to idolise the Caped Crusader on those streets of mid-Seventies Charlton. As such, perhaps I write this section in what Jenkins and Spigel call 'a liminal state', positioned 'somewhere in between child and adult'.[105] Yet while the adults in Spigel and Jenkins' discussion groups – as I shall explore below – forget the show's ambiguities to the extent that they deny ever viewing it as serious, even as schoolchildren,[106] my own reading is far from unique among British critics of the 1990s.

Virtually every reviewer who turned their attention to the British repeats of *Batman* – which was screened regularly during the 1990s, having gained unprecedented ratings when it replaced *TV-am* for several months in 1988[107] – held the programme in a dual vision, harking back to their earlier reading while retaining an 'objective' adult distance. Craig Brown, in the *Sunday Times*, admits that 'as a child, I watched it on tenterhooks, fretting overnight as to how Batman and Robin would escape from that week's deathly conveyor-belt, longing to tune in at the same Bat-time tomorrow. Nearly thirty years on, I find myself laughing out loud at the jokes I would have missed as a child ... girls spooning caviare into their mouths out of large jars marked "CAVIARE" '.[108] Similarly, Allison Pearson 'loved this

---

[105] Spigel and Jenkins, op. cit., p. 142.
[106] Ibid., p. 133.
[107] See Van Hise, op. cit., n.p.
[108] Craig Brown, *Sunday Times Review* (22 August 1993).

series as a child for its rococo alliterations . . . and voluminous camp, which swept me up in jokes I suspected I didn't understand. How right I was. Archer and his boys make their get-away in "the Trojan Hearse".'[109] Victor Lewis-Smith, writing one year after Pearson and two after Brown, echoes their double-edged enjoyment almost precisely. 'As a child, I used to cheer as the dynamic duo routed the forces of evil, and didn't comprehend the rumours I'd heard of smart men in City pubs roaring with laughter at the show. Aged seven, I knew that Gotham City was really New York, but only much later did the penny drop: it's also the City of Fools.'[110]

Of course, it is never easy to say why something is funny, and attempting to do so always risks the kill-joy effect of analysing that humour to death. However, one scene – in fact, one speech – from the episode 'Deep Freeze', which is also discussed by Medhurst,[111] illustrates for me most of the key elements of *Batman*'s comedy. Batman and Robin have been framed by Mr Freeze for the 'theft' of Commissioner Gordon's watch. The two heroes are in the Bat-Cave with Alfred, planning their next move. In an attempt to convey the full effect of Adam West's performance, I shall reproduce all his significant tics and mannerisms as pauses, stresses and stage directions here; the reader will also have to imagine him in full costume, a man in his late thirties[112] in grey tights and matching top, a glossy deep blue cape and a cowl with dinky ears and arch, painted-on eyebrows. The transcription begins with the three characters shown in long-shot.

ROBIN: What do we do now?

BATMAN: . . . The only thing we . . . *can* do, Robin . . . [walks slowly forward, staring into mid-air] . . . hang up . . . our capes . . . and cowls.

---

[109] Allison Pearson, *Independent on Sunday* (1 May 1994).

[110] Victor Lewis-Smith, *Evening Standard* (13 July 1995).

[111] Medhurst, op. cit., p. 149.

[112] West says he was thirty-two when he was cast for Batman; see West with Rovin, op. cit., p. 13. James Van Hise, however, gives his birthdate as 1928, which would make West thirty-eight during the first year of the show's broadcast. See Van Hise, op. cit., n.p.

[CU: BATMAN gazing into space]

BATMAN [cont]: . . . with all this . . . adverse publicity it might be . . . *well* [narrows eyes shrewdly] to let the people . . . think what they *will* [jogs gently on his heels] . . . that we've . . . taken a *'run-out'* . . . powder. That way, maybe we can lull Mr *Freeze* into a [rubs chin, struck by thought] false sense of *security* [gestures with finger] . . . make him . . . overplay his hand, [speeds up rapidly] after all I'm sure he believes [grimace, crosses hands over chest as if cold] that we're

LS of Batman, Robin, Alfred

BATMAN [cont]: Frosty Freezes by now!

ALFRED: You were most ingenious in preventing that, sir!

BATMAN: Thank you, Alfred! [raises one finger, turns] But it will take *more* ingenuity! [wags finger as he walks back to Alfred and Robin] to get us back in the good *graces* of the good *people* of Gotham . . . [turns again, fingers steepled] *City*.

[Dramatic music fades up]

BATMAN [cont]: Aunt *Harriet* [wags finger] asked us to go into the *city* [to Robin, urgently, wagging finger] on an *errand*! [more softly] . . . as Bruce Wayne and Dick Grayson. [to Robin, intimately] Remember?

ROBIN: Mm.

[They turn and walk leisurely out of shot, as dramatic music builds][113]

---

[113] 'Deep Freeze', episode #54, first screened 10 November 1966.

The main ingredients in this comedy lie, I think, in the practice Medhurst identifies at the heart of Batman's suitability for camp: being serious about the ludicrous. Perhaps the outstanding element, which might not have even been realised at the time but is clear to a reader of his autobiography, is that West didn't mean his performance to be comic at all. He thought he was a good actor investing richness into a culturally-important, iconic role.[114] He was proud of his little inflections and of the use he made of gestures to add expression, overcoming what he saw as the drawback of having half his face hidden.

> I told Bill [Dozier] that Batman should muse and connect his ideas and sentences fluidly, similar to the way Basil Rathbone did as Sherlock Holmes, only a bit less tightly wound . . . I also felt Batman should get excited when he hit upon a truth or deciphered a clue, as the adrenaline started to flow. That would help to fire up viewers, too.
>
> [. . .] I couldn't see up or down and lost my peripheral vision totally. I had to compensate by either turning to face whoever was talking, or not looking at them at all. Once we started shooting, I tended to do more of the latter, since it added to the feel of aloofness I wanted to project. The cowl also hid my eyebrows, so I ended up making expressive gestures with my hands: playing with my glove to suggest impatience, jabbing with a finger to underscore a point, rubbing my chin in thought, or toying with the phone cord when I was getting bad news over the Batphone.[115]

West prepared to take on the role of Bruce Wayne/Batman by reading Cervantes;[116] he saw his own lycra costume as 'cold, stony blue and gray [with] lots of sharp, dangerous lines';[117] he likens his performance

---

[114] 'I have helped Batman become a legend, a world-class pop culture icon', he writes in his autobiography; see West with Rovin, op. cit., p. 1.
[115] West with Rovin, op. cit., p. 61.
[116] Ibid., p. 58.
[117] Ibid., p. 60.

to 'a modern-day Hamlet'[118] and 'a real Kabuki experience'.[119] He researched diligently through comic archives, viewed the 1940s serials and studied Jules Feiffer's *The Great Comic Book Heroes* in order to 'discover' his character.[120]

While it would be unfair to claim that he failed to recognise the show's humour, Adam West clearly took Batman extremely seriously, while everyone else saw him as ludicrous. There is a fundamental irony here which makes any of West's scenes inherently and – it seems – unintentionally comic.

Even if we thought West's performance was deliberately self-mocking, though, the humour would in no way be lost. The sheer attention he gives to weighting every single word with some kind of emotional stress, his lengthy pauses and sudden epiphanies, his investment in this most banal of texts, involves a juxtaposition between performance style and subject matter. West is indeed – true to his intention – delivering these lines as if they were Shakespeare, as if they contained ambiguities which his performance must make clear, as if they hid great emotional truths which he must bring out for the audience. He lingers over the dialogue. He lives it. He treats the speech about Mr Freeze as a journey, a process of discovery, and he acts out each nuance in Batman's train of thought, quite literally as if it were one of Hamlet's soliloquies.

So we have the juxtaposition between the actor's sense of his performance and the way we receive it, between an intense investment in the text as 'serious' drama and the ludicrousness of the text itself. The surrounding conventions only echo and emphasise this contrast: the inappropriateness of rising dramatic music on the words 'Aunt Harriet asked us to go into the city on an errand', and the close-up on West's face during most of his dialogue, as if allowing us to follow every intellectual and emotional twist Batman goes through during the Mr Freeze speech. Again, the codes are familiar from 'serious' drama, while the subject matter combines the outlandish with the domestic and winds up with the absurd.

---

[118] Ibid., p. 3.
[119] Ibid., p. 163.
[120] Ibid., pp. 57–58.

Finally, there is an air of camp, in the genuinely 'gay' sense, about some of these moments. Batman crossing gloved hands over his chest, as if Freeze's name alone brings him chills, is markedly 'femme', while the sudden drop in tone as he talks softly to Robin cannot help but suggest the couple's intimacy. Once more, this lends the scene a sense of irony; the idea of a hidden agenda which some viewers – and, it seems, the actors and producers – fail to recognise, a joke about which only 'we' are in the know.

All of these elements are present in other scenes throughout the episode. When a young boy cries 'Boo! Batman!' at a shop window display of the hero, Dick's reaction is shocked dismay, but Bruce's scales the heights of melodrama. Staring after the boy, eyes on the mid-distance, he speaks almost to himself.

> BRUCE: Nothing has ever *cut* me, so deeply . . . to the *quick*. No blow ever struck by any arch villain [DICK looks up at him mournfully] . . . has ever hurt me . . . so acutely . . . as that little boy's boo.[121]

The bathos of that line end is quite beautiful.

The 'feminine' quality of both men's performance in this scene – emotional, vulnerable, wounded by the slightest word – provides another opportunity for camp reading. This aspect is taken still further in later scenes, by which point it becomes hard to believe that neither Dozier, West nor Ward intended *Batman* to be seen as gay. After facing down Freeze's cold gun, Robin declares to Batman 'It was a good idea of yours to wear our "Bat-thermal underwear"'; a few minutes later, Batman explains to Freeze that they took the further precaution 'of processing our crime-fighting costumes with a special Bat-anti-freeze *activating* solution . . . ' Robin points at the villain and adds, fiercely, 'and rubbed some on the rest of our bodies!' You get the feeling Batman would rather he'd kept that detail private.

Neither is portentous over-acting solely confined to West's performance. Commisioner Gordon, played by Neil Hamilton, is almost a match in this respect and shares West's penchant for staring

---

[121] 'Deep Freeze', op. cit.

into space as if lost in thought while delivering grave rhetoric peppered with alliteration.[122] When confronted with Batman's apparent guilt, his faith in the heroes is rocked:

> COMMISSIONER GORDON: I honestly don't know *what* to think, Chief O'Hara . . . but I do fear for Batman's heroic image! . . . I have a feeling the terrible tide of adverse . . . public *opinion* may soon *engulf* our . . . Caped Crusader!

Of course, by the end of the episode Gordon discovers the truth, and admits his mistake; but he takes his time explaining it. This last shot involves a remarkable moment of self-consciousness, almost a Brechtian act of anti-realism in the delivery of the final moral.

> GORDON: False pride is indeed a dangerous thing, Chief O'Hara.
>
> O'HARA: False pride? We-we were talking about beauty contests . . .
>
> GORDON: I'm talking about myself. How hard it is to admit when I'm wrong.
>
> [ZOOM to CU of GORDON]
>
> GORDON [cont] But I was wrong! So wrong! When I even *imagined* I was losing my faith . . . [turns to camera] in *Batman*!
>
> [Fanfare rises: end credits][123]

Of course, viewers of the time did not watch *Batman* as I did for this research, on a videotape in a viewing carrel on the top floor of a library; neither were their episodes of *Batman* edited together in a

---

[122] Ironically, West describes Hamilton's attitude towards the show as overly serious: 'this was straight drama to him'. See West with Rovin, op. cit., p. 120.
[123] 'Deep Freeze', op. cit.

continuous flow of formulaic adventure. *Batman* was part of an evening's schedule, twice a week, and as the *Times'* TV pages demonstrate, it was surrounded by other shows like *I Love Lucy*, *Leave it to Beaver*, *Disc-O-Teen*, *Yogi Bear* and the latest news from Vietnam.[124] Of course, this schedule was not constituted of pure and simple 'Sixties' television; sometimes *Batman* would be slotted next to a movie from the pre-war years, such as Tyrone Power's *Suez* (1938),[125] and some of those sit-coms were re-runs from the 1950s. *Batman*, with its glowing colour and absence of laugh track, looks and plays absolutely nothing like *The Phil Silvers Show*, whose grainy monochrome lends it more similarity to 1930s cinema than 1950s television, and whose every gag is signalled by audience guffaws.

Nevertheless, viewing *Batman* alongside some of its contemporary series – that is, those produced during more or less the same year – it becomes clear even to a one-time naive viewer like myself why the show was readily accepted as a comedy. Apart from the laugh track, the cues and conventions of *Batman* align it far more with *Bewitched* (1964–1971) or *The Monkees* (1966–1967) than with an adventure series like *The Fugitive* (1963–1966). The latter is shot in black and white and lasts the best part of an hour, its narrative broken down into 'Acts' which are announced onscreen with Roman numerals. This solemnity is echoed in the narrative, which focuses on human drama and relationships as much as it does 'action' and plays out a small-scale moral dilemma within the space of each self-contained episode. Apart from Richard Kimble, the eponymous fugitive, the characters are introduced for the space of one instalment only, serving the purpose of this week's passion play before being written out again. The finale of each episode is always the same, with Kimble having to move on and continue his apparently endless run from the law; and just as the narrative never seems to reach closure, so the show's moral stance is always made ambiguous by the fact that its 'hero' is a wanted man. Nothing could be much further from *Batman*'s lurid fist-fights, alternation between cliff-hanger and closure, and frequently reiterated

---

[124] See for instance the television schedules of the *New York Times* (31 March 1966).
[125] Ibid.

condemnation of lawlessness in all its forms, from diamond robbery to jaywalking.

Turning to *Bewitched*, the family resemblance is immediately clearer. The show opens with a flat cartoon of a city skyline at night, almost identical to the image of Gotham from *Batman*'s end titles. Rather than a Bat-signal, though, this sky is lit by a moon from which Tabitha the witch emerges in sleek cartoon form, riding her broomstick side-saddle and wiggling her nose at the viewer. She is soon joined by her husband, the actors' names appearing alongside their animated counterparts, and the sequence ends with a cloud of black smoke filling the screen.

Bewitched's cartoon Tabitha is cutely streamlined, a housewife from contemporary advertising, while those of Batman and Robin are more clunky and reminiscent of Kane's original drawings. Otherwise, the two title sequences could have been produced by the same designer, both in their flat, simple visual style and in the pattern they both follow – introducing the lead actor and key support, showing them in typical activities, whether cooking or fighting, then closing with the names of supporting cast over a still image. Any viewer watching one after the other would immediately place *Batman* in the genre of 'fantastic sit-com', and a few moments of Adam West's delivery would soon confirm this categorisation, even without a laugh track.

The Monkees also has significant echoes of *Batman* in its visual style and quirks of storytelling. The scene transitions which in *Batman* are announced with a Bat-symbol spinning towards the camera are transformed here into a funky graphic of a guitar. The on-screen captions which *Batman* only employed for a cliff-hanger are used here for added gags, captioning a fist fight with 'CASSIUS CLAY WATCH OUT' or flashing '1ST TOPLESS CUSTOMER?' over the shot of a bald gentleman. *Batman*'s Gotham is not so far removed from the comic book world of the Monkees, where every bag of 'QUICK DRYING CEMENT' has to be clearly labelled so we can see the joke coming minutes before it happens; while there are no on-screen sound effects in this show, light bulbs still appear above Peter Tork's head when he has a bright idea, and every bang on the head has a comedy 'dong!' to signify the cartoony level of the violence. We could even draw similarities between *Batman*'s fight scenes, where narrative is suspended for the pleasures of spectacle and the dinna-dinna theme tune, and the combat/chase sequences in *The Monkees* where the boys escape or confound a gang of criminals while playing 'Last Train to Clarksville'.

And yet there are significant differences between these unambiguously comedy shows and the strange fish that is *Batman*. While the latter asks us to believe in a crimefighter in a shiny blue cape fighting costumed villains, its only violation of 'realist' codes is the inclusion of on-screen sound effects. Once we accept this peculiarity, *Batman*'s narratives are not especially unbelievable. Problems are solved using cod-science, characters have to drive to get from place to place, events occur within a reasonable time frame. Even Batman and Robin's costume changes are explained, however weakly, through the 'compressed steam' of the Batpoles.

Bewitched, on the other hand, is not about two crimefighters who happen to wear costumes, but a modern woman who can do magic by twitching her nose. Tabitha can change her clothes in an instant, without the use of compressed steam; she can speed up time so her cleaner finishes work in a matter of seconds; she can enter the pages of her daughter's picture book. *The Monkees* uses all the same tricks to liven up its heroes' adventures, without even the justification of a magical premise. The boys suddenly appear and disappear. They switch from sou'westers and macs to tuxedos in the space of a frame. They zoom off after criminals at double speed. There is no attempt at 'realism' here, despite the mild satire of contemporary fashions and attitudes and the occasional references to surrounding culture. By contrast, the 'Marsha, Queen of Diamonds' episode where Batman and Robin appear to be turned into toads, complete with dinky costumes, quickly exposes the silliness of such an idea when the two heroes reappear and show the illusion to have been achieved with simple ventriloquism.[126]

Unlike *Bewitched*, *The Addams Family*, *The Munsters* and *I Dream of Jeannie*, as well as the *Hard Day's Night*-style zaniness of *The Monkees*, *Batman*'s world operates around strict laws of physics, albeit slightly hokey physics. Like the dialogue, its diegesis is played 'straight',

---

[126] Episode #58, 'Marsha's Scheme With Diamonds', first screened 24 November 1966.

serious, rational. As such, *Batman* is subtly different from the other shows in the genre of 'fantastic sit-com'. It doesn't fit squarely; it escapes the genre and, I will suggest, has one foot in another camp. This, I think, explains its dual address and the difference between the 'adult' and the 'juvenile' reading. Adults saw *Batman* as a fantastic sit-com, like *Bewitched*: children, I will suggest, saw it as science fiction, like *Star Trek*.

The parallels between *Batman* and *Star Trek* – which, like *Batman*, ran from 1966 to 1969 – have to my knowledge never been discussed in academic studies of popular texts. Viewing 'The Tricksters of Triskelion'[127] after 'Green Ice/Deep Freeze',[128] however, the similarities between the two shows – from the faintly camp episode titles on down – seem almost uncanny. Both, of course, centre around a chunky all-American hero and his second-in-command, whose relationship has been subject to extensive gay readings; *Star Trek*'s male couple even lends its initials to an entire body of homoerotic fiction, the Kirk/Spock, K/S or simply 'slash' tale.[129] While Spock's turquoise uniform more closely resembles Batman's outfit, Captain Kirk – mustard-coloured top tight over his sturdy torso, and slacks tucked into shiny boots – looks not a million miles away from Adam West in costume. William Shatner's performance and delivery are also strikingly like those of West. His dialogue and physical movements are characterised by a halting, thoughtful pace which suddenly shifts up several gears at once, breaking the reverie. There is a time for moral pronouncements, delivered with a gaze into mid-air, but that time is abruptly cut short by the call to action. This performance style, 'realistic' within television conventions of the time, has since been read very much as camp: Shatner's LP 'The Transformed Man', featuring his po-faced reading of 'Lucy In the Sky with Diamonds' and other contemporary hits, is now a cult, comedy artefact like Leonard

---

[127] Episode #45, first screened 5 January 1968. Curiously, some listings give the title as 'The Gamesters of Triskelion'.

[128] Episodes #53 and #54, first screened 9 and 10 November 1966.

[129] See ' "Welcome to Bisexuality, Captain Kirk": Slash and the Fan-Writing Community', in Jenkins, op. cit., pp. 185–222.

Nimoy's rendition of the song 'Bilbo Baggins', and indeed West's own LP.[130]

Through its *mise-en-scène*, *Star Trek* offers us a window to re-read *Batman* not as superhero comedy but as science fantasy. The *Trek* episode in question has Kirk facing an arena of gladiators in hand-to-hand combat, watched over by a bald villain in white make-up as a girl in a silver bikini cowers on the outskirts; the *Batman* episode involves an almost identical scenario in its concluding fight scene, with the bald, pasty-faced Mr Freeze observing and Miss Iceland shivering in her swimsuit. Both scenes are primarily in long shot, screening the action theatrically with several figures visible at once, rather than breaking it down into shorter, smaller moments; the only device missing from *Star Trek* is the on-screen sound effects. Even the cliffhanger and voiceover from *Batman* are echoed by *Star Trek*'s fade to an advertisement break at the moment when Kirk is being masochistically whipped, and return to the narrative through the familiar 'Stardate . . . ' recap.

This re-reading is further supported by other shows of the same period. *Man from UNCLE* (1964–1968), another favourite of 'slash' writers for its central relationship between Napoleon Solo and Ilya Kuryakin,[131] clearly shares generic cues with *Batman*. The exaggerated secret-agent narratives involve giant props – a scaled-up game of chess with actors as the pieces – and elaborate death-traps in the style of 1940s serials. The technology here is virtually identical to that in *Batman* – secret cameras, hidden buttons, sliding walls – yet the show is not currently read as especially comic. 'Beginning as a spy spoof in the manner of James Bond,' Meg Garret summarises in 1992, 'later plots became almost comic-book fantastic.'[132] The description could almost suit *Batman* itself, which Garret describes by contrast as 'campy', 'silly', 'overdone', full of 'sight gags' and 'verbal running gags'.[133]

Finally, even *Mission: Impossible* (1966–1972), generally regarded as a 'straight' spy adventure series, relies on many of the same devices as

---

[130] See West with Rovin, op. cit., p. 93.
[131] See Jenkins, op. cit., p. 187.
[132] Meg Garret, Appendix to Jenkins, op. cit., p. 296.
[133] Ibid., p. 289.

Batman. Again, we are in a world where immobilising gas pours from a gun in bright blue clouds, and a hidden alarm button on the side of a petrol pump alerts a scientist in an underground laboratory-cave. As in *Batman*, technology is revered; any speeding car earns lengthy sequences dwelling on its tyres and following its clouds of dust. Criminals are foiled by blinking a secret message in Morse Code, or by subtle clues in a tapped phone conversation. The narrative is built, once more, around two male agents and a pattern of masochistic capture relieved by rescue and bonding. Even the jazz music which accompanies action sequences is not so far from *Batman*'s score.

This is not to suggest that *Batman* 'is' science fiction or spy adventure, rather than sit-com. It isn't entirely a science fiction show or a secret agent drama; but neither is it truly a sit-com. The show contains elements of both television genres, linked by a sense of the 'fantastic' – either technological or magical – which I believe may help to explain how under-twelves were able to read the same show so radically differently from their parents. For such an opposed reading to occur, there must have been cues within the text for this audience to pick up on, and intertextual material to support such an interpretation. I have argued that this support came from a number of surrounding series which a young audience could conceivably have seen as generically related; we might add to the list *Dragnet* (1967–1969) *I Spy* (1965–1967), *The Avengers* (1961–1969) and the unsuccessfully 'straight' *Batman* spin-off, *Green Hornet* (1966).

For a young viewer who missed all these shows the first time round, it is not easy to recall which TV programmes aided my reception of *Batman* as entirely serious; I remember being equally excited by the animated *New Adventures of Batman and Robin*, and by the 'fantastic' drama series *Monkey*, which with hindsight seems very much open to a camp reading. It is difficult to relocate yourself back in the mindset of some twenty-two years ago, especially if your perceptions have fundamentally changed during the intervening years; but even though I can now read *Batman* differently, there is still a residual part of me which remembers that first viewing, a perspective which can be called up and held alongside my current reading for contrast and examination, just as I can balance between an insider 'fan' and a distanced 'academic' position on the more recent *Batman* films. For me – though my first experience of the character was very different from that of Frank Miller – Batman was never funny. And curiously, I suspect my perspective is now shared by the viewers of *Batman* on cable, which was the source of the videotaped episodes I watched for this analysis. The show is not currently screened for an adult audience to laugh at, but for the viewers of The Cartoon Channel. The breaks between cliffhangers advertise upcoming X-Men and Spider-Man cartoons of the kind I used to watch with *Batman* in the 1970s, alongside Playmobil adventure toys, *Star Wars* galactic battle games, Nintendo 64 beat-em-ups and – intriguingly – play make-up, Girl's World hair stylers, Angel Princess Barbies and the anatomically realistic Cocolin Wee-Wee doll, who 'tinkles' on his owner. We can only guess, for the moment, what pleasures little girls of the late 1990s take from the 1966 *Batman*; but it would make an intriguing piece of ethnographic research.

(iii) Merchandise and spin-offs

'I dig, Bats-Man, I dig! Yeah! Yeah! YEAH!' cries the 'Boy Wonderful' in *Mad*'s parody 'Bats-Man' of 1966. Bats-Man has just allowed his sidekick to share some of the profits of their adventures, and they walk off down a high street lined with billboards and neon: 'Bat Cut, $2.25', 'Batcave: Dance the Batusi', 'Bat Toys', 'Bat Bar and Grill', even what looks like a sign for Halal 'Bat Meat'.[134]

The effects Batman had on both the adult- and child-oriented culture of 1966 must have far exceeded Dozier's most optimistic predictions. Batmania, according to Adam West's autobiography, was born on the first evening of broadcast, as West overheard two supermarket customers tell a checkout girl to hurry it up so they could get back in time for the show's debut. Within a week, West was being recognised purely by his distinctive walk; fans shouted 'Batman' after him even when he disguised himself in ski clothes and goggles.

Sales of the comic book quintupled and potential licensees who had failed to tie in with us earlier were running to DC or Fox

[134] Mort Drucker and Lou Silverstone, 'Bats-Man', *Mad Magazine* (September 1966).

with pens drawn, checkbooks open, wanting to do gum cards or soundtrack albums or model kits.[135]

DC and Fox must have snapped up those deals, as gum cards, soundtrack albums and model kits were on sale within the year, along with thousands[136] of other merchandising tie-ins, from toy Batmobiles to vinyl Batcaves to lunchboxes, figurines, roller skates, horns, night lights, baseball caps and toothbrushes. Batman was the hottest product since sliced bread; and indeed, the Bond company did market Batman sliced bread in 1966.[137] By June of that year, the *New York Times* reports, DC Comics was forced to sue five companies, including Woolworth's, for their infringement of copyright in selling Batman 'knock-offs'.[138] The only craze that had come close to Batman was the Davy Crockett fad from ten years previously, 'spinning off popular songs, a movie, and . . . a television serial. As *Life* reported in April, America suffered from a serious inventory shortage of coonskin caps.'[139] Van Hise reports, though, that Batmania was far bigger than the Davy Crockett merchandising boom. 'Kids wanted the hats, cups, costumes, and the dolls.'[140] The *New York Times* confirms that 'having a [Batman] shirt had become a status symbol. Children who didn't have them boasted that they did.'[141]

As vividly illustrated by Chip Kidd's *Batman Collected*, Batman spin-offs were indeed almost exclusively aimed at the younger fans. Kidd's double spreads of colour photography offer a glimpse at the range of 1966 merchandise; a miniature Batman 'parachute figure' alongside a Batphone 'hotline' in authentic red plastic and a colouring book adorned with 'Zap! Crunch!'[142] A kids' Bat-armoury could have included the Batman periscope – 'Holy Scope! Use for Fighting the Forces of Evil' – the Batman dart-launcher, and a water pistol in the

---

[135] West with Rovin, op. cit., p. 92.

[136] Cotta Vaz, op. cit., p. 90.

[137] See Van Hise, op. cit., n.p.

[138] Anon., 'Stores are Sued on Rights to Batman', *New York Times* (23 June 1966).

[139] Gilbert, op. cit., p. 15.

[140] Van Hise, op. cit., n.p.

[141] Eda J. LeShan, 'At War With Batman', *New York Times* (15 May 1966).

[142] Chip Kidd, *Batman Collected*, London: Titan (1997), pp. 48–49.

shape of a doubled-over Caped Crusader.[143] Hidden among the Batman candy cigarettes and the Batman bicycle ornament we even see the 'Photo Rings' which may have inspired Mel Ramos' painting.[144]

Adults brought Batman into their lives in a variety of other ways, which tended more towards a creative 'poaching'[145] than to a straight consumption of official merchandise. A review of the time, advising that 'if you're enthusiastic about pop art, discotheques and tiffany lamps, ABC-TV has a new color show which should appeal to you'[146] set the tone pretty well by locating the program as a light-hearted, fashionable but faddish object for a youthful, educated in-crowd. William Dozier recalls that while students clustered around Batman in their dorm rooms, the clientele of New York's sophisticated '21' Club would gather in groups of up to thirty to watch the show in a TV lounge.[147] The issue of *Life* magazine with Adam West as cover star reported that this activity had been taken to its logical conclusion at the 'Wayne Manor' discotheque in San Francisco.[148] Batman's improvised bop, the 'Batusi', became 'a national dance craze', according to Adam West,[149] while Burt Ward's autobiography claims that men and women were both having 'Batman-style haircuts'[150] – whatever that might mean – and buying replica outfits to spice up their love lives.

At the height of our popularity, it seemed that almost every teenager and adult, both heterosexual and homosexual, wanted to have Batman and Robin in bed, or to dress up like one of the dynamic duo and take someone else to bed. Truckloads of

---

[143] Ibid., p. 49, p. 71, p. 58.
[144] Ibid., p. 62, p. 72, p. 55.
[145] See Henry Jenkins, *Textual Poachers*, London: Routledge (1992), particularly pp. 26–27.
[146] Van Hise, op. cit., n.p.
[147] Eisner, op. cit., p. 11.
[148] *Life* (11 March 1966); see Van Hise, op. cit., n.p.
[149] West with Rovin, op. cit., p. 80.
[150] Burt Ward with Stanley Ralph Ross, *Boy Wonder: My Life In Tights*, Los Angeles: Logical Figments Books (1995), p. 30.

Batman and Robin costumes were sold and they weren't just for kids.[151]

Ward's story is, perhaps surprisingly, backed up to an extent by other accounts of the Detroit hairdresser who 'invented the Bat Cut', and reports that Wayne Manor's *maitre d'* was dressed as the Joker, while the Batusi was led by 'girls dressed like Robin [who] danced behind a plate glass screen'.[152] The trend was apparently taken up elsewhere: the 'Clubs and Restaurants' section in a *Harpers and Queen* of 1968 advises that 'Raffles ... has really good food (don't be put off by Batman opening the door to you)'.[153] While dressing in full Batman regalia may have been too extreme for most fans, it seems possible that the advertisements for a 'Sleek! Zingy! Stretch CAT SUIT: Purrfect for pleasure and comfort',[154] complete with drawing of a feline fatale, may also have reflected the fashion for dressing up as Batman characters, whether for clubs or the bedroom.

By March 1966, according to the *New York Times*, Batman had spawned not just a haircut and dance, but a 'Batman dress, of chrome-coated clear plastic, that will make its debut next month at Paraphernalia, a Manhattan shop that caters to the whimseys of the fashionably youthful'.[155] This designer piece by Betsy Johnson, retailing for $30 at a specialist Manhattan boutique, clearly represents, like the spectacle at Wayne Manor, a use of Batman quite distinct from the 'official' business of Batman marketing which netted ninety companies some $75 million in 1966 alone.[156] While objects like the dress and haircut were more expensive than a Batman periscope or bicycle ornament, they were also more unique, bound up with an aesthetic of individual, imaginative borrowing and appropriative creativity. The adult response to Batman, then, was very much in keeping with the show's reception as Pop and what was perceived as

---

[151] Ibid., p. 36.
[152] Cotta Vaz, op. cit., p. 89.
[153] 'Clubs and Restaurants', *Harpers and Queen* (May 1968).
[154] 'Stretch Cat Suit' advertisement, ibid.
[155] Hilton Kramer, 'Look! All Over! It's Esthetic ... it's Business ... it's Supersuccess!, *New York Times* (29 March 1966).
[156] Ibid.

the tongue-in-cheek, throwaway ephemerality of the Pop aesthetic; after all, there is little doubt that Wayne Manor was a short-lived phenomenon like the novelty haircuts, and Betsy Johnson's designer Batman frock was priced at $10 less than the 'crisp waffle pique cotton dress' on sale at Sak's Fifth Avenue in the same month.[157] None of these adult appropriations was built to last. Batman may have been the best thing since sliced bread, but sliced bread, after all, goes stale after just a couple of days.

(iv) Pop

'We started out to do a pop-art thing,' said *Batman* scriptwriter Lorenzo Semple Jr. in 1966, 'and we're doing it.'[158] We have already seen that the show was selfconsciously, even shamelessly constructed as 'pop' and promoted accordingly to cash in on the contemporary art movement. There was, of course, no guarantee that this intended meaning would be picked up by reviewers; I note below that Adam West's vision of his character contrasts strikingly with the widespread public image of TV's Batman. In this case, however, it seems that the 'pop' associations manufactured by Dozier and his crew were easily spotted by journalists.

An early report from the *New York Times* of 23 January 1966 lists *Batman* alongside other perceived icons of pop, some of which may now seem obscure – 'instant books' and 'the design of the new CBS building on West 52nd St' – while some – 'Andy Warhol', 'a can of Campbell's soup' – retain their cultural resonance.[159] 'The point about *Batman* of course is that the show has been construed as a belated extension of the phenomenon of pop art to the television medium. And contrary to the mournful misgivings of some who felt this act was a ghastly affront to culture, it could be an unforseen blessing of major proportions.' Even though this reviewer welcomes *Batman*'s success

---

[157] 'Crisp Waffle Pique Cotton Dress, $40', advertisement, *New York Times* (31 March 1966).
[158] Quoted in Van Hise, op. cit., n.p.
[159] Anon., 'Too Good to be Camp', op. cit.

only because he sees it as hastening the exhaustion of the pop fad, the references so carefully assembled by ABC's promotion team at their 'cocktail and frug' party have been duly recognised.

Hilton Kramer's later article, 'Look! All Over! It's Esthetic . . . It's Business . . . It's Supersuccess!' suggests both the extent to which *Batman* was instantly viewed not in isolation, but as part of a cultural trend, and the wider discourse around 'pop' in which the show was located. Kramer's discussion positions *Batman* not just as pop, but as representative of a specific phase of pop: the 'comic book craze' of 1966. The intertextual discourse surrounding *Batman* would therefore include the Broadway musicals *The Mad Show* and *It's A Bird, It's A Plane . . . It's Superman*, the comic-strip paintings of Lichtenstein, who was representing America at the Venice Bienniale, 'the most important of the big international art exhibitions',[160] and the parade of newspaper and billboard advertisements employing comic-style typography and effects. Kramer cites the ad for 'No-CAL' soda on display at 42nd and Seventh, showing four teens dominated by the word balloon 'Put POP in your party';[161] we could also look to the *Newsweek* ad based around a Lichtenstein 'POP' explosion, with the caption 'POP! indeed. And also POW! BLAM! and ZAP!'[162] or the 1966 campaign for Canada Dry ginger ale featuring a caped superhero.[163] Kramer's analysis is, however, eloquent enough to speak for itself.

> A new phase in the amazing phenomenon of pop is upon us. Wherever one turns on the cultural, subcultural and pseudo-cultural scene at the moment, something answering to the name 'pop' is visible, if not actually dominant. Just now the principal pop focus is on the comic strip, which, in more forms than one can keep track of, is turning into the biggest bonanza of all.
>
> From billboards to book jackets, from the most prestigious galleries and museums to the most garish souvenir shops, the

---

[160] Kramer, op. cit.
[161] Ibid.
[162] See *New York Times* (5 July 1966).
[163] Ibid.

public is faced with a bewildering variety of comic-strip advertisements, paintings, pinups, posters and all sorts of popular ephemera.

Movie-houses are reviving old serials based on comic-strip adventures, and television producers, responding with alacrity to a universe of discourse they can at last understand, are giving top priority to – and reaping top rewards from – this vogue for pop adventure tales.

Thus the current twice-weekly *Batman* series running – to maximum publicity – on the American Broadcasting Company – will be followed in the fall by an animated cartoon version of Superman over the Columbia Broadcasting System. And still more TV serials, on the Green Hornet and on Tarzan, are in the offing.

What makes this vogue for comic strips so phenomenal is that it cuts across widely disparate levels of commercial, intellectual and esthetic activity. In one form or another, there is – or is about to be – a comic strip idea, style or object to suit every taste.[164]

Batman, then, was perceived as pop partly on the basis of its comic-book origins and style alone. Comic books were inherently pop because they had been embraced by Lichtenstein and Warhol, who, as noted above, had favoured the medium partly because of its aesthetic of flatness, crude execution and mass reproduction. Furthermore, to take the maligned, 'low', juvenile form of comics at all seriously – to elevate it to 'art' and exhibit it at the Venice Bienniale – was itself a typically 'pop' move which only made the comics more perfect examples of the trend; Kramer notes that Jules Feiffer's *The Great Comic Book Heroes*, which 'extolled the virtues of Batman, Superman et. al. with all the sobriety of a learned critic explicating a metaphor in the poetry of John Donne',[165] had served to emphasise comics' pop status through the juxtaposition of superhero adventures with literary

---

[164] Kramer, op. cit.
[165] Ibid.

analysis.[166] The TV show not only adapted from a medium which was already the epitome of pop; it played through its absurd scenarios, in Dozier's words, 'as though we were dropping a bomb on Hiroshima'.[167] Its form was pop; its tone was pop. Its colours recalled Warhol, its effects were straight out of Lichtenstein. Its psychedelic sets littered with stylised props and lit with coloured gels recall pop art's 'Happenings', the use of a 'total space' for a pop environment: Claes Oldenburg's 'Bedroom' in marbled turquoise, leopard-skin and white vinyl,[168] and his huge typewriters, toilets and telephones in vinyl and foam.[169]

Even the superhero names and secret identities of *Batman*'s cast – Edward Nigma aka The Riddler, Selina Kyle aka The Catwoman – echo the alter egos of the second-raters and wannabe superstars of Warhol's mid-1960s Factory: Viva, Ron Vile, Ondine, Candy Darling and Rotten Rita, as photographed by Billy Name aka Billy Linich.[170] *Batman* achieved what Lichtenstein attempted with his ceramic sculptures based on comic book images, their contours shaded with thick outlines and surfaces pitted with Ben Day dots; it brought the two-dimensional into three dimensions, and managed to keep it authentically flat.[171]

---

[166] Feiffer's book was published in 1965. Note that Umberto Eco's analysis of Superman in *The Role of the Reader*, London: Hutchinson (1981) far surpasses Feiffer's in terms of its 'academic' treatment of comic heroes.

[167] Eisner, op. cit., p. 8.

[168] Claes Oldenburg, 'Bedroom' (1963); see Lippard, op. cit., pp. 109–110.

[169] Oldenburg, 'Soft Pay-Telephone' (1963), 'Soft Toilet' (1966), 'Soft Typewriter' (1963). See Tilman Osterwold, *Pop Art*, Koln: Taschen Verlag (1991), pp. 197–200, pp. 22–23.

[170] Elizabeth Young and Billy Name, 'The Broader Picture', *Independent on Sunday* (13 April 1997), pp. 40–41.

[171] Lichtenstein, 'Head with Black Shadow' (1965), 'Ceramic Sculpture 2' (1965) and so on; see Diane Waldman, *Lichtenstein*, New York: Guggenheim Museum Press (1993), p. 315.

(v) Camp

'High camp was happening. Susan Sontag said so.' But what exactly was camp? Andy Medhurst amuses himself with the impossibility of defining the term, offering five attempts from various sources before plumping for the conclusion that 'camp is . . . a great big pink butterfly that just won't be pinned down.'[172] His more sober working definition of 'a playful, knowing, self-reflexive theatricality' is perhaps as good as any, coupled with the notion of a 'dry, self-mocking wit' and Sontag's own maxim that camp is to be 'serious about the frivolous, frivolous about the serious.'[173]

Of course, we don't know if William Dozier really mused about Sontag as he read *Batman* #171 on that airplane, but we can assume that her 'Notes on Camp' played a significant role in shaping the cultural discourse on camp in the mid-1960s, and so in turn had some influence on the *Batman* show's reception and reviews. Constraints of space preclude me from dealing with Sontag's fifty-eight remarks on the subject, but as a sample, here are twelve or thirteen things which the adult viewer might have known about camp when he or she sat down to watch *Batman*.

4. Random example of items which are part of the canon of Camp: . . . the old Flash Gordon comics.

7. All Camp objects, and persons, contain a large element of artifice.

9. Camp responds particularly to the markedly attenuated and to the strongly exaggerated.

16. Thus, the Camp sensibility is one that is alive to a double sense in which some things can be taken.

19. The pure examples of Camp are unintentional; they are deadly serious.

21. So again, Camp rests on innocence. That means Camp discloses innocence, but also, when it can, corrupts it.

22. Considered a little less strictly, Camp is either

---

[172] Medhurst, op. cit., p. 155.
[173] Ibid., p. 156.

completely naïve or else wholly conscious . . .

23. In naïve, or pure, Camp, the essential element is seriousness, a seriousness that fails.

25. The hallmark of Camp is the spirit of extravagance.

26. Camp is art that proposes itself seriously, but cannot be taken altogether seriously because it is 'too much.'

34. Camp taste turns its back on the good-bad axis of ordinary aesthetic judgement.

41. The whole point of Camp is to dethrone the serious. Camp is playful, anti-serious. More precisely, Camp involves a new, more complex relation to the serious.

51. The peculiar relation between Camp taste and homosexuality has to be explained. While it's not true that Camp taste *is* homosexual taste, there is no doubt a peculiar affinity and overlap.[174]

Sontag's list offers guidelines rather than anything so philistine as a dictionary definition, but we can already see how *Batman* would have fitted neatly into this template by virtue of its failed seriousness, its dual meanings, its extravagance, its playfulness and even its source material in comic books. As we see, Sontag also raises the importance of homosexuality to camp, and stresses in her final entries that while no absolute link should be imagined between the two terms, they nevertheless went hand-in-hand during the early 1960s. 'Camp taste is much more than homosexual taste . . . one feels that if homosexuals hadn't more or less invented Camp, someone else would.'[175]

Medhurst develops this connection, drawing the useful distinction between texts which were camp of themselves and those which were transformed into camp through their reception by 'camp audiences'; that is, 'primarily gay male audiences'.[176] Sontag had already suggested these two categories in her discussion of camp as 'pure' and 'completely naïve', or else 'wholly conscious (when one plays at

[174] Sontag, op. cit., pp. 279–291.
[175] Ibid., p. 292.
[176] Medhurst, op. cit., p. 155.

being campy)'.[177] Camp was something which could be deliberately constructed, but was also 'a quality discoverable in objects', a 'way of seeing the world'.[178] As such it was an approach with a transformative power, re-presenting 'straight', serious objects, such as a vulgar Art Nouveau lamp, in a new light.

So if we assume that the Batman comics of the early 1950s were intended by writers and editors as 'straight' action adventures devoid of homosexual associations, these would fall into the category of 'pure' camp: though neither 'knowing' nor 'self-reflexive', they were nevertheless read through their excess of bondage and rescue scenarios as homoerotic narratives. The TV show, as Medhurst observes, overlaid 'this "innocent" camp with a thick layer of ironic distance, the self-mockery version of camp'.[179] Batman had always embodied what we might call a 'latent' camp quality through its very premise – 'it was serious (the tone, the moral homilies) about the frivolous (a man in a stupid suit) . . . and given the long associations of camp with the homosexual male subculture, Batman was a particular gift on the grounds of his relationship with Robin'.[180]

The TV show, then, as Medhurst might put it, merely polished a diamond until its camp facets sparkled. Indeed, *Batman* became a *sine qua non* of camp, almost a definition of the word in living Technicolor: a simple explanation of the slippery term might begin, as Medhurst observes, with 'like the sixties' *Batman* series'.[181] For the wider audience outside that 'homosexual male subculture', it even seems that *Batman* provided the first taste of this knowing aesthetic. 'Most people', Van Hise suggests, 'think that this television show is where the expression "camp" originated. While the show was certainly called "high camp" and the like, they didn't start it. This came out of the press. The term "camp" was an expression used then in the gay

---

[177] Sontag, op. cit., p. 284.

[178] Ibid., p. 279.

[179] Medhurst, op. cit., p. 156. Note that while Dozier apparently intended the irony and saw *Batman* as a 'wholly conscious' camp, Adam West's naïve approach to his performance surely qualifies it as 'pure' camp in the sense of 'failed seriousness'.

[180] Ibid.

[181] Ibid., p. 150.

underground to describe something that was outrageous but cute.'[182]
George Melly's *Revolt Into Style* confirms this interpretation.

> Originally 'camp' was a purely homosexual term. It meant
> overtly and outrageously queer, implied transvestite clothing,
> and was also called into use to indicate the approval of a few
> non-homosexual people, usually actresses who, for one reason
> or another, appealed universally to queans [*sic*]. 'Camp' meant
> 'knowing'. It had undertones of self-mockery. It seemed
> rooted in a certain theatricality. . . .
>
> When, in its turn, pop turned to camp, it redefined the
> word for its own needs. Pop used camp . . . irritating as this
> often was, it had its uses. It allowed pop to expand its terms of
> reference, its bank of images. It gave it (and here it remained
> true to camp's original definition), the confidence to 'come on
> outrageous'. In the end it came to be a repetitious and
> meaningless bore, but, *en route*, it acted as a useful catalyst. It
> helped pop make a forced march around good taste. It brought
> vulgarity back into popular culture . . .[183]

What we have emerging here, then, are two levels to an already two-
faced discourse. On the one hand we have the 'original' camp, the
homosexual camp; on the other the 'appropriated' camp, the straight
camp. It was this second use of the term which became almost
synonymous with 'pop' as the latter art style incorporated camp's
irony, knowingness and elevation of the 'low' or 'vulgar' into its own
practice. Thus the article on *Batman* quoted above, which lists the show
alongside Warhol and Campbell's cans, is titled 'Too Good to be
Camp'. One paragraph refers to *Batman* as 'the extension of pop art to
the television medium'; the next advises that anyone 'insecure in his
judgement of what is camp had to assume the show was important'.[184]
For the purposes of this reviewer, the two concepts seem interchange-

---

[182] Van Hise, op. cit., n.p.
[183] George Melly, *Revolt Into Style: The Pop Arts in Britain*, Harmondsworth: Penguin
(1970), pp. 160–161.
[184] Anon., 'Too Good To Be Camp', op. cit.

able, twin labels for the contemporary 'so bad it's good' trend. There is little connection to homosexuality in this description; nor is it evident in the later article quoting fans who 'describe *Batman* as "camp" and maintain that it is the great social satire of our times'.[185] Again, the equation of 'camp' with 'satire', and subsequently 'wry sophistication', shows no particular awareness of the term's gay origins.

As we saw in the last chapter, however, the 'underground' which had coined the word 'camp' was not slow to reclaim *Batman* for their own enjoyment. Remember Melly's recollection that 'We all knew Robin and Batman were pouves ... over the children's heads we winked and nudged, but in the end what were we laughing at? The fact they didn't know that Batman had it off with Robin.'[186] 'They didn't know': not just the children, surely, but the straight commentators who had only come into contact with camp when it 'swished up out of the ghetto'.[187] Melly and his friends, we know, were not the only ones who knew what Batman and Robin got up to behind the scenes; remember E. Nelson Bridwell pursing his lips about the 'gay set' who 'eagerly seized on' the show,[188] and Steve Beery's reminiscences about his Boy Wonder fantasies.[189]

Medhurst reads the TV show as deliberately camp in this 'gay' sense, suggesting that *Batman*'s producers decided it would be 'more fun' to present the heroes' relationship 'straight'. 'Wertham's reading of the Dubious Duo had been so extensively aired as to pass into the general consciousness ... it was part of the fabric of *Batman*, and the makers of the TV series proceeded accordingly.'[190] Medhurst sees this self-conscious play with the characters' gay overtones in various aspects of the show: in the casting of already-camp actors like Tallulah

---

[185] Eda LeShan, 'At War With Batman', op. cit.

[186] Melly, op. cit., p. 193.

[187] Medhurst, op. cit., p. 155.

[188] E. Nelson Bridwell, *Batman from the 30s to the 70s*, New York: Crown Publishers (1971), p. 12.

[189] Steve Beery, 'One Reader's Story: Holy Hormones! Batman and Robin Made Me Gay!', *Gay Comix* no.8, San Francisco: Bob Ross, publisher (Summer 1986), n.p.

[190] Medhurst, op. cit., pp. 156–157.

Bankhead,[191] in the plotlines which seem to pose heterosexuality as a threat to the heroes' integrity, and in details such as Batman and Alfred driving the Batmobile 'festooned with wedding paraphernalia including a large "Just Married" sign'.[192] To Medhurst, these are deliberate nods to the gay audience, demonstrations of the show's 'commitment to camp'.[193] However, it seems that Dozier would have disagreed. 'I hate the word "camp",' he declared in January 1966. 'It sounds so faggy.'[194]

'When Dozier first used the word "High Camp", he didn't know what he was getting himself into,' writes Van Hise. 'He went out of his way to distance himself from the homosexual connection.'[195] Justifying his use of the term 'camp', Dozier admitted that

> I used it to describe the show. I meant that Batman is so square, he's funny; that there are so many clichés, it's amusing . . . There will be no doubt on TV that Batman and Robin like girls, even though they may be too busy fighting crime to have much time for them.[196]

Adam West, whose autobiography reveals him as something of a scholar and autodidact, claims he 'read Susan Sontag's essay on camp and also looked up the etymology of the word. I found out that camp was short for "camp brothel", a place where gay men met and "flaunted" their sexuality . . . we weren't that.'[197] Although West concluded philosophically that 'with the number of homosexuals in this country, if we get that audience, fine. Just add 'em to the Nielsen ratings'.[198] Dozier and the ABC executives were sufficiently concerned about the resurfacing of Wertham's 'Gay Batman' discourse that they

---

[191] Bankhead's status as 'self-conscious' camp icon had been confirmed by Sontag; see Sontag, op. cit., p. 284.
[192] Medhurst, op. cit., p. 157.
[193] Ibid.
[194] In the *New York Times* (9 January 1966), quoted in Van Hise, op. cit., n.p.
[195] Van Hise, op. cit., n.p.
[196] Ibid., n.p.
[197] West, op. cit., p. 100.
[198] Van Hise, op. cit., n.p.

introduced first Aunt Harriet, then Batgirl, in an attempt to provide both a heterosexual 'family' and potential female love-interest for Batman and Robin. Dozier states it in the plainest terms: 'Aunt Harriet was a character we made up. That was to keep them from looking like homosexuals.'[199] As noted above, Batgirl was also a character they made up; she, like Harriet, was shoehorned into the comic books in order to provide continuity between screen and printed texts. Even the guest starlets, read by Medhurst as camp icons who reinforced the gay interpretation, were apparently intended by the network as 'proof' of Batman's heterosexuality. 'ABC brought in . . . a brace of delectable arch-villainesses, whom Batman destroys only after some all-American ogling.'[200]

These were blatant attempts to impose an 'official' template of meaning over the text and close down the 'subversive' interpretation which had been publicised by Wertham – Aunt Harriet was apparently written in when ABC learnt of the *Seduction* reading[201] – and more recently by Jules Feiffer, whose *The Great Comic Book Heroes* had contributed to the 1960s comic fad. 'Feiffer . . . gave out a couple of interviews when the show was first a hit, implying that there was a homosexual relationship between Batman and Robin', Dozier grumbled. 'So, I made a lot of appearances at that time, when the show was at its zenith, and people would ask me about that. I said, "If Jules Feiffer thinks that, he is just a dirty old man", and that would end the whole discussion.'[202]

But of course it didn't end the discussion. The 1960s series is still Medhurst's favoured text precisely because of the fun it has with Batman and Robin's relationship; another Andy, in *Attitude*'s feature on gay TV heroes, was perfectly capable of projecting his fantasies onto the Dynamic Duo despite Aunt Harriet's continued presence.[203] On the other hand, as indicated above, the contempt for the series on the

---

[199] Eisner, op. cit., p. 8.
[200] Dorothy Storck, *Chicago's American Magazine* (27 February 1966), quoted in Van Hise, op. cit., n.p.
[201] Ibid.
[202] Eisner, op. cit., p. 8.
[203] Murray Healy, 'Tuned In, Turned On', *Attitude* (January 1997), p. 65.

part of so many 'purist' fans is precisely due to its enduring image of
the 'Dark Knight' as the kind of hero who 'clutches a flower to his Bat
chest and sings Gilbert and Sullivan's "I'm Just Little Buttercup" '.[204]
Without the TV show, Wertham's gay reading might have faded and
been successfully rewritten by the 'dark' comic books of O'Neil,
Adams and later Miller. Because of the show, Batman's associations
with camp – in both 'mainstream' and the 'underground' sense – will
never be forgotten for as long as the character survives. It is difficult to
imagine, in this respect, how Dozier's intended meaning could have
gone more awry.

(vi) Effects

Perhaps surprisingly, given the continuing circulation of Fredric
Wertham's arguments in the 1960s,[205] the notion that Batman and
Robin's homoerotic relationship could have adverse effects on children
was never central to the contemporary discourse about the show's
effects. Instead, concern focused on the violent play which Batman
inspired in young children. Perhaps too small-scale to be labelled a
moral panic, this discourse nevertheless ran for some months in the
popular press of the 1960s and, again, prompted Dozier himself to
respond, this time on the letters pages of the New York Times. As Lynn
Spigel and Henry Jenkins discuss at length in 'Mass Culture and
Popular Memory', the controversy which greeted Batman was simply
the latest skirmish in a long-running debate about the 'effects' of
children's entertainment, with its source in concerns over dime novels
at the turn of the century.[206] The 1960s variant on this theme is vividly
epitomised by Eda LeShan's article in the New York Times magazine of
15 May 1966, which is headlined simply 'At War With Batman' and
proposes that the danger of the show lay in its dual address. While
adults are able to interpret the subtle cues of camp and respond to

---

[204] Medhurst, op. cit., p. 158.

[205] He was still actively campaigning in the 1960s, according to West; see West with
Rovin, op. cit., p. 128.

[206] Spigel and Jenkins, op. cit., p. 127.

Batman with an ironic distance, children take the show 'absolutely literally' and see Batman as a figure with carte blanche to hit people and drive fast. Children were coming to school in capes and cowls, viewing road accidents with bland interest and complaining when playground brawls were broken up: 'boy, that was a great fight – just like on Batman'. LeShan argues that

> What comes through to young children, oblivious of the satirical tone, is that those responsible for law enforcement are all complete idiots and that if one wears a mask and a cape, one is invincible and above the law. As one child put it, 'when Batman and Robin get into the Batmobile, they can go as fast as they want to and they can knock everything down.'[207]

Once more, Batman inspired a project of censorship and denial, as LeShan and many of her teaching colleagues across New York declared a ban on all Batman merchandise on school grounds. A fortnight later, Dozier stepped in with a letter refuting LeShan's claims:

> Batman is not 'beyond the law'. It has been stated and restated in the series that Batman is a duly deputized law enforcement officer and operates entirely within the law and as an arm of the law-enforcement body in Gotham City. When Batman and Robin are abroad in the Batmobile, they are always in pursuit of a criminal; and therefore any minor transgressions of traffic ordnances such as excessive speed and veering over a white line on the highway are excusable, just as they are when a police car is roaring down the highway in pursuit of a criminal.[208]

Dozier received unexpected support from a Manhattan clergyman who devoted an entire sermon to Batman on 7 August 1966. Batman, claimed the Reverend Dr Robert E. Terwillinger, appealed to the American penchant for 'practical messiahs'.

---

[207] LeShan, op. cit.
[208] William Dozer, letter, *New York Times* (29 May 1966).

Batman is the savior who comes in from above to rescue the victims of malignant power with absolute goodness. He is called into situations the police can't handle with a special cultic or prayer device called the Bat-phone.[209]

It was very probably thanks to Dozier's shrewd marketing ability that the Reverend Terwillinger was the special guest at a Central Park ceremony, just a few weeks later, where Adam West and Burt Ward were giving out Good Citizen Awards to local children. Forty-three children received the awards: seven thousand turned up to meet Batman and Robin, and, as the *New York Times* sagely reported, 'the crowd of worshippers zoomed off' after the ceremony 'to buy 3000 Batman ice creams, 1000 Batman t-shirts, 1000 Batmasks, 3000 Bataloons, endless mouthfuls of Bat bubblegum and other similar things'.[210] Whatever the influence of educators and critics with regard to Batman's negative effects, it was obvious that the audience of kids, much like the audience of gay viewers, wasn't going to be turned away from its heroes that easily.

(vii) Political satire

'Send Batman to Viet-Nam', read an unauthorised button of 1968.[211] On the face of it, this may seem an odd form of appropriation, and it is difficult to know exactly what was implied by this use of Batman for direct comment on the war. Adam West's Batman, with his podging waistline and painfully slow reactions, would not have been the most obvious choice of soldier against the Viet Cong, while his ponderous moral pronouncements on seatbelts and homework belong more to a rose-tinted 1950s vision of America than to a nation plagued by race riots and student protest. Indeed, it has been suggested that the show's

---

[209] Edward B. Fiske, 'Clergyman Sees Batman's Appeal as Religious', *New York Times* (8 August 1966).
[210] Anon., 'Wow! Bam! Socko! 7000 Children Greet Batman', *New York Times* (25 August 1966).
[211] Kidd, op. cit., p. 149.

obliviousness to its surrounding culture – beyond the spheres of fashion and visual art – was one of the reasons behind its success. James Van Hise notes that this escapism may have been exactly what American audiences wanted at the time; he quotes the *Chicago News*, which spoke warmly of the show's 'welcome, circa-1940s silliness'. 'That was the magic of *Batman*,' Van Hise concludes, contrasting the show to *Laugh-In*'s more topical 'Vietnam jokes' which he argues have not worn so well. 'People are enchanted by that, almost on a Disney level, watching something that's so surreal . . . the *Batman* TV show never made reference to the sixties or to the time or the place. It's very rare that they'd even mention the year.'[212] Adam West himself celebrates the fact that Batman made his fans 'feel secure and happy in a time of chaos and war'.[213]

The contrast between Batman's comic book Gotham and the contemporary news images of New York, Cleveland, Chicago and Haight-Ashbury, not to mention South Vietnam, is vividly illustrated by an anecdote in Spigel and Jenkins' article 'Mass Culture and Popular Memory'. Jim, a computer technician, recalls watching the show as a kid. 'I can remember my sister thought it was really cool . . . and she would sit there and watch it with me. She was a young teenager . . . When she went off to college she became a hippy . . . and completely stopped watching. I was amazed because I always loved the show.'

Notwithstanding the fact that Jim's sister could barely have aged two years between the show's debut, when she was a 'young teenager', and its final episode – which itself provides a telling comment about memory and our perceptions of personal history – the authors' remark that for Jim, his sister's loss of interest in *Batman* was indicative of the 'counterculture's impact' remains perceptive and intriguing. Perhaps the 'Batman to Viet Nam' badge implies a frustration with the mass audience's taste for safe, 'POW! WHAM!' violence and its refusal to engage with 'real' contemporary issues. There was a similar dismay expressed by some commentators at viewers' complaints that their episode of *Batman* was interrupted by newsflashes about the Gemini 8 spaceflight landings in March 1966. During this forgotten controversy

---

[212] Van Hise, op. cit., n.p.
[213] West with Rovin, op. cit., p. 91.

the *Chicago Sun-Times*, which had worried publicly about America's preference for 'entertainment' over 'news', received three hundred letters, '2 to 1 for Batman'.[214]

The parody in *Mad Magazine*, which might have been expected to take up and expand upon any critical readings in circulation, makes no comment about *Batman*'s escapism or lack of topicality: almost the contrary, in fact. In one panel we see Batman spluttering at Robin, who wants to goof off and chase girls, that even if they dealt successfully with crime in Gotham there would still be the international conflict to occupy them. 'What's wrong with you kids today? Your date will have to wait until evil and injustice have been erased from Gotham City! And after that, we've got problems in Asia!'[215] The implication seems to be that Batman would go to Nam of his own free will, if only the problems on his doorstep could be cleared up; rather than condemning or even gently mocking the show's old-fashioned values, this parody seems to accept Batman as an entirely contemporary superhero with a political conscience.

This reading is supported to an extent by stories from the *New York Times* of 1966. Firstly, an editorial of that year makes the light-hearted claim that the Batman show is actually 'un-American' in its subversion of traditional heroic values.

It starts with the basic assumption that the American as Hero (Batman) is a simple-minded ass. As Batman dashes about with flabby stomach bellying against his union suit, he spouts a stream of heroic cliche culled from every American Superman from Tom Mix to John Wayne. The effect is subversive.

Its treatment of Batman's stooge, Robin the Boy Wonder, mocks the national youth cult with the plain implication that boy wonders are insufferable. Besides being dumb, Robin is played as the most odious child hero since Frankie Darro hung up his knickers.

Ridiculing heroism and children would be enough to qualify *Batman* as the most daring TV show in ages, but there is

---

[214] Van Hise, op. cit., n.p.
[215] Drucker and Silverstone, op. cit.

more. It violates two of television's most sacred taboos by depicting the cops as imbeciles and tolerating dialect comedy. On occasion, Batman even commits the ultimate subversion of burlesquing television . . . [the producers] have at last hit on a form which enables television to say . . . that many of our national conventions are ridiculous.

It may be, of course, that the producers do not realise what they have done. Let us hope their sponsors don't catch on.[216]

Whether Dozier realised what he had 'done' is arguable; as we have seen, he fully intended the show to be played so 'square and so serious that adults would find it amusing',[217] but that does not quite constitute planning to burlesque the very idea of heroism or undermine television conventions. Certainly, West did not intend his portrayal of Batman to be a parody or a satire. Although Dozier explained to his lead actor that the show was to be played 'as though we were dropping the bomb on Hiroshima . . . hopefully, it is going to be funny', and confirms 'he got it right away',[218] West treated his role with what seems an entirely sincere gravity and responsibility. 'I revelled in the power and isolation and beauty of the character,' he writes of his first day in costume. 'It's the kind of experience that never leaves you, and creates a very special bond with a character.'[219] A far cry from the American Hero as 'simple-minded ass', and evidence that in this case West's 'authorial' intention for Batman clashed with the journalistic reception.[220]

The *Times* editor begins his analysis with the comment that 'most of the critical response to the television treatment of Batman seems to have missed the point',[221] which suggests – even allowing for the faintly jokey nature of the entire article – that this particular reading of the show was not widespread. Viewers, however, may have had a different perspective to newspaper critics; a later article claims – as

---

[216] Russell Baker, 'Television's Bat Burlesque', *New York Times* (8 February 1966).

[217] Eisner, op. cit., p. 6.

[218] Ibid., p. 8.

[219] West with Rovin, op. cit., p. 68.

[220] And with Burt Ward's notion of the show: he refers to it as a 'spoof'. See LeShan, op. cit.

[221] Baker, op. cit.

noted above – that *Batman*'s adult and teenage fans viewed the show as 'the great social satire of our times'.[222] There is no way we can substantiate or investigate this claim; but the idea of *Batman* as inherently subversive, hiding its satirical edge in apparently harmless, knockabout comedy, casts an interesting light on other uses of the character during the same year.

In a second *Times* article, for instance, *Batman* is cited as the source of a superhero trend which has affected not just merchandising but forms of small-scale political resistance:

> Even committees protesting American policy in Vietnam resort to the vocabulary and typography of the strips to fasten attention on their appeals. And with the publication this week of the 'Great Society Comic Book', featuring such characters as SuperLBJ, Wonderbird, Bobman and Teddy, Gaullefinger and others, this aspect of the pop craze enters the arena of political satire.[223]

While Batman is clearly not the sole factor in this use of comic book forms for political comment – Superman and James Bond are in the mix there too as part of the 'pop craze' – this does seem to represent a use of the character for 'subversive' purposes, again satirising 'national conventions'. We cannot be sure, though, whether the protestors and parodists had this in mind when they chose Batman as an appropriate vehicle for anti-war campaigning or for satirising Bobby Kennedy – assuming, that is, that the 'Bobman' strip ridiculed Kennedy rather than portrayed him as a dynamic hero.

Again, the phrase 'enters the arena' implies that this was a novel use of the character rather than a reading with widespread and established circulation. Perhaps – if Batman's 'subversion' of national ideals went unrecognised by most viewers – the character's mere ubiquity and status as a familiar popular icon were enough to make him a useful campaign tool. Perhaps it was the TV Batman's very flatness, naivety and apparent lack of any inherent political content which

---

[222] LeShan, op. cit.
[223] Kramer, op. cit.

encouraged protestors to adopt him for their own agenda, imbuing this harmless and willing cultural signifier with satirical or resistant meaning. Perhaps turning a hero who seemed the most straight-laced and pedantic of lawmen against politicians and presidency was seen as a neat act of subversion in itself.

Alternatively, it is possible that Batman's immersion in late 1960s culture – the references across journalistic discourse, the very proximity of *Batman* at 7.30 to Walter Cronkite and the 7pm News[224] – had, as the *Mad* parody suggests, already dissolved the boundaries between Gotham and New York and made Batman very much a part of contemporary life, whatever the political innocence of the original text. In this case the use of the character for anti-war protest would have constituted neither the appropriation of a previously empty signifier, nor the subversion of a reactionary icon, nor the deliberate adoption of a figure associated with deft satire, but just another use of one of the period's most recognisable popular figures. Rather than one meaning, Batman probably carried a number of different and contradictory political associations: as a satire or celebration of Bobby Kennedy, as a conservative or a radical, as an anti-war campaigner or an idealised super-soldier, as escapism or subversion. Sending Batman to Viet Nam could have had several connotations, and the button from 1968 simply gives back its ambiguous message, red on white, resisting further interpretation.

(viii) Soviet

If the reading of West's Batman as super-soldier still seems unlikely, consider one further report from the *New York* Times.

> Batman ran into the Russian Communist newspaper *Pravda* yesterday, and – POW! – the collision was earthshaking. The Soviet organ accused the Caped Crusader of brainwashing Americans to become 'willing murderers in the Vietnam jungle'. Furthermore, it said, Batman was 'the representative

---

[224] TV schedule, *New York Times* (31 March 1966).

of the broad mass of American billionaires' who 'kills his enemies beautifully, effectively, with taste, so that shoulder-blades crack loudly and scalps break like canteloupes.' Those responsible for Batman, the article continued, in addition to filling their pockets, 'are striving to brainwash the ordinary American, to get him used to the idea that murder is beautiful.'[225]

ABC officials, the *New York Times* reported, were 'pleasantly amused'.

4. Nostalgia

It is surely clear that Batman's entry into television saw a phenomenal shift in his status as a cultural icon. As already stated, I believe that there are always as many potential interpretations of the Batman as there are individual readers; in this respect the number of 'Batmen' alive in the minds of comic and film serial fans during the early 1940s could rival the league of Caped Crusaders who paraded, each carrying slightly different associations, during the late 1960s. However, if we filter down to those interpretations which reached a certain level of cultural familiarity – those which were picked up by newspapers and magazines, suggested by authors or advanced by producers, editors and actors with a media platform – it becomes obvious that the boom in Batman's popularity led also to an explosion of interpretations which easily outnumbers those of previous decades. I identified perhaps three or four different readings of the character in the early 1940s, based around the interests of authors, editors, producers, readers and censors: in the chapter on the 1950s I dealt, essentially, with Wertham, DC and gay men, each of whom saw the homoerotic element in the Batman–Robin relationship but took a different stance towards it. In this section on the mid- to late 1960s I have already discussed eight interpretations of the TV Batman, some of them mutually contradictory and some, like the 'political satire' reading, themselves containing further complexities and ambiguities. These

---

[225] George Gent, 'Pravda Meets Batman Head On', *New York Times* (30 April 1966).

were simply what I saw as the eight outstanding and most interesting discourses around the character during this decade, taken from documents of or about the period and selected within constraints of chapter length. I have not been able to deal as fully as I would have liked with the subtleties of these chosen readings – for instance, the fact that Adam West was a comic fan, while William Dozier apparently detested the medium[226] – and I have had to omit others.

Bearing in mind this multiplicity of contemporary meanings around the television hero, it becomes even more surprising that retrospective opinions of the series – epitomised by the comic book 'purists' discussed above – tend to reduce all his associations to variations on the single word 'camp'. We have, however, already seen this phenomenon at work in the brief quotation above from a 1960s reviewer. The *Chicago News*, cited by James Van Hise, described the show's humour as 'warm, welcome, circa 1940s' silliness'; a remarkable rose-tinted transformation of the war years into shorthand for a better, simpler time, but one echoed by the film critic who remarked of the rescreened *Batman* serial that it 'shows how much we have lost in innocence even since 1939'.[227] Two or three decades, it seems, has the effect of smoothing the jags and edges of the present into a comfortingly safe 'past'. However real the tensions of 1943 and 1968 seemed to those experiencing them day by day, the complexities of the quotidian are forgotten; 1968 becomes '1968', reduced to two dimensions and rendered in simpler colours like a half-remembered TV show. Many of the comic fans who now deride the 1960s *Batman* as campy and cheap were born in the 1970s and 1980s; their flattening of the complex discourses which surrounded the show to a single characteristic is simply convenient, willful or simple ignorance. Critics like Frank Miller, Jonathan Ross, Paul Sassienie, Mark Cotta Vaz or Alan Moore, who stress the distinction between the 'dark' vision and the unfortunate distraction of the TV show, may be forgetting or repressing the memories of telling their daddies to stop laughing at an Adam West who, at the time, seemed manly and heroic. Yet even those who lived through the decade of the series' debut and now

---

[226] See West with Rovin, op. cit., p. 56.
[227] Anon., '1943 Serial All At Fell Swoop', *The Times* (3 Feburary 1966).

remember it fondly also remember it wrongly; that is, they recall it as the 1960s critics recalled the serial of the 1940s, as souvenir and symbol of a simpler time.

Spigel and Jenkins run through many of the discourses which I discussed above in the introduction to their analysis. The contrast between this scene-setting – recreating the concerns of the 1960s –8 and the 'thick description'[228] which follows as they deal with their correspondents' memories of the period, is extraordinary. The 'effects' discourse of Batman's negative influence on children has been forgotten. The 'merchandising' discourse has been forgotten. The 'dual address' to a juvenile and adult audience has been forgotten. In the space of just twenty years, the complexities which surrounded the show between 1966 and 1968 seem to have passed out of cultural memory, despite the fact that these correspondents see Batman as 'enmeshed . . . in their personal life histories'.[229]

'Our respondents', Spigel and Jenkins report, 'shared few of the earlier critics' anxieties about the program's aesthetic status . . . similarly, any concerns about the suitability of Batman for young viewers had vanished from popular memory. Several people expressed astonishment when learning of the 1960s controversy surrounding the program: "Really! Batman bad for kids. You've got to be kidding," Lori, a Madison game shop owner, declared.'[230]

Lori may have been too young to read the Times articles about parents 'At War With Batman'. We might expect her to remember the banning of Batman capes and masks at school, though, or at least to have seen other kids wearing the coveted Batman t-shirts, even if she never wanted or owned one herself. Yet apparently Lori and the other women of Madison, Wisconsin, never came into contact with Batman t-shirts, gum, periscopes, soundtrack albums, sliced bread or with any of the thousands of Batman licensed products.

Kate, a commercial artist from Madison, 'constrasted her childhood experience of Batman with the consumer-oriented programs preferred by her children: "I can't remember that there even were

---

[228] See Clifford Geertz, The Interpretation of Cultures, London: Collins (1993).
[229] Spigel and Jenkins, op. cit., p. 133.
[230] Ibid.

Batman figures when the show was first on ... I don't remember shows at the time being promoted as such a big package deal.'' Kate's denial of the series' commercialization was shared by other interview participants, most of whom claimed no knowledge or access to Batman spinoff products in the 1960s and saw the commodification of children's television as a relatively new development.'[231] We can either conclude that these four groups of adults from Massachusetts, California and Wisconsin[232] were never allowed out of the house as children during 1966, or that they were singularly unobservant; or else take Spigel and Jenkins' word 'denial' in the psychoanalytic sense of a small repression. It is hard to avoid this conclusion when we read that every correspondent 'insisted that they, like the adult spectators constructed by the 1960s' critical discouse, had always been "in on the joke", had always read the series as camp'.[233]

We could find a rationale for this apparently unconscious rewriting of personal memory. All the adults concerned are re-reading *Batman* according to a new agenda, seeking to hold it up as a bright object against the grubbiness they see in their own late 1980s society. Spigel and Jenkins deftly summarise:

> the program had become emblematic of a purer children's culture against which the offensive features of contemporary mass culture might be judged and condemned ... [w]hile we cannot be sure what any of these people might or might not have known about the cultural past, the general pattern of these memories suggests a simplification of historical contra-dictions in favor of an image of the past as a purer, less complex time, as a place not confronted with our con-temporary problems. What is remembered works to confirm those suppositions, what is forgotten is often information that might challenge such a picture.[234]

---

[231] Ibid.
[232] Ibid., p. 131.
[233] Ibid., p. 133.
[234] Ibid., pp. 133–134.

This response is a precise mirror of the 'comic purist' reading, in that it reduces shades of grey – ambiguities, contradictions – to light and dark. The 1960s TV show is 'light', the newer Batman – of the 1980s comic books and again, Tim Burton's 1989 movie – is 'dark'. The only difference is that in this case the value judgements are reversed.

> Many of the respondents expressed lack of interest in and sometimes hostility to the new *Batman* movie, holding open little possibility for the 1989 release to duplicate the pleasures they found in the TV series. In Kate's words, 'I don't think you could make that series now, I don't think you could make an eighties' version and have it come out the same.' Many found the darker tone of the Tim Burton film emblematic of the loss of innocence and playfulness that their childhood texts had once contained. Reflecting on a recent Batman comic book, Connie suggested, 'Gotham City used to be a much more fun place'.[235]

The pattern emerging here, as Batman evolves from the 1940s to the 1960s and 1980s, and passes from popular consciousness to popular memory, speaks for itself. These viewers of the late 1980s reproduce exactly the process we saw twenty years earlier, whereby the Batman of two decades ago is somehow cleansed of all his sullying contradictions – the censorship, the accusations, the conflicts over meaning – and rehabilitated not just as a simpler, more innocent hero but an emblem of the entire decade. As Batman reappears through the smeary lens of nostalgia, so the 1940s or the 1960s appear around him in turn, less complicated than they ever seemed at the time.

The comic fans who see the TV show as idiotically clownish and camp are therefore performing the same act of revision as these correspondents who remember it fondly as naive and playful. As if looking back with one eye closed, they reduce *Batman* to two dimensions, regarding it as either 'good' or 'bad' object, but at any rate a simple, easily graspable object. It is ironic that the show which arguably succeeded in transforming the comic book page into three

---

[235] Ibid., p. 141.

dimensions now seems, so regularly, to have its complexities flattened by hindsight.

5. The Giant Typewriter

As an academic, I attempt to view each incarnation and interpretation of the Batman objectively, as a valid and interesting text for analysis. But even as a fan, my enthusiasm for Batman – as mentioned above – grew out of both the mid-1970s comic books, which at that stage were going through a relatively 'dark' period, and repeats of the 1960s TV series. It seems curious to me now that, as a child, I saw no incompatibility between the swooping, majestic figure Neal Adams drew in the comics and the character portrayed on TV by Adam West; between the hardboiled dialogue Denny O'Neil gave to his Batman and the TV hero's musings about Frosty Freezes. At the time, I imagine I saw the two as only marginally different angles on the same character; I saw the similarities in costume, setting and supporting cast, and somehow the differences didn't matter. Both offered me the thrilling adventures of the Batman as he fought the Joker and Penguin in Gotham City, and both provided a framework for new Batman games in the back garden.

This open-minded approach to the character, demanding little more than the essentials – Batman is a millionaire who dresses in a bat costume and fights crime – has, I think, informed my position in fandom right up to the present day. I have my personal vision of what Batman would be like if he was 'real', which inevitably provides a standard against which I judge every Batman text; but I retain a loyalty towards the series which introduced me to the character, even though I may only buy the comics which show me Batman as highly intelligent, fundamentally antisocial and deeply cool. I cannot be unique in this. A generation of comic book fans must also have grown up with Adam West alongside O'Neil, Adams and the other architects of the 'dark' 1970s Batman. However, there are to my knowledge no areas of fandom, whether Internet or small press publication, which celebrate the TV hero on an equal footing with the comic book character. The 'Comics In Media' board at *Jonah Weiland's Comic Book Resources*, for instance, would seem a likely site for such fans to congregate but seems far more concerned with ongoing media texts such as the Batman movie franchise and Warner Brothers animations.[236] The Batman message boards on Jonah Weiland's site, as on the sites *Mantle of the Bat* and *The Dark Knight*, are almost universally committed to the Batman of contemporary – post-1970 – comic books; the TV show, as indicated by the quotations earlier in this chapter, is regarded as a gross mistake.[237]

On the other hand, there are sites devoted to the TV Batman, not least Adam West's home page which serves as a gift shop for autographs and memorabilia. Beneath a snazzy, Pop logo, the introductory pages proclaim 'Welcome citizens'.

> As you know, the Bat Cave is my Ultra-Modern crime control center. I have access to files on hundreds of known super criminals. Also, it is here that I develop the various crime control devices which have become my secret weapons in the continuing fight to keep Gotham City safe.[238]

Of course, West probably has no need to write the text for his own site, but this does seem to have his naïve, well-meaning touch; the simple faith of a man who still believes he has a useful role to play as cultural hero and upholder of moral values. Touchingly, the Internet has finally enabled West to reinhabit the role he loved.

West's is not the only site which remembers the TV *Batman* fondly. Andrew Hicks' *Da-da-da-da . . . Batman!* demonstrates its loyalties in the title alone, and provides a number of patiently crafted original scripts in the style of the 1960s series but with a couple of mid-1990s winks. In one episode, 'Aunt Harriet finds out Bruce and Dick's big secret (and no, it doesn't contain the words ''homo'' and

---

[236] See 'Comics in Media' board, *Jonah Weiland's Comic Book Resources*, http://www.comicbookresources.com/.
[237] See *Mantle of the Bat*, http://www.cire.com/batman, and *The Dark Knight*, http://www.darkknight.ca.
[238] *Adam West Batman*, http://www.adamwest.com/home.htm.

"sexuality")'.[239] *The Batcave*'s tone is equally fond, laced with a certain melancholy:

> If you'd have asked me who my favorite actor was in kindergarten, there's no question that I would have snapped back with a definitive 'Adam West'. Little did I know that my hero had been reduced to making appearances at shopping malls and auto shows. Typecasting sucks, plain and simple. It breaks your heart to see . . . an ageing Adam West wearing a cape.
>
> [. . .]
>
> When I was a kid, I took it very seriously indeed. For a time in my life, I was there every day. 'Same Bat-time, same Bat-channel.' Batman didn't jaywalk. Batman drank milk. Batman buckled his safety belt. Batman was a hero. And so is Adam West. I'm still tuning in.[240]

As the URL suggests though – the address is 'entertainment/tv/reruns/batman' – this site really constitutes an outpost of television fandom, rather than comic book readership. The message boards compare *Batman* to *Girl From Uncle* and *Get Smart*, not to contemporary DC titles. These fans have a sense of the show's place in history, of its complex addresses and role in television discourses – 'even back in the day, it was being hyper-analyzed; critics didn't know what to make of it',[241] says the *Bat-Cave*, while Hicks jokingly claims he finds the show to be 'a powerful commentary on the impertinent socialist paradigms of 60's counterculture, while most people just think it's stupid'[242] – but their love for the character apparently doesn't stretch to the comic book medium, or indeed beyond 1968.

So it seems that light and dark, TV and comic book, continue to attract different groups of fans and embody mutually exclusive

---

[239] *Da-Da-Da-Da . . . Batman!*, http://students.missouri.edu/~ahicks/batintro.htm.
[240] *The Batcave*, http://www.taponline.com/tap/entertainment/tv/reruns/batman.
[241] Ibid.
[242] *Da-Da-Da-Da . . . Batman!*, op. cit.

associations, and never the twain shall meet. But that might change. It might be changing now, judging by subtle changes in the way Batman has been envisioned by DC's editors and writers during the 1990s.

It is difficult to identify shifts in the comic book representation of a character while they are still ongoing. Any attempt to pinpoint the exact start of a tentative change in form and theme would be ludicrous; and so my motif may as well be the giant typewriter, and my key text a low-status, little-known Batman miniseries called *Run, Riddler, Run*, created by Gerard Jones and Mark Badger for DC in 1992.

The giant typewriter, along with the giant cash-register, giant clock, giant coffee-cup and giant golf club, was one of the major features of Gotham from the 1940s onwards. Mark Cotta Vaz describes it as 'a notable curiosity that makes Gotham unique among the big cities of the world – the number of over-size advertising props that adorn many Gotham buildings'.[243] Inspired perhaps by the oversized floats in the war bond parades of that decade – Roeder's *The Censored War* shows a giant cash register rolling through Times Square[244] – the comics never missed an opportunity to have Batman and Robin balance on massive scales, swing from the Ajax Golf Club or hang precariously from the rim of that brobdignagian cup of joe. By the 1960s, the gargantuan props had come to signify a playfulness and lightness of touch in the Batman mythos – Claes Oldenburg, of course, had recently put the Pop into props with his giant typewriter, toilet and telephone – and to some fans precisely the camped-up frivolity against which the 'pure' Batman should be defined. Just a glance at the catalogue of deathtraps which provided the TV Batman's cliffhangers makes the association clear. 'Batman is strapped to a giant key duplicator' (Episode 55, 'The Impractical Joker'), '[Catwoman] moves the unconscious duo to a giant echo chamber, where a dripping faucet, magnified ten million times, threatens to destroy their brains' (Episode 63, 'The Cat's Meow'), 'Batman and Robin are bound, tied, and suspended on one side of a giant scale over a vat of sulphuric acid',

---

[243] Cotta Vaz, op. cit., p. 68.
[244] George H. Roeder, Jr. *The Censored War: American Visual Experience During World War Two*, London: Yale University Press (1993), p. 69.

(Episode 52, 'Hizzoner the Penguin'), not to mention the 'giant Frost Freezes' we encountered in Episode 53, 'Green Ice'.[245]

There are no giant typewriters in *The Dark Knight Returns* (1986), nor in *The Killing Joke* (1988), where Batgirl is sexually abused and permanently disabled, nor in *A Death In The Family* (1988), where Robin is slain by the Joker, nor yet in *Knightfall* (1993), in which Batman is crippled and replaced by an even more brutal vigilante. But there is a giant typewriter in *Run, Riddler, Run*, a trap for Batman to tackle before he can help a group of oppressed squatters and radicals; that is, a witty flashback to an earlier aesthetic in the middle of a typically Nineties 'social relevance' story. The giant typewriter returns in a story from 1995's *Two-Face and the Riddler* movie tie-in, this time explicit in its nostalgic function with Edward 'Riddler' Nigma clambering over his huge props as he bemoans the loss of the 1960s: 'It was fun in the old days. That was what it was. There was the old cabal: Catwoman, Penguin and the Joker . . . we hung out together, down at the "What A Way To Go-Go". It was great!'[246] Of course, the club's name shows us where Gaiman's loyalties lie in this story; way back in January 1966, with Adam West looking down at the fallen Jill St John. 'There were all these guys you never see anymore,' the Riddler laments, 'King Tut. Egg Head . . . Book Worm. Marsha, Queen of Diamonds. Where did they all go?' Looking over his yard of rusted, abandoned props, he strikes a defiant pose atop a giant pinball machine. 'You know what they call them now? Camp, kitsch, corny . . . dumb . . . stupid. Well, I loved them – they were part of my childhood.'[247]

This was an unprecented move on the part of a comic book writer, reclaiming the TV show as part of the comic book characters' history and refusing to let the 'camp' and 'kitsch' elements of Batman's heritage be repressed forever. Nigma's manifesto is written by Neil Gaiman as a swan song from an elderly ex-villain; but whether

---

[245] See Eisner, op. cit., pp. 80–84, p. 92.

[246] Neil Gaiman, Bem89 and Mark Wagner, 'When Is A Door', in *Batman: Two Face and The Riddler*, New York: DC Comics (1995).

[247] Ibid.

coincidentally or not, this story can be seen with hindsight as part of a gradual, tentative shift in DC's conception of the Batman 'mythos'.

The giant typewriter resurfaces in Howard Chaykin's one-shot *Dark Allegiances* (1996), for instance, and again signals a playfulness and self-reference which would have been unthinkable for the 'adult'- some would say adolescent – mentality that dominated the Batman stories of the late 1980s. Once more, the giant prop comes hand in hand with a reference to the TV show's aesthetic; not mourning it, this time, but deftly reincorporating an aspect of the Adam West Batman into a story about espionage and political intrigue. This Batman's sinister and violent façade conceals hidden depths, or hidden shallows. 'I'm certain Biggsley's interest in the Batman franchise centers on my dark creature of the night persona,' he muses, preparing to eject an unwelcome guest from the Batmobile. 'So I doubt that the films he intends to make will ... address my academic interest in slapstick comedy.'[248]

It took, perhaps, a creative relaxation within the comic market, a feeling that the eyes of the world had passed away from the medium once more after the 'graphic novel' fad, for DC to allow its writers and artists to unwind and return to aspects of the Batman's rich heritage – like the love between Batman and Robin, evident in scattered moments from recent comics – which had been repressed for at least two decades. It was perhaps this tendency towards increasing self-awareness without self-consciousness which resulted in the *Batman Adventures* comic[249] – based on the Saturday morning Warners cartoon and now, renamed *Gotham Adventures*, one of the healthiest titles on the market.

The *Adventures* aesthetic is flat and sleek in its art, in keeping with the animated style. Paul Dini, the series writer, captures some of the aesthetic's apparent contradictions when he describes it as 'a dark, deco look ... stylized design ... simple, yet elegantly rendered ... ' and the tone as typified by 'straight-ahead action and multilayered

---

[248] Howard Chaykin, *Batman: Dark Allegiances*, New York: DC Comics (1996).
[249] The title debuted 1992 and is now available in Kelly Puckett, Ty Templeton, Rick Burchett *et al.*, *Batman: The Collected Adventures* volumes 1 and 2, New York: DC Comics (1993, 1994).

characterizations'.[250] While Dini still feels he has to stress that 'this is not "Batman lite", it's Batman Classic',[251] emphasising the series' 'darkness' and return to the 'original', the *Adventures* titles do in fact contain more than a hint of 'liteness' amid the dark, as suggested by Dini's own tribute to the 'live-action TV series' alongside Miller's 'magnificent . . . *Dark Knight Returns*' as one of the contributory texts to Batman's 'legend and lore'.[252]

The deliberate Pop flatness and simplicity was joined by a carnival air of camp in the *Adventures*' multiple award-winning spin-off *Mad Love*, a loopy slapstick romance starring a Batman who dares teasingly address the Joker as 'puddin';[253] anathema to the 1980s aesthetic, when all such play was projected onto the villains as deviancy and Batman responded to the Joker's flirtation with the snarl 'filthy degenerate!'[254] More subtly, but equally significantly, the *Adventures* series has led to the resurrection of the Batman 'family', including Batgirl, Nightwing and Robin. Such a notion was also antithetical to the 'dark' 1980s vision of the character, which progressively removed all helpers from Batman's side – Robin murdered, Batgirl crippled, Nightwing estranged – until the Dark Knight became an obsessive loner. For Batman to work not just with a twentysomething partner but a teenage girl and a young boy outdoes even the 'Dynamic Trio' of the TV show in its reassuring conception of the character as protective guardian and symbolic father. We might also note that the mischievous elf Bat-Mite was rehabilitated in an issue of the usually grim monthly *Legends of the Dark Knight*,[255] and that Ace the Bat-Hound now appears regularly in the animated series *Batman Beyond* and its spin-off comic title.[256] The Bat-Hound also made a cameo in a prestigious mini-series

---

[250] Paul Dini, 'Introduction' to Puckett *et al.*, *Batman: The Collected Adventures* volume 1, op. cit.

[251] Ibid.

[252] Ibid.

[253] Paul Dini and Bruce Timm, *Mad Love*, New York: DC Comics (1994).

[254] See Medhurst, op. cit., p. 161.

[255] Alan Grant and Kevin O'Neil, *Legends of the Dark Knight* #34, New York: DC Comics (October 1992).

[256] Hilary J. Bader, Rick Burchett *et al.*, *Batman Beyond* #1, New York: DC Comics (March 1999).

of 1996, *Kingdom Come*; he was accompanied by Batwoman, another product of the 'camp' period whose existence had been written out of Batman's historical continuity and diegesis during the 'graphic novel' years but whose gaudy, bright yellow costume cropped up in no fewer than three titles of the late 1990s.[257] It was also in *Kingdom Come* that Robin uttered his first 'Holy' exclamation in some thirty years, even if this 'Holy God!', from a middle-aged Dick Grayson staring global catastrophe in the face, served as dramatic contrast to the 'Holy Dental Hygiene' of his younger, more innocent days.[258]

Ace and Kathy Kane's returns from comic book limbo may seem trivial, but combined with the other subtle shifts to the Batman mythos detailed above, they arguably constitute a trend which would have seemed inconceivable to both editors and readers during the 'dark age' of the 1980s. Grant Morrison, who now scripts the monthly *Justice League of America* – in which Batman works alongside other DC heroes such as the Flash, Green Lantern and Martian Manhunter – has described it as a 'super-hero renaissance ... a common desire to restore some sense of nobility and grandeur to the super-hero concept ... a fresh and powerful sense of renewed vigor and positivity'. Morrison applauds *Kingdom Come* for having 'rescued the super-heroes finally from the Ghetto of Grim 'n' Gritty' and admits 'I, for one, am relieved and gratified to see the circle finally turn away from the darkness and into the light.'[259]

It is surely no accident that *Kingdom Come* features, in the superhero theme-diner 'Planet Krypton', a display case holding a familiar Batman suit under glass and spotlight: the costume, centrally placed on a pedestal, is unmistakably that once worn by Adam West.[260] And we can surely read wider connotations into this 'renaissance' which turns from darkness towards the light, allowing the return of colleagues and

---

[257] Mark Waid and Alec Ross, *Kingdom Come*, New York: DC Comics (1996); Alan Davis, *Justice League: The Nail*, New York: DC Comics (1998); Mark Waid and Barry Kitson, *The Kingdom: Planet Krypton* #1, New York: DC Comics (February 1999).

[258] Waid and Ross, op. cit.

[259] Grant Morrison, 'Introduction' to Mark Waid and Fabian Nicieza, Jeff Johnson, Darick Robertson *et al.*, *Justice League: Midsummer's Nightmare*, New York: DC Comics (1996).

[260] Waid and Ross, op. cit.

sidekicks who would previously have been derided as the depths of camp, surrounding Batman with a 'family' which hadn't been seen for decades and giving him a taste for slapstick as well as an intolerance for crime. As with the 'gay' associations which, as I suggested in the previous chapter, seem to be finally creeping into a handful of mainstream Batman texts, the reincorporation of 'light', 'camp', 'pop' elements is, I would venture, indicative of a more inclusive vision of the character on the part of DC's editors and writers as Batman reaches the new millennium and ends his first sixty years. Increasingly, DC and its creative staff seem to be coming to terms with the depth and variety of their leading icons' history; sifting through the box of costumes Batman has worn over the years and bringing them out in public as proof of the character's diversity rather than hiding them in disgust at any hint of camp, kitsch or gayness. This, perhaps, will be proof of the comic book industry's 'maturity'; this, rather than the pretensions of the 1980s, the cringing embarassment at previous generations' versions of iconic characters, the obsession with 'literary' status or 'adult' themes. If the readers follow, we may yet see a comic fandom which embraces the contributions of the 1960s TV series even as it celebrates the most recent graphic novel. An obsessively 'dark' Batman, after all, is potentially flatter than any Pop canvas; to achieve any degree of subtle, rounded shadowing, readers and producers alike may have to accept Batman in his costume of 1968 as well as that of 1986, in his camp as well as his sinister mode, in light as in darkness.

4

1986–1997

FANDOM AND AUTHORSHIP

They take the slate-gray Celica, the more Batmobilelike and steely car, on this desperate mission in the dead of the night. (John Updike, *Rabbit at Rest*, Harmondsworth: Penguin (1990), p. 245)

This chapter is divided into seven sections. The first four are about comics. I begin with a brief history of comic book authorship and at the same time with fandom's response to and discourse around that authorship, arguing that the two concepts of comic book 'author' and 'fan' evolved in tandem from the early 1960s. I then focus in more depth on fan discourse during a specifical historical moment, and the ways in which this discourse constructed the author of that period. This case study deals with the lettercolumns of *Detective Comics* during 1965. The subsequent historical overview discusses the ways in which the institutional shift towards 'direct sales' shaped both fandom and the comic author, and considers the role of the Internet in the discourses around comic book fans and authors in the late 1990s. I conclude by suggesting ways in which we could consider the multiple nature of authorship within Batman comics, by looking at the claims for authorship on the part not just of writer or artist, but of letterer, inker and editor.

The final three sections are concerned with the Warners cinema franchise during the years 1989–1998. Again, I deal with issues of authorial style, this time with regard to Tim Burton and Joel Schumacher's two films apiece, and examines critical reception in these terms; and again, I survey fan response to the cinema adaptation of 'their' character, in letter columns, in fanzines and on the Internet.

1. Comics Fandom and Authorship, 1960–1970

The discourses of comic fandom and comic authorship were born as twins and have grown up together over the last few decades, siblings locked into a relationship of debate and mutual dependence. Both originated in the early 1960s. While artists like Kane were lucky enough to enjoy a rare cult of authorship during the 1940s, taking working vacations in Hollywood and posing for publicity snaps with glamour girls on Miami Beach,[1] and the first EC Comics fanzines appeared in the early 1950s, just before the crackdown,[2] these were exceptions rather than early signs of a trend.

According to Gerard Jones in *The Comic Book Heroes*, it was DC that first opened its pages to reader response through the letter columns of *Superman* and *Justice Society of America*, edited respectively by Mort Weisinger and Julius Schwartz.[3] The year was 1960. That September, 'at a Pittsburgh science fiction convention ... two young couples simultaneously conceived fanzines that devoted regular attention to comics'. The editors of *Xero* and *Comic Art* 'were far removed from Weisinger's young letter-writers'.

> the new fanzine publishers were adults looking back, with little emotional investment in the present, while Weisinger's kids were the opposite, all waiting for the next issue of *Superman* with no sense of comics history. Before fandom could have any real effect on the field, the gap between them would have to be

---

[1] See Bob Kane with Tom Andrae, *Batman and Me*, California: Eclipse Books (1989), pp. 120–121, p. 130.
[2] Gerard Jones and Will Jacobs, *The Comic Book Heroes*, California: Prima Publishing (1986, second edition 1997), p. 63.
[3] Ibid.

bridged. And who else could engineer that bridge but Mort's old partner in fandom, Julius Schwartz?

Jones has the journalistic tendency of turning comics history into a comfortable yarn, eliding ambiguity for the sake of a good story teleologically told. It is hard to know, as was the case with his account of William Dozier's epiphany over the *Batman* title, whether the scheme of events was really this simple: but as he relates it, the two fields of fanzine culture and comic book 'letterhacks' were brought together as Julius Schwartz and Gardner Fox invited one of their *JSA* fans, Jerry Bails, into the National Periodicals office in New York. Over lunch, 'Schwartz explained the ins and outs of "fanzines" and fan networking'. The date was now February 1961. That month, a new edition of *Hawkman* comic hit the stands, its lettercolumn bearing – for the first time – the street addresses of every correspondent. Jerry Bails, fired up from his lunch meet, wrote to every fan whose letter appeared in that issue, explaining his vision of 'comics fandom . . . I know now (for sure) . . . that I want to bring out a "fanzine" dedicated to the Great Revival of the costumed heroes.' Within a few months, Bails was publishing *Alter-Ego* with Roy Thomas, a fellow letter-writer.

> Other fanzines popped up like mushrooms all across the country: *Komix Illustrated*, *The Rocker's Blast*, *The Comic Reader*, *Batmania*, and scores more. Most were done by adults, but some came from precocious kids just discovering comics . . . Bails even added two more fanzines to his little home publishing business: *Capa-Alpha*, a sort of communal fanzine called an 'amateur press alliance' or 'apa' and *The Comicollector*, 'the companion to *Alter-Ego*', featuring ads for people selling, buying, and swapping old comics.[4]

The network expanded rapidly, mapping out links between publishing and self-publishing, readers and writers, buyers and sellers; and the relationship between editors and fans was for this time a happy, mutually beneficial one. Bails paid for that lunch in kind by forming an

---

[4] Ibid., p. 64.

Academy of Comic Arts and Sciences whose fan panel awarded every prize to Julius Schwartz and his crew; Schwartz promoted *Alter-Ego* in the pages of his own comics. Prominent fans, writes Jones, 'drove cross-country to visit each other, tally votes, and plan conventions'.[5] A community had been established. 'For years, fans had nurtured their obsessions alone in silence. Now, suddenly, they'd found their lost race.'[6]

The lettercols had made this fan-network possible; and while Jones neglects to mention it, the slippery concept of the comic book 'author' clearly evolved through the same columns and the same process. Julius Schwartz, Jones notes, 'encouraged . . . the controversy over whether Joe Kubert was the right artist for *Hawkman* . . . criticism of *Mystery in Space* . . . and the fight about whether superheroes were better suited for science fiction or human interest stories in *Green Lantern*'.[7] Through the discourse between fan and editor, then, comics 'authorship' was created and debated. The inverted commas are needed here because, as I will suggest, the 'creator' of a comic book – that construction of words, pencils, plots, inks, colours, letters and editing – is especially hard to pin down, and comics fandom, unlike film scholarship, rarely takes the easier option of singling out a single individual from the creative team for sole praise or blame. Even at this early stage, we can see that the responsibility is being jointly attributed to artists as well as writers; and we might also note that Schwartz, as editor, is also responsible in a very real way for the 'creation' – the commission or cancelling, at least – of the stories under discussion. Schwartz's crucial role in the cultivation of the 'authorship' discourse is comparable to the part he played in fandom; for instance, when artist Carmine Infantino made the unprecedented demand in 1964 that the signature 'Bob Kane' be left off his work, it was Schwartz who came through for him.[8]

The culture of the comic fan and accompanying discourse around the comic author went from strength to strength during the 1960s. Fans organised the first New York Comicon in 1964 – a whole

---

[5] Ibid., p. 65.
[6] Ibid., p. 64.
[7] Ibid.
[8] Ibid., p. 97.

convention devoted to comics, rather than just a corner of a sci-fi meet. As Jones reports, most of the professionals invited declined to attend, but Spider-Man artist Steve Ditko's arrival highlighted an important function of the comic book convention: not only did it unite fans from across the country, it brought fans together with producers. Ditko had set a precedent; the second New York Con guest-starred, among others, Mort Weisinger, Gardner Fox and Bill Finger, and the massive annual gatherings of the San Diego Con or Britain's UKCAC today are still built around author signings, sketch sessions from visiting artists and discussion panels where professionals sit alongside fanzine editors and field questions from an active audience.

Comic book authors had remained, for the most part, unknown and unheralded until the 1960s. Julius Schwartz first allowed Gardner Fox and the artists of *The Atom* credit in 1961:[9] readers and writers alike were therefore seeing their names in print for the first time, at the same time. It is perhaps for this reason that comic book fandom has always had a particularly close relationship with the text's creators. The boundaries between comic author and fan, writer and reader, have always been thin and often dissolve entirely.[10]

Even by publishing a mimeographed fanzine for ten people, of course, a fan like Jerry Bails or Roy Thomas was becoming a comic book 'writer'; and often a comic book artist too, as the pages of comic zines were and continue to be filled out with amateur art. The crossovers occasionally became even more dramatic, though, as 'elite' fans actually began to work for the major companies. Roy Thomas was hired to work for Mort Weisinger. E. Nelson Bridwell had already been taken on by Weisinger as an editorial assistant. Both had come to the editor's attention through their letters to *Superman*.[11] 'The signal had been sent', Jones notes. 'Fans could become pros. They could actually *shape* the comics.'

---

[9] Ibid., p. 65.

[10] Not to suggest that this phenomenon is unique to comics. Tulloch and Jenkins note that 'many important science fiction authors came from fandom, while many writers within the genre regularly attend fan conventions.' John Tulloch and Henry Jenkins, *Science Fiction Audiences*, London: Routledge (1995), pp. 187–188.

[11] Jones and Jacobs, op. cit., p. 67.

2. Case Study: Batman Lettercolumns, 1966

In this brief case study I want to step aside from the historical overview for a moment and examine the actual nature of fan discourse within the lettercolumns of *Detective Comics* during 1965. This was a significant cultural moment in terms of fandom's evolution; readers had only recently been given the chance of a public voice, of having their discourse on Batman validated by publication and of joining in debate not just with editors, but with fellow afficionados. One enthuses that 'I seem to be becoming a "regular" in the *Detective* and *Batman* letters pages, and I like it!',[12] and others report that their published comments have led to pen-pal relationships with other fans. It was also a moment of transition in terms of comic book authorship, for – as I'll discuss below – Bob Kane's signature was still appearing on some stories with which he had no connection, while at the same time the names of other artists and writers were beginning to be credited for the first time. This inconsistency led fans into a pleasurable to-and-fro with the editors as they attempted to deduce the identity of unnamed writers and artists, and so effectively shaped the concept of the comic book 'author' – an individual who, whatever his role in the creative process, contributes a recognisable, personal style – at the same time as they were building their own fan-networks.

We saw in the previous chapter that readers had already been invited to play guessing-games with the editors on issues of plot and long-term narrative, as in the 'Outsider' story where letterhacks attempted to identify the mysterious villain – 'is he the American Hydra-Head, as per *Batman* #167, out for revenge?'[13] – until he was revealed as Alfred the Butler. This puzzling over deliberately created narrative enigmas was just part of an extended discourse which dominated the lettercols of the mid- to late 1960s Batman titles; it is tempting to wonder whether this relationship between reader and editor was in any way an unconscious reflection and enactment of the Batman's own role as 'darknight detective', musing over the riddles

---

[12] Letter from Mike Friedrich, *Detective Comics* #335, New York: DC Comics (January 1965).
[13] *Detective Comics* #338, New York: DC Comics (April 1965).

posed by his trickster enemies. It doesn't seem entirely far-fetched to suppose that part of the readers' pleasure in pitting their skills of observation against the comic text came from an identification with Batman and his co-stars, the 'ductile detective' Ralph Dibny, and detective J'onn J'onnz, the Martian Manhunter. In this sense, the title *Detective Comics* referred not just to its featured characters, but to the role of the reader; and it was largely the readers who created this role for themselves.

There was, it seems, no initial editorial invitation to identify the writer or artist on each uncredited story: but this is the task *Detective*'s fans set themselves, performing it with dilligence, shrewdness and a substantial background knowledge of the creators' distinctive styles.

> The artwork was noteworthy in that you've put another inker to work on Carmine Infantino's pencils. I'm not exactly sure, but my guess is that Sid Greene handled the job.[14]

> I am somewhat mystified about the inker. I think it's Infantino himself, with a slightly modified style, yet certain parts look like the work of Murphy Anderson, or even John Giunta.[15]

> Infantino's art-job? Great! It could have been super-great if the great Carmine had inked his own pencils – which leads to an interesting suggestion. How about teaming up Bob Kane and Carmine Infantino as a pencil-ink combo on a Batman story? It should be superb![16]

Note that, in these early days of fan discourse, the concept of 'author', or at least 'creator', is already taken to include the artist as a vital contributor to the construction of the Batman story, and that this role

---

[14] Letter from Mike Friedrich, *Detective Comics* #335, New York: DC Comics (January 1965).

[15] Letter from Kenneth S. Gallagher, *Detective Comics* #336, New York: DC Comics (February 1965).

[16] Letter from Leon J. Tirado, *Detective Comics* #335, New York: DC Comics (January 1965).

is recognised as comprising the two distinct tasks of pencils and inks. Writers receive an approximately equal attention, again with a sometimes astonishing attention to detail.

> the inside story was written with a touch of genius by . . . John Broome?[17]

> I think the author of this story was John Broome, because of the way the Gotham Gladiator stopped in the middle of his sentence in panel 1 of page 5.[18]

Guy H. Lillian, singled out by editor Julie Schwartz as 'our favorite Guy correspondent', receives a lengthy answer to his venture that a particular story 'was written by Gardner Fox, I'll wager'. The reply emphasises the spirit of competition which had emerged in *Detective*, suggests the role of editors in keeping their fans guessing, and indicates the relative complexity which the lettercol discourse of authorship had attained by 1965.

> It wasn't hard for you to tag Gardner Fox as the writer of the Elongated Man yarn . . . especially as he's written all the Elongated Man stories that have appeared so far in *Detective Comics*. Strangely enough, the Elongated Man stories that appeared in *The Flash* were written by John Broome. One of these issues, we're going to give Broome a crack at his original character . . . and then let's see who can tell the difference between a 'Fox' and a 'Broome.'[19]

Note, though, that it was the fans who created the cult of authorship around recognisable styles and creative traits, and the editors who seem to follow, taking up the game and providing new challenges. Clearly,

---

[17] Letter from Doug Potter, *Detective Comics* #337, New York: DC Comics (March 1965).

[18] Letter from Guy H. Lillian III, *Detective Comics* #356, New York: DC Comics (October 1966).

[19] Editorial reply, ibid.

there would be no puzzle if writer, inker and penciller were given full, explicit credit in the pages of *Detective*; and in this regard DC seems markedly different from its rivals, Marvel, who gave enthusiastic billing to everyone from star artist 'Jolly Jack' Kirby down to the secretary 'Fabulous Flo' Steinberg.[20] Although Gerard Jones, as I mentioned above, claims that Schwartz had credited Gardner Fox and his team in *The Atom* from 1960 onwards, my own research suggests that Bob Kane's signature continued to dominate *Batman* up until the mid-1960s, and inconsistencies remain even once his monopoly seems to be broken. Credits for Gardner Fox, Sid Greene and Carmine Infantino begin to appear in *Detective* #357 of November 1966, but the next issue, while correctly attributing the Elongated Man story to Fox and Greene, has Kane's signature returning to Batman artwork which is clearly by another hand. It was presumably this ambiguity which led to comments like the following, as the variable art style of 'Bob Kane' defied the guessing-game:

> I'm writing this because of Bob Kane's magnificent artwork. I can really say I didn't think Bob Kane was much of an artist, with his square-jawed, stiff-looking characters, but in the October *Detective* he really did a good job.[21]

> I must congratulate Bob Kane on his ever improving artwork. However, in some panels, too much of Batman's nose shows below his mask.[22]

Ultimately, though, the discourse around authorship in these columns goes no further than a sophisticated parlour-game of identifying writers, pencillers and inkers. While it constructs each for the first time as a creative individual, vital to the completed work, and associates them with an 'individual stamp' — Broome's unfinished

---

[20] Jones, op. cit., p. 65.

[21] Letter from John Wilson, *Detective Comics* #336, New York: DC Comics (February 1965).

[22] Letter from from Walt Smith, *Detective Comics* #340, New York: DC Comics (June 1965).

sentences, Kane's square chins – the identification is enough; there is no real discussion of what these distinct creative traits contribute to mood, theme or characterisation. The lack of printed credits in *Detective* of the early to mid-1960s creates a mystery, and the fans take pleasure in solving it. It is as though *Cahiers du Cinema* in the 1960s had been made up of letters guessing that 'Gregg Toland is the cinematographer on *Citizen Kane*, I'll wager – his deep focus on the snowstorm scene is unmistakeable', or that 'the music in *Psycho* sounds like Bernard Herrmann. I never enjoyed his repetitive string motifs before, but this theme is more to my taste.' The analysis is in many ways informed and intelligent, but it clearly has its limits; and it was only once the guessing-game was made redundant that lettercolumn fans were able to ask more searching questions of the comic text.

In the Batman comics, then – which, probably because of Kane's sustained monopoly over 'authorship', differ from DC's other titles in their lack of accurate credits until the mid- to late 1960s – the cult around writers and artists as joint authors was born from the combination of fan curiosity and editorial teasing. When full credits began to appear around 1966, fans had the opportunity to direct their discussion around authorship further, beyond mere identification for the sake of it. The guessing-game was over, on one level; but with the identities of writer and artist provided, readers could begin to theorise and conject about the ways in which these authors interpreted the Batman formula, and the differences between them in a wider sense. Consider, just as a brief indication of what followed, these extracts from a *Detective* lettercol of 1980, typical of the contemporary discourse in their discussion of character, narrative, the relation between writing and art and the relative merits of different individual contributions.

> Don [Newton] and Dan [Adkins] are hanging in there, creating page after page of truly beautiful, moody, exciting storytelling artwork. Denny O'Neil's story this time was a little SILLY – a group of assassins killing a nobody on the slim chance that he MIGHT know something about them . . .[23]

---

[23] Letter from Henry R. Kujawa, *Detective Comics* #492, New York: DC Comics (July 1980).

Now the writing. Jack C. Harris is steadily improving, although he still has a way to go to match Bob Rozaki's work. But Jack is doing great things with the Barbara Gordon character, fleshing her out and giving her substance. I am especially delighted with the warm and believable relationship Jack has established between Babs and her father. He also has attained a perfect ratio of action to characterization in his stories. But it is in the plotting that Mr Harris falls down.[24]

Don Newton and Dan Adkins' artistic rendition of the tale by Denny O'Neil shows just how important the artist is in comics. The splash page conveyed the entire feeling of the story in one glance. Throughout the 17 pages the art never faltered even once to convey the storyline and enhance the plot and dialogue. I must also compliment Adrienne Roy for her outstanding coloring, especially the movie theater scene with the shadows playing off of the main figures.[25]

It should be obvious that these letters represent a progression from the spot-the-artist games of the mid-1960s, and show fan discourse engaging with some of the complex issues arising from the nature of comic book storytelling. We can see that the readers are no longer concerned with the identity of the creators, but with what the distinctive talents which those creators bring to the story under discussion, and with the struggle to express the dynamic between several different contributors in terms of the final result.

Leaping forward again, just to show that debate around authorship was still a going concern in the lettercolumns of the late 1990s despite the instant accessibility of Internet boards, here is a comment on Grant Morrison's writing of Batman, published in the *Justice League of America* comic dated July 1998.

Morrison writes the Dark Knight as a double paradox: a sullen

---

[24] Letter from Scott Gibson, ibid.
[25] Letter from Mark Ryan, ibid.

misanthrope devoted to protecting others and a resolutely human figure who nevertheless can perform the impossible. Crucially, Morrison understands that Batman is never a single character, but rather a host of Batmen: a wealth of possibilities existing behind that costume, cowl and symbol.[26]

I'm still quite proud of that letter.

3. Comics Fandom and Authorship, 1970–1999

During the 1970s and 1980s two institutional shifts – 'direct sales', and royalty payments – significantly contributed to both the formation of a dedicated comics fandom and the creation of a 'stardom' within comics authorship. Again, the fates of author and fan were interlinked, their roles within the comic industry evolving during the same period and for the same reasons. As related by Bill Boichel in 'Batman: Commodity As Myth', the 'direct distribution' system was established by fan and convention organiser Phil Seuling in 1974, in order specifically 'to serve the needs of comic book fandom'. It resulted in the creation of the 'direct sales market, which has since grown to dominate American comic book sales'.[27]

The 'direct sales' system meant that, rather than distributing to mom-and-pop stores, newstands and head shops, DC could sell their comics on a non-returnable basis but at a discounted rate to men like Seuling, who in turn would ship them straight to specialist comic dealers. Fans received new titles faster and in better condition than they could hope for elsewhere,[28] and through the specialist outlets they also had somewhere to gather and consolidate their identity.

Denny O'Neil expands on this shift from a writer's perspective, again linking the new stress on 'creators' to the rise of a dedicated readership.

---

[26] Letter from Will Brooker, *JLA* #20, New York: DC Comics (July 1998).
[27] Bill Boichel, 'Batman: Commodity as Myth', in Pearson and Uricchio (eds), *The Many Lives of the Batman*, London: Routledge (1991), p. 15.
[28] Jones and Jacobs, op. cit., p. 209.

When I started out the editor was God because it didn't make any difference who was doing the books, not a bit. Batman sold regardless of who the creative team was ... then DC in particular began to emphasize the creators. The audience became sophisticated and began to demand a certain quality level ... the probable reason was the rise of the direct market. I've heard that the business people here at DC were coming to believe that the direct market was the wave of the future and that this would create a body of knowledgeable readers ... the readers who would care about good material and would notice bylines ... if that's the case, it's just good business to reward the creators who produce higher sales.[29]

O'Neil, speaking in the late 1980s, locates the change 'about ten years ago', which matches with Boichel's account:

By 1981, the direct market had expanded to the point that it could support a company producing four-color comics exclusively for comic book specialty stores. This company, Pacific Comics, offered royalties and shared ownership rights to its creators, an event which produced the first loosening of the iron hold that the old established comic book publishers, especially DC ... had on their talent. Up to this point, creators had received only a flat rate per page produced, with all rights retained by the publisher. Soon, other companies formed and entered the direct distribution market, offering similar terms to creators. As a result, by 1982 both DC and Marvel were forced to institute royalty payments that led to the creation of a comic book writer/artist star system.[30]

It is no accident that Boichel's primary example of this star system at work is the 'luring' of Frank Miller to DC prior to *The Dark Knight Returns*. Miller was both a writer and artist, and had also 'created' his

---

[29] Roberta Pearson and Bill Uricchio, 'Notes from the Batcave', in Pearson and Uricchio, op. cit., p. 27.
[30] Boichel, op. cit., p. 15.

own project with the six-issue series *Ronin*, whose characters and situations DC now offered him the unprecedented right to own for himself. This was a clever bait: DC was plotting to improve their steadily decreasing market share,[31] and after ruthlessly cleaning out their narrative universe in *Crisis On Infinite Earths* they wanted hot writers to offer a new slant to their Big Three characters, Superman, Wonder Woman and Batman. 'Highly lucrative contracts' were offered to 'the most popular comic book creators'[32] for these projects; according to Miller himself, he was originally the only choice for *The Man of Steel* as well as *Dark Knight*, with Steve Gerber pencilled in as collaborator and sole author of the third title, *Amazon*.[33]

The rumours of high-powered deals, the cultivation of Miller as a 'creator' with an 'individual vision', the freedom which DC was now allowing its writers and artists to 'rework' characters with a fifty-year history: all this built a tremendous anticipation which characteristically seems to have brought fandom closer in its shared excitement and common focus, just as it constructed the towering figure of the comics 'author' as star.

> There had been exciting new releases for years, there'd been a star system building for years, but there'd never been releases or stars like this before. Despite the mixed reaction to *Ronin*, every superhero fan and borderline superhero fan was dying to see what Frank Miller would do with Batman. Even the title promised a return to glory: *Batman: The Dark Knight Returns*. When it hit the stores, fans were on the phone to each other instantly – 'Did you get it yet?'[34]

After the revisionist Batman came the revisionist Superman and Wonder Woman: then the second echelon of heroes such as Green Arrow, Blackhawk, the Shadow and the Martian Manhunter, and then

[31] Jones and Jacobs, op. cit., p. 296.
[32] Boichel, op. cit., p. 16.
[33] Frank Miller, quoted in James Van Hise, *Batmania II*, Las Vegas: Pioneer Books (1992), n.p.
[34] Jones and Jacobs, op. cit., p. 296.

the reworkings of ever more obscure figures from the DC archive – Animal Man, the Doom Patrol, Black Orchid, the Sandman.[35] Some of these projects interpreted comics' new 'adulthood' as a licence for sexism and crude violence; some used the characters and costumes as a platform for an esoteric challenging of superhero conventions. All of them privileged the 'author' in a way the industry and the fans had rarely seen before.

Each new 'reworking' was promoted as a meeting of an established formula – say, Batman – with individual creative concerns and styles – say, the cut-and-paste experiment of writer Grant Morrison and painter Dave McKean. Each new Batman graphic novel – with its quality paper, glossy art and on occasion, hard covers – thus became a high concept piece, and the question in each case was the same: what would this creative team 'do' with the Dark Knight? After Frank Miller, what would Alan Moore and Brian Bolland do? After Grant Morrison and Dave McKean, what would Archie Goodwin and Scott Hampton do? And implied in 'do', of course, was 'do different': rather than a functional ticking-over, the industry and the fans now anticipated something radical, or surprising, or at least inflected in some way with the personal, individual style of writer or artist.

When Denny O'Neil wrote a Batman comic in the early 1970s, he was employed to turn out a gripping, self-contained yarn for about twenty pages in each monthly issue, keeping with the current preferences for a 'detective' Dark Knight and satisfying the reader through plot and characterisation; a challenge, of course, but one without intense pressure. There were few reviews, no television and press coverage, no 'highly lucrative contracts', no hype. This was the writer as craftsman, serving the character and the title rather than vice

---

[35] John Byrne, *Superman: The Man of Steel*, New York: DC Comics (1986); Trina Robbins and Kurt Busiek, *Legend of Wonder Woman*, New York: DC Comics (1986); Mike Grell, *Green Arrow: The Longbow Hunters*, New York: DC Comics (1987; Howard Chaykin, *Blackhawk*, New York: DC Comics (1986); Howard Chaykin, *The Shadow: Blood and Judgement*, New York: DC Comics (1986); J.M. DeMatteis and Mark Badger, *Martian Manhunter*, New York: DC Comics (1988); Grant Morrison *et al.*, *Animal Man*, New York: DC Comics (1988); Grant Morrison *et al.*, *Doom Patrol*, New York: DC Comics (1989); Neil Gaiman and Dave McKean, *Black Orchid* (1988); Neil Gaiman *et al.*, *Sandman* (1989).

versa. When O'Neil wrote the five-part series *Shaman* in 1989, it was the first story arc in a brand new monthly title, *Legends of the Dark Knight*. Now O'Neil was being constructed not as a craftsman but as a star, not just allowed but expected to bring something 'individual' to this Batman. What would O'Neil 'do' with his return to the character? DC was releasing the title with different colour covers, promoting it as the first 'solo' Batman comic since 1940. Fans would be on the phone, asking 'Did you get it yet?' By the mid-1990s they wouldn't even need the phone, and the network for fan discussion would have grown to a global scale.

Though lettercolumns still feature in almost every superhero title, the restrictions of space and editorial selection has made the Internet a far more appealing forum for contemporary comic fandom. As I have argued elsewhere,[36] the Internet offers advantages over every form previously available to fans, combining elements of the print fanzine, the convention and the 'real life' discussion group within a global medium, while retaining elements unique to itself.

> Consider firstly the questions of production and audience with relation to print and online fan culture. Even the most modestly produced fanzines ... invoke costs for copying and distribution which have to be covered by subscription, and therefore depend upon a dedicated core readership willing to commit to several issues. The Internet equivalent, on the other hand, allows a potentially infinite audience from around the world to drop in and read articles or features at whim, with no such commitment. Its readership is therefore very different – far larger, more anonymous, more casual – than that of a print 'zine. ...
>
> While debates do of course rage across the letters pages of print zines, the month or more usually three-month gap between issues results in a pace which seems archaic compared to the immediate return provided by the Internet. On the other hand, while many fans relish the informal debates in the

---

[36] Will Brooker, 'Filling In Spaces', in Annette Kuhn, *Alien Zone 2*, London: Verso (forthcoming 1999).

bar at conventions . . . these face-to-face discussions are often months apart, while Internet boards can be accessed during a lunch-break, after homework, even in the middle of the night.[37]

Perhaps most importantly, comics boards on the Internet have eroded more completely than any other form the boundaries between 'reader' and 'writer', amateur and pro, fan and author. As in a print fanzine, there are frequent interviews amid the reviews and articles, but only here can fans interact, on an everyday level, with writers and artists who are also posting from their own home or workplace. Batman group editor Denny O'Neil confesses that he visits Internet boards under an assumed name,[38] and *JLA* writer Mark Waid regularly joins in online discussion on his own books, although his comments are brief and he tends to disappear at the first whiff of criticism.[39] Recently the artists of *The Kingdom* posted an online message announcing that 'Times Are Hard' and trying to sell their original art from the title; an offer which was turned down with the friendly comment that times were harder for most fans.[40] While of course masquerade would be possible, and is no doubt attempted – the appearance of 'Mort Weisinger' alongside Mark Waid seems more suspect – the veteran fans on these discussion groups are canny enough to recognise a fraud, and so far they have all accepted Waid's contributions as the genuine article.

Of course, this does not change the overarching power relation between consumer-fan and writer-producer – the latter is still going to write whatever he likes within editorial constraints, and the former's power is limited to buying or boycotting the title in question – on the Internet board they share a platform in limbo where both voices are equal and the fans stand on an equal footing with the writers, outnumbering them but treating the creators with careful respect for

---

[37] Ibid., pp. 54–56.

[38] Denny O'Neil, personal interview (1 July 1998).

[39] The boards in question, in Waid's case, are at *Jonah Weiland's Comic Book Resources*, http://www.comicbookresources.com/boards.

[40] The artists were Matt Haley and Tom Simmons, posting to *Comic Book Resources* in January 1999 shortly after the publication of their art in *The Kingdom: Nightstar*.

fear that a stray insult will send them off in a huff and so deprive the boards of their presence. Once again, though, the comic book industry remains fairly exceptional in this respect; there are few media forms in the late 1990s whose creators regularly choose to participate in an informal online forum, discussing their own work and treating their critics as peers; where the gap between author and fan, in short, is still so narrow.

4. The Many Authors of the Batman

My question here is simple. In what ways do the multiple comic book authors of the Batman during the 1980s and 1990s 'construct' the character, inflecting the basic formula – millionaire in Bat-costume fights crime – through the tools available to them?

(i) Writers

Comic scripters, as we might expect, shape the Batman with words. In some ways, their role is far more like that of a scriptwriter for film or television than of a novelist, for the majority of text in any comic script constitutes instructions to the artist which will never appear on the completed comic page. As such, the comic writer's task is, partly, to communicate his own creative 'vision' of a scene – composition, setting, atmosphere, action – to the artist, rather than directly to the reader. However, certain textual elements of the script do carry through – via the letterer – to the final page, where they stand as a prose representation of what in cinema and television would be voiceover and dialogue.

Firstly, then, comic writers can shape their own interpretation of the Batman through a narrational 'voiceover', or an 'internal monologue'. This first device was dominant in Batman stories, from my reading, from the late 1930s until the mid-1980s. You will remember the opening caption of the first Batman story, describing 'a mysterious and adventurous figure fighting for righteousness', and the way this portentous tone was echoed in the 1943 serial's narration, then parodied in Dozier's TV voiceover in 1966. The same device was still being used in 1980, by Marv Wolfman – 'The Batman's hands are a sudden *blur* of action – and less than a *heartbeat* later . . . a perfectly aimed *batarang* flashes forward at lightning speed' [41] – and by Denny O'Neil – 'Like a dark-clad wraith, he swoops down from the giant tree . . . '[42]

Clearly, these expository captions give us a sense of the author's vision of Batman through an added description of character, action and movement, and the opportunity for metaphorical overtones. 'Like a twisted freak . . . ', 'Like a costumed idiot . . . ' or 'Like a giant ape . . . ' would obviously have lent Dan Adkins and Don Newton's picture a completely different association.

More common in contemporary comics, however, particularly those which style themselves for an older audience, is the 'internal monologue' caption, which gives us entry into Batman's mind moment-by-moment, or permits us to read his journal entries. Given the pulpy, faintly comical rhetoric of the 'expository' caption, it is unsurprising that this device should be valued for its more serious, literary overtones; it also, of course, brings us closer to the character by making us privy to his own thought patterns. This is the device used by Frank Miller throughout *Dark Knight Returns* – 'This should be *agony*. I should be a *mass* of aching muscle – broken, spent, unable to *move*. And, were I an *older* man, I surely *would* . . . '[43] – and employed again in *Year One*.

Through this device, Miller is able to suggest Bruce's state of mind, from lucid observation to fading consciousness – 'made it . . . somehow . . . must've made it here . . . to the car . . . '.[44] Bruce's 'internal' captions occasionally explain events which the artwork leaves unclear, adding a wry commentary which in turn shows us this Batman's mordant perspective: 'Leaving the world no *poorer* – four men die', 'I

---

[41] Marv Wolfman, 'Twice Dies the Batman', *Batman* #329, New York: DC Comics (November 1980).

[42] Denny O'Neil, 'The Riddle of the Golden Fleece', *Detective Comics* #491, New York: DC Comics (July 1980).

[43] Miller, *The Dark Knight Returns*, op. cit., Book One, p. 26.

[44] Frank Miller and David Mazzucchelli, *Batman: Year One*, London: Titan Books (1988), p. 16.

make him eat some *garbage* — then I help him *swallow* it', 'I watch them kick him around for a minute. I've had *worse* times.'[45]

Compare this hard-boiled vigilante with the Batman in Alan Moore's *The Killing Joke*. Moore opts not to use narrational or 'internal' captions here, instead constructing his version of the character through dialogue: in this case, with the Joker.

> Hello. I came to talk. I've been *thinking* lately. About you and me. About what's going to *happen* to us, in the end. We're going to *kill* each other, aren't we? Perhaps you'll kill me. Perhaps I'll kill you. Perhaps sooner. Perhaps later. I just wanted to know that I'd made a genuine attempt to talk things *over* and *avert* that outcome. Just *once* . . . I don't fully understand why ours should be such a *fatal* relationship, but I don't want your *murder* on my . . . hands . . . [46]

While the actions and behaviour of this Batman are not so different from those of Miller's *Dark Knight* — the Batman fights the Joker hand-to-hand, as he is destined to, and even the setting of a fairground hall of mirrors is identical to that of Miller's climactic showdown — the dialogue could never be transposed to Miller's Batman without seeming glaringly out of place. Miller's Batman simply does not deliver such long speeches. He talks in a flat, efficient shorthand — 'To the stables, Robin'[47] — rather than in such measured, thoughtful, self-deprecatory language. He would never give his arch-enemy the offer 'Maybe I can *help*. We could *work* together. I could *rehabilitate* you . . . you needn't be *alone*.'[48] When Miller's Batman faces Superman in their final conflict, he scorns the Man of Steel's attempts at last-ditch talks as

---

[45] Miller, *The Dark Knight Returns,* op. cit., Book One, p. 46; Book Two, p. 23; Book Four, p. 36.

[46] Alan Moore, Brian Bolland and John Higgins, *The Killing Joke*, New York: DC Comics (1988).

[47] Miller, *The Dark Knight Returns*, op. cit., Book Four, p. 17.

[48] Moore *et al.*, *The Killing Joke*, op. cit.

'more wind . . . Now he's talking – trying to *reason* with me. I can't *hear* him, of course.'[49] Dialogue defines these two Dark Knights as very different characters.

Even if Batman never speaks, barely appears throughout the story or simply makes a brief cameo, the writer has the opportunity to cast his own 'vision' of the character through a focus on others' reactions – grudging respect when Batman guest-stars with Aztek[50] and Chase,[51] the awe tinged with faint dislike experienced by the younger heroes in *JLA*,[52] and even mockery, when Hitman greets the Dark Knight with 'Inform the troops! Lord Vader has arrived!'[53]

Of course, a comic book writer has control over his characters' actions as well as their speech, directing them as if they were performers and trusting to the artist to visualise the scene. Some writers, like Alan Moore, go into notorious amounts of detail for every single frame. 'His description for the first panel of *The Killing Joke*, one ninth of a page', says Denny O'Neil, 'is two and a half single space pages. It took me a day to read the script of *The Killing Joke*. It was a pretty good day, though.'[54] O'Neil, on the other hand, writes brief, often irreverent descriptions of each panel which leave the artists a great deal of creative space:

1. MIDNIGHT. WINTER. ROOFTOP. BATS IS ON A PARAPET, OR PERCHED ON A GARGOYLE, OR WHATEVER BATMANLIKE PLACE YOU WANT TO PUT HIM . . .
CAPTION: Soon he will act. Soon, he will leave this cold perch above the city, fall through the November night –

2. FLASHFORWARD (AND IF WE WERE ANY MORE

[49] Miller, *The Dark Knight Returns*, op. cit., Book Four, p. 38.
[50] Grant Morrison *et al.*, 'A Dark Knight in Vanity', *Aztek* #7, New York: DC Comics (February 1997).
[51] D. Curtis Johnson *et al.*, 'Shadowing the Bat', *Chase* #7, New York: DC Comics (February 1997).
[52] Grant Morrison *et al.*, *JLA*, New York: DC Comics (1999).
[53] Garth Ennis and John McCrea, *Hitman*, New York: DC Comics (1997).
[54] Pearson and Uricchio, 'Notes from the Batcave', op. cit., p. 32.

ARTY, WE'D BE WEARING BERETS): BATS CRASHING
THROUGH A SKYLIGHT IN BATMAN-LIKE FASHION.
SEE COPY.[55]

'We're not curing cancer', O'Neil replied when I questioned him
about this offhand, jokey tone.[56] Note, though, that the lack of
pretension in the panel descriptions stands in contrast to the grandeur
of the narrative captions: it is clearly in this area of traditional,
'literary' narration that O'Neil's 'voice' will come across most strongly
in the final text.

O'Neil concludes his script with a further show of humility,
admitting the problems he had with the script and offering the artist
free reign to suggest other solutions: 'I finally decided on the falling
metaphor. If that doesn't work for you, or if you want me to change
any of the other artsies (the dialogue-in-caption shtick, for instance),
you need but holler. I live to serve.'[57] As a veteran scripter brought up
on the craft of writing quickly and effectively, rather than the hoo-ha of
graphic novel 'stardom', O'Neil is perhaps exceptional in his sharing of
creative responsibility. Even here, though, we can see that the writer
decides the number of frames per page, their size and their layout –
'suggest the crash thru the window take up the top half of the page and
the rest of these punky panels be strung out across the bottom'[58] – as
well, of course, as describing the scenes they contain and their order
within the story.

Thus Moore's characteristic use of a strict grid system in *The Killing
Joke*, dividing the page into regularly sized panels, lends the story a
sense of order and measured pace which matches this conception of the
Batman and echoes Moore's controlled, structured approach to
writing. The layout and page design is 'neutral', designed not to be
noticed; our eye flicks easily from frame to frame, taking in the panel's
content rather than its form. Deviations from this strict grid, as in the

---

[55] Denny O'Neil, 'Batman Origin', unpublished script. This draft ultimately saw
print as 'The Man who Falls' in *Secret Origins*, New York: DC Comics (1990).
[56] Denny O'Neil, personal interview (1 July 1998).
[57] O'Neil, 'Batman Origin', op. cit.
[58] Ibid.

scene where Gordon is faced with images of his violated daughter and the artwork escapes the panel borders, therefore help to convey a lack of order and reason through the very abnormality of the page design.

Miller's *Dark Knight* is on the whole more free with its layouts, sometimes employing a 'filmic' grid like a storyboard to break scenes down into tiny, individual moments – the slow fall of pearls from the neck of Bruce's mother – and frequently overlaying scenes with small television panels which offer a constant background discourse. Sound effects frequently break the borders of frames or even occupy entire frames themselves, forming an integral part of the page. The most radical change in pace, however, comes from the 'splash' panels which present us with huge images of Batman in towering, iconic poses – cradling a dead general in the American flag, leaping through the sky with Robin, rearing his horse as he rallies a gang of urban youths. These serve as landmarks in the story and in the character's development, lending the scene a pivotal, mythic status.

The comic book writer therefore takes on a role perhaps equivalent to film scriptwriter, director and editor – at once the author of dialogue and voiceover, the architect of plot, the supervisor of action and the organiser of shot sequence. Paradoxically, though, once the script has left his hands he will usually have no control: the realisation of the comic's visual elements is entirely in the hands of others.

(ii) Artists

The simplest way to understand the importance of Brian Bolland's pencils and inks to the Batman of 'Alan Moore's' *The Killing Joke*, or the contribution of Dave McKean's painted art to 'Grant Morrison's' *Arkham Asylum*, is to imagine the situation reversed.

Arkham Asylum is a deliberately ambiguous narrative which juxtaposes the journal entries of the asylum's architect – telling the story of his family's murder and his subsequent madness – with the 'present day' plot which has Batman trapped in the asylum with the inmates. The book makes frequent reference to psychology, literature and mythology, drawing parallels with *Psycho*, *Alice In Wonderland*, the Bible and the Tarot. Dave McKean's paintings, accordingly, mix media – pencil sketches, photographs, collages of lace, hessian and nails – into an often blurred, obscure, literally 'dark' vision of the Batman's physical and emotional journey through the asylum.

The Killing Joke, as suggested above, is a story about control, structure, rules and order – represented by Batman and Gordon – being put to the test by insanity. The Joker captures Gordon and forces him to view images of his naked, paralysed daughter in an attempt to break his reason. As he explains to Batman, 'Gordon's been driven *mad*. I've proved my point. I've demonstrated *there's no difference* between *me* and everyone *else*! All it takes is *one bad day* to reduce the *sanest man alive* to lunacy.'[59] But Gordon struggles through, insisting 'I want him *brought in* . . . and I want him brought in by the *book*! We have to *show* him! We have to show him that our way *works!*' Bolland's artwork is in the traditional comics mould, built around detailed pen lines and solid blacks. Sometimes criticised as stilted, his figure-drawing tends towards the static, frozen moment even when characters are in movement, and he relies on 'speed lines' to convey action. There is no ambiguity about the content of each frame, and the art is contained within strict panel grids – except, as noted above, during brief moments associated with the Joker's temporary dominance. Here the image escapes its frame and spreads across the page, uncontrolled; but on the next page the grid system is reinstated, indicating long before the conclusion that it is Batman's system of order and control which will ultimately prevail.

Had Dave McKean provided his impressionistic, painted art for this story, the implications would have been completely different. McKean's Batman is a devil-eared shadow rather than a concrete human figure, while his Joker, all swirling fluorescent hair and gleaming white face, remains a blur who refuses to be pinned down. McKean's abandon with different materials, styles and visual references suggests anarchy rather than control. Put simply, the Joker 'aesthetic' would have dominated every page of *The Killing Joke*, and Batman's failure to resolve their 'fatal relationship' through dialogue would have seemed to mark victory for the forces of unreason. On the other hand, Bolland's stiff inks would have illuminated every corner of *Arkham Asylum*, turning ambiguity to stolid detail and making the lunatic house

---

[59] Moore and Bolland, *The Killing Joke*, op. cit.

a 'real' place of objects and rooms rather than the state of mind implied by McKean's painting.

This artistic influence over the story's characters, tone and meaning is by no means confined to McKean and Bolland. Kelley Jones, for instance, always draws Batman as a demonic creature with a cloak made up of jagged shadows and ears like scimitars extending some four feet from the top of the cowl;[60] whatever measured, rational tones an Alan Moore put in this Batman's mouth, he would still look like a crazed vampire. Kevin O'Neil, whose jagged, cartoony style was condemned in the 1980s never to bear a Comics Code seal of approval, whatever the content, makes Batman an angular parody of heroic masculinity, lantern-jawed and blank-eyed.[61] It would be difficult to take this Batman seriously as the protagonist of Morrison's self-conscious, referential and faintly pretentious journey through the psyche.

Less obviously, perhaps, inkers still have a crucial role in creating and maintaining tone. We may have to peer hard from Kelley Jones' pencils on Red Rain to the same artist's work on Bloodstorm in order to spot any difference between the inks on the former – by Malcolm Jones – and those on the latter, by John Beatty.[62] Likewise, only a second glance would suggest that Brian Kitson's pencils, which he inked himself for the first two issues of JLA: Year One, were overlaid with Michael Bair's slightly more fussy inks for the rest of that title's twelve-issue run.[63] However, this is sometimes exactly the point: as Bruce Timm points out in his introduction to Batman Adventures, the comic adaptation of Warners' animated series, 'inker Rick Burchett has been doing superlative work on the book . . . maintaining a consistent "look" over the work of three very different pencillers, and yet

---

[60] See for instance Doug Moench, Kelley Jones and John Beatty, Batman: Bloodstorm, London: Titan Books (1995).

[61] See Alan Grant, Kevin O'Neil et al., 'Legend of the Dark Mite', Legends of the Dark Knight #38, New York: DC Comics (October 1992).

[62] See Doug Moench, Kelley Jones and Malcolm Jones III, Batman: Red Rain, London: Titan Books (1991); Moench, Jones and Beatty, Batman: Bloodstorm, op.cit.

[63] See Mark Waid, Brian Augustyn, Barry Kitson, JLA: Year One #1, New York: DC Comics (January1998); Mark Waid, Brian Augustyn, Barry Kitson and Michael Bair, JLA: Year One #12, New York: DC Comics (December 1998).

playing up the strengths of each'.[64] When Brad Rader takes over the pencils on issue #4 and provides a far less confident line than the previous artist, it is Burchett's job to overlay this new style in a manner that irons out some of the differences between the two artists, retaining the standard features of the TV show's Batman while refraining from completely stamping out Rader's idiosyncrasies. 'Not an easy feat', Timm concludes; and one which is seldom recognised if performed well. Only bad inking stands out from the page. 'A good inker can take a mediocre pencil job and make it great', observes Denny O'Neil, 'and, conversely, a bad inker can take a pretty good pencil job and make it awful.'[65]

The same is true of letterers and colourists, although these contributors have if anything more influence over the atmosphere, characterisation and even narrative of a comic book story. O'Neil notes that 'the colorist can be part of the storytelling process. If the vase in the corner is going to be very important to the story, they will color the panel in such a way to subtly emphasize that vase without a little arrow pointing to it saying "important clue".'[66] Lynn Varley's colours on Dark Knight undeniably contribute to the book's feel of 'gritty realism', providing subtle tones and textures which contrast with the traditional 'four-color' comic palette just as Miller's morally ambivalent characters contrast to the clear-cut heroes and villains of earlier comics. The colour in Dark Knight also suggests a psychological and physical state, as when a sick and staggering Batman sees his world in shades of muddy grey and dull crimson,[67] and plays a crucial role in clarifying the various internal monologues which make up the book's narration. Batman's thoughts appear in grey captions, Robin's in bright yellow, and Superman's in blue – and again, Superman's internal narration pales to a weak, washed-out colour when the character loses strength, only returning to its full turquoise as he recovers.[68] John

[64] Bruce Timm, Introduction to Batman: The Collected Adventures volume 2, London: Titan Books (1994).
[65] Pearson and Uricchio, 'Notes from the Batcave', op. cit., p. 26.
[66] Ibid.
[67] Miller, The Dark Knight Returns, op. cit., Book Three, pp. 41–42.
[68] Ibid., Book Four, p. 26.

Higgins' colour in *The Killing Joke* even shows us when the story is entering flashback, as scenes from the Joker's past are filtered through the sepia shades of old photographs.[69]

'Lettering is a great unacknowledged art form', says O'Neil. 'The minimum requirement is that the lettering should be neat and very legible, but we are getting sophisticated to the point that we actually use it as part of the story ... what I designate on scripts as spooky lettering.'[70] Spooky lettering is a vague term, typical of O'Neil's casual approach to scripting; it might include the handwritten diary entries of Bruce Wayne and Jim Gordon in *Year One*, or the lunatic, almost illegible scrawl of red on white which represents the Joker's speech in *Arkham Asylum*. Once more, colour becomes important here: Gordon's neat penmanship in *Year One* stands in buff captions and Wayne's more flowing text in white, distinguishing the two even when they appear alongside each other. In *Arkham Asylum* colour and lettering again come together as Batman's dialogue is stamped on the page in an inverse of the normal speech balloons, white on a black background. That this same device had already been used by Neil Gaiman for the Dark Knight's cameo in *Black Orchid* and was borrowed again for Batman's dialogue in Jamie Delano's *Man-Bat*[71] surely indicates the potency of the convention; through it, Batman's voice becomes unmistakeable, a dark imprint across all the scenes he walks through. 'It adds visual texture,' O'Neil concludes, 'and I think in your mind you hear it differently. At least I do.'[72]

(iii) Editors

O'Neil has probably considered the role of letterists, inkers and colourists longer and harder than most comic book scripters. While he still writes the occasional Batman story, Denny O'Neil is currently

---

[69] Moore and Bolland, *The Killing Joke*, op. cit.

[70] Pearson and Uricchio, 'Notes from the Batcave', op. cit., p. 25.

[71] See Neil Gaiman and Dave McKean, *Black Orchid*, New York: DC Comics (1988); Jamie Delano and John Bolton, *Batman: Man-Bat*, New York: DC Comics (1995).

[72] Pearson and Uricchio, 'Notes from the Batcave', op. cit., p. 25.

Group Editor of the ongoing Batman titles, supervising not just the Dark Knight but his 'universe' – the monthly exploits of Catwoman, Robin and Azrael, as well as the various inflections of the Bat-mythos in *Legends of the Dark Knight*, *Shadow of the Bat*, *Gotham Adventures*, *Detective* and *Batman*. O'Neil's personal vision of the Batman, then, is imposed on every use of the character across the board, and extends to cameos and guest-starring appearances in other titles like *Chase*, *Hitman*, *Aztek* and *JLA*. To all intents and purposes, O'Neil is God in the Batman universe, and his rules, or 'guidelines', for what the Dark Knight can and cannot do, are set out in the document he calls the *Bat-Bible*. This set of codes did not exist until the mid-1980s; O'Neil instigated it some three months into his appointment as editor in 1986.[73] Rather than an indication of his personal control, however, O'Neil argues that the *Bat-Bible* came about as a response to dedicated fandom and its insistence on 'continuity' between stories.

> Julie Schwartz did a Batman in *Batman* and *Detective* and Murray Boltinoff did a Batman in *The Brave and the Bold* and apart from the costume they bore very little resemblance to each other. Julie and Murray did not coordinate their efforts, did not pretend to, did not want to, were not asked to. Continuity was not important in those days. Now it has become very important . . . continuity is something our audience demands. I think maybe the audience is more cohesive . . . the current fans read a great deal more intently and with a great deal of care. Also, thanks to the direct market, it is now possible to get every issue of everything . . . also, letter columns did not exist back then so there was no arena to exchange opinions, nor were there conventions . . .[74]

Nevertheless, the preferences of a single man who wrote Batman in the early 1970s now take precedence over the interpretation of every contemporary scripter and artist who deals with the character. Most obviously, 'Wayne/Batman is not insane . . . and he never kills. Let's

---

[73] Denny O'Neil, personal interview (30 June 1998).
[74] Pearson and Uricchio, 'Notes from the Batcave', op. cit., p. 23.

repeat that for the folk in the balcony: *Batman never kills.*'[75] While O'Neil insists that 'Continuity should not be the boss . . . the *Bat-Bible* is a ball-park with wide boundaries, and if a writer transgresses them with a great story, I'll find a way of fitting them in', we can safely assume that during O'Neil's time as editor, no writer or artist will be able to show Batman taking a life.

More subtly, there are 'guidelines' pertaining to the Batman's relationships. Commissioner Gordon '*does not know Batman's true identity*'. Bruce has 'never had a serious affair', and is 'celibate' but 'appreciates women'. Again, then, while O'Neil is editor no story will ever be published which shows Batman acknowledging sexual feelings for another man: not because of any conservatism on the editor's part, but 'because of the tabloid backlash, although I'm a token liberal. I'm not sure if it's a fight worth fighting. The heat we would take would be too heavy, and it could set back gay rights.'[76] Yet whatever the motivation the result is still the same, and O'Neil's 'guideline' clearly limits the possibilities for creative and political expression through the Batman.

In terms of Batman's place within the DC Universe of superheroes, O'Neil has to struggle with his vision of the character against the more fantastic powers and situations of the other comic titles. 'I'm a realist. Batman should not exist in the same world as Superman and Green Lantern. You've got Superman, who can juggle planets, and Batman, who is . . . quite strong!' When Batman is obliged to take part in a 'planet-hopping' storyline across the DC Universe, O'Neil follows the same compromise employed by the scriptwriters of the 1943 serial: if Batman has to take part in a war, let's bring the war to Batman in the form of a Gotham City spy column. If Batman has to be part of an interplanetary crossover, 'let's play it so the visiting alien is after a gadget in an alleyway'.[77] In turn, when Batman becomes caught up in science fiction through his integral role in Grant Morrison's *JLA* stories, it is O'Neil who has the ultimate control – if he sees the script and art in time.

---

[75] Denny O'Neil, *The Bat-Bible*, unpublished document.
[76] Denny O'Neil, personal interview (1 July 1998).
[77] Denny O'Neil, personal interview (30 June 1998).

If an editor borrows any of my characters – Robin, Catwoman, Azrael – I should see the script and artwork. I have veto power. Theoretically, I can get a project killed at any stage. The first three issues of *JLA* were about right. But when I saw Grant Morrison had put a teleporter in the Batcave, it made my teeth ache. If I'd seen it before publication, I would absolutely have stopped it. I would absolutely have killed the teleporter, because it so violates our concept of the character.[78]

Artwork, on the other hand, is less rigorously policed. No official visual guidelines exist, though a creator may be given xeroxes of *Year One* for reference – Miller and Mazzucchelli's vision of the character having therefore become the 'dominant'. However, the more idiosyncratic styles of the artists mentioned above are allowed the space to express their own interpretation of the Dark Knight; more space, it seems, than that given the scripters. 'I just say, there are two hundred Batsuits . . . so when Kelley Jones draws him, he's wearing the costume with huge ears. It's a different suit.'[79]

Perhaps surprisingly, O'Neil has no great love of fandom, and seems prejudiced by his encounters with Batman readers. His attitude also suggests his own investment in the commercial aspect of Batman as a franchise, and his recognition that the 'hardcore' of fans constitutes only a vocal minority instead of representing the paying audience as a whole.

The people we hear from are mainly the fanboys and the heavy breathers . . . people with high emotional investment . . . very vocal, very vehement . . . a minority. We have [in the past] been working for that audience, and alienating everybody else to serve the fan agenda.

If we choose to continue with a failing title, it is because we think it's good, of artistic merit or with film and TV potential . . . because we like it, not because of a loyal fanbase. If we cancel a title, I know it will lead to two hundred letters saying

---

[78] Denny O'Neil, personal interview (1 July 1998).
[79] Ibid.

'You are a rat bastard and I don't like your mother.' I've visited Internet chatrooms and I'm astonished by the vehemence there. I'm like, 'Check out the sunlight! Get out of your mother's basement!' We just can't allow ourselves to pay unstinting attention to the fans.[80]

In the hierarchy of control over Batman, though, O'Neil knows full well that there are bigger players than him. Whether he approves of Paul Dini's *Batman: The Animated Series* more than Joel Schumacher's *Batman and Robin* is irrelevant; when Schumacher suggests that Batman appreciates Dick Grayson more than Poison Ivy, or Tim Burton shows Bruce spending the night with Vicki Vale, O'Neil can do nothing but throw up his hands. The *Bat-Bible* has its limits, and those limits end when DC Comics ends and Warner Brothers, the overarching conglomeration, begins. There can be no continuity enforced between DC's comics and Warners' films. 'Both sides would go nuts,' O'Neil concludes, 'And they're the bigger side.'[81]

5. *Batman* and Fandom: Anticipation and Rejection

Camille Bacon-Smith and Tyrone Yarbrough identify four distinct audience groups who attended the early screenings of Tim Burton's *Batman* in June 1989. Respectively, they list 'Long term fans of the comic books', 'Short term fans', 'Fans of the television series' and 'Audiences who were not fans of Batman in any sense'. The last group attended the movie as an 'event' and summer blockbuster. These viewers were there out of curiosity piqued by hype, but had little emotional investment in Batman as a character or interest in the movie's 'fidelity' to a specific comic book 'original'. This group, we can generalise, wrote few letters to the national or fan press about Burton's conception of the character; they did not protest the casting of Michael Keaton in the title role, or campaign for the casting of Adam West. As such, then, they offer far less to academic discussion than do

---

[80] Ibid.
[81] Ibid.

the more 'active' fans; but paradoxically, this was by far the single most important audience group in terms of the film's treatment, script, casting, promotion, marketing and commercial success. This paradox is central to any major Batman film, and probably to any big-screen adaptation of a 'cult' text. The movie will be tailored for those who care least about the character, while those with the greatest emotional investment become a powerless elite, a vocal minority whose voice is rarely loud enough, and who are fated to watch helplessly as 'their' treasured posession is given over to the whims of the majority.

The first group to face this defeat was, intriguingly, the lobby for Adam West; a group which included West himself and pal Wally Wingert, whose song 'Adam West' – a parodic cover of 'Wild West', by The Escape Club – spearheaded the campaign to get West back on-screen as the Caped Crusader. 'He's so bitchin', he's so brave', proclaimed the lyric, 'it's back to the batcave. He's got cool and savoir faire, in his cape and cowl and his gray underwear.'[82] Perhaps surprisingly, West was actually offered a role in Burton's feature, as Bruce's father Dr Thomas Wayne; but the actor demanded Batman or nothing, and got the latter. 'I cried for an hour, but then I was okay,' West admitted on a May edition of the entertainment show *A Current Affair*. 'I wanted it!'[83]

Support for West was more widespread than might be imagined, bearing in mind the fact that the actor was sixty years old at the time of filming.[84] *Comics Scene* magazine published a letter proclaiming that

> I think I speak for many when I say that the most remembered Batman is from the classic 1960s TV show with Adam West and Burt Ward. This is the Batman we all know and love so much. We do *not* need a serious, melodramatic, or violent Batman film to help ruin the legend . . . [85]

---

[82] 'Adam West', by Wally Wingert and the Caped Club, quoted in Van Hise, op. cit., n.p.

[83] Ibid. n.p.

[84] Van Hise gives his birthdate as 19 September 1928; Ibid. n.p.

[85] Letter from Michael Schilling, *Comics Scene* #6, quoted in Van Hise, Ibid. n.p.

Comics Feature had received similar letters: 'What does everyone have against Adam West? He's an awesome actor ... if you want a good movie that'll be a hit, hire Adam West for the job, he won't let you down.'[86] A nationwide petition for West's reinstatement as Batman echoed these sentiments. West, of course, heartily encouraged this campaign. During 1988 and 1989, as noted in the previous chapter, he did the rounds of conventions and TV talk shows to protest at his treatment by Warner Brothers, who had recently banned him from wearing his home-made costume for public appearances.

Related to the audience groups who specifically wanted West to return were those who believed more generally that Burton's movie would, or should, be a comedy. Less focused than the West campaigners, these were presumably non-comic fans who, unlike the first group, were not particuarly invested in TV fandom either, but whose memories of Batman were irrevocably tied up with West: similar people, perhaps, to Kate, Connie and Susan in Spigel and Jenkins' study, who fondly recalled the TV show from childhood and regretted the 'lack of innocence' they saw in Burton's 'darker' vision of Gotham.[87] Thus a theater owner in Arizona is reported as having researched his regular customers for their expectations of the *Batman* movie, and announced 'I can tell you right now *they will come expecting to see a comedy and will be angry if it is not one*,'[88] while an article by Joe Desris in the *Comic Buyer's Guide* warned that 'those expecting a humorous Batman will be disappointed'.[89]

Among comic fans, the issue was similar but the context very different. Again, there was one key question: was *Batman* going to be a comedy? As in the introductions to those 1980s graphic novels quoted in the previous chapter; as in the discourse surrounding Neal Adams and Denny O'Neil's early 1970s work; as in the debates over Joel Schumacher's two *Batman* movies, the oppositions were clearly drawn. On the one hand were 'comedy', 'light', 'TV series', 'camp',

---

[86] Letter from Eric Grignol, *Comics Feature* #5, quoted in Van Hise, Ibid. n.p.

[87] See Lynn Spigel and Henry Jenkins, 'Mass Culture and Popular Memory', in Pearson and Uricchio, op. cit., p. 141.

[88] Quoted in Van Hise, op. cit., n.p.

[89] Ibid., n.p.

'aberration'. On the other, 'serious', 'dark', 'comics', 'straight', 'original'. The comic fans' attitude toward Tim Burton's movie in the months before release were entirely dependent on whether the current leaked information indicated that the film was to fall on one side or the other of this binary structure.

The first response was shaped by the initial announcement in July 1988 that Tim Burton was to direct. James Van Hise explains:

> On the surface this seemed an odd choice as his only two features prior to *Batman* had been *Pee Wee's Big Adventure* and *Beetlejuice*, both bizarre comedies. But what really heated up the controversy was the casting of Michael Keaton in the title role. Out of all the actors fans had ever considered a possibility for the lead, this is one name which never made the short list . . . it was like sending up a flare, and what the burst seemed to reveal was that *Batman* was destined to be a comedy – a retread of the little lamented 1960s television series.[90]

The feelings of betrayal on the part of comic fans were voiced within a week in the *Comic Buyer's Guide*. 'Remember that empty, hollow feeling that you got in the pit of your stomach when your girlfriend wanted to break up with you? That same lump-in-the-throat yucky feeling which brings on the ''dark night of the soul'' attacked me this morning . . . '[91] In *Comics Scene* the complaints were equally heartfelt: 'Why would anyone choose a short, balding wimpy comedian to portray the Dark Knight?' 'Michael Keaton is not a serious actor. I fear that the comic talent behind *Mr Mom*, *Gung Ho* and *Night Shift* will desecrate the Batman legend beyond repair.'[92] Even Nicholson, generally a more popular choice than Keaton, was criticised by a writer to *Comic Buyer's Guide*: 'Jack Nicholson is not the right choice to play the Joker. He does not physically resemble him and I do not think he will take the character seriously.'[93]

---

[90] Ibid., n.p.
[91] Ibid., n.p.
[92] Ibid., n.p.
[93] Ibid., n.p.

Fans extended their complaints beyond the comics press to the national papers. One letter in the *Los Angeles Times* announced that 'by casting a clown, Warner Bros and Burton have defecated on the history of Batman',[94] while *Premier* magazine carried a similar comment:

> Casting '*Mr Mom*' Keaton as Batman because of his dramatic success in *Clean and Sober* makes about as much sense as casting Mary Tyler Moore in the same role because of her success in *Ordinary People*. Michael Keaton is in no way suited to play the role of the Dark Knight. His personality, screen image and physical makeup are the absolute opposite of the time-honored character of Bruce Wayne/Batman, regardless of what cartoonist Bob Kane might think . . . [95]

We might have expected Kane's authorial intention for the character to have carried the ultimate weight in the eyes of comic book fans, but clearly another interpretation was now taking precedence over Kane's 'original'. In this case, the source is surely Miller's Batman, the 'Dark Knight' of the 1986 graphic novel, and the template of serious, grim, adult crimefighting it implies; Kane is relegated to the role of 'cartoonist'.

Interestingly, though, it seems that Kane did have some veto power over the shaping of Tim Burton's Batman, and that his first reaction to Keaton's casting was similar to that of the fans. 'I was . . . stunned by Tim's choice . . . I expressed my discontent to Tim and the Warner executives.'[96]

> I wrote a 'Bible' for the movie script. A 'Bible' is show-biz jargon for a list of do's and don't's in writing a screenplay. By outlining my suggestions, I hoped to put the writer on the right track . . . I critiqued one of the first versions of [Sam] Hamm's

---

[94] Mark Salisbury (ed.), *Burton on Burton*, London: Faber (1995), p. 72.
[95] Letter from Daniel T. Lappen in *Premiere* (February 1989), quoted in Van Hise, op. cit., n.p.
[96] Kane with Andrae, op. cit., pp. 146–147.

script. There were flaws in it that I spotted, and they were corrected.[97]

However, when Kane went to Burton to complain about the casting of Michael Keaton, it seems he had to swallow his big talk pretty swiftly with a portion of humble pie. 'After digesting Tim's explanation, I began to re-evaluate my own concept of Batman and came to accept the movie adaptation as a valid and correct image.'[98] After this meeting, it seems there were no more complaints: 'Nicholson's portrayal of the Joker', Kane concludes, 'was exactly what I had in mind . . . and was the piece de resistance of the film . . . .I can honestly say that this film had me spellbound from beginning to end.'[99]

There remains a certain ambiguity around Kane's influence over the meaning of this 1989 Batman. Just as was the case with the 1966 series and the balance of power between DC editors and TV producers, we can only guess at the precise institutional relationships. On the one hand, Kane relishes the story of his spotting the 'flaws' and having them 'corrected' by Warners, with all the influence that implies; on the other, he seems to accept that his 'Bible' was merely a set of guidelines, 'suggestions' which he 'hoped' would come through in the final product. As I suggested, there is a strong sense from the above report that when it came to a conflict of interpretations around the casting of Michael Keaton, Kane was ultimately persuaded into subscribing to a version of the Batman which was very different from his own.

My own opinion is that the seventy-two year-old Kane was very probably given the job as 'consultant' on Batman mainly as a courtesy and a shrewd publicity move.[100] By inviting this veteran onto the team, by asking him to draw up a 'Bible' and allowing him to design posters and costumes which were never used,[101] by flattering and courting him and keeping him sweet, Warners were shrewdly ensuring that he

---

[97] Ibid., p. 144.
[98] Ibid., p. 147.
[99] Ibid., p. 148, p. 151.
[100] He was born on 24 October 1916.
[101] There is a faint sadness behind the self-aggrandising of Kane's autobiography,

wouldn't become another Adam West, a loose cannon shooting his mouth off against the forthcoming production on whatever talk show would take him. With Kane as consultant, Warners had the stamp and approval of the 'creator'; without him, they could have earned themselves another aggrieved and bitter enemy who might well have swung the opinion of the comic fans and press even more vehemently against the motion picture.

In fact the fan protests, while apparently not organised, did have some quantifiable impact on Batman's producers. The 29 November 1988 issue of The Wall Street Journal 'reported that there were financial jitters concerning the Batman feature film because of the vociferous fan backlash to the casting of Michael Keaton'. Producer Jon Peters later admitted, in Newsweek of 26 June 1989, that 'every analyst I knew sent that to me the day it came out. It just deflated everybody.' According to James Van Hise, 'it was in response to this single event that Warners decided they had to counteract the waves of criticism by cutting together a ninety-second trailer of coming attractions to demonstrate just what Batman would be like'.[102]

Peters' own view of the Batman and his surroundings would have come as a firm reassurance to those fans who feared any return to campiness; the producer stated his dislike for the TV show, and revealed his taste for 'straight' heroes. 'All those pinks. I didn't like it. I wanted the guy to be New York, to be street.'[103] Comments like these, coupled with an interview with Tim Burton in the Comic Buyer's Guide – 'you will see a very interesting, surprising action story set in a dark, Gothic, timeless American city'[104] – and Joe Desris' article of September 1988 – 'this movie will go back to Batman's roots: mysterious, brooding, dark, somber ... ',[105] – helped to calm fan anxieties and create a second discourse around the forthcoming movie, one which hoped for the best rather than fearing the worst. A letter in

---

[102] Van Hise, ibid., n.p.
[103] Ibid.
[104] Ibid.
[105] Ibid.

the *Comic Buyer's Guide* admitted 'I'm starting to like the idea of Michael Keaton as the ''everyman'' hero. It's not such a bad idea,'[106] while a similar comment in *Amazing Heroes*, enthusing that the trailer was 'perfection . . . of all surprises, Michael Keaton is perfect as the Batman' was headlined 'So Now We Can All Shut Up'.[107]

The comic fanzine *Speakeasy* ran several features on the movie in early 1989, again within a mode of cautious optimism. 'We were reassured by someone who has been closely involved with the project: ''It's a grim film . . . they have tried to do it seriously.'' ' This article consistently stresses 'fidelity' to the original – 'the story will stick quite closely to the comics' – distance from the TV show – 'thankfully we are spared the Hotline' – and 'darkness' in tone and visual style.

> You'll be relieved to hear that he's being portrayed as a creature of the night, with elongated ears and a massive cloak . . . he's still got the yellow emblem, though unlike the 60s series, it doesn't look like a stick-on, it's actually part of the costume. The yellow is played down and the costume is slightly darker than in the comics. There is a utility belt, which is a dirty yellow, and the size of a soldier's ammo belt.[108]

This slowly building confidence in Burton and enthusiasm for the movie was evident in the lettercolumns of *Batman*, the comic book, during the months just prior to the film's release.

> I . . . saw a scene where Batman crashed through a skylight. He looked just as he should, just like in the comic books. Keaton and Nicholson will be great, I tell ya!![109]

> My congratulations go to you and Warner Brothers! Superb! Bruce Wayne has never looked so debonair, Jack Nicholson's

---

[106] Letter from Lon Wolf, *Comic Buyer's Guide* (January 27 1989), quoted in Van Hise, ibid., n.p.

[107] Letter from Kenneth Chisolm, *Amazing Heroes* #162, quoted in Van Hise, ibid.

[108] Dick Hansom and Alan Mitchell, *Speakeasy* (February 1989), pp. 30–32.

[109] Letter from George Crawford, *Batman* #438, New York: DC Comics (1989).

Joker is chilling and the Batmobile is awesome. This is going to be a blockbuster! I've seen the previews, and the characters appear true to their comics form.[110]

Denny O'Neil himself, though, betrays a note of ambivalence in an editorial column written at the time of *Batman*'s first preview screenings.

the halls are quiet, the doors closed. Today is the day of the screening. DC staffers are seeing that movie. The B-word movie. I've seen it already, so I'm sitting as lonely as a pacifist in the Pentagon, doing a little of this and a little of that. Clearing my desk, mostly, getting ready to take a long swing around the country. I'll be travelling somewhere in Louisiana when the B-word movie opens here in New York ... in a couple of weeks, I'll get around to the reviews ... and by then, I'll know what I really think.[111]

For most comic fans, O'Neil's tone would with hindsight seem to have hit the mark pretty well. As Bacon-Smith and Yarbrough discover, the responses of most comic readers emerging from the first screenings of *Batman* ranged from disappointed to only vaguely satisfied. Members of Philadelphia's Anime Society told the researchers 'the movie stank', 'I think they kept it fairly faithful to what was expected of it', 'it just didn't work', it was 'all right', it was 'mediocre'.[112] Another fan concluded 'I thought it was really disappointing',[113] while DC staff writer Martin King had to wrestle to 'rehabilitate' the movie, justifying its failings: 'things that didn't work the first time did work the second time ... I said, you know, "now it does make sense" ... and then, it worked, you know.'[114]

This process of rehabilitation was typical of comic fandom's

---

[110] Letter from Mike Kuker, *Batman* #437, New York: DC Comics (1989).

[111] Denny O'Neil, 'From the Den', *Batman* #438, New York: DC Comics (1989).

[112] Bacon-Smith and Yarbrough, op. cit., pp. 106–109.

[113] Ibid., p. 101.

[114] Ibid., pp. 104–105.

approach to the movie. 'Fans . . . returned to see the film many times in its first run in spite of serious misgivings . . . and fans discussed the movie endlessly, trying to reconcile the conflicting images of the film to the pre-existing model of the characters and setting they already had in their heads.'[115] Ultimately, though, the researchers conclude that the movie *Batman* failed to enter into fan 'continuity' as an 'authentic' representation of the character: 'no fans talk about the movie as part of the repertoire of Batman representations accepted as "real" in the community.'[116]

Similarly, an editorial voice distanced the comic character from the movie hero in the public forum of *Batman* #442. 'The BATMAN movie (as well as the BATMAN MOVIE ADAPTATION) IS NOT a part of Batman continuity.'[117] There is no signature on this declaration, but from its firm tone and decisiveness it seems that someone at *Batman*, sensing the mood of his readers, realised it was time to declare loyalty and come down down on the fans' side. After months of anticipation and growing optimism, comic fandom, like the diehard supporters of Adam West, was feeling rejected, even betrayed.

'There might be something that's sacrilege in the movie,' admitted Tim Burton. 'But I can't care about it . . . this too big a budget movie to worry about what a fan of a comic would say.'[118] Yet as Van Hise notes, 'Comic book fans are enthusiasts who feel deeply about their interests . . . to the fans, the forthcoming *Batman* movie was viewed as an *event* and was discussed in terms otherwise reserved for presidential elections. This was a movie which would put something *we care about* on the big screen! Would they blow it?'[119] Bacon-Smith and Yarbrough echo this sense of anticipation: 'Fans awaited the finished product with equal shares of excitement and forboding – would the producers get it right?'[120]

To many fans, they got it wrong. They blew it. And, worse, they

---

[115] Ibid., p. 111.

[116] Ibid., p. 112.

[117] 'Continuity Corner', *Batman* #442, New York: DC Comics (1989).

[118] Quoted in Pearson and Uricchio, 'I'm Not Fooled By That Cheap Disguise', in Pearson and Uricchio, op. cit., p. 184.

[119] Van Hise, op. cit., n.p.

[120] Bacon-Smith and Yarbrough, op. cit., p. 111.

didn't care. 'This is too big a budget movie to care ... ' Yet as Van Hise stresses, the fans cared. Batman was 'something *we care about*'. In such a struggle over meaning, one side has to lose; and as O'Neil noted of Warner, 'they're the bigger side'. In the summer of 1989, fans of the comic book Batman were forced to realise that the character was no longer their property. He wasn't Denny O'Neil's property, or DC Comics' property. He was Tim Burton's property this summer, and he was the property of Time-Warner; and beyond that, because of that, he was now the property of the global audience, of the non-fans.

6. *Batman*: A Tim Burton Film

'I was never a giant comic fan', Burton cheerfully admits in *Burton and Burton*, a study of the director as auteur. 'I could never tell which box I was supposed to read. That's why I loved *The Killing Joke* ... it's my favourite. It's the first comic I've ever loved.'[121] Curiously, though, Burton announces in *Speakeasy* that he had read both *The Killing Joke* and *The Dark Knight Returns* prior to filming, and that 'of the two books, *Dark Knight* is my favourite'.[122] We can assume that Tim Burton really is not the world's biggest comic fan.

As I have argued elsewhere,[123] Burton's *Batman* is not an 'adaptation' as we would use the term to describe, say, Ang Lee's *Sense and Sensibility* or Kenneth Branagh's *Hamlet*. It does not rely for its narrative structure on a specific text, its dialogue is not based on the dialogue of an 'original', it does not refer back to any particular comic for its characterisation, its tone or its visualisation of Batman and his surroundings. The origin of the Joker in Burton's film is similar to that given in *The Killing Joke*, in that the character falls into a vat of acid, and the scene where Batman suspends a criminal off the ledge of a roof recalls a similar moment in *The Dark Knight Returns*. Batman's appearance and costume, however, are explicitly based on Burton's

---

[121] Salisbury, op. cit., p. 71.

[122] Alan Mitchell, 'Burton's Big Adventure', *Speakeasy* (February 1989), p. 28.

[123] Will Brooker, 'Batman: One Life, Many Faces', in Deborah Cartmell and Imelda Whelehan, *Adaptations*, London: Routledge (1999).

concept that Bruce Wayne would be a fairly puny man who armours himself in sculpted musculature – 'he's trying to become something that he's not'[124] – and as such contradict the standard comic book visual of Bruce Wayne as a formidably built, highly trained athlete. The Joker's costume in the latter stages of the movie – top hat, formal jacket and mouth prissily lipsticked into a constant pout – is very similar to his outfit in the last chapter of Jim Starlin, Jim Aparo and Mike DeCarlo's *A Death In The Family*.[125] However, the other aspects of his appearance and identity run against established comic book convention. Nicholson as the Joker is short and stocky rather than tall and spindly; he is given a name, Jack Napier, and identified as the killer of Bruce Wayne's parents; he is killed in the final scene. Finally, the implication that Batman/Bruce has a sexual relationship with reporter Vicki Vale is clearly antithetical to the *Bat-Bible*'s ruling that Batman is celibate.

These are not, to a fan of the comic Batman at least, minor changes. They roughly equate to Kenneth Branagh casting Hamlet as a man of sixty, or Baz Luhrman having Romeo and Juliet survive at the end of the story, or Ang Lee deciding that Marianne Dashwood and Lucy Steele should have a lesbian affair. *Batman*, then, is not an 'adaptation' either of *The Killing Joke* or *The Dark Knight Returns*, and neither is it an adaptation of the comic book 'mythos', as O'Neil's *Bat-Bible* defines it. While O'Neil generously suggested in early 1989 that the movie could never attempt to literally translate the comic books – 'what you have to do is recreate it in your own medium' – Burton's film, as argued above, is really not concerned with its source material or with fidelity to any 'original'. What it constitutes, perhaps, is the adaptation of late-1980s discourses around the comic book Batman into the medium of cinema: firstly, the notion of Batman as 'dark', 'adult', 'serious' and defined against the TV show, and secondly, the notion of creative freedom around authorship, of a new creator 'doing different' with the character.

By all accounts, the film would not have been made were it not for

---

[124] Salisbury, op. cit., p. 76.
[125] Jim Starlin, Jim Aparo and Mike DeCarlo, *Batman: A Death in the Family*, New York: DC Comics (1988).

the circulation of these discourses; more specifically, were it not for
Dark Knight, which most epitomised them. Van Hise's chapter on
Miller is entitled 'Prepping The Batman for the Movies' and subtitled
'He didn't know it, but he was preparing a new version for the movie
screen.'[126] Miller didn't know it, and the fans didn't know it: but
Warner Communications Inc. knew it. Eileen Meehan's account of the
movie's prehistory, which dates back to Warners' acquisition of DC in
1971, has almost a sense of undercover conspiracy: the negotiations
towards a movie *Batman* began more or less at my birth, and went on
well above the heads of readers, writers and editors.

> The mid-1980s marked the beginning of a process in which
> WCI both tested the waters and began building towards the
> release of *Batman*. By issuing *The Dark Knight Returns* in comic
> form, WCI essentially test marketed a dark reinterpretation of
> Batman with an adult readership . . .
>
> Besides WCI earning revenues twice from *The Dark Knight
> Returns*, WCI tapped different systems of distribution, placing
> the *Dark Knight* in different kinds of retail outfits, tapping the
> markets of fandom and general readers to determine if the grim
> version of Batman could gain acceptance from both specialized
> and generalized consumers.[127]

Burton was handed the movie after the success of *Beetlejuice* in 1988,
comparatively late in the project's eighteen-year history.[128] The
market for a 'dark' Batman had, as Meehan affirms, been established:
but the choice of Burton as director implies that Warners had also
taken notice of the second discourse I mentioned. *Superman* director
Richard Donner would most likely have given the Batman myth a
straight, 'faithful' adaptation; Mark Goldblatt, then working on *The
Punisher*, could have been relied on for a violent, comic-based actioner.
Instead, Warners chose a director whose previous two features, *Pee-*

---

[126] Van Hise, op. cit., n.p.
[127] Eileen Meehan, 'The Political Economy of a Commercial Intertext', in Pearson
and Uricchio, op. cit., p. 53.
[128] Salisbury, op. cit., p. 70.

Wee's Big Adventure (1985) and *Beetlejuice*, had been quirky, faintly surreal black comedies with a distinctive visual style and a miscellany of recurrent personal tics: 'these include a model town, characters patterned with black and white stripes, and a graveyard setting'.[129] Warners knew they were not just getting Batman, but Tim Burton's Batman, and surely the choice of such a director rested partly on the recently established discourse of creative authorship in comic books; it was the impulse behind 'Miller's Batman' and 'Moore's Batman' that enabled 'Burton's Batman'. Rather than a neutral, well-crafted adaptation, Warners surely sensed – from the popularity of *Dark Knight* and *Killing Joke* – the market for a 'personal vision'.

> So, while I was never a big comic book fan, I loved Batman, the split personality, the hidden person. It's a character I could relate to. Having those two sides, a light side and a dark one, and not being able to resolve them . . . I also see aspects of myself in the character. Otherwise, I wouldn't have been able to do it.
>
> [. . .]
>
> I'd worked with Michael before and so I thought he would be perfect, because he's got that look in his eye. It's there in *Beetlejuice*. It's like *that* guy you could see putting on a bat-suit; he does it because he *needs* to, because he's not this gigantic, strapping macho man. It's all about transformation. Then it started to make sense to me.
>
> [. . .]
>
> The Joker . . . he's the best character . . . I just love the idea of a person who's turned into a clown and is insane. The film is like the duel of the freaks. It's a fight between two disfigured people. That's what I love about it. I was always aware of how weird it was, but I was never worried about it in any way . . . any character who operates on the outside of society and is deemed a freak and an outcast then has the freedom to do what they want.[130]

---

[129] Ibid., p. 65.
[130] Ibid., pp. 72–80.

'It's there in *Beetlejuice*'; it's also there in *Edward Scissorhands* (1990), *Pee-Wee's Big Adventure*, *Ed Wood* (1994) and *Tim Burton's The Nightmare Before Christmas* (1993), and it's there in *Batman Returns* (1992). *Batman* is, like all Tim Burton films,[131] a story of freaks and clowns, dressed up a little like Narnia and a little like Edward Lear, with the spookily pretty swoops and twinkles of Danny Elfman's soundtrack laid over shots of spires and snowfalls.

Comic fans had seen 'personal vision' before, though, and embraced it. Dave McKean's Batman was a swirling wraith; Moore's Joker was originally a stand-up comic with a pregnant wife. Miller's Robin was a girl, and his Joker died by twisting his own spinal column. Why should Burton's departures from the comic book mythos invoke feelings of disappointment, rejection or betrayal? As a comic book fan who experienced precisely those feelings without being sure of the reasons, I feel Bacon-Smith and Yarbrough offer at least part of the explanation. 'For comic book fans ... the movie serves one vital purpose: it represents them to the outside world.'[132] Tim Burton's Batman was not, like *The Killing Joke* and *Dark Knight*, 'outside continuity'; it was not an 'Elseworld' story of what could possibly have happened.[133] It was not one narrative among the many which appear in comics every month. It was *Batman: The Movie*, a supposedly definitive representation, and the world was watching it. Tim Burton's Batman had become, as far as the wider audience was concerned, 'the' Batman, and all the movie's idiosyncrasies and infidelities to the comic text – the sex life, the stocky Joker, the skinny Bruce – were now considered gospel in the eyes of the viewing public. *Batman* now belonged to a multi-national conglomeration and the global audience who bought the tickets and the merchandise, rather than to the dedicated comic readers and the community of writers, artists and editors who had themselves emerged from the ranks of fandom. Worse still, any fan who recognised the extent of Warners' controlling interest behind DC from

---

[131] With the possible exception of *Mars Attacks* (1996).
[132] Bacon-Smith and Yarbrough, op. cit., p. 112.
[133] That *Killing Joke* and *Dark Knight* were both outside regular continuity was stressed in the 'Continuity Corner' mentioned above; see *Batman* #442, New York: DC Comics (1989).

1971 onwards faced the realisation that it had been thus for at least the past eighteen years.

7. Joel Schumacher's Batman

From the British reviews of *Batman Forever* (1995) and its sequel *Batman and Robin* (1997) you would hardly know that Joel Schumacher had directed other films previously; that is, the Batman movies were not discussed within any context of authorial style in relation to, say, *The Lost Boys* (1987), *Flatliners* (1990), *Dying Young* (1991), *Falling Down* (1993), *The Client* (1994) or *A Time To Kill* (1996). It would certainly be possible to follow an interest in beautiful, death-marked youth through Schumacher's earlier movies to *Batman Forever*, to trace the homoeroticism in *The Lost Boys* and the fanciful gothicism of *Flatliners* through to *Batman and Robin*, or to ask why the issues of race so evident in *Flatliners*, *Falling Down* and *A Time to Kill* are so strikingly absent in Schumacher's Gotham; but no review I saw made reference to this earlier work. There were, however, plenty of references to Burton's 'authorial style', which as we have seen is more recognisable and easier to discuss; tellingly, Faber does not publish a volume entitled *Schumacher on Schumacher*.

Batman Forever and *Batman and Robin* were, therefore, identified in the press primarily by what they were not; that is, by their difference from the previous Batman. They were not Tim Burton films, they were not 'dark', they were not a world away from the TV show; they were not played 'straight'. These distinctions, especially the last, became most explicit with *Batman and Robin*. By this point the oppositions were clearly being drawn up between the two films under Burton's helm and those directed by Schumacher: and the binary structure discussed above was firmly in place.

> Four films in, and the Dark Knight has finally become an extra in an elongated Village People video . . .
> . . . journey with Schumacher on his personal odyssey to create the campest *Batman* movie ever; so much so that it makes the 60s TV series seem like a radical exploration of existential angst. In fact, short of casting John Inman as Batman and

wrapping him in a pink feather boa, Schumacher couldn't really have made it more camp. As such, we're treated to Gothic pantomime. Tim Burton's black visions are swapped for a steady flow of double entendres and some heroically atrocious acting ... Uma Thurman totters around on Day-Glo sets ... Schumacher doubtless sees all this as an ingenious attempt to subvert mainstream audiences with homosexual imagery ...[134]

The *New Musical Express* review covers all the bases in its identification of Schumacher's Batman as 'other' – radically opposed to Burton's, but also by implication to the 'Dark Knight' of the 1980s graphic novels. This Batman is 'camp', compared to the Village People and effeminate actor John Inman; he is associated with 'homosexual imagery' – 'it starts with a lingering close-up of Batman's rubber bottom', begins the review – and equated to the Batman of the TV show. Burton's 'black visions' have been replaced by another 'personal odyssey', this time informed more by day-glo pantomime than dark cabaret.

Other reviews of the time confirm that this discourse of oppositions and otherness around Schumacher's Batman was widespread.

From the opening shots – close-ups of rubber-clad butts and groins – it's clearly no *Free Willy* ... if this is a straightened out version, then the original cut must have been more camp than Liza Minelli's knicker drawer. True, removing the ear-ring that Chris O'Donnell (Robin/Dick Grayson) wore in *Batman Forever* has made him look less like Wayne Manor's resident catamite, but Akiva Goldsman's script bulges with so much tongue-rolling *double entendre* that the cast look badly in need of a Barbara Windsor masterclass ...

Clooney's Batman marks a departure from the depressive navel-gazing of his Keaton and Kilmer incarnations, and harks back to Adam West's more self-consciously ditzy TV interpretation. Rather than being a tormented loner, apt to stare moodily into the distance at the clang of a Batarang, the

---

[134] James Oldham, 'Bun Lovin' Criminal', *New Musical Express* (28 June 1997).

Caped Crusader now seems to be pursuing more domestic interests . . .

. . . if they regroup for a fifth caped crusade, expect the Dark Knight to confess to a life-long passion for interior decorating.[135]

Again, the suggestion that Schumacher's Batman is closer to the TV hero than to Burton's 'depressive', 'tormented' character, and the stressing of *double-entendres* and, obliquely, homosexuality in this Batman's make-up. The surprisingly coy identification of gayness through 'hidden' clues such as an interest in color schemes – very reminiscent of those secret signs of the 1950s – return in a further review, which again associates homosexuality with interior design and subtly distances Burton's 'gothic', 'troubled' protagonist from Schumacher's through references to 'drag', 'fashion tips' and 'swooshy' dust. Even the reviewer's turn of phrase – 'don't worry your pretty head', 'a mite too large to be wearing the gym-slip' – seems informed by a camp sensibility.

It's time to put Batman to bed. The first two under the direction of Tim Burton had some distinction, thanks to the vast and gloomy gothic sets and a Batman (Michael Keaton) who was clearly troubled by some unnameable worries beneath his rubber mask . . . but Burton gave way to Joel Schumacher, a very average sort of journeyman . . .

You might wonder what ice-hockey is doing in here? Don't worry your pretty head, it all gets much, much worse. Uma Thurman then turns up out of nowhere as Poison Ivy, clad in a slinky green leotard and acting like a drag queen doing a bad impression of Mae West . . . what she mainly does is breathe some swooshy red dust over men . . .

Alicia Silverstone also puts in an appearance, looking a mite too large to be wearing the gym-slip they have given her. But in no time she is sheathed in black rubber . . . proving that girls

---

[135] Matthew Sweet, 'Dark Knight of the Soul-Destroying', *Independent On Sunday* (29 June 1997).

can be just as moronic as men when it comes to fashion tips.

Incidentally, I am assured by a colleague that Joel Schumacher began life as a window dresser.[136]

The same distinctions emerge in *Time Out*'s review: remote from Tim Burton's vision in its lack of 'gloom' and 'existential melancholia', Schumacher's Batman involves fetishised male bodies ('bigger codpieces') and is once more linked to a vague 'gayness' through costume design, masquerade and catwalk shows. Again, the reviewer almost seems to adopt a camp persona in the neat, faintly bitchy rhyme of his concluding phrase.

> For the first two films, Tim Burton at least supplied a sense of occasion – a grand, gloomy *schadenfreude* ... when Joel Schumacher replaced Burton behind the camera on *Batman Forever* Warners apparently got the franchise it required: a brighter, breezier incoherence; more cameos, bigger codpieces ...
>
> Michael Keaton's existential melancholia has been supplanted by George Clooney ...
>
> 'Joel Schumacher – he's a great costume designer,' a rueful Warners executive once admitted to me. If only he'd stuck to his original occupation ... *Batman and Robin* isn't so much a movie as a giant masquerade, a catwalk show, all dressed up with no place to go.[137]

Reviews from across the United States echo this pattern of response. Where the identification of homoeroticism in Schumacher's *Batman and Robin* is less explicit, the comparisons drawn – Broadway shows, circus acts, Ice Capades, Disney parades and the 1960s TV show – nevertheless have overtones of baroque camp. In the US journalistic response, too, we find repeated comparisons of Burton's 'vision' with the less coherent project of Joel Schumacher, and more references to Schumacher's supposed talent for design rather than direction.

---

[136] Anon, 'Holy Baloney! It's a dodo!', *Daily Express* (27 June 1997).
[137] Tom Charity, 'The Big Chill', *Time Out* (2 July 1997).

Thanks to director Joel Schumacher, *Batman and Robin* is less like a comic book and more like the most flamboyant Broadway musical ever staged – imagine a cross between Ice Capades and the Disney World Main Street Electric Parade. Granted it's got more in common with the campy 60s TV series than it does with the brooding comic book; but once that's understood, things clip along at an entertaining pace . . . I'm guessing if you're a hard-core Batman purist, then you've given up on these circus tent shenanigans long ago.[138]

. . . whatever one's feelings for Tim Burton's first two gothic tales of Batman, they were at least consistent. There was a vision behind them – brooding, gloomy, sexy – a nerdy fantasy of transformation, through rubber suit, from dud to superhero. If there's a vision behind *Batman and Robin*, it is of big stacks of money. The sets, like the movie, are an overwhelming mess. Impressive at first, by virtue of size and number alone, one is quickly numbed by them, beaten into sensory submission by the busyness and clash of styles. *Batman and Robin* is like a big, cheesy Broadway musical where every number is a show-stopper. Each piece is mildly entertaining but the whole enterprise goes nowhere.[139]

Burton used the Batman myth as a framework to hang one of his typically wan, existential 'outsider' fashion shows. Schumacher has turned his two passes through Gotham into incomprehensible swirls of mayhem and art direction.[140]

It's only as an exercise in set design that Batman & Robin succeeds, though it's all so over the top that it's more of an exercise in what not to do than anything else. Schumacher has chosen to light his film with outlandishly garish neons and brilliant blues and pinks, which unfortunately make this look

---

[138] Devin D. O'Leary, review of *Batman and Robin*, *Weekly Alibi* (2 July 1997).
[139] Zak Weisfeld, review of *Batman and Robin*, *Metro Pulse* (2 July 1997).
[140] Noel Murray, review of *Batman and Robin*, *Nashville Scene* (8 July 1997).

more like some ridiculous Batman on Ice escapade than anything else. It's all too much too often, a smorgasbord of boredom, a cavalcade of crap. (And, hey, enough with the nipples on the Batsuits already, okay? Geez . . .)[141]

Schumacher's Batman had, as noted at the start of my third chapter, become associated with all the qualities many comic fans had learned to abhor – camp, gayness, the aesthetic of the TV show. In a curious but perhaps inevitable twist, Burton's Batman therefore became something of a 'good object' within the Internet debates of 1997. The campaign against Michael Keaton's casting and the discrepancies between 1989's screen *Batman* and the comic book *Dark Knight* it was meant to resemble were apparently forgotten – by these fans at least – in the face of Schumacher's reinterpretation. Fewer than eight years had passed since *Batman*'s release, but already a nostalgic revisionism had settled around the movie and by association, the summer of 1989.

Everybody, I'm writing WB about future Bat-Flicks . . . I'm sick of seeing dark, somber villains such as Two-Face portrayed as goofy idiots!! Does everybody remember the feeling during the summer of 89? It was great . . .[142]

That summer of 89 was cool . . . I remember what it was like seeing *Batman* on opening day . . . Jack Nicholson's performance was clearly one of his best and Michael Keaton surprised everyone in that he pulled off the feat of making Bruce Wayne and Batman believable . . . the first film wasn't perfect but it was clearly the best one. And it was the one that captured the dark mood the best.[143]

I'll never forget the summer of 89, I hope to bring that feeling

---

[141] Anon., review of *Batman and Robin*, *Austin Chronicle* (20 June 1997).
[142] Posted by J.Grayson, *Mantle of the Bat: The Bat-Board*, http://www.cire.com/batman (27 February 1997).
[143] Posted by Harley Quinn, *Mantle of the Bat: The Bat-Board*, op. cit. (27 February 1997).

back once more. Nostalgia floods me . . . [144]

I wish Tim Burton would return as director. His vision of Batman was much closer to the comics than Joel Schumacher's. [145]

I was floored at just how campy [*Batman and Robin*] is shaping up to be . . . like most of you, I felt that the original Batman was by far the best of the series . . . I really liked *Batman Returns* because of its even darker take on Gotham . . . I really prefer the darker Batman as opposed to the light campy Batman. [146]

Please bring Tim Burton back . . . Burton's Batman was dark, mysterious, shadowy and gothic. Schumacher's Batman was campy and cartoonish. I prefer Burton's Batman 10-0. If you agree email me. [147]

I still don't think Joel Schumacher is the right man as I really hate the campyness of the 60's Batman that seems to be slowly trickling into the 90's series . . . [148]

I think that every Batfan has been disappointed with all 3 films so far, with the first being the best . . . will someone tell Warner Brothers that even little kids prefer Darknight Batman compared to Caped Crusader Batman as offered in the 60s . . . [149]

Note that emerging from these posts is a dislike of the 'campiness' Schumacher brought to the movies, and in turn a fear of any return to

---

[144] Posted by J. Grayson, *Mantle of the Bat: The Bat-Board*, op. cit. (28 February 1997).

[145] Posted by Thatman, *Mantle of the Bat: The Bat-Board*, op. cit. (27 February 1997).

[146] Posted by Nightwing, *Mantle of the Bat: The Bat-Board*, op. cit. (3 March 1997).

[147] Posted by The Dynamic Trio, *Mantle of the Bat: The Bat-Board*, op. cit. (21 February 1997).

[148] Posted by BatDan, *Mantle of the Bat: The Bat-Board*, op. cit. (27 February 1997).

[149] Posted by Mike, *Mantle of the Bat: The Bat-Board*, op. cit. (25 February 1997).

the 1960s television aesthetic. The points raised by Internet fans during these months of anticipation, then, were very similar to those covered in press reviews of *Batman and Robin* on its release.

Like all contributions to fan boards, these posts were part of 'threads' which branched off from discussion points and so led into various sub-debates. For instance, the argument about a 'gay Batman' discussed in my second chapter was partly informed by speculation about Schumacher's 'camp' Batman and the director's own sexuality.

> Batman is not gay but I do wonder about Schumacher. All his butt shots and crotch shots tell me that he is a little camp himself. And he keeps raving about how Val and George looked great in rubber . . .[150]

As already seen, this argument seemed fuelled by homophobia in the quite literal sense – a fear of homosexuality, and a determination to 'protect' Batman from such associations.

A further debate spinning off from the nostalgia for Burton's movie concerned the power of fandom to affect Warner Brothers' decisions on direction, casting and scriptwriting, and returned to the paradox of the fan as part of a powerless elite.

> I think the problem is that the non-batfans can only identify with the 60's series especially the gadgets, thus they look forward to some kind of 'nostalgia' along with a 90's penchant for special effects and a technological update of the 'gimmicks' . . . the others being more in number than us batfans seem to be getting more of Warners' attention. Remember people watch movies like *The Terminator* . . . just for the special effects and action . . . thus anyone who doesn't even care for the Batman as a character would like to see this movie. We're mistaken in the belief that this movie is being made to bring the comic book character to life . . . all that's being done is another summer movie is being made on which you could put any title

---

[150] Posted by Number Two, *Mantle of the Bat: The Bat-Board*, op. cit. (8 May 1997).

... the only difference is the characters seem oh so familiar to some of us ...[151]

This melancholy resignation was echoed by other contributors:

> The problem is non-batfans and bad script writing. The glorious history of Batman that most batfans treasure is being replaced by some writer or executive's interpretation of it. The only way this will change is if the next movie bombs at the box office. Even if that happens (which I doubt) the true Batman fan will probably have to look to the comics and not the movies to enjoy Batman the way it was intended.[152]

This line of discussion in turn went two ways; towards despair when fans saw previews of *Batman and Robin* and accepted that the control of 'their' character was entirely out of their hands, and in a more optimistic direction prompted by fans who claimed they did have some power to affect the future of the movie franchise. The first response is epitomised by Mike Higgins and Nightwing respectively: note that while the Bat-Board is usually characterised by mild language out of respect to younger visitors, the movie drove these fans to full-on cursing both in the theatre and on the Internet forum.

> This is without a doubt one of the worst movies I have ever seen! When the film ended the audience all shouted obscenities at the screen. I didn't pay a dime to see it and I feel cheated! Everybody was horrible! Uma was the absolute worst of anyone. Clooney was nowhere near as good as Keaton or Kilmer. This was the worst I've seen Chris O'Donnell, Arnold was awful as well ... this is the worst of the series, it made *Batman Forever* look as good as the first film. Commissioner Gordon was reduced to a role very similar to O'Hara from the

---

[151] Posted by Nikhil Soneja, *Mantle of the Bat: The Bat-Board*, op. cit. (26 February 1997).
[152] Posted by Nightwing, *Mantle of the Bat: The Bat-Board*, op. cit. (26 February 1997).

60's TV show. It's that bad. *Batman and Robin* is pure shit![153]

> You have got to be fucking kidding me. This movie was the absolute worst of the series. I hope they crucify Schumacher and hang him from the tallest building in Hollywood. Uma's performance was so over the top it was like watching the campy 60's show . . . I can't write anymore, I'm just too damn disappointed.[154]

However, some argued that fandom did have some leverage if properly organised, and tried to identify the ways in which a message of protest could be sent to Warners. This approach originated with the post from J. Grayson cited above – 'everybody, I'm writing WB about future Bat-flicks' – and drew in issues of institution and audience, even recalling previous examples of successful fan campaigns.[155]

> I would like each and every one of you to help figure a way that we can do this. I do plan to try and e-mail WB and write them for this very reason. Also, I plan to ask other Bat-sites for their support. If you folks could help I think we would see a movie that would knock our very Bat-socks off . . .[156]

> As I said, I'm going to write and e-mail WB . . . I encourage all of you to do the same and I implore you to do so . . . also, if you e-mail me I have Jack Nicholson's address, so we may write him with the notion of the Joker's return . . . this will be like Star Trek and it could work if we all participate.[157]

---

[153] Posted by Nightwing, *Mantle of the Bat: The Bat-Board*, op. cit. (20 June 1997).
[154] Posted by Mike Higgins, *Mantle of the Bat: The Bat-Board*, op. cit. (20 June 1997).
[155] For more on the original *Trek* 'letter-writing campaign' which protested the cancellation of the first series, see Tulloch and Jenkins, op. cit., pp. 8–10.
[156] Posted by J. Grayson, *Mantle of the Bat: The Bat-Board*, op. cit. (27 February 1997).
[157] Posted by J.Grayson, *Mantle of the Bat: The Bat-Board*, op. cit. (28 February 1997).

Other contributors saw a vote of protest in simply refusing to contribute to *Batman and Robin*'s box office, and held out some hope for 'non-Batfans' doing the same.

> I'm sorry, but WB is not gonna control me, I am still gonna boycott *Batman and Robin*. We have done so well against the powers that be. Don't let the suits at WB win.[158]

> I think we underestimate the non-Batfans understanding of Batman . . . they seem to be just as interested in good taste as we are . . .[159]

> This movie, if it's as bad as I think it will be, will fade pretty fast. It'll probably peak at about $125 million and disappear. VERY BAD NEWS for Joel since Warners is expecting at least $165 million. All I can say is BYE, BYE Joel.[160]

At its most optimistic, this approach saw small victories for fandom in every change Warners seemed to make to the forthcoming movie.

> Did anyone see the NEW trailer . . . two words describe it, IMPROVEMENT and STUNNING . . . definitely looks to have changed from the original . . . where that one looks like a hiphop, day-glo Disney trailer, this one looks like a dark, sexy spectacular . . . our criticism seems to have paid off. Sometimes you have to be cruel to be kind. WB have ordered the 'feel' to be amended . . . expect this new one to be up on the official website soon.[161]

While, as Mike Higgins and Nightwing's reviews indicate, the final product was by no means 'dark' enough for many fans and was 'sexy' mainly in its nudges about Batman and Robin's relationship – again, an

---

[158] Posted by Brandon, *Mantle of the Bat: The Bat-Board*, op. cit. (8 May 1997).
[159] Posted by Nikhil, *Mantle of the Bat: The Bat-Board*, op. cit. (8 May 1997).
[160] Posted by Mad Hatter, *Mantle of the Bat: The Bat-Board*, op. cit. (1 May 1997).
[161] Posted by Andy, *Mantle of the Bat: The Bat-Board*, op. cit. (7 May 1997).

unwelcome development for many of the contributors to Internet Bat-
boards – the belief that fan protest can genuinely affect institutional
choices persists across Internet fandom, which at the time of writing is
gearing up for the potential affront of a fifth movie.

There are currently at least three Internet sites explicitly dedicated
to campaigning against Joel Schumacher's involvement in the Batman
franchise and notching up small victories at every apparent move away
from the *Batman and Robin* aesthetic, whether George Clooney's '*mea
culpa*' publicity tour on which he apologised constantly for 'killing the
franchise',[162] Alicia Silverstone's retort with regard to *Batman 5* that
'I hear Joel Schumacher will be playing Batgirl',[163] or the
announcement of a re-released, 'much darker, and less confusing'
cut of *Batman Forever* on video. This last was claimed by the 'Anti-
Schumacher Site' as a direct case of the director bowing to fan
pressure; Schumacher's decision about a director's cut was made,
according to a press release quoted by the site's creators, 'due to
"angry Internet fans and their responses" to his bat-films'.[164]

Campaigning is not the sole purpose of the 'Anti-Schumacher Site',
nor of 'The Anti-Schumacher Society', nor 'Bring Me The Head of Joel
Schumacher'. As the latter title suggests, these forums also serve
simply as sounding boards for the very real fury and despair experienced by fans who have watched 'their' property, the Batman and
his mythos, being publicly vandalised. 'Bring Me The Head' opens with
a statement of intent: 'This site is dedicated to getting off our chests all
the things that made us really PISSED OFF about this movie. Why did
it piss us off so much? We grew up on Batman, and to see him exploited for the commercial marketing (which is just what is happening)
is infuriating.'[165] That the webmasters of this site are far from alone is
demonstrated by the thirty or more pages of complaint against
Schumacher which fill the guestbook of 'Bring Me The Head ... '

---

[162] See 'Batman 5 ... Don't Believe the Hype', http://www.cinescape.com/
features/981030a.shtml (10 March 1999).

[163] Reported in 'Update!', *Empire* magazine (April 1999), p. 37.

[164] Aaron Koscielniak and Adam Rosen, announcement on the *Anti-Schumacher Site*,
http://members.aol.com/BatmanLite/frameni.htm (10 March 1999).

[165] *Bring Me The Head of Joel Schumacher*, http://www.cgicafe.com/~ajrosen/batman
(10 March 1999).

One entry reads 'Batman and Robin was filth',[166] another remarks that 'My mother made me go and see the crap with my brothers and sister and I was disgusted.'[167] A third is so emotionally fired-up that I believe it warrants quoting in full, as an example of the sheer impotent rage that can boil up within a fandom denied any real power to influence the way its treasured icons are represented to the mass public.

> Schumaker you little piss ant! Who the fuck gave you the right to direct anything remotely as cool as Batman? I'm a film major in my freshman year, and I can tell you right now I can direct a better film on crack with my mouth stitched closed and my eyeballs plucked out! I don't know what the fuck you were thinking . . . pick up a Batman comic book you assinine fool? Does Gotham City look like Club Expo to you? Do you see any neon? What the fuck? And NIPPLES? This isn't a fucking joke! Batman isn't some two-bit circus freak like your bearded lady of a mother! He is the essence of gothic darkness, a man ripped between reality and fantasy, teetering on the brink of insanity with only his partner and butler and his mission to keep him from going crazy! Did you capture any of these elements? Of course not, because obviously you must have gone to Ronald McDonald School of Film? Who's the next villain, Schumacher, you schmuck, you prick . . . the Hamburglar? FUCK YOU![168]

I don't believe Jeff Shain's entry above is a prank, an exercise in elaborate insult for the sake of it, a Tourette's outburst intended to shock. Jeff knows his comments will only reach a jury of his peers, but still he needs to express this anger. 'This isn't a fucking joke.' Jeff has his own clearly defined vision of the way Batman should be, and in his

---

[166] Fatboy, guestbook entry, *Bring Me The Head of Joel Schumacher*, op. cit. (10 March 1999).
[167] Gregg, guestbook entry, *Bring Me The Head of Joel Schumacher*, op. cit. (10 March 1999).
[168] Jeff Shain, guestbook entry, *Bring Me The Head of Joel Schumacher*, op. cit. (10 March 1999).

eyes that ideal is being bastardised, violated, humiliated. Whether his comments – say, as part of a thirty-page document of complaint forwarded to Warners – could actually affect the development of *Batman 5* is, to my mind, arguable. The changes which, so far, seem to have been implemented because of fan dissatisfaction are on the whole tokenistic and trivial; one trailer released before its scheduled date, another reshuffled while the actual movie remained intact. That said, the Batman franchise is currently in question; the original December 1999 release date for *Batman 5* has been scrubbed out, while the identities of both cast and director are being left open. The relationship between fan pressure and institutional response is, therefore, hard to call at present. The anti-Schumacher webmasters may have some justification in claiming that campaigns like theirs have halted the progress of the Warners juggernaut; on the other hand, the multinational may roll on with another day-glo spectacular of a Batman sequel, oblivious to the protests of idealists like Jeff Shain. As Batman enters his sixty-first year, the future of the movie franchise – and in turn, the conflict between fandom and Time-Warner's subsidiaries for 'ownership' of the character – hangs very much in the balance.

$$\boxed{\text{Conclusion}}$$

1999

'I'm in charge of a national icon. Will he be around in sixty years? Will the planet survive sixty years? He'll survive another decade, I guess.' (Denny O'Neil, personal interview (1 July 1998))

1. A Death, a Birthday, and Two Months of Minor Celebrity

A funny thing happened on the way to the conclusion. Bob Kane died on 4 November 1998. Batman turned sixty some time in February 1999. And in between, around 28 January of the same year, I became almost famous.

Curiously, there remains a certain ambiguity around all of these dates. Kane was being remembered by 5 November, but obituaries were still reporting the death as news on Saturday the 7th,[1] while there were other claims, dating back to the 4th, that 'Bob Kane . . . passed away yesterday . . . November 3rd'.[2] Batman, of course, was born in *Detective Comics* #27, with a May cover date; but at least one documentary celebrated the anniversary in February, claiming –

---

[1] For instance, Martin Wainright, 'Prince of Gotham', *Guardian* (7 November 1998).
[2] Posted by Derek at *Jonah Weiland's Comic Book Resources*, http://www.comicbook-resources.com (4 November 1998).

probably correctly – that the comic in question actually hit newstands two months earlier.[3] Perhaps unsurprisingly, there was little media attention around this February birthday, partly because of its vagueness and perhaps because the May cover date is still taken as the marker for Batman's anniversaries: at least two newspapers interviewed me for a May 1999 'birthday' story.[4]

My own minor celebrity began in the *Mirror* of January 28 – though I was interviewed and photographed on the 7th – and at the time of writing, early in April, the story still seems to have legs; two newspapers and two television companies have contacted me in the past week.

Of course, I could only have predicted one of these events when I began this research. Certain aspects of their media treatment, however, came as little surprise. I could have foreseen, for instance, the tributes to Bob Kane across comic book Internet sites, from both webmasters and individual contributors. Beau Yarbrough's announcement on *Jonah Weiland's Comic Book Resources* was typical; and intriguingly reminiscent, in its portentous opening, of the first scenes of *Citizen Kane*. 'The Bat Signal will be dark over Gotham tonight . . . Kane died Tuesday of a heart attack . . . Kane created comic book characters before and after, but it was his creation of Batman in 1939 that forever made him part of pop culture history . . . '

In turn, the notes left by individual visitors were often autobiographical and quietly touching, as the Batman board became, temporarily, an online book of condolence.

> Twenty-eight years ago a little boy turned off the afternoon television, tied a towel around his neck, and started running around the house and yard, singing the Batman theme song and fighting the Joker, the Penguin and whatever other villains had been on that day.
> Thanks to Bob Kane that was the start of a long ride that made my life a little brighter.
> Last night my son turned off the TV, tied a towel around his

---

[3] 'Happy Birthday Batman', BBC Radio 2 (23 February 1999).
[4] Alison Stokes for the *Western Echo* and Jenni Zylka for *Die Tageszeitung*.

neck and went down to his playroom to fight whatever Bat-
villain had appeared on Cartoon Network last night.
Thank you, Bob Kane. Someday I'll tell my son about you and
how you were responsible for the good times we have both
had.
Slam Bradley
feeling a little melancholy and a lot misty.[5]

The newspaper obituaries of Bob Kane, on the other hand, made
frequent and ludicrous mistakes – 'Batman never left the brooding
towers of Gotham City', 'Kane . . . came up with the idea of
"Birdman" . . . his friends laughed' – which I as a fan I had anticipated,
and saw fit to correct in a faintly pompous letter to the *Guardian*.

> You are wrong in suggesting that Batman's 'monkish co-
> existence with Robin' was seen as 'sinister' during the early
> years. The Dynamic Duo's relationship was, however,
> condemned as a homoerotic fantasy during the McCarthyite
> 1950s, a crucial turn of events which you neglect to mention.
>
> Finally, with all due credit to Kane, Batman's creator, it is
> misleading to state that he 'learned successfully to share his
> creation with many other artists.' Kane consistently played
> down the contributions of his art assistant, Jerry Robinson, the
> writer Gardner Fox, and most crucially, Batman's co-creator
> Bill Finger – not Fingers – without whom the character would
> never have become the cultural icon he is today.[6]

I was familiar, too, with the popular media's tendency to gently mock
the academic study of pulp culture, and so was prepared for my
research to be trivialised a little when it was picked up by the *Mirror*. I
wasn't disappointed by the quality of the puns.[7]
The story was headed with a photograph of me looking like a

---

[5] Posted by Slam Bradley, *Jonah Weiland's Comic Book Resources*, op. cit. (6 November
1998).
[6] Will Brooker, 'Jolly Batman', letter to the *Guardian* (9 November 1998).
[7] Jeremy Armstrong, 'Degrees? Will has Gotham', *Mirror* (28 January 1999)

He's doctor of Batman

WILL Brooker is about to become the first man in the world with a degree – in Batman.

The 28-year-old is studying for a PhD on Gotham City's comic and movie superhero.

Will's "doctor" qualification will make him one of the world's leading experts on the Caped Crusader, who has his 60th birthday in May.

"I will be the only person in Britain with this qualification, if not the world," said Will, a student at Cardiff University.

"But I do take a lot of stick from my friends.

"Whenever I tell people what I do, you get all the 'Holy Smoke' gags.

Hero

"So I started saying I was doing cultural or American history instead.

"It can be a bit of a burden, but I work hard at the subject and take it all with a pinch of salt," added Will, who plans to write a book on his hero.

London-born Will, who became a Batman fan aged just six, admitted that he had trouble

EXCLUSIVE
By JEREMY ARMSTRONG

finding somewhere to complete his PhD once he had completed his first degree in English.

But he found Dr Roberta Pearson at Cardiff who had written essays on the topic.

"People have studied everything from Robin Hood, James Bond, Dracula, the Avengers to EastEnders in the past, but not Batman," said Will.

Since first appearing in DC comics in 1939, the superhero and sidekick Robin have won millions of fans world-wide in a series of blockbuster movies.

However, Will holds a view on Batman's sexuality which may disappoint some of them.

"I think in real life he would be gay," he said.

10 BAT FACTS

1. LEWIS Wilson first played Batman in the 1943 serial for cinema houses.

2. TV's Batman and Robin, Adam West and Burt Ward, both changed their names — from William West Anderson and Bert Gervis.

3. ONE of West's first TV jobs was with as side-kick to a monkey in Honolulu.

4. BATMAN had a dog, Ace, the Bathound.

5. THERE was also "Bat-mite" — an insect.

6. BATMAN comic artist Bob Kane died last year, aged 83.

7. IN a 1986 comic, there was a female Robin.

8. ROBIN was killed by the Joker as a result of a comic readers' poll in 1988.

9. IN some comics, Batman married Batwoman and the had a Bat-daughter.

10. BATMAN has met Dracula, Sherlock Holmes, Robin Hood — and, in 1943, he beat up Hitler.

crazed ten-year-old, grinning over an issue of *Batman* and sporting a mortar board – it was captioned 'No Joker: Will is serious about his subject' – and finished with ten half-true 'Bat Facts'. The article concluded with me cryptically adding that 'I think in real life he would be gay.'

As noted, I had expected the nature of my research to undergo a translation process as it passed from the private sphere to the public. I had subjected myself to this treatment with the intention of studying the result. What I didn't expect was the extent to which this tabloid version of my work – and, indeed of myself – would be picked up not just across the national and regional press, but in radio and television, on the Internet and even, for some reason, in the German media.[8]

On Thursday, 28 January, I was called by the *Western Mail*, BBC Choice, Radio 1, Radio Wales, UK Living and RDF. By Friday I had been asked to appear on HTV's *Moneyspinners*, Sky's *Guilty* and BBC1's *The Vanessa Show*. Later that day, I was being debated on *Jonah Weiland's Comic Book Resources*:

> He sure as Hell won't get any respect but he will be laughed at.
> What do you have your doctorate in?
> My PhD is in BATMAN.
> Response: hahahahahahahahahaha!!!!
> What a f$@king moron/idiot wasting his money. He has nothing intellectual to do with his time.[9]

> Why not do a PhD in Batman? He must be doing his degree on Literature. Comics ARE a form of literature, despite what others may tell U . . . just because it's a 'popular' medium doesn't mean it's less valid than the classical medium.
> Batman is a great character, on many levels, and has a rich and complex history to draw upon. What does the Batman represent? Why is he so popular? How has he changed over the

---

[8] By RDF and in Jenni Zylka, *'Von Fledermausen und Menschen – Batman wird 60'*, *Die Tageszeitung* (May 1999)
[9] Posted by Von-El, *Jonah Weiland's Comic Book Resources*, op. cit (29 January 1999).

years?

Is it really such a stretch to conceive of a thesis on Batman?[10]

On Monday morning Channel 4's *Big Breakfast* show ran their usual competition during which a celebrity guest was asked to identify objects from Johnny Vaughan's frantic descriptions. Mid-way through, Vaughan offered the clue 'rats of the air'. The guest faltered 'pigeons'; the answer was a bat. The next object was a mortar board. I wondered if I was just imagining the connection; but when a student told me later that day that a quiz on Radio 1 had included the question 'Will Brooker is about to get a PhD in what subject?', I realised I had been subtly appropriated by the British media.

Over the space of three days, I had acquired an alter ego, a ghost-self: the 'Dr Batman', the 'Will Brooker' – or 'Booker'[11] – who was doing 'Batman Studies'[12] and planned 'to write a book about his hero'.[13] Things I had never said began reappearing in newspapers; I kept hearing myself repeat 'I'm no Batman anorak'[14] and confess that I had looked into buying a Batman suit for '£150, or up to £300 for a deluxe version'.[15] This version of me 'decided that Batman would be the perfect cultural icon to study' immediately after completing 'his BA in film and tv studies'[16], or alternatively 'his first degree in English'.[17] He was 'a f$@king moron/idiot wasting his money'. He was 'Cardiff's Batman Boffin',[18] 'specialising in the man in tights';[19] 'the world's first academic superhero . . . arrived fresh from

---

[10] Posted by Damocles, ibid. (29 January 1999).
[11] According to Julian Carey, 'Happy Birthday, Batman', op. cit.
[12] Interview on Radio 5 Live (28 January 1999).
[13] Armstrong, op. cit.
[14] For instance, Rachel Harvie, 'To the Bat-Lecture, Robin!', *Gair Rhydd* (8 February 1999).
[15] For instance, Michelle Bower, 'Award me the Bat-doctorate, Boy Wonder', *Western Mail* (29 January 1999).
[16] Harvie, op. cit.
[17] Armstrong, op. cit.
[18] Harvie, op. cit.
[19] Interview, Radio 5, op. cit.

the Batcave in Cardiff'.[20] 'I will be the only person in Britain with this qualification,' crows the Batman boffin proudly, 'if not the world' – according to *Empire*'s feature on the 'Caped Crusader collegian'.[21]

Phil Jupitus announced that 'these days, you can even get a degree in Bat Studies. In fact, British student Will Booker is currently completing the world's first PhD in Batman'.[22] Cam Winstanley, from *Total Film* magazine, lambasted my work as 'preposterous . . . it just doesn't seem the sort of thing that you should be spending three years at college doing'.[23] Zoe Ball scoffed at me for the benefit of her early-morning listeners.[24] Terry Wogan invited listeners to call in with puns about me 'Robin the taxpayer'.[25] Vanessa Feltz invited me on her show, but in the excitement over Glenn Hoddle's resignation forgot that I was there to be interviewed.[26] I had become a face, a concept, a set of quotes. I knew what it meant to be interpreted, reproduced, to become an Aunt Sally and scapegoat, to circulate in various, sometimes mutually contradictory incarnations, to be debated by audiences, to lose your original referent. That is, I think I knew what it meant to be Batman – to be a cultural icon, however minor.

I had also had it confirmed that the popular media do not like academics writing about popular texts; that they feel threatened by research like mine, and begin to guard their property jealously. For the most part they sought ways to ridicule my study, trying to force me into the ready stereotypes of dry academic, geeky fanboy or money-wasting student; often I seemed to be tagged with two or even three of these labels. 'So go on, speaking as an academic, what's Batman *really* about?' asked the Radio 1 presenter with more than the trace of a sneer. Following my game attempt to condense one hundred thousand words into ten seconds, Cam Winstanley was called in to deliver a rabbit punch. 'It just doesn't seem the sort of thing that you should be spending three years at college doing, really . . . doing something that

---

[20] *Newsbeat*, Radio 1 (28 January 1999).

[21] William Thomas, 'Riddle Me This!' *Empire* magazine (April 1999).

[22] Carey, 'Happy Birthday, Batman', op. cit.

[23] Ibid.

[24] *Zoe Ball*, Radio 1 (28 January 1999).

[25] *Wake Up With Wogan*, Radio 2 (28 January 1999).

[26] *The Vanessa Show* (2 February 1999)

most people just sort of talk about . . . down the pub.'[27] I was at once up in my ivory tower babbling about cultural icons, and down in the union bar drinking the taxpayers' money.

Even those reports which I felt were favourable followed a similar pattern. The *Western Mail* began 'it's been a tough three years for Will Brooker – hundreds of comics to read, countless hours of TV viewing and the odd trip to New York . . . ', and while the copy ran 'no bat-geek repellent required', 'Will insists he is not a Batman anorak', the fan-as-nerd label was still there for readers to pin on me if they liked. Similarly, when Touch Radio opened its interview with the presenter asking his girl assistant 'you told me about a gentleman who was doing a serious, high-level study on Batman . . . and I didn't believe you! And you've actually found him!' the stage was set for parading a freak. Again, this was a sympathetic interview which allowed me to talk at length about my research, and yet it led into a phone-in on Batman collectables and their prices, rather than, say, a discussion about the role popular heroes play in our culture.[28]

There was nothing personal in my media treatment, of course, and there is nothing personal in my complaint. I set myself up for this and for the most part expected to be presented as little better than the 'I Grok Spock' Trekkies in the *Saturday Night Live* parody discussed by Henry Jenkins.[29] By my second interview, though, I was already honing my own soundbites and potted justifications, calling on a tradition of work about Robin Hood, James Bond, soap operas and romance novels and stressing Batman's role in top-ten moments of American history. I would argue, then – I would hope – that my brief stint of fame did more to help than to hinder the cause of Cultural Studies.

With hindsight, though, I was still surprised by the fact that the British media, in the final year of the twentieth century, found it so difficult to conceive of academic research on one of that century's most significant icons; and that serves perhaps as the ultimate justification of my project. When a student newspaper opens its report on a cultural

---

[27] *Newsbeat*, op. cit.
[28] Interview, Touch Radio (16 February 1999).
[29] Henry Jenkins, *Textual Poachers*, London: Routledge (1992), p. 9.

studies doctorate with the words 'three years of serious television viewing is about to come to an end for a Cardiff PhD student';[30] when *Empire*, 'the movie magazine', cannot discuss the academic study of film texts without calling me a 'Batman boffin' and going into hysterical alliterative fits – 'Cardiff commends culpably capable Caped Crusader collegian'[31] – then the case for Batman's role in the lives of audiences and the culture of the last six decades surely still needs to be proven. Even the *Western Echo*, picking up on the story late in the day for its May 1999 article, was unable to hold back from the same recycled gags about 'a tough three years . . . with hundreds of comics to read', while the headline asserted triumphantly 'Will is a Bat Swot'. The report faithfully included my argument that 'a PhD in Batman [is] a professional qualification and just as relevant as doing a PhD in . . . satellite television in Saudi Arabia or World War Two propaganda',[32] but still I doubt that researchers in those latter fields would have been labelled 'Saudi Swot' or 'Propaganda Swot'. The serious study of popular, contemporary, familiar texts – as opposed to those old enough or obscure enough to be recognised as properly 'academic' – is evidently still regarded as a contradiction in terms by the mass media. From national TV news through phone-in radio debate to local newspapers, the very idea of work like mine – in its problematising of distinctions between work and play, the serious and the trivial, the academic and the everyday – seems to unsettle this popular discourse, and its embarassment manifests itself in ridicule and attack.

Cultural Studies clearly still has its work cut out for it, then, and seems destined for the moment to still be treated as a novelty discipline, the home of trick-pony research. However, my experience provides a convincing reason for its continued ventures into research like this current project, whatever the jeers; Cultural Studies has to do it, because the popular media are clearly not prepared to treat popular texts with anything like the attention they deserve.

---

[30] Harvie, op. cit.

[31] Thomas, op. cit.

[32] Alison Stokes, 'Will is a Bat Swot', *Western Echo* (22 May 1999).

2. Batman's Future

I hope that each chapter so far has reached its own conclusions about the issues surrounding Batman in the specific historical moments already covered – the origins and war years, the period of censorship and gay reading, the decade of camp and Pop and more recently the time of the Batman author-as-star and the ever more vocal fanbase. Towards the end of the second and third chapters, though, I began to suggest ways in which the issues circulating around Batman during the 1950s and 1960s were being reworked in the 1990s; the occasional nod towards a possible romantic love between Batman and Robin, for instance in the stories 'A Great Day For Everyone' and 'Fear of God' cited above, and the embracing of the 'camp' Batman of the 1960s, giant typewriters and all, in stories like 'When Is A Door' and 'Dark Allegiances'. I suggested that these moments seem to imply a loosening of the official definitions around DC's vision of Batman, a gradual tendency towards openness and experiment. We are, I suggested, beginning to see a more fluid history where present versions recall and replay earlier moments, rather than adhering to strict chronology and continuity. I want to explore these issues further in this section, and ask what vision DC seems currently to hold of Batman's future.

It hardly seems coincidental that the last few years have seen an unprecedented number of DC projects which actually project Batman forward in time – nothing extravagant, just a few decades – as if actually to road-test possible models for the character in the new century and see how the readers take to them. By surveying these speculative fictions of an older Batman, I will discuss the ways in which DC seems to be preparing the ground for inevitable changes and progression in the Batman mythos, altering the role of Bruce Wayne while always retaining the concept of the Dark Knight.

The notion of the audience – a fictional audience of Gothamites standing for the actual readership – is surprisingly prominent in DC's conceptions of the future Batman. I will end this chapter by considering the importance of Batman's readership – the active fans, the wider non-participatory group, and the millions who may rarely pick up a comic but still know the character intimately – in maintaining the Batman myth into the new millennium, regardless of what DC and Warners decide to do with their franchise.

(i) Batman and institution: taking stock of Batman

Issue #94 of the monthly *Legends of the Dark Knight* was simply called 'Stories'.[33] A group of Gotham residents – young and old, situated within various social and ethnic interpretive communities – are trapped in an elevator by a terrorist group. They begin to share their tales of the Batman, but each experience is radically different and illustrated in affectionate pastiche of the art and writing style of the appropriate period. Elderly Julie Madison remembers the vampire-fighting Bat-Man of the 1930s. A middle-aged black cop recalls a bizarre case of the 1950s, full of gags and gimmicks. An ageing hippy swears he saw Batman thwart 'Age O'Quarious' in 1967, and the cop's teenage son tells of the armour-plated, ultra-violent vigilante he spotted only recently.

As in 'The Batman Nobody Knows', each participant argues for his or her own interpretation over the others, regardless of its improbability – Julie Madison's hero would be eighty years old, after all – and when Batman, shadowy and noble, appears to free them, each reads from him only what suits them: the beauty of a former sweetheart, a 'faar out' old amigo or a dude in 'wicked armor'. It is a sweet, generous story and, I think, in some ways symptomatic of DC's current willingness to allow a little play with the rules of the Dark Knight. It stands in marked contrast to the ethos of 1986, when the multi-part, crossover story *Crisis on Infinite Earths* imposed a strict framework of continuity over all DC characters and insisted that most of the events of the past fifty years or so had never happened. In Batman's case, this meant no Batwoman, no Bat-Mite, no Batman Genie or Rainbow Batman, no time-travel or spacefaring; from one point of view, no fun. It was time to stop play: it was, after all, the time of *The Dark Knight Returns* and *The Killing Joke*, of the graphic novel, the comic as literature, the hardback, painted Prestige Edition subtitled 'A *Serious* House on *Serious* Earth'.[34]

---

[33] Michael T. Gilbert, 'Stories', *Legends of the Dark Knight* #94, New York: DC Comics (May 1997).

[34] This being the achingly pretentious subtitle to Grant Morrison and Dave McKean's *Arkham Asylum*, New York: DC Comics (1989).

As I have suggested in previous chapters, though, times have been changing for Batman in the 1990s. *Legends of the Dark Knight* #100 brought Robin back into a resolutely 'solo' title. The Bat-Mite had, as noted above, already returned in *Legends of the Dark Knight* #34. Batwoman's costume was brought out of mothballs in *The Nail*, a three-part series from 1998,[35] and in *Planet Krypton* Batman actually came face to face with his old partner for the first time in decades, breathing 'Kathy?'[36] Finally, while the first Bat-Girl is still out of continuity and the second, crippled by the Joker in 1988, still operates from a wheelchair as 'Oracle', current issues of *Batman* and *Detective* show a third Batgirl, her face concealed and identity as yet unrevealed.[37]

I want to draw three points from these changes to the mythos and attempt to project from them what I see as DC's possible attitude toward the character's current position and his future as a comic book franchise.

First, the concept of Batman as a solitary vigilante which dominated the late 1980s – as epitomised by the 'Death in the Family' murder and the 1989 Burton film – has effectively been replaced with a new-model Batman as team player. The Dark Knight in current continuity works not just with Robin and the new Batgirl, but with the twentysome-things Oracle and Nightwing, previously known as Batgirl and Robin. The team is completed by Azrael, 'Agent of the Bat' – the Canadian martial artist who temporarily replaced Wayne as Batman during the *Knightfall* storyline – and Huntress, a marginally more law-abiding version of Catwoman. Batman looks less like a lonely avenger and more like the boss of a well-honed outfit; and this is before he teams up with Superman, Wonder Woman and the other big guns in the regular title *Justice League of America*. I will suggest below that this model of 'Batman' as a concept rather than an individual seems vital to DC's

---

[35] Alan Davis, *Justice League: The Nail*, New York: DC Comics (1998).

[36] Mark Waid and Barry Kitson, *The Kingdom: Planet Krypton* #1, New York: DC Comics (February 1999).

[37] For instance, Greg Rucka and Frank Teran, 'Mosaic', *Detective Comics* #732, New York: DC Comics (May 1999). Batgirl II was revealed in *Legends of the Dark Night* #120 (June 1999) to be the Huntress. The Batgirl mantle was subsequently passed to Cassandra Cain, a mute Asian-American teenage assassin who gained her own solo title in February 2000.

projections of the future Dark Knight – that is, both in the fictional twenty-first century Gotham, and in the real world of twenty-first century markets and audience.

Second, this remaking of Batman as a team player has another significant implication in terms of institutional branding. As discussed in the third chapter, the Batman animated series and its related comics have constituted a highly successful franchise since their inception in 1992, providing Warners with that rare gem, a TV show which appeals to both children and adults, and a platform for spin-offs ranging from feature films to ice creams, action figures and birthday cakes.[38] 'Animated series' continuity, however, has always worked on a slightly different level to 'DC Universe' continuity. The original comic tie-in was titled *Batman Adventures*, and differed only from the world of *Detective* in its distinctively simple yet elegant cartooning. The second title, however, was called *Batman and Robin Adventures*: its Robin was Dick Grayson, who in regular continuity had been operating for years as Nightwing. The third title was *Gotham Adventures*: it featured Barbara Gordon as Batgirl. Barbara Gordon, of course, was 'officially' in a wheelchair, and regular continuity hadn't seen a Batgirl since 1988. There were, therefore, marked discrepancies between Batman 'regular' and 'lite'; both successful, the DCU Batman and the animated Batman nevertheless remained different brands. A kid coming from the TV show to *Batman* or *Detective* would find a significantly grimmer world, missing out some of his favourite characters and evoking a very different style. It seems to me that this might have struck Warners as bad business.

While I have no way of second-guessing Time-Warners, I would venture that the construction of a Batman Family, including a new Batgirl, within *Batman* and *Detective* – while meanwhile in the 'Adventures' universe a flashback entitled *The Lost Years* neatly shows us Dick Grayson graduating to Nightwing and Tim Drake taking over as

---

[38] See for instance Batman and Catwoman, *The Animated Series*-based ice lollies, from Wonderland Ice Cream (1997); 'A Guide to Celebration Cakes' including *Batman and Robin Adventures* design, from Sainsbury's supermarket (1997); Sue Webster, 'All Dolled Up', review of 'Rocketpak Batman and Air Strike Robin' toys, *Independent on Sunday* (13 April 1997).

Robin, in keeping with regular continuity[39] – may be part of a grand plan to bring the two brands into conjunction and enable unification some time in the near future. An Internet rumour has it that Warners plan to relaunch and rebrand the entire Batman group of comics for the new millennium, stamping *Batman* and its sister titles with the same typography and logo as the *Adventures* series and so presenting a cohesive and accessible front for the young reader. This move would provide a more inviting way into Batman for the juvenile audience reared on the cartoon, offering a whole spread of appealing Batman titles rather than just the single dedicated spin-off, and making *Gotham Adventures* the norm, even the template, rather than the exception. Of course, I may be proved wrong within the next two years;[40] but it seems a canny idea and no more radical than the restyling of the two Bat-titles in 1966 to keep them in tune with the TV show and provide an entry for the new wave of fans. If this change did occur, the Batman titles would, as Denny O'Neil hinted to me in 1998, 'lighten up';[41] by coming into line with animated continuity and a younger audience, the regular comics would surely tend towards snappy one-shot adventures and an element of teen humour, rather than the lumbering multi-parters and social comment which O'Neil seems to prefer.

Finally, whether this strategy is implemented or not, there is no doubt that DC has made a substantial change in its attitude to Batman

---

[39] See Hilary Bader, Bo Hampton *et al.*, *Batman Adventures: The Lost Years*, New York: DC Comics (January–May 1998). Harley Quinn entered DCU continuity in 1999 with the *Batman: Harley Quinn* one-shot by Paul Dini and Yvel Guichet, the photorealist cover by Alex Ross easing her transition from 'cartoon' to 'official' Batman mythos. She subsequently appeared alongside the Joker in 'No Man's Land' and is apparently working with the Catwoman in current continuity. Thanks to Viceroy-Batman from *Batman.net*, *http://batman.fanhosts.com/archives.html* (June 2000).

[40] At the time of going to press (June 2000) this prediction has been proved half-right. The Batman stable of comics was entirely rebranded for DC's millennium celebrations, giving the titles a consistent identity, and the tendency is indeed toward shorter, more accessible stories following the conclusion of O'Neil's socio-political ramble through 'No Man's Land'. O'Neil's announcement in June that he was soon to retire as Batman group editor confirms the sense that the shift towards a 'lighter' Batman is still ongoing, albeit gradually.

[41] Denny O'Neil, personal interview (1 July 1998).

continuity very recently. The house-clearance so diligently and ruthlessly performed by *Crisis On Infinite Earths* in 1986 was undone by another multi-part crossover in 1998, called *The Kingdom*. Without going into the arcana of DC's universe, suffice it to say that all the embarrassing and silly aspects of superhero history which 'never happened' following *Crisis* have now been allowed back in, with the proviso that they occurred on various alternate timelines. It was this 'Hypertime' device which allowed Batman to come face to face with Kathy Kane as Batwoman, a character who until that point didn't 'exist'; and potentially, it allows DC's writers and artists to wish even more impossible things.

The two-page spread at the climax of *The Kingdom* shows Batman and his colleagues looking out over a universe of events from the past sixty years of DC Comics; events which from 1986 onwards had been written out of history. We see the ginger-haired 'Robin II', son of Robin, from the 1960s, and the teenage 'Son of Batman' from the 1970s; we see Batplanes, and the Bat-Mite, and Batman as a knight in armour, and Batman on the trail of Jack the Ripper.[42] Everything which had been forbidden was now possible, even if it was understood from the DC press releases to Internet boards that travel across these alternate universes would be used sparingly.

That said, *The Kingdom* has radical implications for Batman narrative. All the stories told by the Gothamites in that elevator – or indeed by the boys on Mr Wayne's camping trip – can now be true, all at once; not within the safety of an 'Elseworld' or an 'Imaginary Story', but within regular continuity. The concept of an 'aberration' within the Batman mythos must by extension now have lost its meaning: just as the memory of a Batman who fought around giant typewriters and muttered 'What a way to go-go' can no longer be denied, so the possibility of a Batman in love with Robin, or Kathy Kane, or Selina Kyle, must be equally valid, and we must also assume that at least one of those alternate timelines houses the real 'Black Batman'. It is, I think, a wise and warm-spirited gift from DC's editors to its writers, artists and above all its fans; this decision at the end of

---

[42] Mark Waid, Mike Zeck and John Beatty, *The Kingdom* #2, New York: DC Comics (February 1999).

sixty years to embrace and include all the Batmen that have ever been since 1939, in all their difference and variety, rather than closing down that notion to a single rigid design of the 'pure' Dark Knight.

It hardly needs noting, perhaps, that Hypertime is a textbook example of postmodernism, following Fredric Jameson's influential definitions. Steeped in nostalgia, *The Kingdom*, like 'Stories', revisits the Batman museum and evokes earlier periods through a pastiche of their characteristic art style – literally trying on the masks of previous Batmen, and evoking a more fluid sense of history through its bending of strict chronological rules.[43]

To detect traces of a postmodern aesthetic in DC comic books is nothing groundbreaking in itself. *Arkham Asylum*, to give just one example, blurred distinctions between high and low culture by employing hardback production, glossy, painted art and self-conscious references to psychoanalysis, mythology and literature in a story about Batman fighting the Joker. However, rather than just a formalist adoption of postmodern styling – perhaps in an attempt to relaunch DC comics as 'sophisticated', 'adult' entertainment – *The Kingdom*, as I have suggested, epitomises a wider, equally postmodern trend towards fluidity and play, towards an interpretive pluralism in place of the restrictive grand narrative. Instead of attempting to force continuity on the character and ruling that earlier, incompatible versions 'never happened', the *Kingdom* approach seeks to reconcile difference – Batman's rich cultural history – with the unity implied by the character's consistent 'template' and the need for a recognisable brand. As such it implies a new flexibility on the part of the producers which could in turn be read as a bending to the demands of fans, particularly those vocal Internet campaigners who bemoaned the Crisis and longed for the return of 'infinite earths'.

On the one hand, then, DC seem to have responded to their audience by loosening the reins of continuity around Batman and allowing the character to embody various different, mutually contra-dictory forms and meanings, rather than imposing a tight 'official' narrative. From another angle, though, we could argue that the

---

[43] See Fredric Jameson, *Postmodernism, or, the Cultural Logic of Late Capitalism*, London: Verso (1991).

decisions behind *The Kingdom* still lay with DC's editors, and that the fans, however vociferous, remain powerless subjects who are expected to be mollified with a gift from 'above'. The rulers may have adopted more liberal policies, but the balance of cultural power is intact.

Finally, the situation is complicated by the fact that, while adult fans make up a vocal minority whose resistance only threatens DC if it becomes organised, the far larger juvenile audience for Batman comics holds the genuine power to make or break a title. While the producers can choose to ignore the older fans, then, the younger readers must ultimately be catered for to ensure the continued commercial success of the comic books. As such, then, we might argue that it is the children who wear the crown of cultural power; Ziggy, Mickey and Ronnie telling Mr Wayne how they see the Batman, and Mr Wayne having to change accordingly or lose his job. The extent of this young readership's influence, and its relation to DC's current reshaping of the Batman mythos, is explored in my next section.

(ii) Future Batmen: Batman as genre

It is not surprising that the years 1996–1999 have seen several visions of the 'future' Batman. As we approach our anniversaries or landmark birthdays, we often look forward as well as back, and wonder where we will be twenty, thirty years from now. What is more striking is that the most significant of these visions – those which project Batman into the near, rather than far future[44] – are so very similar to each other. The first was written by Grant Morrison, in the *Justice League of America* comic: I quoted from it at the start of this chapter. Morrison is currently one of DC's two star writers, and *JLA*, starring all the 'Big Gun' superheroes, one of its flagship monthly titles. The second was written by Mark Waid, in the prestige edition, gorgeously painted *Kingdom Come*. Waid is the other of DC's two star writers, and *Kingdom Come* perhaps the company's biggest critical and fan success of the 1990s; it spawned a trade paperback, hardcover with slipcase and

---

[44] For visions of the far-future Batman, see *DC: One Million* and 'Legend' in *Batman: Black and White*, cited below.

annotations, set of trading cards, poster collection and ultimately the spin-off series *The Kingdom*. The third was written by Hilary Bader, in *Batman Beyond*. *Batman Beyond* is 'based on the hit animated series on Kids' WB';[45] that is, it serves as an adaptation of the latest Warners cartoon series, and as such is part of a wider franchise. These three texts, then, are not obscure, throwaway what-ifs hidden in the backwaters of the DC Universe; they are highly visible experiments, test-runs in front of a crowd of both dedicated fans, more casual readers and lastly, the audience of the TV show who may rarely pick up a comic. That they all seem to have so much in common suggests to me that these prominent visions of the 21st century Batman may in fact be running by us on their way to becoming the dominant.

In 'Imaginary Stories' from *JLA* #8, Bruce Wayne is a grim, grey-haired man of around sixty, married to Selina Kyle and living in Wayne Manor. Tim Drake, once Robin, has grown up to adopt the mantle of the Batman; his sidekick is 'Bruce Jr', once more the ginger-haired Robin II. Bruce broods around the cave while a new Dynamic Duo stand guard over a darker Gotham: because 'as long as Gotham needs them, Batman and Robin can never die'.[46] He communicates with Tim by means of a headset, and when Robin is captured by the Joker he provides backup by strapping himself back into the suit and the Batmobile, thundering through Gotham for a last stand with his nemesis.

In *Kingdom Come*, Bruce Wayne is a sardonic, grey-haired man of around sixty, supported by an exoskeleton and living under the ruins of Wayne Manor. Gotham is under a system of martial law, the Batman's law: it is patrolled by an army of robotic 'Bat-knights', giant machines and winged guardians. He orders his mechanical regiment from the Batcave through microphones and closed-circuit screens – 'Twenty-five and thirty-two . . . resume *patrol* . . . Maneuver twelve'[47] – but when society is threatened by the new wave of anarchic metahumans, he

---

[45] Bader *et al.*, *Batman Beyond* #1, op. cit.

[46] Grant Morrison, Oscar Jiminez *et al.*, *JLA* #8, New York: DC Comics (August 1997).

[47] Mark Waid and Alec Ross, *The Kingdom* #2, New York: DC Comics (1996).

straps himself back into the suit and soars down from the sky for the final battle.

In *Batman Beyond*, Bruce Wayne is a misanthropic, grey-haired man of around sixty, living as a hermit with his dog Ace in the run-down Wayne Manor. The Batman suit – an all-black miracle of technology enabling flight and super-strength – has been appropriated by teenager Terry McGinnis. Bruce guides, advises and chastises McGinnis from the Batcave – 'there's a radio receiver in your cowl'[48] – as his new protégé fights organised crime, corrupt institutions and the gang of thugs calling themselves the Jokerz.

My own overwhelming sense from these three glimpses into a 'possible' future for the Batman is that we may in fact be seeing the Batman's probable future. Robin and Batgirl – in all their incarnations – have always grown up, learned from mistakes, taken on new names and identities, faced death or paralysis. Perhaps DC have decided that Bruce Wayne, forever in his 'early 30s' these days, must also grow older and change. Perhaps, if the Batman line of comics really is being brought more into line with the animated series and its younger audience, Warners have realised that to a kid of twelve, a man in his early thirties might as well be a sixty-year-old in terms of appeal, charisma and possibility for identification. Perhaps Batman at sixty will become, for the first time, a real sixty-year-old.

In the current Batman team, the twentysomething Nightwing and Oracle serve as the 'good' big brother and sister, Azrael and Huntress the 'bad'. Robin/Tim Drake, like Terry McGinnis in the future fiction, is the only character anywhere near the age of the teenage and juvenile market. If Batman is to be the dark father, guiding a younger team of dynamic heroes – as seems to be the case both in the animated and regular continuity – why not take this model to its logical end, push Wayne forward to his 'real' age and play to the strengths of this 'Team Batman' concept? It worked in the 1960s for Marvel's *X-Men*, that motley group of superheroes under Professor Xavier; and it worked in the 1970s and 1980s for TV shows like *Charley's Angels*, *The A-Team* and *Knight Rider*. It worked in the 1990s for pop groups like Take That and the Spice Girls, both projecting themselves as carefully assembled

---

[48] Bader *et al.*, *Batman Beyond* #2, New York: DC Comics (April 1999).

teams operating under an older svengali.[49] As I write, the model is about to be reworked once more in the form of *S Club 7*, a cross-media phenomenon consisting of seven young people aged between 17 and 22, each with a subtly different appeal – cheeky, thoughtful, crazy, cool – and managed by the Spice Girls' producer.[50]

If Batman is going to sell not just to the diehard minority who follow *Detective*'s year-long sagas and the artistic departures of *Legends of the Dark Knight*, but to a younger audience accustomed to instantly accessible continuity between comics, t-shirts, video games, the Internet, TV and cinema, then the 'Team Batman' would be a way to go; and it looks as though this may be the way DC is heading with the concept, following what it sees as the juvenile market's demands. Again, altering the Bat-brand to pull in a younger audience would hardly be an unprecedented step: Bill Finger and Bob Kane did it in 1940, and the readership doubled. If DC can pull that trick again by moving the younger team to centre stage and locating Bruce Wayne as a concerned father in the background, it will be worth all the inevitable criticism from older fans.[51]

If this move does occur, 'Batman' comics will take on a new meaning. Already, as noted, there exists a 'Batman group' of titles – *Robin, Azrael, Catwoman, Nightwing* – under Denny O'Neil's control, just as in the fictional world the Batman team operates under the Dark Knight; both men, as a point of interest, turn sixty in 1999. 'Batman', then, already means more than just *Batman* and *Detective*, or even the more obviously related titles *Shadow of the Bat* and *Legends of the Dark Knight*. If Bruce Wayne moves toward a background, organisational role within continuity, 'Batman' will have to take on a wider meaning within the comics themselves. As in the *JLA* story and *Batman Beyond*,

---

[49] Even after the Spice Girls had sacked their producer, Simon Fuller, the svengali figure was incorporated into their *Spice World* movie as Richard E. Grant.

[50] Nicholas Barber, *Independent on Sunday* (4 April 1999).

[51] Again, in June 2000 the notion of Batman as mentor to a young team is still proving a popular model. Paul Dini comments that the whole concept of the 'Batman' narrative has indeed changed, in the *Adventures* at least: 'It's really Batman as the cornerstone of a group that encompasses Nightwing, Robin and Batgirl' (*http://www.batman-superman.com*). However, we should note that the *Adventures* series is still distinct from the 'DC Universe' mythos.

the word will connote a concept rather than a single man – 'Batman and Robin can never die' – and will no longer simply mean Bruce Wayne. Rather than Batman as an individual, we might have to start thinking of the 'Batman genre';[52] and this would also tally with the new boundaries set by *The Kingdom*.

Within a 'Batman genre story', variation would be allowed, indeed expected, within a set of familiar rules, just as was the case in the classical Hollywood genres. Some of the codes would always remain – a Bat-costume, gadgets, crime-fighting, Gotham – but some would be missing or altered. Batman might not be Bruce Wayne; he might be Bruce Wayne and Terry McGinnis, or Barbara Gordon, or Ziggy and Ronnie. Just as the boundaries of the Western genre have stretched to include the comedy-Western, musical Western and science fiction Western without losing the basic identifying characteristics of theme, if not iconography, so we could see – as indeed we have already seen – the science fiction Batman story, the comedy Batman story, the romantic Batman story. 'Batman' as a genre could embrace variation and improvisation around its core template, adapting to survive as Batman has always adapted to survive, both in Gotham and the real world. The concept can, as the past sixty years have shown, undergo a lot of changes and still be recognisable as Batman; just as 'Star Trek' has for many years meant more than Mr Spock and James T. Kirk, and 'Star Wars' no longer relies for its identity on Luke Skywalker and Darth Vader, so 'Batman', I would venture, is bigger than Bruce Wayne in a costume. As the Batman of the 853rd century remarked in Grant Morrison's far-future extravaganza *DC: One Million*, 'One Batman? You believe there can only be one Batman? Batman is not a *man*. I'm an *ideal*.'[53]

The success of this broadening of 'Batman' would depend, of course, on audience; on audience recognition and acceptance. Significantly, this notion is recognised and incorporated into the third issue of *Batman Beyond*. Terry McGinnis turns up to help a group of

[52] I'm indebted to Harry Hood, Kevin Gater and Nick Forrer, students at the Southampton Institute, for suggesting this concept to me.
[53] Chuck Dixon, Greg Land *et al.*, *Detective Comics* #1,000,000, New York: DC Comics (November 85,271).

young people, wearing the black and red Batman suit. 'Who are you?' asks their leader, a black man in his twenties. 'What do you want? Answer me!' It is a drowsy toddler in his mother's arms who mumbles 'Batman? Batman. That's the Batman.'

'Batman? Ain't no such animal as a Batman,' snarls the man, Akira. 'Someone made him up to scare little kids into being good. I ain't no little kid. And I don't scare.'

McGinnis dodges Akira's blow with a clean swoop through the air. The kids cry out in pleasure. 'Look. He's flying. So cool. He's Batman.' 'Yeah,' another affirms, 'that's Batman.'

'Play nice, Akira', McGinnis warns. 'You're setting a bad example . . . if I wanted to hurt someone, they'd already be hurt. Now chill out.' The kids are convinced, and cluster round: 'Can you take me flying?' 'Do you have any gum?'

'Akira, leave them alone', says the toddler's mother. 'He's not going to hurt us. I can tell. You know I can. Look. They trust him. And they're never wrong.'[54]

The confirmation of Batman's identity lies with the young audience, the audience of under-tens. He doesn't have to be Bruce Wayne; he just needs the suit and the gadgets, the abilities, and most importantly the morality, the humanity. There's just a sense about him: 'they trust him. And they're never wrong.' As in 'Stories' and 'The Batman Nobody Knows', it's a self-conscious moment, this time apparently expressing a wish on the part of the creators that the real-life young audience will be open to a new Batman in the next century, just as the Gothamites accept him here.

And if they aren't? What if *Batman Beyond* fails to catch on adequately, if the road-test is judged unsuccessful, if the young readers never tune into Batman and the films continue to flop, and the comic books become a cultish minority for an audience of twentysomethings before eventually folding? 'He'll survive another decade, I guess,' was all O'Neil would venture.[55] What if, in 2010, Batman has vanished from DC's racks and Warners' merchandising; if – institutionally – he

[54] Bader *et al.*, *Batman Beyond* #3, New York: DC Comics (May 1999).
[55] O'Neil, personal interview, op. cit.

no longer exists? Then I conjecture that he will become not a genre, but a myth: and he will endure, but in a different way.

(iii) Batman and audience: Batman as myth

The first story in issue #2 of the limited-series *Batman Black and White* was simply called 'Legend'.[56] 'It is the future,' begins the voiceover. 'And in a stainless steel city of light . . . as they have done since time immemorial . . . a mother is telling her child a bedtime story.'

> Once upon a time, the city was a gothic realm of eternal night. Full of pain, and grief, and a people broken by evil. Muggings. Beatings. Shootings. Killings. The four horsemen of the apocalypse raged unchallenged across an illimitable domain.
>
> And then, from the darkest pit of hell, a champion arose. No one knew how, or from where. He was as black as the villainy he sought, and he stood in harm's way, between the good and the evil. He did things no mortal man could do. Some say he could fly. Some say he could breathe underwater. Some say he had a secret fortress and slept there to recover from his never-ending battles. Some say he never slept at all.
>
> And in the end, he destroyed the dark . . . banishing evil forever. It was the beginning of the dawn, and with the coming of the light, he was gone. No one knew where. But many believe that he withdrew into his secret fortress, to sleep. And if that evil ever returns, he will awaken again . . . to save us . . . his people.

'Sleep tight, my love', the mother whispers, a tear on her cheek as she closes the bedroom door. 'My little love.' We pull back from the window and see the new city of light, and its price: martial law, soldiers on the corner, tanks on the street and the icon of a raised fist

---

[56] Walter Simonson, 'Legend', *Batman: Black and White* #2, New York: DC Comics (July 1996).

mounted on giant banners. And in the final frames, we close in on one of the soldiers; he looks around as the shadow of a bat falls over his face, and then 'KLOKK!' The Batman has woken again.

Again, the story provides a metaphor for the real world of institution and audience. Batman could 'die' in the comic book, or fold as a comic book – just as he seems now to have failed as a movie franchise – but by now, I think, his legend could not be killed. Perhaps if *Batman* and *Detective* had ceased publication in 1965, as was almost the case, or even if the titles had tailed off in 1985, putting an end to the development of Warners' movie, Batman would have been fated to the same role as Dick Tracy, Doc Savage and the Shadow: nostalgia pieces, pulp heroes with a corny appeal and a dedicated fandom of collectors. Thanks in great measure to the ABC show and to the Warners series of features, though, Batman is bigger than that. Batman, his logo, and the details of his city, colleagues and foes are familiar to those who neither know nor care that the character is still running in DC comics; and I would suggest that if those comics ceased publication tomorrow, I could ask a representative sample of adults twenty years from now what they knew of Batman and still get the same enthusiastic replies Spigel and Jenkins recorded in 1989,[57] the same replies I would receive today: 'Adam West ... Robin ... Catwoman ... the Bat-Signal ... Gotham City ... the Joker.' Batman would, like Sherlock Holmes, Robin Hood and Dracula, live on in popular memory, in his many and often mutually contradictory forms.

Neither, I think, would the more minority field of active Batman fandom die off with the publication of monthly comics. As John Tulloch and Henry Jenkins have shown, the fans of shows like *Star Trek* and *Doctor Who*, *Starsky and Hutch* and *Man From Uncle*, even of lesser-known series like *Beauty and the Beast* and *Alien Nation*, have both kept the faith and kept 'production' going in a very real sense – through a small industry of homemade art, videos and fiction – years after the

---

[57] See Lynn Spigel and Henry Jenkins, 'Mass Culture and Popular Memory', in Roberta Pearson and William Uricchio, *The Many Lives of the Batman*, London: Routledge (1991).

cancellation of the 'official' text.[58] The Internet sites dedicated to Batman already provide a home for fans who want to propose their own ways forward for the mythos, fill in the gaps in narrative and explain inconsistencies, or simply write more stories than the DC comics have time and space for:

> I have a personal timeline I play with sometimes, regarding the 'real time' eras of heroes. My version does not 'knock Batman out of the picture', but it gives Bruce Wayne a believable, worthwhile and fitting death. Great legends are not complete without an ending . . . my point is not that I am a great writer, or that my story is the only way to do this, but that even a hack fan like myself could conceive of ways to see superheroes as generational sagas.[59]

If this fan wanted to post his Batman 'generational saga' on the web, he would instantly reach an audience which potentially stretches into the millions; readers could access it free, print it out, suggest changes which could then be incorporated, offer illustrations, jointly author the next chapter. The possibilities of the Internet as a means of production are so vast that I have little hesitation in proposing that, were DC to scrap its Batman titles as a commercial loss, new Batman stories would nevertheless be forthcoming immediately, regularly and in great number; and that this global fan-factory for Batman narrative could sustain itself for many years. Bear in mind also that these stories would in no way be 'inferior' to the official texts, except perhaps due to the technical limitations of monitor resolution and printer quality: comic book authors and artists have for decades been recruited from fandom, and the Internet as an industry merely allows more creators to make their work public without submitting to the gatekeepers of DC and Warners.

If he is dropped from the 'official' text, then, this may even be a

---

[58] John Tulloch and Henry Jenkins, *Science Fiction Audiences*, London: Routledge (1995), and Henry Jenkins, *Textual Poachers*, London: Routledge (1992).
[59] Posted by Dr Manhattan, *Jonah Weiland's Comic Book Resources*, op. cit. (21 July 1998).

liberation for Batman rather than his death. As noted, this would not always have been the case — in 1965 or 1985, I think things would have been very different — but the nature of Batman and his audience is now such that they could gladly and easily carry him if his institution handed him over. Like Robin Hood and Dracula, Batman would truly become a myth, a legend, his roots in the ur-text often forgotten; he might be revived every ten years or so in a feature film, either live-action or animated, dramatic, romantic, satirical or comic. We might, depending on patterns of ownership and how tightly Warners continued to hold copyright, see the Bat-equivalent of Disney's *Robin Hood* (1973), taking anthropomorphic liberties with the text, or of Kenneth Branagh's *Mary Shelley's Frankenstein* (1994), claiming to return us to the 'original' source; of Richard Lester's *Robin and Marian* (1976) with an older Batman facing his last days, or of Martin Campbell's James Bond film *Goldeneye* (1995), reworking the myth for a new generation.

'He'll survive another decade, I guess': in comic books, perhaps. But it is not merely a romantic notion to assert that for as long as I live, at least — which could give him another sixty years — there will always be a Batman.

Bibliography

Note: Books, journal articles and reviews are listed in alphabetical order by author, where known. Primary texts such as films, comics and merchandise are listed chronologically, by date of publication or production.

1. Method

Popular texts and audiences: specific case studies

Martin Barker, 'Taking the Extreme Case: Understanding a Fascist Fan of Judge Dredd', in D. Cartmell, I.Q. Hunter, H. Kaye and I. Whelehan (eds), *Trash Aesthetics*, London: Pluto Press (1997)

Tony Bennett and Janet Woollacott, *Bond and Beyond*, London: Macmillan (1987)

Will Brooker, 'Batman: One Life, Many Faces', in Deborah Cartmell and Imelda Whelehan (eds), *Adaptations*, London: Routledge (1999a)

Will Brooker, 'Filling in Spaces: Internet Fandom and the Continuing Narratives of *Blade Runner*, *Alien* and *Star Wars*', in Annette Kuhn (ed.), *Alien Zone 2*, London: Verso (1999b)

Will Brooker, 'Containing Batman: Rereading Fredric Wertham and the Comics of the 1950s', in Nathan Abrams and Julie Hughes (eds), *Containing America*, Birmingham: University of Birmingham Press (forthcoming)

Susan J. Clerc, 'DDEB, GATB, MPPB and Ratboy: The X-Files' Media Fandom, Online and Off', in David Lavery, Angela Hague and Marla Cartwright (eds), *Deny All Knowledge: Reading the X-Files*, London: Faber and Faber (1996)

Ken Gelder, *Reading the Vampire*, London: Routledge (1994)

Henry Jenkins, *Textual Poachers*, London: Routledge (1992)

Henry Jenkins, 'Do You Enjoy Making The Rest Of Us Feel Stupid?

alt.tv.twinpeaks, the Trickster Author and Viewer Mastery', in David Lavery (ed.), *Full of Secrets: Critical Approaches to Twin Peaks*, Detroit: Wayne State University Press (1994)

Henry Jenkins, 'Dennis The Menace, The All-American Handful', in L. Spigel and M. Curtin (eds), *The Revolution Wasn't Televised: Sixties Television and Social Conflict*, London: Routledge (1997)

Stephen Knight, *Robin Hood*, Oxford: Blackwell (1994)

Toby Miller, *The Avengers*, London: BFI (1997)

Roberta E. Pearson and William Uricchio (eds), *The Many Lives of the Batman*, London: Routledge (1991)

William Uricchio and Roberta E. Pearson, *Reframing Culture*, New Jersey: Princeton University Press (1993)

Roberta E. Pearson, 'It's Always 1895: Sherlock Holmes in Cyberspace', in D. Cartmell *et al.* (eds), *Trash Aesthetics* (1997)

Roberta E. Pearson, 'White Network/Red Power: ABC's Custer', in Lynn Spigel and Michael Curtin (eds), *The Revolution Wasn't Televised: Sixties Television and Social Conflict*, London: Routledge (1997)

Richard Gid Powers, *G-Men: Hoover's FBI in American Popular Culture*, Carbondale: Southern Illinois University Press (1983)

John Tulloch and Henry Jenkins, *Science Fiction Audiences*, London: Routledge (1995)

Imelda Whelehan and Esther Sonnet, 'Regendered Reading: Tank Girl and Postmodernist Intertextuality', in D. Cartmell *et al.* (eds), *Trash Aesthetics* (1997)

Texts and audience: further studies

Umberto Eco, *The Role of the Reader*, London: Hutchinson (1981)

John Fiske, *Television Culture*, London: Routledge (1989)

John Fiske, *Understanding Popular Culture*, London: Routledge (1991)

John Fiske, *Reading the Popular*, London: Routledge (1991)

John Hartley, *The Politics of Pictures*, London: Routledge (1992)

John Hartley, *Popular Reality*, London: Arnold (1996)

David Morley, *The 'Nationwide' Audience*, London: BFI (1980)

Janice Radway, *Reading the Romance*, Chapel Hill: University of North Carolina Press (1991)

Lynn Spigel and Michael Curtin (eds), *The Revolution Wasn't Televised: Sixties Television and Social Conflict*, London: Routledge (1997)

New Criticism and reception theory

Timothy Bagwell, *American Formalism and the Problem of Interpretation*, Houston: Rice University Press (1986)

Stanley Fish, *Is There A Text In This Class?*, Cambridge, MA: Harvard University Press (1980)

Elizabeth Freund, *The Return of the Reader*, London: Methuen (1987)

Eric D. Hirsch, *The Aims of Interpretation*, Chicago: University of Chicago Press (1976)

Robert C. Holub, *Reception Theory*, London: Methuen (1984)

Roman Ingarden, *The Literary Work of Art*, Evanston: Northeastern University Press (1973)

Wolfgang Iser, *The Implied Reader*, Baltimore: Johns Hopkins University Press (1974)

Susan R. Suleiman and Inge Crosman, *The Reader in the Text*, Princeton: Princeton University Press (1980)

Jane P. Tompkins, *Reader-Response Criticism*, Baltimore: Johns Hopkins University Press (1980)

Theory: miscellaneous

Michel Foucault, *Discipline and Punish: The Birth of the Prison*, London: Allen Lane (1977)

Clifford Geertz, *The Interpretation of Cultures*, New York: Basic Books (1973)

Fredric Jameson, *Postmodernism, or, the Cultural Logic of Late Capitalism*, London: Verso (1991)

2. American History and Intertextual Frames

General, from 1940s

William H. Chafe, *The Unfinished Journey: America since World War Two*, New York: Oxford University Press (1986)

Walter LaFeber *et al.*, *The American Century: A History of the United States Since 1941*, New York: McGraw-Hill (1992)

BIBLIOGRAPHY

1940s propaganda and war bond promotion

Thomas Doherty, *Projections of War: Hollywood, American Culture and World War Two*, New York: Columbia University Press (1993)

John W. Dower, *War Without Mercy: Race and Power in the Pacific War*, New York: Pantheon (1986)

Anthony Rhodes, *Propaganda, the Art of Persuasion: World War Two*, London: Angus and Robertson (1976)

George H. Roeder, *The Censored War: American Visual Experience During World War Two*, New Haven: Yale University Press (1993)

Phillip M. Taylor, *Munitions of the Mind*, Manchester: Manchester University Press (1995)

1940s audience research studies

E. Cooper and H. Dinerman, 'Analysis of the Film "Don't Be A Sucker"': A Study in Communication', *Public Opinion Quarterly* vol. 15 no. 2 (Summer 1951)

E. Cooper and M. Jahoda, 'The Evasion of Propaganda', *Journal of Psychology* vol. 23 (1947)

S. Flowerman, 'Mass Propaganda in the War Against Bigotry', *Journal of Abnormal and Social Psychology* vol. 42 (October 1947)

Paul. F. Lazarsfeld *et al.*, *The People's Choice: How the Voter Makes Up His Mind in a Presidential Campaign*, New York: Columbia University Press (1944)

Robert Merton *et al.*, *Mass Persuasion: The Social Psychology of a War Bond Drive*, New York: Harper and Brothers (1946)

L.E. Raths and F.N. Trafer, 'Public Opinion and "Crossfire"', *Journal of Educational Sociology* vol. 21 (February 1948)

I. Rosen, 'The Effect of the Motion Picture "Gentlemen's Agreement" on Attitudes Towards Jews', *Journal of Psychology* vol. 26 (October 1948)

1940s newspaper articles on comics

Anon., 'Educators Uphold Children's Comics', *New York Times* (2 February 1944)

Anon., 'Japan Plans to Crush Us With a Flood of Comics', *New York Times* (25 March 1944)

Anon., 'Influence of Reading on Youth Discussed', *New York Times* (16 December 1945)

Anon., 'Some Comics Books [*sic*] Are Called Shocking', *New York Times* (14 February 1946)

Anon., ' "Comics" Denounced by South Africans', *New York Times* (6 May 1946)

Anon., 'Crime Comics Under Attack', *New York Times* (28 August 1946)

Anon., 'Priest Warns of Perils in Comic Books', *New York Times* (24 August 1946)

J. Donald Adams, 'Speaking of Books', *New York Times* (16 December 1945)

Theo J. Harmitz, ' "Comics Have a Place', letter, *New York Times* (6 August 1944)

Lieut. J.G. 'Nudes Preferred', letter, *New York Times* (2 August 1944)

Catherine Mackenzie, 'Children and the Comics', *New York Times* (11 July 1943)

Catherine Mackenzie, 'Parent and Child: Positive and Negative', *New York Times* (31 October 1943)

1950s censorship

Martin Barker, *A Haunt of Fears*, London: Pluto (1984)

James Gilbert, *A Cycle of Outrage: America's Reaction to the Juvenile Delinquent in the 1950s*, New York: Oxford University Press (1986)

Robert Griffiths, *The Politics of Fear: Joseph R. McCarthy and the Senate*, Lexington: University Press of Kentucky (1970)

C. Wright Mills, 'Nothing to Laugh At', review of *Seduction of the Innocent*, *New York Times* (25 April 1954)

Amy Kiste Nyberg, *Seal of Approval: The History of the Comics Code*, Jackson: University Press of Mississippi (1998)

Athan Theoharis, *Seeds of Repression: Harry S. Truman and the Origins of McCarthyism*, Chicago: Quadrangle Books (1971)

Fredric Wertham, *Seduction of the Innocent*, London: Museum Press (1955)

Homosexuality in the 1950s

Alfred C. Kinsey *et al.*, *Sexual Behavior in the Human Male*, Philadelphia, W.B. Saunders Company (1948)

Judd Marmor *et al.*, *Sexual Inversion: The Multiple Roots of Homosexuality*, New York: Basic Books (1965)

D.J. West, *Homosexuality Re-Examined*, London: Duckworth (1977)

Gay experience from the 1950s

Howard Brown, *Familiar Faces, Hidden Lives: The Story of Homosexual Men in America Today*, New York: Harvest (1977)

Donald W. Cory, *The Homosexual in America*, New York: Paperback Library Inc (1951)

Hall Carpenter Archives, *Walking After Midnight,* London: Routledge (1989)

Peter M. Nardi, David Sanders and Judd Marmor (eds), *Growing Up Before Stonewall: Life Stories of Some Gay Men*, London: Routledge (1994)

Kevin Porter and Jeffrey Weeks (eds), *Between the Acts: Lives of Homosexual Men 1885–1967*, London: Routledge (1991)

Jeffrey Weeks, *Coming Out: Homosexual Politics in Britain from the Nineteenth Century to the Present*, London: Quartet Books (1977)

Queer readings: general

Paul Burston and Colin Richardson (eds), *A Queer Romance: Lesbians, Gay Men and Popular Culture*, London: Routledge (1995)

Alex Doty, *Making Things Perfectly Queer: Interpreting Mass Culture*, Minneapolis: University of Minnesota Press (1993)

Richard Dyer (ed.), *Gays And Film*, New York: New York Zoetrope (1984)

Richard Dyer, *Heavenly Bodies: Film Stars and Society*, New York: St Martin's Press (1986)

Andy Medhurst, ' "It's As A Man That You've Failed", Masculinity and Forbidden Desire in "The Spanish Gardener" ', in Pat Kirkham and Janet Thumim (eds), *You Tarzan: Masculinity, Movies and Men*, London: Lawrence and Wishart (1993)

Vito Russo, *The Celluloid Closet: Homosexuality in the Movies*, New York: Harper and Row (1987)

Queer readings of Batman

Anon., 'Pass Notes No 640: Batman', *Guardian* (July 1995)

Steve Beery, 'Holy Hormones! Batman and Robin Made Me Gay', *Gay Comix* no. 8 (Summer 1986)

Paul Burston, 'Together Forever', *Attitude* (July 1995)

Paul Burston, 'Holy Homo', *Time Out* (26 July 1995)

Mort Drucker, 'Batman Fershlugginer', *Mad Magazine* (July 1995)

Murray Healy, 'Tuned In, Turned On', *Attitude* (January 1997)

David Jays, interview with Chris O'Donnell, *Attitude* (July 1995)

Freya Johnson, ' "Holy Homosexuality Batman": Camp and Corporate Capitalism in "Batman Forever" ', *Bad Subjects* no. 23 (December 1995), http://english-server.hss.cmu.edu/bs/23/johnson.html

Adam Mattera, 'Batman Unmasked', *Attitude* (July 1995)

Adam Mattera, 'Batty Boys', *Attitude* (November 1996)

Andy Medhurst, 'Batman, Deviance and Camp', in Pearson and Uricchio (eds), *The Many Lives of the Batman* (1991)

Andy Medhurst, review of *Batman and Robin*, *Sight and Sound* vol. 7 no. 8 (August 1997)

Megan Radclyffe, 'Comics'r'Us', *Gay Times* (November 1996)

Scott Shay, 'Scott's Chris O'Donnell Page', http://www.clark.net/pub/sshay/chris.html (June 1997)

Amy Taubin, 'House of Bats', *Village Voice* (27 June 1995)

Various, 'Battyman', 'Buttman Returns', 'Bats-Man', *Mad Batman Spectacular* (July 1997)

Bryan Vickery, 'Shrine to Chris O'Donnell', http://rs2.ch.liv.ac.uk/biry/batman.html (June 1997)

Ivan Waterman, 'Mr Nice Guy?', interview with Chris O'Donnell, *Attitude* (June 1997)

Pop Art and Camp

Van M. Cagle, *Reconstructing Pop/Subculture: Art, Rock and Andy Warhol*, London: Sage (1995)

Janis Hendrickson, *Roy Lichtenstein*, Cologne: Taschen Verlag (1994)

Klaus Honnef, *Andy Warhol*, Cologne: Taschen Verlag (1993)

Lucy R. Lippard *et al.*, *Pop Art*, London: Thames and Hudson (1966)

George Melly, *Revolt into Style: The Pop Arts In Britain*, Harmondsworth: Penguin (1970)

Tilman Osterwold, *Pop Art*, Cologne: Taschen (1991)

Susan Sontag, 'On Camp', in *Against Interpretation*, New York: Dell (1969)

Diane Waldman, *Roy Lichtenstein*, New York: Guggenheim Museum (1993)

Elizabeth Young and Billy Name, 'The Broader Picture', feature on the Factory, *Independent on Sunday* (13 April 1997)

1960s newspaper articles on Batman

Anon., 'Too Good To Be Camp', *New York Times* (23 January 1966)

Anon., 'Batman Dilemma', *New York Times* (17 April 1966)

Anon., 'Stores are Sued on Rights to Batman', *New York Times* (23 June 1966)

Anon., 'Russians Call Batman "Idealised FBI Agent"', *New York Times* (12 September 1966)

Russell Baker, 'Television's Bat Burlesque', *New York Times* (8 February 1966)

William Dozier, 'Batman: Menace or Hero', letter, *New York Times* (29 May 1966)

Edward B. Fiske, 'Clergyman Sees Batman's Appeal as Religious', *New York Times* (8 August 1966)

George Gent, 'Pravda Meets Batman Head On', *New York Times* (30 April 1966)

Helen Heineman, 'Batman: Menace or Hero' (letter), *New York Times* (29 May 1966)

Hilton Kramer, 'Look! All Over! It's Esthetic ... It's Business ... It's Supersuccess!', *New York Times* (29 March 1966)

Eda J. LeShan, 'At War With Batman', *New York Times* (15 May 1966)

Howard Thompson, 'TV Heroes Stay Long', review of film, *New York Times* (25 August 1966)

Vartanig G. Vartan, 'Batman Fad Aids Stock Rise', *New York Times* (20 March 1966)

British reviews of Batman film serial (rescreened)

Anon., '1943 Serial All At Fell Swoop', *The Times* (3 February 1966)

Jeffrey Blyth, 'Batman Flies Again for 4 1/2 Hours Non-Stop', *Daily Mail* (28 December 1965)

Patrick Gibbs, 'Low Camp', *Daily Telegraph* (4 February 1966)

Nina Hibdin, 'Here's a New Cult for Suckers', *Daily Worker* (3 February 1966)

Virginia Ironside, 'Hiss! Boo! Cheers! We Want Batman', *Daily Mail* (16 February 1966)

David Robinson, review, *Financial Times* (4 February 1966)

Alexander Walker, 'Stop for a Meal or a Chat!', *Evening Standard* (3 February 1966)

British reviews of Batman TV series (first screening)

Anon., review, *Morning Star* (25 June 1966)

Nancy Banks-Smith, review, *Sun* (6 July 1966)

Stewart Lane, review, *Morning Star* (8 June 1966)

Richard Last, review, *Sun* (21 July 1966)

Joan Seddon, review, *Sun* (23 May 1966)

Milton Shulman, review, *Evening Standard* (27 July 1966)

David Wilsworth, review, *Sun* (19 October 1966)

British reviews of Batman TV series (repeats)

Craig Brown, review, *Sunday Times Review* (22 August 1993)

Christopher Hudson, review, *Evening Standard* (18 September 1978)
Victor Lewis-Smith, review, *Evening Standard* (13 July 1995)
Allison Pearson, review, *Independent on Sunday* (1 May 1994)

Autobiographies and interviews

Richard Ashford, 'The Year of the Bat', interview with Denny O'Neil, *Speakeasy* magazine (February 1989)

Tim Burton with Mark Salisbury, *Burton On Burton*, London: Faber (1995)

Richard Houldsworth, 'Robin Returns', interview with Chris O'Donnell, *Starburst* vol. 7 no. 2 (August 1995)

Alison James, 'Holy Kilmer', 'Chris the Boy Wonder', *More* magazine (July 1995)

Bob Kane with Tom Andrae, *Batman and Me*, California: Eclipse (1989)

William Keck, 'Pow! TV's Robin Blasts New Batman Stars', *National Enquirer* (11 July 1995)

Alan Mitchell, 'Burton's Big Adventure', *Speakeasy* magazine (February 1989)

Alan Mitchell and Dick Hansom, 'Behind the Scenes on *Batman* The Movie', *Speakeasy* magazine (February 1989)

Stephen Rebello, 'Number One With A Bullet?', interview with Val Kilmer, *Movieline* vol. 6 no. 9 (June 1995)

Peter Sheridan, interview with Adam West, *Daily Mail* (14 August 1993)

Burt Ward with Stanley Ralph Ross, *Boy Wonder: My Life in Tights*, Los Angeles: Logical Figments Books (1995)

Adam West with Jeff Rovin, *Back to the Batcave*, London: Titan Books (1994)

Alan Woollcombe, 'Byrne Takes the Bat', interview with John Byrne, *Speakeasy* magazine (January 1989)

Comics: histories and debate

Clive Bloom, Greg S. Cue, *Dark Knights: The New Comics in Context*, London: Pluto (1993)

Joe Desris, *The Golden Age of Batman: The Greatest Covers of Detective Comics from the 30s to the 50s*, New York: Artabras (1994)

Mike Edwards, 'Batman: The case of the caped crusader', in Barbara Connell, Jude Brigley and Mike Edwards (eds), *Examining the Media*, London: Hodder & Stoughton (1996)

Joel Eisner, *The Official Batman Batbook*, London: Titan Books (1987)

Dennis Gifford, *The International Book of Comics*, London: Hamlyn (1988)

Ron Goulart, *Ron Goulart's Great History of Comic Books*, Chicago: Contemporary Books (1986)

BIBLIOGRAPHY

Amy Handy, *Bat Man in Detective Comics*, New York: Abbeville Press (1993)

Gerard Jones and Will Jacobs, *The Comic Book Heroes*, California: Prima Publishing (1997)

Chip Kidd, *Batman Collected*, London: Titan (1996)

Scott McCloud, *Understanding Comics: The Invisible Art*, New York: HarperPerennial (1994)

Dennis O'Neil, 'A Brief Bat-Bible: Notes on the Dark Knight Detective', unpublished document (June 1998)

George Perry and Alan Aldridge, *The Penguin Book of Comics*, Harmondsworth: Penguin (1967)

Reinhold Reitberger and Wolfgang Fuchs, *Comics: Anatomy of a Mass Medium*, London: Studio Vista (1972)

Richard Reynolds, *Superheroes: A Modern Mythology*, London: B.T. Batsford (1992)

Roger Sabin, *Adult Comics: An Introduction*, London: Routledge (1993)

Paul Sassienie, *The Comic Book*, London: Ebury Press (1994)

William W. Savage Jr, *Comic Books and America, 1945–1954*, Norman: University of Oklahoma Press (1990)

James Van Hise, *Batmania II*, Las Vegas: Pioneer Books (1992)

Mark Cotta Vaz, *Tales of the Dark Knight: Batman's First Fifty Years 1939–1989*, London: Futura (1989)

Journal articles on Batman

Thomas Andrae, 'From Menace to Messiah: The Prehistory of the Superman in Science Fiction Literature', *Discourse* no. 10 (Summer 1980), reprinted in Donald Lazere, *American Media and Mass Culture*, California: University of California Press (1987)

Alyson Bardsley, 'Batman/Election Returns', *Bad Subjects* no. 3 (November 1992), http://english-server.hss.cmu.edu/bs/03/Bardsley.html

Alec McHoul and Tom O'Regan, 'Batman, Glasnost and Relativism in Cultural Studies', *Southern Review* vol. 25 no. 1 (March 1992)

Kim Newman, 'Who Are His People – Batman', *Sight and Sound* vol. 56 no. 68 (September 1989)

Andrew Ross, 'Ballots, Bullets or Batmen: Can Cultural Studies Do The Right Thing?', *Screen* vol. 31 no. 1 (Spring 1990)

British press reports on Batman, 1989

Anon., 'Bat-Rayed! They've Made Him A Limp-Wristed Queen', *Sun* (11 May 1989)

Anon., vox pop with fans, *Mirror* (16 June 1989)

Anon., 'Battle of the Caped Crusaders', *Sun* (21 June 1989)
Anon., 'Batman Zaps Box Offices', *Mirror* (12 August 1989)
Anon., 'Batman's £100,000 Dreamer', *Mail* (22 August 1989)
Anon., 'Batman zaps into the big records', *Daily Mail* (13 October 1989)
Ian Brandes, 'Kerpow! Batman Faces the Censor', *Today* (27 February 1989)
Dick Hansom and Alan Mitchell, 'Behind the Scenes on Batman: The Movie',
    Speakeasy magazine (January 1989)
Carol Leonard, 'Batmania', *The Times* (2 September 1989)
Peter McDonald, 'Batman's £50m Cliff-hanger', *Evening Standard* (20 June 1989)
Lester Middlehurst, 'Sex-Mad Batman Needs a Shrink', *Today* (21 June 1989)
Piers Morgan, 'Here's Batman and Throbbin: Caped Crusader Has Sex for 1st
    Time', *Sun* (1 February 1989)
Piers Morgan, 'Bat Special', *Sun* (15 August 1989)
Mark Tran, 'Fans Batty over Caped Crusader Film', *Guardian* (23 June 1989)
Warner Bros production notes, *Batman* (1989)
Barry Wigmore, 'Batman's Foxed the Joker', *Mirror* (17 August 1989)
Peter Willis, 'Holy Scoop, Batman', *Sun* (12 January 1989)
David Wooding, 'Evil of the Bat-Drugs', *Sun* (19 August 1989)

British reviews of Batman, 1989

Anon., review, *NME* (12 August 1989)
Sean French, review, *Observer* (13 August 1989)
Allan Hall, 'Jack's A Cracker', *Sun* (23 June 1989)
Clive Hirschhorn, 'Stylish Batman Plays an Ace with the Joker', *Sunday Express*
    (13 August 1989)
J. Hoberman, 'Night and the City', *Village Voice* (4 July 1989)
Tom Hutchinson, review, *Mail on Sunday* (13 August 1989)
George Perry, 'The Man Behind the Batmask', *Sunday Times* (13 August 1989)
Charles Shaar Murray, 'Holy Authentic', *Daily Telegraph* (15 August 1989)
Kevin O'Sullivan, 'Batman's £2 Million Zap at Censors', *Today* (29 July 1989)
Christopher Tookey, review, *Sunday Telegraph* (13 August 1989)
Shawn Usher, review, *Daily Mail* (8 August 1989)
Adam West, 'Joker's Bat-Tastic', *Sun* (4 August 1989)

British reviews of Batman Returns, 1992

Mark Amory, 'Gloom Merchant', *Spectator* (11 July 1992)
Nigel Andrews, 'Further Adventures of the Caped Crusader', *Financial Times* (9
    July 1992)
Anne Billson, 'Twilight of the Gothamites', *New Statesman* (10 July 1992)

Phillip French, 'Gothic Revival', *Observer* (12 July 1992)
Marshall Julius, 'Batman Go Home', *What's On In London* (8 July 1992)
Adam Mars-Jones, 'Rubber Soul, Plastic Passion', *Independent* (10 July 1992)
Sheridan Morley, review, *Sunday Express* (12 July 1992)
Terrence Rafferty, 'Masked Ball', *New Yorker* (29 June 1992)
Jeff Sawtell, 'Crusading Goth Capers', *Morning Star* (11 July 1992)
Phillip Thomas, review, *Empire* magazine #38 (August 1992)

British reviews of Batman Forever, *1995*

Stephen Amidon, 'Reaching for the Stars', on comic adaptations, *Sunday Times* (18 June 1995)
Nigel Andrews, 'High-Intensity Junk', *Financial Times* (13 July 1995)
Anon., 'Robin Muscles In on Movie Action', *Daily Mail* (29 April 1995)
Anon., 'This Batman is Not For Real', *Asian Age* (20 June 1995)
Anne Bilson, 'Caped Crusader Dishes It Up With Lashings of Ham', *Sunday Telegraph* (16 July 1995)
Alison Boshoff, 'Holy Film Premieres Batman', *Daily Mail* (13 July 1995)
Geoff Brown, 'Gross Profit from Cash and Carrey', *The Times* (13 July 1995)
Tom Charity, review, *Time Out* (12 July 1995)
Roger Clarke, 'Stripped Down', on comic adaptations, *Sunday Times* (18 June 1995)
Quentin Curtis, 'Wholly Boring, Batman!', *Independent on Sunday* (16 July 1995)
Phillip French, 'Flash! Crash! Splash! Cash!', *Observer Review* (16 July 1995)
Brigit Grant, 'The Cape of Great Hype', *Sunday Express* (16 July 1995)
William Leith, 'Planet of the Capes', *Mail on Sunday* (16 July 1995)
Adam Mars-Jones, 'Holy Neurosis, Batman', *Independent* (13 July 1995)
Jonathan Romney, 'The Comic Strip Tease', *Guardian* (13 July 1995)
Tom Shone, review, *Sunday Times* (16 July 1995)
Alexander Walker, review, *Evening Standard* (13 July 1995)

British reviews of Batman and Robin, *1997*

Anon., 'Actors Bury Cinema Time Capsule', news item, *Guardian* (24 June 1997)
Anon., review, *The Big Issue* (27 June 1997)
Anon., 'Holy Baloney! It's a Dodo!', *Express* (27 June 1997)
Tom Charity, 'The Big Chill', *Time Out* (2 July 1997)
Quentin Falk, review, *Sunday Mirror* (29 June 1997)

Nick Fisher, 'Boring Batman isn't in Sexy Ivy's League', *Sun* (27 June 1997)
Derek Malcolm, 'Holy Baloney', *Guardian* (27 June 1997)
James Oldham, 'Bun Lovin' Criminal', *New Musical Express* (28 June 1997)
John Patterson, 'Testing, Testing', on audience previews, *Guardian Guide* (21 June 1997)
Jonathan Rose, 'Arnie's Chiller Thriller', *Mirror* (26 June 1997)
Matthew Sweet, 'Dark Knight of the Soul-Destroying', *Independent on Sunday* (29 June 1997)
Dan Wakeford, 'The Bat Pack', *Mirror* (26 June 1997)
Martin Walker, 'Comin' at Ya!', on summer blockbusters, *Guardian* (29 April 1997)
Alexander Walker, 'Arnie Breaks the Ice, George Flops', *Evening Standard* (26 June 1997)
Ivan Waterman, 'Gotham Knights', *Flicks* magazine vol. 10 (June 1997)
Matthew Wright, 'Batman and Mobbin'', *Mirror* (24 June 1997)

American reviews of Batman and Robin

Anon., review, *Austin Chronicle* (20 June 1997)
Noel Murray, review, *Nashville Scene* (8 July 1997)
Devin D. O'Leary, review, *Weekly Alibi* (2 July 1997)
Zak Weisfeld, review, *Metro Pulse* (2 July 1997)

'Dr Batman'

Jeremy Armstrong, 'Degrees? Will has Gotham', *Mirror* (28 January 1999)
Zoe Ball, BBC Radio 1 (28 January 1999)
Michelle Bower, 'Award me the bat-doctorate, Boy Wonder', *Western Mail* (29 January 1999)
Julian Carey, 'Happy birthday Batman', BBC Radio 2 (23 February 1999); *Newsbeat*, BBC Radio 1 (28 January 1999)
Rachel Harvie, 'To the bat-lecture, Robin!' *Gair Rhydd* (8 February 1999)
Alison Stokes, 'Will is a bat swot', *Western Echo* (22 May 1999)
William Thomas, 'Riddle me this!', *Empire Magazine* (April 1999)
The Vanessa Show (2 February 1999)
Wake Up With Wogan, BBC Radio 2 (28 January 1999)
Jenni Zylka, 'Von fledermausen und menschen – Batman wird 60', *Die Tageszeitung* (May 1999)
Interview, Touch Radio (16 February 1999)

Internet sites

Adam West Batman, http://www.adamwest.com/home.htm

Anti-Schumacher Site, http://members.aol.com/BatmanLite/frameni.htm

The Batcave, http://www.taponline.com/tap/entertainment/tv/reruns/batman

Bring Me The Head of Joel Schumacher, http://www.cgicafe.com/~ajrosen/batman

Da-Da-Da-Da . . . Batman!, http://students.missouri.edu/~ahicks/batintro.htm

The Dark Knight, http://www.darkknight.ca

Mantle of the Bat: The Bat-Board, http://www.cire.com/batman

Jonah Weiland's Comic Book Resources, http://www.comicbookresources.com/boards

3. Key Primary Texts

Comics, 1989 onwards

Hilary Bader *et al.*, *Batman Beyond*, New York: DC Comics (March 1999–)

John Byrne, Jim Aparo and Mike deCarlo, *The Many Deaths of the Batman* #1–3 (*Batman* #433–435), New York: DC Comics (1989)

Howard Chaykin and Daniel Brereton, *Batgirl and Robin: Thrillkiller*, New York: DC Comics (1996–1997)

Chuck Dixon, Graham Nolan and Scott Hanna, *Detective Comics* #700, New York: DC Comics (1996)

Larry Hama, Jim Balent and Ray McCarthy, *Legends of the Dark Claw* #1, New York: DC Comics (1996)

Peter Milligan, Kifron Dwyer and Dennis Janke, *Batman: Dark Knight, Dark City* #1–3 (*Batman* #452–4), New York: DC Comics (1990)

Grant Morrison, various artists, *JLA*, co-starring Batman, New York: DC Comics (1996–)

Grant Morrison, Mark Miller, Steven Harris and Keith Champagne, *Aztek* #6–7, co-starring Batman, New York: DC Comics (1997)

James Robinson, Tony Harris and Mark Buckingham, *Starman* #33, co-starring Batman, New York: DC Comics (1997)

Ty Templeton and Rick Burchett, *Dark Claw Adventures* #1, New York: DC Comics (1997)

Steve Vance, John Delany, Ron Boyd, *Adventures in the DC Universe* #1, New York: DC Comics (1997)

Various, *Batman: Legends of the Dark Knight*, New York: DC Comics (1989–)

Various, *Batman: Black and White* #1–4, New York: DC Comics (1996)

Various, *The Batman Chronicles* #5, New York: DC Comics (1996)

Various, *I Love to Read: Batman* #7, London: Redan (1996)

Various, *Batman: Secret Files and Origins* #1, New York: DC Comics (1997)

Mark Waid, Brian Augustyn and Barry Kitson, *JLA Year One*, co-starring Batman, New York: DC Comics (1997–1998)

Mark Waid *et al.*, *The Kingdom* #1–2, New York: DC Comics (January–February 1999)

Marv Wolfman, Pat Broderick and John Beatty, *Batman Year Three* #1–4 (*Batman* #436–9), New York: DC Comics (1989)

Marv Wolfman, George Perez, Jim Aparo and Mike deCarlo, *Batman: A Lonely Place of Dying* #1–5 (*Batman* #440–2), New York: DC Comics (1989)

Prestige format comics

Brian Augustyn and Mike Mignola, *Batman: Gotham by Gaslight*, New York: DC Comics (1989)

Howard Chaykin, John Moore and Mark Chiarello, *Batman/Houdini: The Devil's Workshop*, New York: DC Comics (1993)

Howard Chaykin, *Batman: Dark Allegiances*, New York: DC Comics (1996)

Jamie Delano and John Bolton, *Batman/Manbat* #1–3, New York: DC Comics (1995)

Neil Gaiman and Dave McKean, *Black Orchid* #1–3, co-starring Batman, New York: DC Comics (1989)

Alan Grant, John Wagner and Simon Bisley, *Batman/Judge Dredd: Judgement on Gotham*, New York, Fleetway Comics/DC Comics (1991)

Gerard Jones, Mark Badger and Willie Schubert, *Batman: Run, Riddler, Run*, New York: DC Comics (1992)

Jeph Loeb and Tim Sale, *Batman: The Long Halloween* #1–13, New York: DC Comics (1996–1997)

Peter Milligan, Tom Grindberg and Dick Giordiano, *Catwoman Defiant*, New York: DC Comics (1992)

Doug Moench, Kelley Jones and Malcolm Jones III, *Batman/Dracula: Red Rain*, New York: DC Comics (1992)

Doug Moench, Kelley Jones and John Beatty, *Batman: Bloodstorm*, New York: DC Comics (1995)

Alan Moore, Curt Swan and George Perez, *Superman: Whatever Happened to the Man of Tomorrow*, co-starring Batman, New York: DC Comics (1986, reprinted 1997)

Alan Moore, Brian Bolland and John Higgins, *Batman: The Killing Joke*, New York: DC Comics (1988)

Kelley Puckett, Matt Haley and Karl Kesel, *Batman: Batgirl*, New York: DC Comics (1997)

Mark Waid and Alec Ross, *Kingdom Come* #1–4, co-starring Batman, New York: DC Comics (1996)

Matt Wagner, *Batman/Grendel, Devil's Masque/Devil's Riddle*, New York: Comico/DC Comics (1993)

Marv Wolfman, *History of the DC Universe*, New York: DC Comics (1986)

Graphic novels

Mike Barr, Alan Davis, Todd McFarlane *et al.*, *Batman: Year Two*, New York: DC Comics (1990)

John Byrne, *Batman 3D*, New York: DC Comics (1990)

Paul Dini and Bruce Timm, *Batman Adventures: Mad Love*, New York: DC Comics (1994)

Garth Ennis and John McCrea, *Hitman*, co-starring Batman, New York: DC Comics (1997)

Dave Gibbons and Steve Rude, *Superman/Batman: World's Finest*, New York: DC Comics (1992)

Keith Giffen, J.M. deMatteis, Kevin Maguire *et al.*, *Justice League: A New Beginning*, New York: DC Comics (1987)

Archie Goodwin and Scott Hampton, *Batman: Night Cries*, New York: DC Comics (1992)

Mary Z. Holmes (ed.), *The Super Dictionary*, New York: Holt, Rinehart and Winston (1978)

Jeph Loeb and Tim Sale, *Batman: Haunted Knight*, New York: DC Comics (1996)

Frank Miller, Klaus Janson and Lynn Varley, *Batman: The Dark Knight Returns*, New York: DC Comics (1986)

Frank Miller and David Mazzucchelli, *Batman: Year One*, New York: DC Comics (1988)

Grant Morrison and Klaus Janson, *Batman: Gothic*, New York: DC Comics (1990)

Grant Morrison and Dave McKean, *Arkham Asylum*, New York: DC Comics (1989)

Dennis O'Neil, Joe Quesada and Kevin Nolan, *Batman: Sword of Azrael*, New York: DC Comics (1993)

Kelley Puckett *et al.*, *Batman: The Collected Adventures* vol. 1, New York: DC Comics (1993)

Kelley Puckett *et al.*, *Batman: The Collected Adventures* vol. 2, New York: DC Comics (1994)

Jim Starlin, Jim Aparo and Mike deCarlo, *Batman: A Death in the Family*, New York: DC Comics (1988)

Various, *Superman and Batman Annual*, New York: DC Comics (1976)

Various, *The Greatest Superman Stories Ever Told*, New York: DC Comics (1987)

Various, *The Greatest Batman Stories Ever Told*, vol. 1, New York: DC Comics (1988)

Various, *The Greatest Joker Stories Ever Told*, New York: DC Comics (1988)

Various, *The Greatest Team-Up Stories Ever Told*, New York: DC Comics (1990)
Various, *The Greatest Batman Stories Ever Told*, vol. 2, New York: DC Comics (1992)
Various, *Batman: Knightfall*, vol. 2, New York: DC Comics (1993)
Various, *Batman: Featuring Two-Face and the Riddler*, New York: DC Comics (1995)
Mark Waid, Fabian Nicieza *et al.*, *Justice League: A Midsummer's Nightmare*, co-starring Batman, New York: DC Comics (1996)

Key filmography

Batman, dir. Lambert Hillyer (1943); aka *The Batman*; re-released as *An Evening With Batman and Robin* (1966)
Batman and Robin, dir. Spencer Gordon Bennet (1949); aka *New Adventures of Batman and Robin*; rereleased as *An Evening With Batman and Robin* (1966)
Batman, TV series, dir. Robert Butler *et al.* (1966–1968)
Batman, dir. Leslie H. Martinson (1966)
New Adventures of Batman, TV series, dir. various (1977–1978)
Batman, dir. Tim Burton (1989)
Batman Returns, dir. Tim Burton (1992)
Batman: The Animated Series, TV series, dir. Kevin Altieri *et al.*, (1992–1993)
Batman: Mask of the Phantasm, dir. Eric Radomski and Bruce W. Timm (1993)
Adventures of Batman and Robin, TV series, dir. Kevin Altieri *et al.* (1994–)
Batman Forever, dir. Joel Schumacher (1995)
Batman and Robin, dir. Joel Schumacher (1997)
Batman & Mr. Freeze: SubZero, dir. Boyd Kirkland (1998)
Batman Beyond, TV series, dir. various (1999)

Miscellaneous: Batman as promotional material or intertextual reference

The Who, version of 1960s, *Ready Steady Who* EP (1966)
The Kinks, version of 1960s, *Live at the Kelvin Hall* (1967)
'Raffles', club with Batman-costumed doorman, review, *Harpers and Queen* (May 1968)
'Sleek! Zingy! Stretch Cat Suit', advertisement, *Harpers and Queen* (May 1968)
The Jam, 'Batman Theme', *In the City* LP (1977)
Batman Returns, giant poster magazine series #3, Titan Books (1992)
'Don't Wait Forever', promotion for video release of *Batman Forever*, Playhouse video store (1995)

Batman Forever, official movie souvenir magazine, Titan Books (1995)

'Catwoman . . . seeks her very own Batman', *Guardian* Soulmates (2 September 1995)

'Catwoman seeks Batman to find the woman behind the cat', *Guardian* Soulmates (16 September 1995)

'Purr-fect it's Kitty Lips', Catwoman flyer for Kitty Lips gay club, London (1996)

'You'd Better Ring the Royal', Batmobile advertising hoarding from Royal motor insurers (1996)

Batman and Robin: The Costumes, exhibition at Museum of the Moving Image, London (June–October 1996)

'Only Fools and Horses' Batman episode, BBC (December 1996)

Batman and Catwoman, *The Animated Series*-based ice lollies, from Wonderland Ice Cream (1997)

'A Guide to Celebration Cakes' including *Batman and Robin Adventures* design, for Sainsbury's (1997)

'Der Dunkle Ritter', semi-pornographic German postcard of Batman (1997)

'Missing This Would Be a Crime', *Batman and Robin* promotion for Barclays Bank (1997)

'The Funky Kitten', Catwoman poster for Warm As Toast club night, Cardiff (1997)

'Mandy Capp' Batman cartoon, *Mirror* (1997)

Batman and Robin sticker promotion, Kellogg's Frosties (1997)

Sue Webster, 'All Dolled Up', review of 'Rocketpak Batman and Air Strike Robin' toys, *Independent on Sunday* (13 April 1997)

Richard Phillips, 'London Theme Park Axed', item on Batman roller coaster, *Independent on Sunday Business* (1 June 1997)

'Gala Premiere of *Batman and Robin* in Support of Special Olympics', flyer promoting Capital Odeon (23 June 1997)

'Batman', daily comic strip in *Express* (7 July 1997)

'Poison Ivy searching for Bat Man to give a poisonous gift of love to', Greenwich *Mercury* personal ads (21 August 1997)

'Freezed to See You', 3D comic pull-out promoting *Batman and Robin* video release, *News of the World* (16 November 1997)

'Batman, 28, seeks soulmate with own cape', *Guardian* Soulmates, 'Men Seeking Men' section (29 November 1997)

'Peter Andre is turning up as Batman', *Guardian Guide* report on Smash Hits Poll Winners' Party (29 November 1997)

'Free Batman and Robin Glow-In-The-Dark Yo-Yo', Wimpy promotion (December 1997)

Batman Forever / Batman and Robin latex costumes, Internet promotion from The Nightmare Factory mail-order company, http://www.nightmarefactory. com/bat3.html (1997)

'Grab Some Caped Action', promotion for Batman figures, vehicles, watches, caps, pogs, from Official Batman Gear company (1997)

Index

ABC (television network) 5, 16, 41, 160, 171, 178, 179, 184–8, 192–6, 214, 217, 218, 226, 235, 334

Ace the Bat-Hound 155, 246

Adams, Neal 7, 150, 175, 226, 240, 281

Adkins, Dan 258, 267

Alfred 10, 76, 90, 103, 155, 166, 185, 187–9, 199, 201, 224, 254

as The Outsider 187, 254

Alter-Ego fanzine 251

Anderson, Murphy 255

Andrae, Tom 61, 79

Arkham Asylum 275, 323

Armitage, Simon 24

Asherman, Alan 59, 186

Attitude magazine 163, 164, 167, 226

audiences 12–13, 29, 30, 35, 63, 79, 182, 194, 195, 209, 221, 235, 237

Augustyn, Brian 55

Aunt Harriet 10, 166, 188, 200, 225, 226, 241

Austin, William 89

Authorship (comic) 249, 250, 252, 254, 255–8, 259

Azrael / Jean-Paul Valley 319, 326, 327

Bacon-Smith, Camille 279, 287, 288, 293

Bader, Hilary 325

Badger, Mark 243

Bails, Jerry 251–3

Bair, Michael 273

Barker, Martin 107

Bat-Bible 37, 277, 279, 290

Batgirl / Barbara Gordon 10, 150, 151, 166, 185, 187, 225, 246, 259, 319, 320, 326, 328

as Oracle 319, 326

Bat-Girl / Betty Kane 145, 150–8, 319

Batgirl III / Cassandra Cain 319

Batman (1943) 41, 83, 84, 162, 266

Batman (1966) movie spin-off 192

Batman (1966) TV series 4, 49, 150, 153, 160, 162, 167, 171, 173, 174–7, 180, 185, 186, 188, 190, 193, 194, 216, 221, 222, 224, 226, 231, 233, 235, 236, 238–40, 266, 282, 284, 297, 303

Batman (1989) 49, 149, 161, 176, 238, 279, 287

Batman 5 307–10

Batman and Robin (1997) 30, 41, 164, 166, 167, 279, 294, 297, 298–9, 300–4, 306

Batman Beyond 42, 325, 326, 327–9
Batman Black and White 330
Batman Forever (1995) 30, 108, 164, 167, 294–5, 302, 305
Batman Returns (1992) 300
Batman: The Dark Knight Returns 7, 50, 55, 172, 176, 244, 246, 261, 262, 267–8, 271, 274, 290–1, 292, 293, 299, 319
Batmobile 85, 189, 211, 228, 244
Batwoman / Kathy Kane 10, 145, 146, 150, 152–3, 155–8, 319, 322
Beatty, John 173
Beery, Steve 141, 224
Beetlejuice 292, 293
Bennett, Tony 8, 9, 11, 12
Bewitched 184, 191, 195, 207, 208
Blyth, Jeffrey 159
Boichel, Bill 35, 85, 145, 145, 149–50, 260–2
Bolland, Brian 263, 271, 272, 273
Bond, James 8–11, 80, 153, 196, 209, 233, 333
Bordieu, Pierre 7
Bridwell, E. Nelson 105, 162, 224, 253
Broome, John 256–8
Brown, Howard 124, 125, 129, 136
Burchett, Rick 273–4
Burnley, Jack 86
Burton, Tim 4, 17, 27, 96, 149, 161, 166, 174, 177, 239, 250, 279–82, 283–4, 285, 286, 288, 289–90, 292–3, 294, 297, 298, 300, 319

camp 12, 14, 16, 155, 160, 161, 167, 168, 174, 177, 178, 180, 183, 185, 186, 190, 196, 197, 199, 202, 219–25, 236, 238, 244, 248, 294–5, 301
Catwoman / Selina Kyle 38, 51, 137, 164, 219, 243, 244, 276, 278, 319, 322, 325, 331

CBS (television network) 195, 218
Chaykin, Howard 245
Clayface 51, 150, 152, 156, 157
Clooney, George 166, 295, 297, 302, 305
Collins, Jess 181
Columbia 34–6, 39, 41, 47, 84, 85, 86, 94
Comics Code 143–7, 149, 152–4, 155, 156, 158
Commissioner Gordon 44, 46, 47, 89, 135, 139, 157, 192, 199, 203, 204, 272, 277, 302–3
communism 117, 118, 120
Cory, Donald 136, 137
costume 27, 37, 40, 43, 45, 57, 160, 167, 175, 199, 201, 203, 207, 208, 214, 215, 247, 248
costume (gay associations) 129, 132
Cotta Vaz, Mark 57, 67, 72–7, 79, 89, 105, 148–50, 175, 177, 188, 236, 243
Craig, Yvonne 187
Croft, Douglas 86, 88
Crosman, Robert 22–4

DC Comics 5, 10, 14, 17, 29, 31, 36–8, 42, 47, 51, 53, 60, 61, 63, 65, 66, 72, 74, 79, 80, 82, 86, 87, 95, 106, 141, 144, 146, 147, 152, 168, 177, 179, 181, 186–8, 211, 212, 235, 242, 244–7, 250, 257, 258, 261–2, 264, 284, 287, 291, 293–4, 317–20, 321–6, 332
de Certeau, Michel 5, 15, 28
Dibny, Ralph 255
Dini, Paul 279
Dozier, William 87, 184–8, 193–8, 201, 203, 211, 214, 216, 220, 225–9, 232, 236, 251, 266
Dracula 8, 9, 10, 40, 43, 45, 95, 331, 333
Drake, Tim 37

dual identity (gay associations) 136, 137

EC (Entertaining Comics, aka Educational Comics) 144, 250
Ellsworth, Whitney Frederick 60–2, 74, 75, 79, 82

fandom 13, 16, 17, 249–56, 260, 261, 263–6, 278, 279–81, 289, 307
Feiffer, Jules 202, 218, 226
fight scenes (1966 TV series) 190, 191, 205, 206
Finger, Bill 43, 48, 51–2, 56, 58–62, 64, 74, 78, 81, 83, 85, 89, 146, 253, 310, 327
Fish, Stanley 15, 20, 21–6, 28, 29, 116
Fiske, John 13–15, 27–9
Flash, The 181
Fox, Gardner 52, 251, 253, 256, 257
Fraser, Harry 96
Fugitive, The 205

Gaiman, Neil 243
Gaines, William M. 144
Gay Comics 141
Gelder, Ken 8–10, 13
Gerber, Steve 262
Gibbons, Dave 55
Gifford, Denis 77
Gilbert, James 113, 118
Giordano, Dick 53
Giunta, John 255
Goldsman, Akiva 174
Goodwin, Archie 263
Gorshin, Frank 175, 195
Gotham City 23, 28, 37, 38, 40, 47, 49, 76, 79, 84, 87, 93, 94, 106, 139, 140, 148, 199, 206, 228, 231, 234, 238–40, 243, 331
Goulart, Ron 106
Green Arrow, the 134, 262
Green Hornet 210, 218

Green Lantern, the 144, 247, 252, 277
Greenaway Productions 185
Greene, Sid 255

Hall, Stuart 28
Hamilton, Neil 203
Hampton, Scott 263
Handy, Amy 77
Harris, Jack C. 259
Hillyer, Lambert 85
Hirsch, E.D. 15, 20, 21
Hitler, Adolf 8, 61, 70, 72, 77, 78
homosexuality 12, 14, 13, 25, 31, 100–37, 141–7, 151, 153, 155, 156, 158–64, 166, 167, 169, 175, 187, 198, 214, 227, 235, 247, 295, 296
homosexuality and camp 221–3, 225
Huntress, the / Batgirl II 320, 326

iconography 37, 42, 43, 45, 52
Infantino, Carmine 252, 255, 257
Ingarden, Roman 15, 19, 20
Internet 3, 15, 17, 30, 31, 104, 164, 241, 250, 264–5, 305, 321, 332
Internet fan boards 174, 175, 240–2, 259, 265, 279, 302, 305
intertextuality 9, 11, 14, 198, 217
Iser, Wolfgang 15, 20

Jameson, Fredric 327
Japanese stereotypes 96, 97, 99, 122, 159
Jenkins, Henry 12, 13, 15, 28, 30, 180, 181, 194, 198, 227, 230, 237–8, 281, 315, 331
Johnson, Freya 107, 109
Joker, The 27, 38, 40, 49, 51, 52, 76, 84, 86, 135, 157, 166, 215, 240, 246, 268, 272, 275, 287, 289, 290, 309, 323
Jones, Gerard 184, 185, 243, 250–2, 253, 257

Jones, Kelley 273, 278
Jones, Malcolm 273
Justice League of America (JLA) 273, 276, 325, 327

Kane, Bob 25, 27, 35, 41–3, 47–53, 56, 57, 58–60, 64, 65, 74, 78, 81, 82, 84, 85–9, 106, 146, 174, 175, 179, 183, 198, 206, 250, 252, 254, 255, 257–8, 283–5, 308, 309–10, 327
Kaye, Stan 82
Keaton, Michael 279, 282, 283–4, 285, 286, 292, 295, 296, 299, 300, 302
Killing Joke, The 177, 243, 289–93
Kilmer, Val 295, 301, 302
Kingdom Come 325
Kingdom, The 323–5, 328
Kitson, Barry 273
Knight, Stephen 13
Kramer, Hilton 217–18
Kubert, Joe 252

LeShan, Eda 228
Lichtenstein, Roy 135, 180–2, 184, 191–3, 217–19
Liebowitz, Jack 59, 81

McCarthy, Joseph 120, 122
McCarthyism 41, 117, 120, 310
McKean, Dave 40, 41, 263, 271–2, 273, 293
McLeod, Victor 96
Man from UNCLE, The 209, 331
Many Lives of the Batman, The 9, 11, 13, 37–8
Martian Manhunter, the / J'onn J'onnz 255, 262
Mazzucchelli, David 278
Medhurst, Andy 4, 12, 13, 25, 107, 109–11, 122, 124, 126, 127, 131, 149–51, 152, 154, 156, 160, 161, 166, 171, 199, 200, 221, 222, 225–6

Meehan, Eileen 13, 291
Melly, George 163, 223–4
merchandise 36, 211–15, 228, 229, 236, 237
Miller, Frank 3, 7, 8, 27, 41, 55, 172–7, 210, 227, 236, 261–2, 267, 268–9, 274, 278, 283, 291
Mintz, Robert 193
Mission: Impossible 209
Monkees, The 208–9
Moore, Alan 172–5, 236, 263, 268, 269, 270, 271
Morley, David 28, 29
Morrison, Grant 39, 41, 247, 259–60, 263, 271, 273, 277–80, 324, 328
Mr Freeze 199–201, 202, 203, 208

National periodicals *see* DC Comics
Nazism 70–2, 76, 90, 91, 106
NBC (television network) 195, 196
Newton, Don 258, 267
Nicholson, Jack 282, 284, 286–7, 290, 299, 303
Notes on Camp 180, 220
Nyeberg, Amy Kiste 61, 143, 147

O'Donnell, Chris 14, 164, 166, 295, 302
O'Neil, Dennis *see* O Neil, Denny
O'Neil, Denny 7, 27, 37, 40, 42, 48, 55, 81, 95, 148, 150, 169, 175, 226, 258, 260–1, 263–4, 265, 267, 269, 270, 274, 278–9, 281, 287, 289, 290, 308, 321, 327, 329
O'Neil, Kevin 273
Oldenburg, Claes 243

Pearson, Roberta E. 8, 12, 15, 29, 37, 38, 41, 42, 53–5, 145
Penguin, the / Oswald Cobblepot 5, 51, 75, 76, 84, 86, 137, 242, 244, 309

Peters, Jon 285
Pfeil, Fred 4
Poison Ivy 296
Pop 7, 12, 14, 160, 177, 178, 180,
    181, 186, 187, 191–4, 196, 214,
    216, 218, 222, 223, 225, 234,
    241, 243, 245, 248
pop Art 4, 16, 41, 180–4, 193, 194,
    214, 216, 218, 223
propaganda 2, 16, 35, 36, 67–70, 73,
    84, 87, 88, 141
Puckett, Kelly 170

queer readings 8, 14, 16, 25, 101,
    104, 105, 108, 123, 125–7,
    132–5

Radway, Janice 4, 14, 15, 27–9
Ramos, Mel 182, 214
Reitberger, Reinhold 105
Reynolds, Richard 48
Riddler, the / Edward Nigma 49, 176,
    182–4, 219, 243, 244
Robin / Dick Grayson (as Nightwing)
    5, 10, 14, 16, 25, 30, 34, 37,
    38, 40, 41, 56–60, 65, 75, 77,
    81, 82, 84, 85, 87, 89, 93, 98–
    103, 105–10, 126, 129, 132–5,
    137–42, 145, 146, 148–51,
    153–6, 160, 162, 163, 167–9,
    183, 187–92, 198–200, 203,
    206, 214, 222–6, 228, 230, 231,
    235, 243, 245, 246, 271, 274,
    276, 278, 310, 319, 320, 322,
    326, 327
Robin Hood 9–11, 41, 63, 331, 333
Robin II / Jason Todd 167, 169
Robinson, James 168, 169
Robinson, Jerry 51–3, 74, 86, 310
Roeder, George H. 67–9
Ross, Andrew 25, 27
Ross, Jonathan 173, 174, 236
Roy, Adrienne 259
Rozaki, Bob 259

Russo, Vito 131, 132

Sabin, Roger 106
Sassienie, Paul 105, 174, 176, 177,
    236
Savage, William W. 70, 72, 106
Schiff, Jack 82, 83
Schumacher, Joel 17, 27, 30, 41, 96,
    164, 166, 167, 173, 175, 178,
    250, 279, 281, 294–302, 303,
    305–6, 307
Schwartz, Alvin 82
Schwartz, Julius 185, 187, 188, 250–
    3, 256, 257
Seduction of the Innocent 12, 16, 56,
    101–3, 112–15, 117, 118, 120,
    122, 123, 141, 147, 148, 160,
    162, 163, 166, 170, 226
Semple Jnr, Lorenzo 216
Seuling, Paul 260
Shadow, the 61
Sherlock Holmes 9, 40, 44, 79, 133,
    201, 331
Siegel, Jerry 65
Silverstone, Alicia 296–7, 305
Slash fiction 13, 209
Sontag, Susan 180, 185, 220–1, 225
Spiegel, Lynn 12, 13, 180, 181, 193,
    195, 198, 227, 230, 237–8, 281,
    331
Sprang, Dick 82
Star Trek 13, 210, 209, 307, 328, 331
Superman / Clark Kent 43, 46, 55,
    65, 73, 82, 112, 134, 144, 169,
    181, 217, 218, 233, 250, 253,
    262, 268–9, 274, 277, 319
Swabacker, Leslie 96
Szasz, Thomas 121

Thomas, Roy 251, 253
Thurman, Uma 296, 302, 303
Tulloch, John 331
20th Century Fox 185, 211

Two-Face / Harvey Dent 51, 137
Tynan, Kenneth 159

Uricchio, William 8, 11, 15, 29, 37,
    41, 42, 53–5, 145

Van Hise, James 85, 86, 90, 177, 189,
    193, 222, 225, 230, 236, 282,
    285, 289, 291
Varley, Lynn 274
Vertov, Dziga 12
Vietnam War 231–3, 234

Waid, Mark 179, 265, 324–5
Ward, Burt 108, 109, 160, 163, 166,
    172, 190, 191, 203, 214, 229
Warhol, Andy 180–2, 191–4, 216,
    218, 223
Warner Brothers 8, 10, 13, 17, 30,
    41, 49, 166, 176, 196, 241, 252,
    276, 279, 281, 283, 284–5, 291,
    292, 293–4, 297, 299, 301, 303,
    304, 307, 317, 320, 331, 332,
    333

Weisinger, Mort 250, 253
Wertham, Fredric 12, 16, 39, 41,
    56, 61, 100–17, 119, 122–7,
    133, 134, 136, 137, 141–7,
    149, 150, 152, 158–64, 166,
    168, 170, 171, 174, 188, 224–7,
    236
West, Adam 7, 12, 42, 160, 163, 166,
    171–8, 180, 189–92, 199, 201,
    202, 203, 206, 210, 211, 214,
    218, 227, 229, 230, 232, 234–6,
    240–2, 245, 247, 279, 280–1,
    285, 288, 295, 331
Willis, Paul 4
Wilson, Lewis 86, 87
Wolfman, Marv 267
Wonder Woman 144, 262, 319
Woollacott, Janet 8, 9, 11, 12
World War Two 4, 16, 34, 35, 41,
    67, 73, 80, 84

Yarbrough, Beau 309
Yarbrough, Tyrone 279, 287, 288,
    293